Gendered Mobilizations and Intersectional Challenges

Gendered Mobilizations and Intersectional Challenges

Contemporary Social Movements in Europe and North America

Edited by Jill Irvine, Sabine Lang, and Celeste Montoya

ecpr PRESS

ROWMAN &
LITTLEFIELD
INTERNATIONAL
London • New York

Published by Rowman & Littlefield International, Ltd.
6 Tinworth Street, London, SE11 5AL
www.rowmaninternational.com

In partnership with the European Consortium for Political Research, Harbour House, 6–8
Hythe Quay, Colchester, CO2 8JF, United Kingdom

Rowman & Littlefield International, Ltd., is an affiliate of Rowman & Littlefield

4501 Forbes Boulevard, Suite 200, Lanham, Maryland 20706, USA
With additional offices in Boulder, New York, Toronto (Canada), and Plymouth (UK)
www.rowman.com

British Library Cataloguing in Publication Data

A catalogue record for this book is available from the British Library

ISBN: HB 978-1-78552-290-1
       PB 978-1-78552-289-5

Library of Congress Cataloging-in-Publication Data Available

ISBN: 978-1-78552-290-1 (cloth)
ISBN: 978-1-78552-289-5 (pbk.)
ISBN: 978-1-78552-291-8 (electronic)

We dedicate this book to our children (Andy, Julie, Keagan, Kylissa, Oliver, and Nicky),

and to all those working toward the arrival of a more intersectionally just world.

Contents

List of Figures and Tables   ix

Preface   xi

Introduction: Gendered Mobilizations and Intersectional
Challenges   1
Jill Irvine, Sabine Lang, and Celeste Montoya

PART I. INTERSECTIONALITY WITHIN GENDERED SOCIAL MOVEMENTS   23

1   The Limits and Potential of Solidarity: Activism on
Reproductive Rights in Ireland   25
Pauline Cullen

2   Feminist Policy Mobilization and Intersectional
Consciousness: The Case of Swedish Domestic Services Tax
Reform (RUT)   42
Andrea Spehar

3   The Politics of Intersectionality in Activism against Domestic
Violence in Hungary and Romania   56
Raluca Maria Popa and Andrea Krizsán

4   Counter-Intersectionality: The Politics of Conservative
Women's NGOs in Turkey   74
Ayşe Dursun

5   Political Opportunities and Intersectional Politics in Croatia   92
Jill Irvine and Leda Sutlović

6 Intersectional and Transnational Alliances during Times of
Crisis: The European LGBTI Movement   111
Phillip M. Ayoub

**PART II. INTERSECTIONALITY ACROSS SOCIAL JUSTICE
MOVEMENTS**   **133**

7 From Identity Politics to Intersectionality? Identity-Based
Organizing in the Occupy Movements   135
Celeste Montoya

8 Navigating Transnational Complicities: Expanding
Frameworks of Intersectionality in the Deadly Exchange
Campaign   154
Rachel H. Brown

9 Enacting Intersectional Solidarity in the Puerto Rican Student
Movement   171
Fernando Tormos-Aponte

10 Activists as Political Translators? Addressing Inequality and
Positional Misunderstandings in Refugee Solidarity Coalitions   189
Nicole Doerr

11 Equality and Recognition or Transformation and Dissent?
Intersectionality and the Filipino Migrants' Movement in Canada   208
Ethel Tungohan

12 Sistas Doing It for Themselves: Black Women's Activism and
#BlackLivesMatter in the United States and France   226
Jean Beaman and Nadia E. Brown

13 A Mountain Skyline? Gender Equality and Intersectionality in
Supranational "Equality CSOs"   244
Petra Ahrens

References   263

Index   295

List of Contributors   309

Figures and Tables

FIGURES

6.1   Key Terms in Delegate Packets for the Annual ILGA-
      Europe Meetings, 2005–2016   123

13.1 Network Map Example   247

TABLES

6.1   LGBTI Movement: Intersectional and Transnational
      Alliances in Times of Financial Crisis, Average Reponses   118

6.2   Collaboration among INGOs in Europe   121

9.1   Student Movement Demands and Policy Outcomes by
      Administration, 2005–2018   177

13.1 Annual EU Funding of CSOs (Self-Reported)   252

Preface

The origins of this book go back a number of years, when the editors participated in a workshop organized by Celeste Montoya, which was funded and hosted by the Colorado European Union Center of Excellence (CEUCE) at the University of Colorado Boulder. At this workshop, the editors started to think about unifying the artificially separate research on feminist activism, women's movements, and women in movements, by way of developing the concept of gendered mobilizations. It evolved to its current focus on intersectionality, when the majority of contributors to this volume came together at a follow-up workshop in 2015 organized by Sabine Lang at the Center for West European Studies (CWES) and EU Center of the Jackson School of International Studies at the University of Washington, Seattle. We would like to acknowledge the generous support of both universities and their centers as well as the European Union's financial support through European Union Centre of Excellence funding. Along with this evolution in focus, we expanded our query from European gendered mobilizations to include movements in the United States and Canada.

Subsets of authors came together to advance their manuscripts during a number of conferences over these past three years. We would like to thank all those who gave us a platform to meet and debate, in particular, the European Conference on Politics and Gender, the European Consortium for Political Research, the Council for European Studies, and the Western Political Science Association. During these workshops and conferences, many colleagues have commented and contributed to the ideas in this volume. Besides all the authors, we would like to extend particular thanks to Akwugo Emejulu, Sara De Jong, Myra Marx Ferree, Eléonore Lépinard, Silke Roth, Birgit Sauer,

Laurel Weldon, and the many activists who have shared their experiences and insights with us.

We are deeply appreciative of the continuous encouragement and patience of Dhara Snowden, Natalie Bolderston, and Rebecca Anastasi at Rowman & Littlefield International and Madeleine Hatfield at ECPR Press. We also thank Ildi Clarke for compiling the index and Sathya Shree for overseeing the book into production.

Introduction

Gendered Mobilizations and Intersectional Challenges

Jill Irvine, Sabine Lang, and Celeste Montoya

On January 21, 2017, the first full day of Donald Trump's presidency, millions of people participated in the Women's March, in the United States and beyond, as a powerful demonstration of resistance. Trump's campaign had been characterized by racialized nationalistic rhetoric and accusations of sexual assault. The mobilization was likely the largest single-day protest in US history (Chenoweth and Pressman 2017). A notable facet of the Women's March was the attention given to intersectional inclusion. While white women appeared to be leading the initial call to action, a more diverse group of women was quickly recruited to organize the national march. The result was global protests representing people of different gender, race, ethnicity, sexuality, class, faith, ability, and nationalities. The speakers on stage and the signs in the crowd, in Washington and elsewhere, spoke to issues of not only women's rights but also immigrant rights, LGBTQ rights, racial justice, and social justice issues more broadly. While not all demonstrations organized that day, or afterward, exhibited the same level of intersectional awareness and conscientious inclusion, this moment represented the possibility of a new, more intersectional women's movement. In the face of rising white, masculinist politics in both the United States and Europe, we argue in this book that attention to intersectionality has become all the more salient and necessary.

An enduring challenge for feminist movements, and social justice movements more broadly, has been how to address and work across difference. Traditional strategies have often emphasized universalizing messages and common identities as means of facilitating collective action. Feminist movements, LGBTQ movements, racial justice movements, immigrant rights movements, and labor movements have generally focused on one dimension of oppression. Each has called on diverse groups of people to mobilize, by strategically emphasizing commonalities in ways that sometimes eclipse other relevant and intersecting dimensions of marginalization or oppression. While strategically focusing on commonality can be an effective means of mobilization, suppressing difference can create rifts over time and ultimately weaken movements. Overemphasizing one form of oppression while deemphasizing others can lead to the marginalization and exclusion of groups in already precarious positions.

Activists located at the intersection of multiple marginalities and movements have long advocated for more inclusive approaches that acknowledge the significance and complexity of different social locations. While the term "intersectionality" was coined by Kimberlé Crenshaw (1989, 1991) as an intervention to counter legal analysis that failed to address adequately the simultaneity of gender and racial discrimination as experienced by black women, the idea of attending to multiple and interconnected forms of oppression has a much longer history, emerging in the "border space between social movements and academic politics" (Collins 2011, 92; 2015). Scholar-activists of color in the United States wrote of the struggles of those located at the intersections of oppression related to gender, race, class, and sexuality as well as the liberation movements created in response (e.g., Anzaldúa 1987; Collins 1990; Combahee River Collective [1977] 1993; Davis 1981; Lorde 1982; Min-Ha 1989; Moraga and Anzaldúa 1981; Sandoval 1991; Smith 1983). In Europe, feminists also discussed race, class, and gender as co-constitutive (e.g., Amos and Parmar 1984; Anthias and Yuval-Davis 1983; Carby 1982; Mirza 1997; Wilson 1978). Intersectionality's political genealogy connects to these struggles to eradicate inequality, with an emphasis on collective action as an instrument of meaningful contestation (May 2015, 48). Over the past several decades, the importance of intersectionality increasingly has been recognized and articulated as a normative goal and mode of mobilization (Chun, Lipsitz, and Shin 2013; Emejulu and Bassel 2017; Evans 2015; Lapperière and Lépinard 2016; Verloo 2013; Weldon 2008), yet it is still far from the norm in social movements or in social movement scholarship. Continued popular critiques of "identity politics" demonstrate the tendency toward oversimplified approaches to understanding societal inequalities and efforts to overcome them (Hancock 2011 and 2017).

As intersectionality has gained recognition and resonance, it has rapidly expanded into a burgeoning field of study such that it has gained multiple and sometimes contested definitions. Patricia Hill Collins and Valerie Chepp (2013, 58) provide a working definition that captures some of this expanded purview while still maintaining the integrity of core genealogical components:

> Intersectionality consists of an assemblage of ideas and practices that maintain that gender, race, class, sexuality, age, ethnicity, and similar phenomena cannot be analytically understood in isolation from one another; instead these

constructs signal an intersecting constellation of power relationships that produce unequal material realities and distinctive social experiences for individuals and groups positioned in them.

As such, intersectionality is a means of delving into the complexities of lived realities and the processes that shape them.

While intersectionality emerged out of social movements, the study of intersectionality has not been a central feature of social movement scholarship (Broad-Wright 2017; Chun, Lipsitz, and Shin 2013; Roth 2017). There are a number of reasons for this. For one, social movement scholarship developed within mainstream academic disciplines (i.e., political science, sociology, psychology) has not been consistently attentive to issues of gender, race, and sexuality. Scholarship that does address such issues has often been held apart from, rather than a part of, the perceived canon. Outside of mainstream academic disciplines, feminist, critical race, and queer studies have usually developed in separate and often siloed academic units in ways that have hindered the study of intersecting and overlapping movements and issues. The field of women's studies has traditionally focused on feminist movements, ethnic studies on anti-racism movements, and sexuality studies on the LGBTQ movements. Intersectional considerations have garnered much attention at the theoretical level, but their presence in and influence on empirical work is more measured (Mügge et al. 2018).

Disciplinary biases also come into play in considering the limited application of intersectionality in social movement research. In fields such as political science, psychology, and sociology, there is a bias toward more positivist approaches to social science. The emphasis on parsimony and generalization is already a challenge when studying the complexity of social movements: they are not always temporally bounded; they rarely involve a fixed set of actors; and they cut across societal groups, organizations, and institutions. Their messiness can make finding causal connections challenging (Roggeband and Klandermans 2017; Tarrow 1998, 199). Theorizing intersectionality within social movements only adds to this complexity. Intersectionality asks scholars (and activists) to complicate their understanding of the world, moving from an oversimplified single-axis analysis of oppression to a more complete and nuanced examination of multiple, interacting, and dynamic dimensions.

Within the field of intersectionality studies, there are debates about how intersectionality is or could be articulated across and within disciplines. Scholars such as Hancock (2007a, 2007b) have characterized intersectionality as both a normative theoretical argument and a research paradigm, an approach to conducting empirical research that emphasizes the interaction of categories of difference (including but not limited to race, gender, class, and sexual orientation). Yet, there is some concern about this dual characterization of intersectionality. Conceiving of intersectionality as a research paradigm is a means of formalizing its methodological or theoretical foundations within disciplines. Some scholars and practitioners have raised questions about whether the attempt to mainstream intersectional scholarship within a power-laden and unrepresentative academy may depoliticize or minimize the political project of intersectionality, particularly as it pertains to its roots in centering women of color (Alexander-Floyd 2012; Bilge 2013; Jordan-Zachery 2007 and 2013). Cho, Crenshaw, and McCall (2013) caution that in the process of developing intersectional projects and literacy within fields (a project they support), it is important to be mindful that disciplinary conventions "import a range of assumptions and truth claims that sometimes contribute to the very erasures to which intersectionality draws attention" (Cho, Crenshaw, and McCall 2013, 793). May (2015) and Bilge (2014) remind us that intersectional scholarship emerged as an "activist scholarship" and "insurgent knowledge" developing from the collective action of feminists and lesbians of color.

In this book, we uphold the importance of developing intersectionality as a research paradigm that provides vital insights into the understanding of social movements but one that is grounded in an epistemological demand "to make visible" experiences that are obscured by single-axis conceptualizations of power (Carastathis 2008). Furthermore, we posit that intersectionality, as a social movement ethic and practice, plays a vital role in contemporary social movements. While studying intersectionality in and between social movements is a difficult, messy, and sometimes fraught task, we seek to identify conditions that facilitate or inhibit it from being acknowledged and practiced.

Within the volume, we explore intersectionality as it is understood and exercised in contemporary movements. We consider how social movement scholars might better work to identify and understand intersectionality in social movements, and how intersectionality might be better employed within research practices. We place an emphasis on gendered mobilization, as an entry point to studying the presence or absence of intersectional activism. Consistent with the work of feminists of color, however, we also expand our purview to movements where the central organizing focus is not around gender. Comparative studies of gender and social movements have generally focused on women's movements, feminist movements in particular. Much scholarly attention has been directed toward how to conceptualize and classify these types of movements, to be used as a basis of comparison. For example, Karen Beckwith (2007, 313), discusses women's movements as movements that involve "women as the primary core actors" and "where women make gendered identity claims as the basis for the movement, where they explicitly organize as women, or mothers, or as daughters, asserting a female gendered identity, distinguished from other possible (overlapping or competing) identities." This, she argues, does not preclude a recognition of women's political activism external to women's social movements (such as in race-based movement) but rather helps to distinguish between *women's movements* and *women in movements*. Feminist movements, she goes on to argue, can be distinguished from the larger set of women's movements on the basis of goals and aims. Citing Weldon (2004, 3), she argues that feminist movements are a type of women's movement that challenge patriarchy and contest political, social, and other power arrangements of domination and subordination on the basis of gender.

When focusing on intersectionality, these types of classifications pose some interesting and important challenges. Intersectionality, by definition, resists the prioritization of one form of oppression or identity over another. While movements that are classified as "women's movements" or "feminist movements" are not inherently precluded from being intersectional, there are some tensions that may arise depending on how rigidly scholars (and perhaps activists) adhere to or interpret such typologies. As argued by Ferree and Roth (1998), constructions of ideal-typical movements (be they based on race, gender, or class) tend to exclude those organizing at (or on) the intersections of multiple marginalities. Blackwell (2011, 26–27) argues that feminist practices of women of color, lesbians, and working-class women are not clearly registered in dominant frames because they involve political subjects with multiple identities who most often engage in multi-issue organizing or work on several political fronts, not all of which put gender at the center. Thus, when we focus on gender, but not class, we run the risk of considering movements that only appeal to the upper or middle classes. When we focus only on gender and not race, we may highlight movements that appeal mainly to white women. When we focus on gender and not sexuality and gender identity, we might focus on movements for straight cisgender women. This is not to say that focused studies are not important or are inherently problematic, but that given our interest in investigating intersectionality, an expanded purview is necessary.

We propose to broaden our inquiry by expanding what is generally considered gendered mobilization by not only making less rigid distinctions between women in movement, women's movement, and feminist movement but also expanding upon what is understood as gendered (such as the inclusion of LGBTQ) movements. Expanding our purview to include "women in movement" means examining movements that are not ostensibly about gender but are sites for gendered (and intersectional) claims to be made. Anti-poverty, anti-war, and anti-racism movements may not be overtly gendered but have important gendered implications.

Drawing upon this broader understanding of gendered mobilization, we have organized this volume into two main sections. The first section of the volume includes chapters examining intersectionality (or the lack thereof) within movements organized centrally around gender and sexuality. The second section of the volume looks beyond these movements to other sites of gendered and intersectional activism. These include movements focused on democracy, migration, education, economic and racial justice, and beyond. This approach is a means of expanding our understanding of what might (and should) be considered gendered mobilization and of better demonstrating what intersectionality might look like in practice. This approach also provides a broad and unique means of examining the extent to which issues of gender, race, ethnicity, class, sexuality, nationality, and ability are addressed in contemporary movements.

We focus on North America and Europe, as places where movements have often been siloed and where the need for intersectional practices to counter neoliberal, populist, and reactionary politics is urgent. We also investigate the degree to which recent economic and refugee "crises" have impacted intersectional consciousness, imagination, and actions within movements and organizations. The chapters in this volume offer diverse perspectives on how to study the political practice of intersectionality and better identify the opportunities and obstacles to its success. Ultimately, we hope that this book will generate more interest in intersectional social movement scholarship, recognizing that this journey is ongoing, with much more to learn along the way.

SOCIAL MOVEMENT INTERSECTIONALITY

As stated above, social movement scholarship on intersectionality has been relatively sparse; however, important developments have emerged in recent years as scholars continue not only to theorize intersectionality but also to engage with it empirically. Building upon this work, we propose a broad framework for thinking about and studying intersectionality empirically within the context of social movements. Constructing a more inclusive and empirically sound analysis of today's social movements starts with the expansion of our current analytical frameworks. What does social movement intersectionality look like? What forms does it take? Who employs it? When, why, and to what impact? How do shifting political environments shape the form or even possibilities of intersectionality? If intersectionality is both an analytical framework and a political practice, much work remains to be done toward conceptualizing a framework of social movement intersectionality and collecting the empirical evidence of its practices.

Scholars who have undertaken the study of social movement intersectionality, or the logic of intersectionality inside an organized movement for social change, argue that it may take many different forms (Broad-Wright 2017; Chun, Lipsitz, and Shin 2013). Generally, the literature exploring social movement intersectionality focuses on two distinct but overlapping conceptualizations: First, and perhaps foremost, are *intersectional movements*. Broad-Wright (2017) specifies *intersectional movement* as a specific type of *social movement intersectionality* where a movement is mobilized more centrally by those similarly situated at the intersection of two (or more) forms of oppression. While Broad speaks most directly to groups organized around the intersections of race and gender, explicitly Black feminisms and Chicana feminisms in the US context, this definition might extend into other groups at the intersection of various marginalities.

A second type of social movement intersectionality is *intersectional movement praxis. Intersectional movement praxis* pertains to *intersectional movements* but extends beyond them. Townsend-Bell (2011) uses the term "intersectional praxis" as a means of looking beyond intersectionality as an analytic or orientation to the actual practices that are deployed on the ground by social justice groups. While it might be generally assumed that *intersectional movements* will be engaged in *intersectional praxis*, this is not necessarily the case. Critics have argued that organizations or movements premised on multiple marginalities might replicate overly simplistic and essentialized understandings of identity and oppression (Ernst 2010). In this volume, Celeste Montoya's chapter on the Occupy movement discusses how identity-based groups within the movement made intersectional interventions in the movement but did not necessarily adopt intersectional praxis internally. Whether and what forms intersectional praxis take, then, are open empirical questions. Such questions are also essential when looking beyond "intersectional movements" to movements less centrally organized around intersections.

What, then, might comprise an intersectional praxis? Tormos (2017a) argues that intersectionally conscious political praxis requires both recognizing *and* representing intersectionally marginalized social groups. This dual requirement is important. While an intersectional consciousness or "recognition" might be a necessary component of intersectional praxis, by itself it is insufficient. Lépinard (2014) highlights this, differentiating between a social movement repertoire offering "intersectional recognition" and a social movement offering "intersectional solidarity." Using her examples, the former might include the recognition that racialized women have specific needs and interests and that minority women are better placed to respond to these needs. Intersectional recognition does not require that a given group or movement actually change its behavior or mode of organizing. A repertoire of "intersectional solidarity," on the other hand, might involve feminist organizing that includes the political priorities of minority women and works to improve their representation within the movement. The former is a limited form of intersectionality that recognizes the significance of multiple identities but potentially keeps movements fragmented and some groups marginalized. The latter is a form of recognizing difference and incorporating it in ways that meaningfully broaden a purportedly "universal" agenda.

Intersectional praxis in this context might include assessing/reassessing and then forming/changing the internal structures, norms, and practices of social movements in light of recognizing group differences (Greenwood 2008). This might include organizing an inclusive decision-making structure and leadership, supporting the autonomous organization of distinct groups within the movement, and advocating for social policies that address multiple forms of organization (Lapperière and Lépinard 2016; Roberts and Jesudason 2013; Strolovitch 2007; Tormos 2017a; Weldon 2006). It might also include the praxis of "political translation," as Nicole Doerr argues in her investigation of social movement alliances in Europe and the United States (Doerr 2018a). Political translation points to a set of disruptive communicative practices developed by activists to address intersectional inequalities in movements and correct for positional imbalances in deliberation.

Another way in which intersectional praxis might be conceptualized is through coalitional politics or transversal politics. Coalitional politics allows for groups to focus on and organize around single dimensions of oppression or particular (even intersectional) positions but in a way that does not preclude intersectional praxis. Yuval-Davis (1997, 2006a) discusses *transversal politics*, a method of activism developed as an alternative to universalistic politics (that overemphasize commonalities to the neglect of differences), on one hand, and particularistic politics (that overemphasize differences to the neglect of commonalities), on the other. Transversal politics envisions more dynamic interaction, a constant flow of communication between groups and individuals, both horizontally and vertically, so as to avoid reification. Yuval-Davis talks about *rooting* and *shifting* as an exercise in empathy, in which participants bring with them a reflexive knowledge of their own positioning and identity (*rooting*) but can also *shift* to put themselves in the situation of those with whom they are in dialogue and who are different from them.

This conceptualization of rooting and shifting might be pushed beyond an exercise in empathy when combined with intersectional theorizing. Crenshaw (1991), for example, conceptualizes any one identity (or dimension) as a coalition of differentially located individuals organizing along a particular dimension. Such a conceptualization emphasizes that this organizing is not inevitable, nor is it the only possibility for coalescing. Patricia Hill Collins (1990) uses the "matrix of oppression" analogy to demonstrate that while there are some dimensions that divide groups, there are others that unite them. Groups that maintain an intersectional consciousness might organize along or *root* in certain identities or dimensions without forgetting about the other dimensions, thus being able to *shift* along other dimensions in a coalitional fashion. This type of politics is important for maintaining internal cohesion as well as building broader coalitions, networks, and movements. Recognition or consciousness is a central component of transversal politics but so is choice and action.

COMPARATIVE FRAMEWORK OF SOCIAL MOVEMENT INTERSECTIONALITY

While the above discussion of social movement intersectionality points to some of the ways in which intersectionality has been conceptualized in the context of social movements, here we are interested in developing a broader framework of social movement intersectionality that more fully engages with the extensive research on social movements. This approach allows us a means to better interrogate, examine, and compare the (intersectional) modes of mobilization. Three main approaches map the activities that are necessary for creating and sustaining effective social movements. Resource mobilization theory points to the process of creating capacity, the aggregation of material, social-organizational, and human resources necessary to produce collective action (Edwards and McCarthy 2004; McCarthy and Zald 1987, 2001). Cultural theories of social movements stress identity formation and issue framing, creating a voice that resonates with participants and populace alike (Johnston and Klandermans 1995; Rose 1997; Ryan and Gamson 2006). Political process theories emphasize the importance of political opportunities and allies and the dynamics of coalitional politics (McAdam, Tarrow, and Tilly 2001; Meyer 2004; Tarrow 1998). All social movement theories focus on the necessity of political action—in the streets, in government, or on social media, to name just a few sites of resistance.

We argue that intersectional politics and analysis encompass dynamic strategies to create capacity, find voice, form alliances, and act politically. Mapping the concepts of intersectional politics and analysis onto these four dimensions of political mobilization may help us to study it empirically. Intersectional political practice involves most centrally the recognition of diverse identities and experiences, their relation to structures of power, and methods of mediating difference and increasing inclusivity. The emerging literature on intersectionality and social movements can help us identify possible obstacles and opportunities to intersectional political practices as well as strategic dilemmas in mediating the tension between recognizing difference and fostering common identities and goals. Building upon this research, we can provide a comparative research framework for examining intersectional politics and practices in creating capacity, finding voice, forming alliances, and acting politically.

Creating Intersectional Capacity

Resource mobilization theory alerts us to the importance of material, socio-organization, and human resources for the ability of social movements to create capacity. Perhaps the most important aspect of intersectional capacity involves the commitment to addressing intragroup inequalities through the recognition of marginalized identities and their relation to power structures within social movement groups. This involves the fostering of intersectional consciousness, an awareness of the identities and needs of the most marginalized members of the movement as well as a sense of the particular, and multiple challenges they face. Intersectional scholarship further highlights the challenges of creating capacity across difference. As Crenshaw (1991) warned early on, political groups and movements organized around a single axis of identity and oppression run the risk of erasing or ignoring intragroup differences. Increasing intersectional capacity means finding ways to recognize intragroup inequalities and responding to them.

While intersectional consciousness through the recognition of different social locations may be a necessary condition for creating an inclusionary intersectional politics, it is not a sufficient one. Rather, gendered mobilizations must adopt decision-making practices that ensure the representation of their most marginalized members. Several chapters in this volume describe a host of practices intended to increase the intersectional capacity of groups and movements. For example, Pauline Cullen assesses how the Abortion Rights Campaign in Ireland attempted to ensure marginalized groups within the women's movement a "seat at the table" through working groups and rotating membership and leadership roles. In her chapter on refugee solidarity activism in Germany and Denmark, Nicole Doerr describes how the practice of political translation can help provide a meaningful voice to refugees in setting the agenda for the refugee solidarity movement. She also reminds us that meeting times, locations, and structure can be a means to include or exclude members with fewer resources of time and mobility. Creating intersectional capacity may also involve facilitating the formation of identity-based subgroups informed by intersectional consciousness within movements, which, as Celeste Montoya in her chapter on the Occupy movement reminds us, should not be viewed as a sign of movement breakdown but potentially of its health.

Creating intersectional capacity often relies directly on the ability of organizations and movements to secure material resources, and we are attentive in this volume to the ways in which donors' priorities and practices provide opportunities or obstacles for intersectional capacity. Indeed, as several chapters in this volume indicate, coalitions and movements that fail to secure funding or bring enough of their own funding to the table face severe challenges. Although a robust critique of funding practices has emerged that points to the ways in which they often serve to depoliticize the discourse, practices, and aims of social movements (Bernal and Grewal 2014; Lang 2013), very little has been written about the ways in which these practices facilitate or hinder intersectional organizing and activist strategies (Irvine and Halterman 2018).

A complex picture of the impact of funding practices on intersectional capacity emerges from the studies presented here. For example, while previous research suggests that a more competitive funding environment often fragments movements by causing competition among groups, Ayoub argues that the economic crisis has increased intersectional awareness and capacity of the LGBTQI movement in Europe through an increased sense that in a time of reduced funding all groups will benefit from cooperation rather than competition. Andrea Krizsán and Raluca Popa similarly find evidence that EU funding practices increased the intersectional capacity of women's groups in their campaign against violence toward women. Nevertheless, Jill Irvine and Leda Sutlović in their chapter in this volume describe the constraints imposed by EU funders in determining what constituted legitimate intersectional interests and groups, while Petra Ahrens finds that equality civil society organizations access to the EU is organized along class, gender, and race and this order is replicated in networks among the organizations themselves. Numerous activists in a variety of settings have called for a move away from a reliance on professionalized organizations and a greater investment in other forms of nonmaterial resources such as volunteers' labor and time. In any case, in order to act intersectionally, activists must devise strategies for garnering human, socio-organizational, and material resources that strengthen their capacity to do so.

Finding Voice

Finding voice involves consciousness raising and the creation of a collective identity around shared interests that can inspire political action (Evans 2015; Luciak 2001; Okeke-Ihejirika and Franceschet 2002; Razavi 2001). This is done through a process of framing issues and identity and through the related, but distinct, practice of political discourse (Agustín 2013; Siim and Mogre 2013). Much of the literature on intersectionality has centered on the challenges of recognizing difference while seeking common ground in the framing and articulation of identity, issues, and claims. Focusing on the process of finding voice can shed new light on when and how actors involved in gendered mobilization seek to root in particular gender and intersectional identities and when they shift toward new, broader frames that incorporate different perspectives and concerns (Yuval-Davis 2006a). It can also help us understand who is left out and why (Verloo 2006). Investigating intersectionality in the process of finding voice means identifying when and why actors involved in gendered mobilization shift message/tropes; what kind of equality arguments they adopt and why; and the issues and identities they deploy in shifting frames. The contributions to this volume add to previous scholarship on intersectionality, revealing both the challenges of creating inclusionary interests, frames, and claims in the process of finding voice and the possible benefits and drawbacks of particular strategies for achieving these aims.

Several possible intersectional strategies have been identified in the literature for creating common identities while acknowledging difference. The first is what we might call a *common identity strategy*. This strategy is based on efforts to increase the inclusion of marginalized groups of women, differentiated by a host of markers such as race, class, gender, or citizenship status. Dara Strolovitch (2007) has identified a number of "affirmative advocacy" approaches that are designed to achieve the inclusion of minority groups in social movements through outreach and other programs. As Lapperière and Lépinard (2016) point out, this strategy of inclusion often results in a minimalization of difference as advocates seek to incorporate new groups into movements with already articulated identities and interests. Pauline Cullen in her chapter in this volume makes the distinction between intersectional consciousness arising from a sensitivity to differences stemming from the intersection of social identities and intersectional blindness that insists on highlighting a single, shared identity. In this case, a strongly unifying emphasis on, for example, shared gender identity hinders the deeper fostering of intersectional consciousness and perspective. Moreover, it runs the risk of focusing on the most privileged voices within the movement since, as Andrea Spehar's study of the mobilization around the Swedish Domestic Service Tax Reform (RUT) in this volume demonstrates, political strategies that focus on one axis of identity are not somehow neutral toward others.

A second strategy addresses the explicit recognition of power differentials based on group identities and their inclusion in the process of constructing identities and interests. This strategy of finding voice does not seek mere recognition of marginalized individuals but a broadening of the perspectives and issues of different groups within gendered mobilizations. In this second *politicized identity strategy*, the politicization and mobilization of racial, ethnic, and other identities and subgroups within the women's movement requires a tolerance for difference and willingness to support new ways of framing identities and issues (Lapperière and Lépinard 2016). For example, in her chapter on the Jewish Voice for Peace Deadly Exchange campaign, Rachel Brown describes how combining the frameworks and perspectives of abolition, settler colonialism, and critiques of anti-blackness can enrich the understanding and framing of movement issues and help build new alliances.

A third intersectional strategy for finding voice, one that seeks to overcome the "logic of separation" (Bassel and Emejulu 2010) while not privileging one strand of identity over others, is what might be called an *interest-based strategy*. Elizabeth Cole argues for a process of framing based on commonality of interests rather than a commonality of identity (2008). Pauline Cullen in this volume illustrates how reproductive rights activists "shifted from a rooted form of identification toward collective action on a transversal set of claims where shared goals, rather than shared identities, anchor mobilization," exploring what is lost and what is gained when such a strategy for finding voice is employed. Interests can take a variety of forms, from support for particular policies to a shared interest based on a common experience of marginalization in relation to power. While supporting particular policies may be most appropriate for finding voice in broader coalitions among social groups, a focus on a common experience of marginalization might make most sense for building alliances among different groups within the women's movement. Nevertheless, movements may experience deep disagreements over their common interests; for example, as Ethel Tungohan's chapter on the Filipino migrant's movement suggests, between those advocating for legal equality and those responding to structural forces of oppression through a vision of "radical futurities."

A persistent challenge in finding voice, particularly in broader coalitions, involves the process of shifting or challenging already fixed frames and framing logics. Scholars have pointed to the dilemmas involved in articulating a frame that might resonate better with the majority population or articulating a set of issues, concerns, and demands that represent the interests of marginalized groups from intersectional social positions. While the first opens up greater potential for coalitional politics and political success, it may also stifle intersectional claim making. As Andrea Krizsán and Raluca Popa demonstrate in this volume, identity-based groups that have ways of framing their claims in terms of a particular logic, for example the logic of inequality, or the logic of protection, may find that their claims are fundamentally at odds with one another. In resolving competing or incompatible frames and claims within alliances, the group that can make the more widespread, popular appeal usually wins, relegating to the margin those groups whose social identities cause them to reside there.

Forming Alliances

Forming alliances gets at the heart of intersectional activism, which points to the necessity of building alliances across both "intracategorical difference" within groups as well as across "intercategorical difference" among different social movements (McCall 2005).

In this section, we are primarily concerned with building intersectional alliances across movements. Even single-axis identity groups engage in intersectional alliance building, but the broader and more diverse a coalition becomes, the more difficult it may be to find a common framework and set of political goals, and the larger the risk that groups at the intersection will find themselves marginalized or ignored. Scholars of women's movements have pointed out that in forging alliances, women's organizations must balance the risk of being subordinated to the strategies and goals of other political actors with the need for political support (Friedman 2000; Seidman 1999; Verloo 2013). Yet, as Celeste Montoya demonstrates in her study of the Occupy movement in this volume, broad coalitions or social movements also offer opportunities for intersectional exploration and activism as identity-based subgroups draw attention to new issues and perspectives (Bassel and Emejulu 2014; Hancock 2011).

As bridge builders, individuals and groups at the intersections, what Chun, Lipsitz, and Shin (2013) call "strategic group positions," play a critical role in envisioning and facilitating new coalitions and collaborations. These positions "while always partial perspectival and performative" can be used strategically to "recognize split and conflicting identities not as obstacles to solidarity but as valuable evidence about problems unsolved and new coalitions that need to be formed" (Chun, Lipsitz, and Shin 2013, 923). Several chapters in this volume point to the crucial role played by bridge builders. In their chapter on the BlackLivesMatter movement, Bauman and Brown point to the critical role black women play in organizing within their own communities and in reaching across to other communities in fostering advocates and alliances. Nicole Doerr similarly points to the importance of second- and third-generation immigrants who engage in political translation practices that help bridge communities and movements. Chapters by Phillip Ayoub and Andrea Krizsán and Raluca Popa describe how transnational organizations, such as International Lesbian and Gay Alliance (ILGA) and the transnational Roma group (EERC), acted as bridge builders in forming alliances across borders, though these had more limited impact in particular national contexts.

This raises the question of whether certain forms of alliance or coalition are more conducive to intersectional politics. Social movement scholars have long been concerned with coalition typologies and the various political goals they best serve (McAdam, Tarrow, and Tilly 2001). In contrast, little attention has been given to this question in the literature on intersectionality. Some scholars have argued that the more established and institutionalized coalitions become, the more likely they are to resist demands for recognition from those groups with less power (Lyshaug 2006). Suzanne Staggenborg (2015) warns, however, that while the relative absence of hierarchy may be more conducive to intersectional politics, "there is also a danger of exclusivity in informal alliances." Other scholars have tackled the question of identity-based subgroups, which break away from single or multiple axis movements to form their own groups. The risk of fragmenting women's movements through separate, identity-based organizing has long concerned feminist scholars and practitioners (Hancock 2011; Yuval-Davis 2011). While some scholars highlight this risk, others argue that separate organizing based on group identities increases intersectional consciousness and benefits the women's movement as a whole (Chun, Lipsitz, and Shin 2013; Weldon 2011). Celeste Montoya's chapter demonstrates that subgroups with intersectional consciousness and capacity can and do play a positive role in building and maintaining healthy alliances in broad-based social justice movements.

In short, forming alliances is perhaps *the* crucial element in intersectional political practice. Mere empathy is not enough in building alliances, although it can provide a useful starting point. Rather, the recognition of cross-cutting cleavages and intersectional identities and interests provides a firmer basis on which to build coalitions, networks, and alliances. This recognition signals a dynamic notion of rooting and shifting, in which the roots of one's commitment to a cause are denaturalized as constant shifting in order to build alliances becomes part of a movement's DNA. While intersectional strategies might involve "staying close to home" in the selection of allies, they may also involve moving into a larger regional or global network of transnational actors. Similarly, they may involve only women's movement allies or involve class, race, and ethnically diverse movements. Using an intersectional lens may lead to the search for unlikely allies, resulting in fruitful coalitions or more enduring movements.

Acting Politically

The capacity for and modalities of intersectional political action depend on institutional and contextual factors as well as on strategic choices and agency. Intersectional organizing is shaped by political institutions and structures and shifting political opportunities, but it is also the result of strategic choices and agency. Thus, while particular practices influence the emergence of intersectional activism, these practices are crucially shaped both by the institutional structures within which they occur and the political opportunities created by shifting social, economic, and political contexts. Economic uncertainty and forced migration, for example, may have impacted the intersectional consciousness, imagination, or actions of movements and organizations. For example, the economic crisis in Europe may increase solidarity among and between different identity-based groups as a result of a realization that "we are all in this together," as Phillip Ayoub documents in his study of LGBTQ activism. Similarly, chapters by Ethel Tungohan and Nicole Doerr indicate that the recent waves of migration and forced migration have opened up opportunities for new forms of solidarity and intersectional activism, even as they have raised new tensions between groups with different social locations.

In investigating how intersectional consciousness and practices shape political action, we tackle three major questions. First, when it comes to strategic choices and agency, we are concerned with the twin questions of how the choice of political strategies shapes the possibilities of intersectional politics and, in turn, how the emergence of intersectional consciousness shapes the action repertoires of movements. For example, in their chapter on Croatia, Jill Irvine and Leda Sutlović investigate how different political strategies shape intersectional politics, contrasting the different possibilities of mass "disruptive" political strategies with more legalistic, "routinized" political strategies. Ethel Tungohan similarly juxtaposes two different political strategies that have divided the Filipino migrants' movement, arguing that while a strategy of focusing on gaining legal equality may garner more allies, only a more radical strategy that considers the underlying structural causes of interlocking oppression can ultimately achieve intersectional goals.

While the choice of strategies affects possibilities for intersectional action, intersectional consciousness also shapes the modes of action movements embrace. Acting intersectionally can alter repertoires as new approaches to protest get added to approaches more familiar to a particular group. For example, an alliance between women's organizations and labor movements may result in a fusion of two different protest repertoires by adding strikes to street protests. Incorporating youth movements and concerns into gendered mobilization may result in new social media strategies and modes of action. Aligning LGBT issues and groups with women's movement activism can result in the adoption of Pride Parades as a more central mode of action. As Fernando Tormos-Aponte's chapter on student activism in Puerto Rico demonstrates, including the voices, and incorporating into the leadership groups at the intersection of identities within movements, changes not only the goals and frames employed but also the modes of action.

Second, when it comes to political institutions, we are concerned with how these shape, constrain, and preclude particular forms of intersectional political action. When movements act politically, they engage with institutions that try to impose their own policy logics and policy-making pathways (Tarrow 2011). These logics and pathways might acknowledge one ground of discrimination but not others; or they might encourage specific collaborations while precluding others. Institutional logics can thus impede or enable intersectional political action. In effect, intersectional gendered mobilization often relies not just on outside activism but also on feminist insiders within political institutions.

Within the EU, many of these feminist insiders, or femocrats, however, have historically defined their role first and foremost as fighting women's discrimination and second as mainstreaming gender into all government units and policy fields. Some now see their budgets cut or distributed differently to multiple discrimination causes, in effect pitting discrimination grounds and their institutional advocates against each other. As Petra Ahrens demonstrates in her chapter on transnational equality organizations, EU institutions privilege certain identity groups over others when it comes to access to resources and influence. When political institutions invite what Elizabeth Martinez (1993) has called the "Oppression Olympics," those who mobilize for intersectional claims are particularly vulnerable to losing their ability to act politically. Ethel Tungohan warns of the "drawbacks to prioritizing engagement within 'state regulated institutions and economic systems' which themselves foster 'exploitation and violence'" since without an awareness of how these institutions are flawed, the gains will primarily benefit the most privileged members of the Filipino community. In short, proximity to the state can result in significant policy gains but often at the expense of deeper intersectional engagement.

Third, we investigate the impact of scaling from the local to the transnational (Lang and Sauer 2016) and its impact on intersectional activism and movement building. Previous research on social movements has shown how transnational action repertoires expand upon forms of protest enacted only at the national level (Tarrow 2011). Whether and how transnational forms of intersectional activism emerge and differ from intersectional activism at the nation and local levels is a question we address in this volume. While political action may involve local or national coalitions, which include gender equality as only one of several issues, it may also mean mobilizing transnational alliances to leverage political action focused exclusively on gender equality. In this case, rooting and shifting may involve strategies of scaling and finding modes of action most appropriate to them. As Phillip Ayoub demonstrates in his chapter in this volume, LGBT intersectional consciousness and activism has been fostered most centrally at the transnational level, with diffusion to the national contexts in varying degrees of success. In their chapter on Black-LivesMatter, Beaman and Brown stress that the boundaries of black women's activism are not nation-state based, since racism and colonialism are two sides of the same coin, and several of the social movements considered in this volume similarly engage in transnational political action to address these issues.

OVERVIEW OF THE BOOK

In this volume, we asked our contributors to engage with different components of social movement intersectionality by asking a series of questions. In what ways have activist groups mobilized around various facets of identity and how do they work together? To what extent have various movements addressed the issues of race, ethnicity, class, sexuality, and nationality? What are the power structures within and across movement alliances? In what way have shifts in the political environment, such as the economic downturn and the perceived immigration crises, impacted the intersectional consciousness or praxis of these movements and organizations? What are the dynamics of intersectional praxis, and how might groups roots and shift in different ways? And ultimately, what are the ways in which intersectional praxes manifest or are manifested through creating capacity, finding voice, forming alliances, and acting politically.

As discussed earlier, the book is divided into two sections. In the first section of the volume, authors examine intersectionality (or the lack thereof) within movements organized centrally around gender and sexuality. In chapter 1, Pauline Cullen investigates activism for reproductive rights in Ireland, focusing on the dynamics of collaboration and contestation between state feminist organizations, on the one hand, and student and radical feminist groups, on the other hand. She shows that campaigns such as "Repeal the Eighth" and "Together for Yes," while playing a central role in delivering the votes to repeal the constitutional antiabortion amendment of 1983, did so at the expense of marginalizing young, working-class, and minority women. Thus, temporary alliances led to successful political action—at the prize, however, of sustained intersectional activism. With a focus on attracting rural, middle-class, and nonfeminist constituencies to vote for the repeal, intersectional claims were dampened strategically to orchestrate a unified voice.

In chapter 2, Andrea Spehar considers the challenges of employing an intersectional approach in the policy-making process in Sweden through investigating the case of the Swedish Domestic Services Tax Reform (RUT). The RUT reform of household-related services powerfully highlights intersectional dilemmas feminists encounter when organizing around public policy reforms. In the case of domestic work, class and immigrant status informed feminist positions in politically significant ways. In particular, the voice and the political activities of civil-society actors (e.g., immigrant organizations and labor unions) and their relevance in agenda setting and policymaking were insignificant. Rather, state feminists, mostly women and men representing different political parties and governmental bodies for gender equality, led agenda setting and policymaking. Moreover, domestic workers in general and migrant domestic workers in particular constituted a largely invisible and underrepresented collective in the policy process. In order to pursue effective intersectional policymaking, representatives of intersectionally defined target populations should be included in the policy process.

In chapter 3, Raluca Popa and Andrea Krizsán provide a comparative analysis of intersectional politics in activism against domestic violence in Hungary and Romania, investigating meeting points between different inequality claims and mobilizations with the aim of assessing their potential for intersectionality. Their comparative analysis of the dynamics of intersectional politics in the two countries highlights important factors that facilitate intersectional alliances and action. They find similarities in that a gradual openness to diversity took place over the fifteen years of their analysis with organizations and activists increasingly representing multiple social locations, in particular Roma women, lesbian women, and disabled women. The two countries, however, are markedly different in the type of political intersectionality dynamics that emerged in domestic violence activism. Intersectional groups are conspicuously missing from the mobilization against domestic violence in Hungary, while they are included throughout the mobilization process in Romania from 2010 onward. These differences are due to (1) the respective capacity of intersectional women's groups for shaping the politics of intersectionality, (2) the importance of resource pulling in building intersectional alliances, and (3) the role played by transnational organizations such as the European Women's Lobby.

In chapter 4, Ayşe Dursun focuses on what she calls "counter-intersectionality," a mode of politics that seeks to dismantle intersectional discourses and practices. While this volume focuses primarily on socially progressive organizing (by feminists, LGBTQ rights, and anti-racist activists), assessing the manner in which they pursue intersectional mobilization, this chapter focuses on one set of actors aiming to do the opposite. Dursun theorizes and demonstrates the counter-intersectional mode of politics by examining conservative women's activists in Turkey, who, under the impetus of a reactionary government, have worked to undo the intersectional advances made by feminist, Kurdish, and LGBTQ movements. They do this by using a "gender justice frame" of gender equality that reinforces rather than challenges traditional (and religiously based) gender roles. Dursun concludes by calling upon scholars to study how intersectionality is currently being undone in the context of globalization and rising right-wing movements in order to develop strategies to circumvent counter-intersectional attacks that threaten to marginalize the knowledge on inequality and solidarities laboriously produced by generations of multiple marginalized groups

In chapter 5, Jill Irvine and Leda Sutlović investigate how shifting political environments in Croatia shape social movement strategies and approaches and how these, in turn, may open or close opportunities for intersectional politics. They identify three periods of feminist activism: the first characterized by the disruptive politics of a pro-democracy, oppositional movement; the second by a legalistic approach focused on formulating and passing gender equality policies and legislation required by the EU accession process; and the third period characterized by new forms of intersectional politics emerging in response to economic crisis and protest. They argue that the pro-democracy movement's electoral strategy of maximizing the number of voters during the first period fostered the inclusion of rural women, even as it failed to prioritize intersectional awareness or claims. These claims became more possible during the second period, when with EU accession new channels of influence emerged but were constrained by the legalistic mode of politics adopted by the women's movement and by the EU's narrow definition of what constituted valid intersectional claims.

In chapter 6, Phillip Ayoub investigates the conditions that enable cross-organizational and cross-movement alliances in his exploration of the European LGBTI movement during the financial crisis. Drawing upon survey data he collected from LGBTI organizations, he argues that the financial crisis has worked to increase intersectional consciousness, particularly at the transnational level, where the potential for brokering cross-movement relationships is high. Although groups on the ground struggle with realizing the political potential of intersectionality, times of scarcity have served to heighten awareness by generating a sense of shared threat and by challenging INGOS to think pragmatically about cooperating for access to limited resources. Lack of resources, however, is also a factor in avoiding intersectional mobilization, as his interlocutors point to the material costs of implementing intersectional approaches to activism.

The second section of the volume looks beyond movements focusing on gender and sexuality toward inclusion of gender and intersectional mobilization in other activist causes. In chapter 7, Celeste Montoya examines the role of identity-based organizing as a potential site for making intersectional interventions in mass movements, by studying groups organized around gender, race, and sexuality within the US Occupy mobilizations. Using examples from this research, she argues that intra-movement "identity politics" serve not as a cause of movement failure, as is often argued, but instead as a symptom of social movement failures arising from false universalisms and exclusionary practices. Identity-based groups formed when groups felt underrepresented, marginalized, or even threatened. She argues that identity-based groups might also provide a remedy for such failures, when they develop intersectional practices and avoid replicating fragmenting single-axis approaches.

In chapter 8, Rachel Brown examines the insurrectionary potential of intersectionality, particularly when it is deployed alongside other analytic frameworks. In her autoethnographic study of Jewish Voice for Peace, a US-based national organization campaigning for justice in Palestine, Brown highlights how theorization of settler-colonialism labor might work with logics of intersectionality to more effectively and thoroughly challenge police brutality, anti-black violence, militarization, and land colonization in the United States and Palestine. Utilizing an intersectional approach in tandem with a colonial framework, she argues, also helps unpack the dangers of feminist universalist solidarity claims by insisting on the complicity of queer settlers in the violence against indigenous people.

Fernando Tormos-Aponte, in chapter 9, explores the role that intersectional solidarity played in transforming the Puerto Rican student movement. Using a participant observation approach, Tormos-Aponte assesses the differing impact of student activism on higher education policy. He demonstrates how from 2005 to 2017, the Puerto Rican student movement shifted its agenda, leadership, and structure to include and prioritize the issues of intersectionally marginalized groups. He argues that it was only after the movement developed an intersectional solidarity approach that it was able to successfully seize political opportunities and effectively mobilize for change. Adopting this organizing approach allowed the movement to sustain coalitions across different identity groups and increase their legitimacy in the public eye.

Nicole Doerr ethnographically studies intersectional gendered inclusion in German and Danish refugee solidarity activism in chapter 10. She argues that lack of intersectional awareness in broad and heterogeneous coalitions may create what she calls positional misunderstandings, in which cultural differences are highlighted while structural inequalities are overlooked. Doerr advances her concept of political translation as a set of collective practices that enable intersectional capacity, alliances, and political action. In order to develop such political translation capacity, she argues, insight into and experiential knowledge of positional misunderstandings is key. While many queer activist group members had developed that capacity, the mainstream refugee organizations she studied in many cases marginalized those articulated positional power differentials and resulting exclusionary dynamics.

In chapter 11, Ethel Tungohan examines the politics of intersectionality in the Filipino migrants' movement in Canada. Employing autoethnographic and participant observation approaches, Tungohan analyzes the movement's attempts to grapple with the intersecting social locations of its members, to articulate and advocate for its diverse needs, and to build intra- and cross-movement coalitions. She argues that the Filipino migrants' movement in Canada is divided between organizations that adopt a notion of intersectionality that adheres to vision of radical futurities, one that places a critique of interlocking powers at the center of their work, and those organizations that prioritize legal equality. She concludes by discussing the challenges the migrants' movement faces in building alliances across movements, arguing that working in solidarity with other oppressed groups "remains an important" and only partially realized goal of the Filipino migrants' movement.

Jean Beaman and Nadia E. Brown highlight the role that intersectional consciousness plays in shaping black women's activism, in their exploration of the US and French #BlackLivesMatter movements in chapter 12. They argue that while black women's precarious social location has often led to their marginalization, it has not impeded their ability to mobilize their communities. Exploring how black women draw on their race and gender identities as a primary means of connecting with their communities and advocating for social justice in various political environments, they argue that intersectional consciousness can be articulated and practiced inside as well as outside the state. Whereas in France, black activists mostly organize from the margins and outside of state institutions, US activists combine political work inside the state with community activism. In both cases, however, a single-axis focus on sexism or racism has proven to be insufficient to address discrimination and marginalization of black women.

In chapter 13, Petra Ahrens investigates the interface between civil society organizations and European Union institutions in terms of allowing for supranational intersectional policy claims and outputs. Drawing on the political opportunity structure that the EU provides for civil society engagement, she asks if and how EU-level organizations are pushed to work within intersectional frameworks as well as how civil society actors try to shape the kinds of intersectional activism they practice within these institutional confines. EU institutions, Ahrens argues, do shape intersectional civil society mobilization by inviting and positively sanctioning it. EU-level equality organizations, however, resemble a mountain skyline, in which a clear hierarchy exists with class at the top, followed by gender and race. In effect, some organizations have developed substantial capacity to act intersectionally, but they do so from the top, in the process contributing to the marginalization of other, smaller, often race-based civil society actors.

Part I

INTERSECTIONALITY WITHIN GENDERED SOCIAL MOVEMENTS

Chapter 1

The Limits and Potential of Solidarity

Activism on Reproductive Rights in Ireland

Pauline Cullen

This chapter explores advocacy for reproductive rights in Ireland to pose questions about the dynamics of collaboration and contest, inclusion, and exclusion in gendered mobilizations. In this case study, I examine the reproductive rights activism of the state feminist organization, the National Women's Council of Ireland (NWCI), and of student and radical feminist groups. Working from the theoretical framework of this edited collection, I focus on the factors that shape the capacity, resources, voice, alliances, and forms of political action open to feminist social movements and forms of gendered mobilization. In emphasizing patterns of collaboration and contestation between different organizations and collectives, I reflect on elements of inclusion and exclusion that narrow or widen the possibilities for intersectional awareness and action. In the Irish context, complex intersectional claims making is often stymied by a political culture most open to single-issue populist campaigns. Forms of situated solidarity, however, have arisen between diverse groups of women alongside elements of exclusion where poor and ethnic minority women remain less represented.

In what follows, I detail the broader conceptual frameworks within feminist and social movement studies that support this analysis. I then outline the contemporary context within which feminist and gendered mobilizations occur, describing the organizations taking a central role in advocating for reproductive rights in Ireland and their efforts to mobilize separately and in common campaigns to repeal the Eighth Amendment[1] of the Irish constitution. This constitution granted the fetus the right to life and maintains a constitutional restriction on abortion. I further investigate the changing political opportunity structure on reproductive rights in Ireland and the ways in which pro-choice organizations and the NWCI responded in transversal campaigns aimed at securing a yes vote on a constitutional referendum to repeal the Eighth Amendment. Ultimately, the campaigns documented here were successful in achieving their goal, when on May 25, 2018, voters returned a two-thirds majority to secure a constitutional referendum for repeal.

The contribution made here is to offer an empirical study that allows for a nuanced assessment of how gendered mobilizations are complicated by external political constraints and opportunities and the presence of diverse actors with different levels of power and resources in the organizational field. These factors have implications for the tactical choices made and for what women and whose issues and interests gain most visibility. Examining campaigns to repeal the Eighth Amendment makes visible the challenges present in addressing a highly polarizing issue of morality politics in a conservative gender regime. In addition, this case illustrates specific challenges for the pro-choice movement in creating capacity in their efforts to counterbalance a well-resourced, pro-life movement supported by the Catholic Church and to find voice in the context of the historical opposition and/or ambivalence of the state and ruling centrist parties toward the issue. While the campaign illustrated intersectional awareness, intersectional action and inclusion were constrained by power dynamics within and across organizations in generational and racialized terms and as a consequence of an inhospitable political context for complex intersectional claims.

My analysis draws primarily on secondary sources and primary data collected from public sources, including governmental and nongovernmental organizations, media websites, social media, and organizational publications. This is supplemented with twelve semi-structured interviews conducted between 2014 and 2018. Interview participants were selected using purposive sampling from the staff and volunteers in the main organizations advocating for reproductive rights. Interviewees include activists with the anarchist feminist Abortion Rights Campaign (ARC), leaders of pro-choice Action on Choice, the NWCI and allied left-wing politicians, and members of civil society organizations. The data also include participant observation of three organizing meetings for the pro-choice campaigns held during 2017 and 2018 and two "marches for choice" in September 2016 and September 2017.

THEORIZING GENDERED MOBILIZATIONS

Research on gendered mobilizations as outlined in the introduction to this volume asks us to reflect on how women's organizations rooted in specific identities and focused on specific issues can, through collective action, shift to build capacity and alliances that aim to deliver forms of political intersectionality. Analyses of the coalition politics involved in organizing on women's rights also indicate the range of difficulties faced by women's groups in accessing resources, avoiding co-optation, and practicing inclusionary and intersectional forms of mobilization (De Jong and Kimm 2017; Fraser 2016; Motta et al. 2011). Analysis of women's movements and organizing has clearly identified the limits of white liberal and neoliberal feminism in constructing women in ways that fail to address intersectional realities (Bassel and Emejulu 2017; Motta et al 2011) and the co-optation of feminist projects by neoliberal and market forces (Fraser 2016; Griffin 2015; Rottenberg 2014). Asserting the dearth of intersectionality in women's movements in terms of the existence of hegemonic unthinking forms of action, however, may miss important attempts made to collaborate across difference where conscious decisions are made to minimize difference for collective ends. Forging such alliances, where critical mass may strengthen campaigns, is important in the context of creating capacity to demobilize strong counter movements. The pro-choice case study here illustrates these dynamics and can help us adjudicate what is lost and gained when moderate forms of feminism engage alongside more radical elements to secure gendered social change. In these encounters, different feminist groups bracket their ideological differences, shifting in ways that allow for a common, if broad, platform that illustrates the political solidarity of women and the deep conflicts between them.

Adopting the concept of voice here reveals the frameworks and identities at play when activists shift from a rooted form of identification toward collective action on a transversal set of claims where shared goals, rather than shared identities, anchor mobilization. In conceptual terms, forms of transversalism can be identified, as a dynamic practice of "rooting" and "shifting" along different dimensions of intersecting oppressions as both a normative and strategic commitment to inclusion. Weaker allies, however, may be overshadowed by stronger coalition members that can erase or weaken voice and reproduce exclusions while offering opportunities to secure forms of systemic change (Irvine et al. in this volume). Greater empirical and conceptual specification of campaigning between mainstream and autonomous women's organizations that involves the process of shifting from specific rooted identities to shared programs may reveal possibilities to secure movement goals, while offering opportunities to achieve forms of political intersectionality. In what follows, I map these theoretical conceptualizations of intersectionality onto established dimensions of political mobilization, applying an analytical framework that focuses on the role intersectionality plays in creating capacity, finding voice, forging alliances, and acting politically.

GENDER EQUALITY AND WOMEN'S MOVEMENTS
IN IRELAND

Ireland is an open and highly globalized economic regime with a hybrid welfare system that combines strong liberal characteristics with conservative and Catholic features and a strong variant of the male breadwinner regime (Murphy 2017). As a low-tax economy, Ireland also lacks capacity to fund socially necessary reproductive and care work. As a result, such work remains feminized in the sphere of the private household. This is exacerbated by the economic crisis and more permanent forms of austerity. Irish political culture is characterized by forms of progressive incrementalism and consensus policymaking (Kirby and Murphy 2011) as well as anti-intellectualism and a strong ideology of both the market and charity (Lynch, Cantillon, and Magaret 2016, 23). The apparatus of Irish policymaking includes a bicameral parliament, and the 1937 constitution which only weakly articulates social and economic rights is heavily gendered in style and content. As such, the constitution is a focus of feminist campaigns for reform as detailed here.

Despite the introduction in 2016 of a gender quota for national electoral candidates, Ireland occupies eightieth place when it comes to women's representation. Women comprise 22 percent of the national parliament and 16 percent of local government bodies (IPU 2018). The gender pay gap increased from 12.2 percent in 2012 to 14.1 percent in 2014, and the pension gap is 34 percent (IHREC 2017). Only 20 percent of Irish women earn more than €50,000 per year (Murphy 2017). Limited state-funded childcare and crisis-related labor market policy responses have also heighted the likelihood that women are locked into combining unpaid care work and low pay. This is particularly the case for single parents and for migrant and young women (Collins and Murphy 2016). Austerity-related cuts to state funding (in the order of 40 percent) for some women's groups have also meant that the overall feminist architecture is under-resourced, with major challenges for feminist resistance and mobilization (Harvey 2014).

Conflict and fragmentation are key elements in understanding the development of feminism in the Irish context (Cullen 2016). Efforts to construct a unified women's movement in the 1970s had created forms of exclusion where differences on issues including nationalism, class, religion, and abortion led to significant divisions (Connolly 2006). The mainstreaming of the women's movement from the early 1990s, with the establishment of the state-funded NWCI, offered a platform for some women's organizations to pursue common aims. The NWCI became an umbrella under which to consolidate the activities of predominantly liberal women's organizations, while small radical and anarchist groups persisted on the margins (De Wan 2010, 524–5). At the same time, working-class women and ethnic minority women established their own organizations and have operated in parallel, in alliance, or in contest with the more formalized arm of the Irish women's movement (De Tona and Lentin 2011) The existence of these later groups marks a challenge to the former boundaries of Irish feminism rooted largely in white middle-class terms, but their members often remain marginalized and excluded from

Irish society and Irish feminist activism. At the same time, recession and austerity measures that cut gender equality infrastructure, funds, and services have rendered migrant-led women's organizations and working-class women's groups based in the community more dependent on mainstream women's organizations (Cullen and Murphy 2016).

Activism on gendered issues has proved most successful when it has used maternalist messages and when it targets single issues with broad public appeal. This is most evident in a series of gendered campaigns that experienced some successes in resisting austerity-related cuts to services and supports for single parents and children with disabilities (Cullen and Murphy 2016). Spillane (2015) recounts how, while absent feminist messaging, women in public sector teaching and nursing unions led resistance to public sector wage cuts and negative changes in flexible working conditions. Women were also vocal in the successful 2015 marriage equality referendum. As such, gendered and feminist mobilizations manifest a range of frameworks both liberal and radical, creating different alliances with the state and left politics. These resistances and contradictions, however, reflect the multiple realities experienced and strategies employed by different classes of women and the varying modes of intersectionality, raising questions about what women and whose interests count (Bassel and Emejulu 2017; Murphy and Cullen 2018).

REPEAL THE EIGHTH AMENDMENT AND REPRODUCTIVE RIGHTS

Ireland has a poor record on intimate citizenship rights for women. Denied access to safe, legal and affordable termination of pregnancy in Ireland, Irish women had continually mobilized for a constitutional amendment to repeal the 1983 Eighth Amendment. Various UN committees[2] had made detailed recommendations on legal and policy frameworks on reproductive rights.

In a break from past political consensus, a May 2017 Citizen Assembly recommended legislative and constitutional reforms to government, which, if enacted, would amount to safe legal abortion in Ireland. A parliamentary committee began deliberation in September 2017 and made recommendations in December 2017 that called for a repeal of the amendment, a referendum on the constitutional ban that took place on May 25, 2018, and a liberalization of access within the first trimester (Oirechtas 2017). Repeal of the Eighth Amendment garnered governmental support, although polling in advance of the referendum indicated a close margin between both those supporting and opposing repeal (Leahy 2018a). A decline in the moral authority held by the Catholic Church has played a role in an increased support for repeal and is, in part, a function of revelations of historic institutionalized child abuse and cruelty toward pregnant women and the reluctance of the church authorities to provide for victims through reparations. At the same time, broader cultural shifts associated with the emergence of new feminist organizations encouraged women to speak out about their experiences of crisis pregnancy and abortion. Analysis also suggests that the return of Irish emigrants from more liberal countries has driven change (McKay 2018).

While activism for reproductive rights has waxed and waned in the past forty years in Ireland, more proximate events are key to understanding this wave of mobilization. A series of European Court of Justice (ECJ) rulings on reproductive rights cases in 2006 and 2010 and the twentieth anniversary of a significant legal development in the Irish reproductive regime (the X case, decided in 1992)[3] contributed to the consolidation of abortion rights campaigning (Quilty, Kennedy, and Conlon 2015). This movement was galvanized by the tragic death of thirty-one-year-old Savita Halappanavar following the denial of her request for a termination of her pregnancy. In response to her death, 15,000 people marched in a "Never Again" protest in Dublin on November 17, 2012. A revised, if restricted, legal regime on the issue followed in 2013. In 2012, in part as a response to these events, the ARC, an anarchist and autonomous organization advocating for a liberal abortion regime, was established.

The first main activity of the ARC was a mass protest entitled the "March for Choice" in September 2012, which is now an annual event. The ARC's demand for a radical liberalization of abortion in Ireland, its connections to anarchist organizations, and its predominantly younger feminist membership profile have placed it at odds with organizations such as the state feminist NWCI, which has pursued a more moderate agenda. The ARC has worked to facilitate forms of intersectional dialogue and voice aimed at "building solidarity and communication between groups of marginalised women in Ireland" (ARC 2015, 16). In concrete terms, they have produced materials in culturally sensitive formats for ethnic minority women. In organizational terms, the ARC is a volunteer-led and grassroots-based organization. It makes strong claims to work according to anti-hierarchical structures and a commitment to represent "those disproportionately affected by these laws including women who are marginalised by poverty, racism, immigration status and disability" (ARC 2016). The ARC is organized in a series of working groups and committees that rotate membership and leadership roles. Although few members of marginalized groups are featured in the organization, this absence is justified by the organization in terms of "the significant structural barriers at a societal and organizational level which prevent marginalized groups participation and involvement in ARC" (ARC 2015, 13).

The organization, though headquartered in Dublin, has worked to build an infrastructure in different regions through student feminist collectives and anarchist spaces. Efforts to mobilize in rural areas have been stymied by "the conservative stance of some members of boards of organizations that did not participate because of our perceived radical stance" (ARC 2015, 15). Voice is thus, in this context, characterized by a majority of younger female activists identifying as radical feminist and/or anarchist. The ARC demonstrates intersectional consciousness and commitment to supporting intersectional voice in its stated efforts to "avoid tokenism, engage with minority representative groups and provide diverse opportunities to enhance a wide range of participation sensitive to issues of class, ethnicity and race and disability" (ARC 2018). The ARC relies on volunteers and they have accessed resources from an initiative entitled the Workers Beer Company, where activists (mostly students) work as bartenders at outdoor musical festivals and donate their wages. This has allowed them to remain independent of national and international pro-choice donors they view as a constraint on issues including ARC's pro-sex work platform (ARC 2015, 13).[4]

Another important player in pro-choice activism has been the organization Action for Choice, led by long-serving second- and third-wave feminists and focused on building a broad alliance for the removal of the Eighth Amendment. ARC and Action for Choice have had a conflictual relationship, competing for political and overall fundraising space for reproductive rights. When asked about the relationship between the organizations, leaders of Action for Choice and other veteran, pro-choice activists indicated their appreciation for the creativity and imagination of the ARC, yet also communicated their frustration at their controversial messaging, viewed as politically naïve.[5] At the same time, ARC members felt that older activists had worked to marginalize their influence, excluding them from the organizing efforts of the NWCI where Action for Choice had enjoyed access. The NWCI, dependent on state funds from centrist political parties, in the past has been cautious about collaboration with the ARC due to its association with largely male-led, socialist opposition political parties.[6]

By 2017, however, as the political opportunities to change the abortion regime evolved, the ARC and Action for Choice allied with the NWCI to form a new alliance known as the Coalition to Repeal the Eighth. The Coalition to Repeal the Eighth is made up of over 100 organizations and includes trade unions, student societies, LGBTQI and women's community development organizations, left minority political parties, and medical and faith-based, pro-choice groups.[7] The decision to form the broader coalition is an indication of efforts to shift toward an alliance in order to consolidate capacity, strengthen voice, and design forms of political action. A central objective of the Coalition was to secure 1 million votes in the referenda held in May 2018, an objective they ultimately realized. Their key areas of work included raising awareness of why and how the Eighth Amendment should be repealed, working with groups countrywide and supporting them to raise awareness of the need for repeal, and facilitating connections and networking between the broad range of groups and individuals who wanted the Eighth Amendment removed (Coalition to Repeal the Eighth 2017).

The impetus for this alliance was a function of the proliferation of smaller pro-choice groups and actions in the year leading up to the proposed referendum, characterized by veteran feminist activists as "chaotic with overlapping and contradictory messaging" (Interview with director of NWCI, December 2017). Asked to comment on the direction of the movement during this phase, a co-convenor of the coalition commented, "There is a balance to be struck between energizing the base of committed activists and appealing to the wavering centerground. For the moment, the repeal campaign seems to be focusing on the first of these" (Leahy 2017a).

Faced with a well-resourced, pro-life countermovement and eager to seize this historic break in the status quo on abortion, pro-choice leaders worked to move the movement from mobilization of committed members toward reaching a broader set of constituents. Veteran activists recognized that the ARC had organized successfully, if less strategically, in this phase and if incorporated into a broader alliance had an important cadre of biographically available younger activists and a regional infrastructure that could be exploited. Activists from all contexts reported a series of "tough" conversations in the process of forming the coalition (Trapped in Time Event, Repeal the Eighth October 2017). This process of coalition building marked a shift in the campaign toward the cultivation of a messaging discipline and focus largely absent from its early stages.

A focus on one specific goal, repeal of the Eighth Amendment, rather than any prescription on what should replace the ban, allowed the coalition to host organizations across the ideological spectrum. Initially, the ARC maintained its demand for "free, safe, and legal" including late-term abortion while the NWCI, supporting a twelve-week limit for most cases, adopted a "safe, rare and legal" message. As the referendum neared, however, the coalition shifted to create a universalizing message that de-emphasized the specific provisions to replace the repealed amendment, emphasizing instead merely the removal of the constitutional article. This was deemed essential to convince those undecided or middle-ground voters.[8]

The success of the "Yes Equality" campaign that secured marriage equality by referendum in 2015 is widely recognized as an important motivator and exemplar. Securing gay marriage in Ireland by popular vote is seen a remarkable feat given the long tradition of Catholicism and restrictive gender politics (Healy, Sheehan, and Whelan 2016). Activists advised, "The repeal movement needs to take a leaf out of the marriage equality campaign book, particularly its focus on personal stories which deliberately dialled down the visibility of some LGBTQ figures" (Trapped in Time Event Repeal the Eighth, October 2017).[9] Eager to avoid the polarizing debates evident on social media, specifically younger pro-choice activists baited by pro-life social media accounts, veteran feminist activists referred again to the Marriage Equality campaign and its strict discipline and training that had helped to avoid confrontation with the Catholic right.[10]

A central tactic of "Yes Equality" was the use of personal accounts including of parents of gay and lesbian children to secure a yes vote, a strategy widely critiqued for its exclusion of trans, intersex, and bisexual communities (Healy, Sheehan, and Whelan 2016). Drawing on personal stories was interpreted in different ways and became a source of tension early on in the repeal coalition. The more radical elements of the repeal movement had long drawn on the tactic of personal testimony, with a social media campaign that included the abortion stories of young women and a live tweeted journey of young woman traveling to the United Kingdom to obtain a termination. These tactics were viewed with exasperation by some within the coalition eager to de-emphasize the stories of younger women making "choices" and any specific feminist framing and favoring the stories of parents experiencing a pregnancy with a fatal fetal abnormality, obstetricians testifying to the legal constraints in the care they provide, or the predicaments of rape or incest victims.[11]

Class, generation, and spatial dynamics were also evident. Analysis of the success of marriage equality indicated that support from working-class urban areas was essential (Healy, Sheehan, and Whelan 2016). Some activists worried that the coalition's reliance on technical and expert arguments and the predominance of students mobilizing for a liberal regime was in danger of alienating working-class supporters. Sympathetic rurally based politicians also warned against complacency, noting weak support among local councilors fearful of losing their seats in rural constituencies.[12] While church attendance has waned in Ireland, declining from 91 percent identifying as Catholic in 2006 to 78 percent in 2016 (CSO 2017), cultural identification with Catholicism remains significant particularly outside of large urban centers. ARC campaigns including their reframing of Saint Brigid, an important Irish Catholic icon, as an early abortionist, drew ire from second-wave activists working to construct a less contentious platform to advocate for constitutional change.[13] Much focus was placed on de-emphasizing late-term abortion as "we need to acknowledge that some of those who want to repeal the amendment are not pro-choice."[14] Here more radical elements of the pro-choice movement were signaled as potentially problematic in "spooking the middle of the road voter and center-right politicians."[15] Overall, the coalition leaders suggested that the campaign "must know when to de-emphasize specific identities, particularly those considered outside the mainstream in order to make the campaign *all Ireland*."[16]

A strong universalizing strategy was put in place aimed at cementing a winnable campaign. Some, however, were uncomfortable with the implications of this strategy for undermining political and generational solidarity. Leftist actors, veterans from the anarchist movement, noted that while focusing on repeal rather than abortion was strategically necessary, it was essential that "whatever we do now in positively elaborating reasons for repeal we must do so without doing damage to those who want to expand choice later."[17] Another dissenting veteran noted, "We need to accept that there is a lot of really angry young women out there and that they have never had the opportunity to vote and they want to be heard and we can't tone them down or silence them—we have had enough of the silence."[18] Younger activists supporting the coalition also drew attention to the risks of employing a narrow conceptualization of women's rights that might deny gender fluid or bisexual women a stake in the campaign.[19] Voice remained contested in this context as the coalition worked to craft a coherent message while navigating the diverse range of positions.

EVERY WOMAN AND TOGETHER FOR YES: CAMPAIGNS TO REPEAL THE EIGHTH

Alongside the coalition, the state feminist NWCI initiated its own campaign, "Every Woman," that made most ground in terms of political party support. Notably the NWCI, established as the state feminist organization in 1974, had not taken a specific position on abortion until 2012. Position within the NWCI membership that ranged from opposition to or ambivalence about abortion had contributed to the absence of a coherent and consistent message (Cullen 2008). The "Every Woman" campaign, launched in December 2017, downplayed the focus on abortion arguing for better access to a new model for reproductive health care. Abortion was referred to as "a necessary element of obstetric care." The CEO of the NWCI stated, "We looked at what the coalition was doing and we realised as the national representative women's organization we could align with their efforts to broaden the appeal of the campaign and create political party support" (Interview with NWCI CEO, January 2018). She outlined how the organization had informed its strategy with expertise from the New York–based Center for Reproductive Rights and an extensive set of grassroots consultations with rural constituencies and women from different generations. NWCI materials state, "Our hope is to build a sensitive and inclusive consensus that acknowledges people's experience of pregnancy and family life in all its diversity and complexity" (NWCI 2018, 3). Campaign materials invoke an intersectional assessment and include messaging such as,

> Every pregnancy is different and every decision is personal. Women are different. We are Traveller women, we are rural women, we are migrant women, we are women with disabilities, we are older women, we are young women. We have different needs based on our different circumstances, our backgrounds, our beliefs, our socioeconomic circumstances and our ethnicity. It's time as a country we reclaimed our women's reproductive health service from the polarised political sphere that it has been in. Women's healthcare should not be a cause, we should not need marches. Women are not a minority. (NWCI, Every Women, 2018)

Here the national representative organization for women, with a mixed record on representing ethnic minority and indigenous women, aimed to project an intersectional political claim while removing the trope of repeal as a polarizing issue. The effort made here was to situate the mobilization in a broad set of gendered health policy-focused demands, avoiding explicit feminist frameworks. Notably the NWCI, although a member of the Coalition to Repeal the Eight, initiated "Every Woman" independently and as a precursor to a specific referendum-focused campaign tied to the scheduling of the actual vote. The decision was also motivated by a sense that as the official representative organization for women in Ireland, the NWCI should be the one to claim the space to articulate a framework to advance repeal and to define the parameters for future mobilization. "Every Woman" was also initiated as a way to demobilize the more radical and what was perceived as unwinnable demands emerging from ARC and others.[20]

Asked about the decision to create their own campaign, the NWCI CEO remarked that "polling data suggests broad support for changing the current legal context, but it is much less certain that there is wide support for expansive and late term access. The predominant center-right political establishment including the ruling party do not comprehensively support a liberalized abortion regime."[21] Her analysis is supported by the fact that although the center-right ruling and opposition parties supported a repeal, neither engaged in comprehensive campaigning and both allowed party members a free vote on the issue.

The "Every Woman" campaign was critiqued heavily on social media by more radical feminist and hard left organizations and actors for pandering to the political establishment. In effect, universalizing messages characterize both the Coalition to Repeal the Eighth and NWCI campaigns, with tensions between broad gendered frames of "Every Woman" or narrow legal objectives such as "repeal" and a recognition of other relevant dimensions of identity and oppression. Despite the discomfort of radical feminist groups, leaders of the ruling and opposition center-right endorsed the planned amendment drawing on the narrative and reasoning of the "Every Woman" campaign (Bardon 2018). Working from this political party support and a specific date agreed for the referendum, the Coalition to Repeal the Eighth launched its official campaign in March 2018, entitled "Together for Yes." The launch statement read "Together for Yes is the National Civil Society Campaign to remove the Eighth Amendment from the Constitution. Together we are campaigning for a more compassionate Ireland that allows abortion care for women who need it" (Together for Yes Campaign 2018). Emphasizing care, compassion, and change, showcasing women's experiential knowledge and testimony rather than pro-abortion language of bodily autonomy or choice, marked a break from past repeal campaigns.

A central organizing tactic of "Together for Yes" included door-to-door canvassing including a traveling canvass entitled "The National Conversation on Repeal" aimed at reaching outside large urban populations. Carefully staged social media postings documented the route and stopping points while inputting into local media coverage. ARC activists played a central role in this strategy, providing their regional network of unpaid volunteers to populate the canvass. This team traveled to specific regional hubs, convening town hall meetings with a uniform branding and scripted message. Town hall meetings mandated a mix of representatives from Together for Yes, a local politician, a medical representative or representative from Catholics for Yes and a member of Parents affected by Fatal & Severe Foetal Anomalies (TMFRIRE). A focal point of the meetings was the testimony of women who had to travel to the United Kingdom to terminate a fetus diagnosed with a fatal anomaly. Interviews with a leader of the traveling canvass indicated that these powerful testimonies drew the largest crowds and attracted the most emotive responses. Repealing the restriction on abortion in this context was framed as a merciful solution for those parents seeking a termination of an non-viable pregnancy. This was deemed particularly effective in "putting a face to the argument and pulling people towards the idea of mothers and families requiring better health care."[22]

Given the influence of localism in Irish politics, the support of political parties at the local level was also deemed crucial, especially middle-aged men whose position "had evolved" toward supporting a yes vote. Cross-party support in local canvasses was evident between left-wing parties, although less so between center-right party members. In effect, despite the official support of the largest center-right parties for a yes vote, there was a marked absence of high-profile national politicians from the center-right mobilizing on the local level. Local political support was seen as contingent on a strict branding and family-oriented messaging. As such, while ARC members were crucial to the canvass, their participation was carefully managed.[23]

Tensions were evident between younger ARC activists and older Together for Yes coordinators. One leader characterized ARC activists "as organized anarchism, all peers no leader, endless amount of discussion on whatsapp, but few decisions made, really a difficulty in translating this structurelessness into disciplined on brand messaging."[24] ARC activists had to be instructed to wear commissioned Together for Yes T-shirts and badges, rather than their own branded clothing from earlier campaigning, and those less conventional-looking activists were edited out of photographs. Two of the ARC activist coordinators commented that they were aware that their anarchist and radical persona was a poor fit for the campaign, as such they purchased more conservative clothing to align with the campaign image more closely. Shifting is evident here as compromises were made to construct a palatable framework to appeal to those outside of core pro-choice constituencies.

The ARC's connections to leftist politics, while downplayed in campaign messaging, did provide opportunities for capacity building. Notably, the ARC acquired a large and centrally located building to use as campaign headquarters in Dublin. This space was gifted on a temporary basis by a British far-left trade union, the GMB, an offer unlikely to be made to more moderate and centrist feminist organizations. Despite the diminution of their "voice" in the campaign, ARC's presence was essential, providing revenue-neutral human capital, its grassroots networks, and physical space, all essential resources for mobilization.

Although minority women are featured in a minor way in published campaign materials, they were not visible in the regional campaigning. In the final weeks of the campaign, the Together for Yes did use a Twitter hashtag whoneedsyouryes#, which elicited a significant response from those claiming to be migrant women without the right to vote asking for support from the majority population for their specific circumstances.[25]

TOGETHER FOR YES:
ETHNIC MINORITY AND MIGRANT WOMEN

While intersectional framing was used by the pro-choice movement, ethnic minority, migrant, asylum seeker, and traveler women remained the least visible in campaign leadership and organizing. This is notable in that both high-profile legal cases on abortion, the X case and the 2017 case of a suicidal women forced to undergo early-term C-section, were respectively a young traveler and a young female refugee. Ethnic minority and migrant women involved in reproductive rights activism expressed their frustration that their voices were absent from most mobilizations on abortion (Interview with ethnic minority activists, March 2016). Unhappy with how migrant women had been neglected by the larger organizations, in April 2018 a small group of ethnic minority women formed Migrants and Ethnic-minorities for Reproductive Justice (MERJ). MERJ launch statement stated, "We believe in self-organizing and self-determination and autonomy—we will not be white washed or erased from this movement" (MERJ Launch statement, 2018). While mainstream migrants' rights organizations formally supported repeal of the Eight, MERJ represents one of a small number of migrant-led organizations focused on reproductive justice.

Citing statistics that "25% of women having babies in Ireland are migrants and 40% of all maternal deaths happen to ethnic minority women," MERJ activists made the link between racial stereotyping and the discriminatory experience of women of color in Irish health services (MERJ 2018). After placing pressure on key members of the Repeal the Eighth coalition, MERJ activists were invited to join the "Together for Yes" campaign in April 2018. In their contribution to a large fundraising event they stated, "We've had to fight for a seat at this table and now that we're here we are claiming our space, shoulder to shoulder with every woman in Ireland."[26] A specific issue for MERJ and other migrant organizations was their disenfranchisement in the referenda process and the fact that as undocumented persons, they could not travel to access services in the United Kingdom. From their perspective, "We all have one thing in common we are all disproportionately affected by the Eighth Amendment—migrant women face more barriers than their Irish sisters" (MERJ 2018).

Notably, MERJ activists expressed their determination to continue their campaign beyond the more limited horizon of "Together for Yes," stating, "We will continue to pursue an intersectional approach because we do not live single issue lives, we hope that the repeal of the Eighth will not mark the end of our struggle for autonomy but be the beginning. Do not forget about us when the campaign is over we need you by our side until the very end" (MERJ 2018). Other ethnic minority and migrant organizations that formally participated in "Together for Yes" include the European Network of Migrant Women, based in Brussels, and the African women's rights organization in Ireland, AkiDwA. AkiDwA's support derived from its individual campaigns to publicize maternal deaths of specific African women in Irish hospitals, which they have attributed to the restrictions of the Eighth Amendment (AkiDwA 2018).

Finding voice for the range of perspectives on reproductive rights in this context remains challenging. Coalitional dynamics were carefully managed, with significant contests behind the scenes, yet a choreographed form of unity displayed in public events was maintained for the most part alongside a common message to reach the "middle ground." Through the act of coalition building, more radical elements of the pro-choice movement and different generations of women worked together to secure a repeal of restrictive legislation. Radical feminists moved to the center, at least temporarily, while minority women, due to their own efforts, gained some visibility in forms of political action. Overall though, intersectional voice was limited in this context by campaigning that aimed to neutralize specific claims and pull from the middle ground to attract rural, middle-class and nonfeminist constituents seen as essential for electoral support.

CONCLUSION

Gendered mobilizations offer an important conceptual framework to interrogate the limits and possibilities of mobilization across social divides in pursuit of inclusive and progressive gendered social change. In the case under consideration here, women from different generations and commitments to different feminist formations grappled with ideological, identity, and power dynamics to forge a common platform to secure reproductive rights. Tensions persist, yet shifting is also evident along different dimensions of intersecting oppressions as alliances were constructed to create capacity, find voice, and act politically. The Coalition to Repeal the Eight and the Together for Yes campaign illustrate how the weight of a well-resourced countermovement[27] and political culture resistant to gendered social change galvanized diverse actors to seek constitutional and legal reform. Through collective action, ideological and generational cleavages were bracketed to produce a moderated set of demands that gained mainstream political support. This strategy can be understood as an effort to forge a common understanding of how and when to take political action in a highly politicized and historically polarized context.

External factors, however, can also limit the potential for political intersectionality. Publicized maternal deaths and pressure from activists on the political system to reopen the issue for consideration were crucial. Yet, a center-right and gendered political party culture while nominally in favor of repeal and still reliant on rural and older voting blocs maintained their opposition against a broad liberalization of reproductive rights in Ireland. Reflecting their feminist and leftist perspectives, coalition members employed intersectional discourse, yet in working to reach a broad constituency, eschewed radical feminist framing, marginalizing the perspectives of many young, working-class, and minority women. This framework aimed to cultivate a form of gendered mobilization that could demobilize morality-based arguments of anti-choice actors and interests while recruiting "middle Ireland" and retaining centrist party political support. While strategically astute, these forms of engagement strained the limits of intersectional solidarity. They may, however, be an inevitable consequence of feminist organizing across generational, ideological, class, and ethnic and racial lines in the broader neo-liberal context that supports complex and fragmented public spheres (Ellison 2000). Strategies that can find common ground between gendered mobilizations, different forces of feminism, and ethnic minority and migrant women may require a fundamental rethinking of solidarity and intersectionality.

The Together for Yes campaign is acknowledged to have played a major role in delivering the sizable margin by which the referendum passed alongside broader attitudinal change on the issue that neither polling nor political elites predicted (Leahy 2018b). In the end, grassroots mobilization, largely delivered by ARC, tactical learning gleaned from moderate feminists, including middle-ground messaging, alongside an emigrant home to vote campaign and the support of relevant political party elites all contributed to deliver the successful outcome. Legislation to enact access to abortion tabled for early 2019 became the new front for mobilization. ARC, in particular, continued to campaign for free and less restrictive conditions on access to abortion stating, "The referendum in Ireland was one of the most intersectional issues the country faced. Abortion affects disabled people, Trans people & migrant people in uniquely challenging ways, we must be vocal and present to ensure the legislation we deserve & need will be enacted" (ARC August 2018).[28] Despite the successful outcome of the referendum, internal cleavages between those advocating for "free, safe, and legal" and those advocating for "safe, legal and rare" may undermine longer-term efforts to construct an inclusive intersectional gendered mobilization on an Irish reproductive rights regime and more broadly on intersectional gendered social change.

NOTES

1. Article 40.3.3, known as the Eighth Amendment, was voted into the Irish Constitution by referendum in 1983; it restricts abortion in almost all circumstances, including cases of fatal fetal abnormality and rape and gives an equal right to life to both mother and unborn child; until 1992, it also restricted a woman's right to travel abroad for a termination. This was only permitted after a case reached the Supreme Court involving a fourteen-year-old girl who was raped and became suicidal. It's estimated that approximately 5,000 Irish women access abortion annually, by either traveling abroad or using unregulated abortion pills purchased online.

2. UN Committee on Economic Social and Cultural Rights, Convention Elimination of Discrimination against Women and Committee against Torture.

3. The X case involved a Supreme Court judgment in 1992 that forced the Irish state to allow a pregnant teenage rape victim with suicidal ideation to travel to the United Kingdom for a termination.

4. George Soros Open Society Foundation is a significant source of funding to pursue pro-choice activism. This has been a point of significant controversy given strict guidelines that prohibit foreign donors making donations to groups involved in elections or referendums. ARC also underlines its independence in contrast to organizations such as the NWCI that receive state funds.

5. Interview with leader of Action for Choice, 2015.

6. Interviews with ARC and NWCI activists, 2015.

7. These include the Repeal Project, London-Irish ARC, X-iles project, Speaking of Imelda, Repeal the Eight Global, Midwives for Choice; Doctors for Choice; Know Your Repealers; TFMR Ireland (Terminations for Medical Reasons); Catholics for Choice, strike4repeal.

8. Interview with NWCI leader of the Coalition to Repeal the Eighth, December 2017.

9. Two leaders of the Marriage Equality are also leading figures in the Repeal the Eight movement.

10. Trapped in Time Event, Repeal the Eighth, October 2017.

11. Interview with leaders of Together for Yes campaign.

12. Trapped in Time Event, Repeal the Eighth, October 2017.

13. Interview with CEO of NWCI, November 2017.

14. Trapped in Time Event, Repeal the Eighth, October 2017.

15. Trapped in Time Event, Repeal the Eighth, October 2017.

16. Marriage Equality Activist at Repeal the Eighth, October 2017.

17. Trapped in Time Event, Repeal the Eighth, October 2017.

18. Trapped in Time Event, Repeal the Eighth, October 2017.

19. Trapped in Time Event, Repeal the Eighth, October 2017.

20. Interview with the NWCI CEO, December 2017.

21. Interview with NWCI CEO, January 2018.

22. Interview with Leader of the National Conversation, May 2018.

23. Interview with Leader of the National Conversation, May 2018.

24. Interview with leader of Together for Yes traveling canvass.

25. The largest ethnic minority population in Ireland is from Eastern Europe, specifically Poland. The campaign reported only minor advances in campaigning and canvassing within this traditionally Catholic community.

26. MEJR activist speech at "Together for Yes" fundraiser, April 2018.

27. The pro-life countermovement, well funded by international pro-family Christian organizations, draws on the expertise of the marketing team that delivered the Brexit vote and uses framing such as "Both Lives Matter' and "LoveBoth."

28. Despite trust gained between organizations, other fundamental cleavages have reappeared on issues including ARC's support of sex workers that places them in direct conflict with the NWCI support for the prohibition of prostitution.

Chapter 2

Feminist Policy Mobilization and Intersectional Consciousness

The Case of Swedish Domestic Services Tax Reform (RUT)

Andrea Spehar

This chapter discusses the challenges of utilizing an intersectional approach in mobilizing around public policies in Sweden. Despite worldwide advancement of gender equality policymaking, the priorities of the most socially and economically disadvantaged women are often not included in public policy. This is also the case in Scandinavian welfare states that are often cited as examples of far-sighted gender equality policy and outcomes. In 2007, Sweden joined a number of other European countries in introducing a tax deduction on domestic services for private households RUT, following years of fierce debate about the proposed reform's consequences for the egalitarian aspirations of the Swedish gender equality model. Already in the early 1990s, concerns had been voiced about the effects that such legislation might have on society by reinforcing the traditional gender roles of both women and men (Öberg 1999). Furthermore, some feared that, if implemented, these reforms would lead the country along a path toward a bygone era of a "maid society" (Platzer 2006, 217).

This chapter aims to highlight the intersectional issues involved in feminist mobilizing around different visions of RUT. To what extent was the RUT reform problematized from a class and/or ethnicity perspective and by which feminist actors? What were the major lines of agreement (and disagreement)? What can organizing for and against RUT reform tell us about intersectionality and intersectional dilemmas? I argue that the RUT reform of household-related services powerfully highlights intersectional dilemmas feminists encounter when organizing around public policy reforms (see, e.g., Fraser 2009; Tronto 2002). First, in the case of domestic work, class and immigrant status informed feminist positions in politically significant ways. The RUT reform demonstrates that building feminist alliances in order to push for intersectional perspectives in policymaking can be very difficult to accomplish given different feminist ideologies and, as in the case of RUT, the left-liberal divide. Moreover, according to previous research, the creation of intersectional policy requires the presence and empowerment of women's groups in civil society that are dedicated to advocating for marginalized sub-groups of women (e.g., Bustelo 2009; Walsh and Xydias 2014). In the case of RUT reform, the voice and the political activities of civil-society actors (e.g., immigrant organizations and labor unions) and their relevance in agenda setting and policymaking were insignificant. Rather, state feminists, mostly women and men representing different political parties and governmental bodies for gender equality, led agenda setting and policymaking. Finally, in order to pursue effective intersectional policymaking, representatives of intersectionally defined target populations should be included in the policy process (Bishwakarma, Hunt, and Zajicek 2007). In the case of RUT, domestic workers in general and migrant domestic workers in particular constituted a largely invisible and underrepresented collective in the policy process.

The materials used for this study consist of various kinds of public documents (government bills, official reports, election manifestos) as well as records of parliamentary and media debates. The selection of documents was based on a constructed timeline that identified the key moments of the debates among feminists and other political actors during the period of study (the 1990s and the 2000s). In addition, I relied on official gender equality statistics as well as previous research relating to the Swedish market for domestic services. The section that follows outlines the theoretical and empirical insights used in this study. Thereafter, the contrasting ways in which left and liberal leaning feminists framed and voiced arguments for and against the RUT reform are presented and analyzed. In the concluding discussion, the findings of this study are summarized and discussed more broadly in terms of what the Swedish debates about the domestic and household services may tell us about the intersectional dilemmas related to gendered mobilizations in a context where "women" do not constitute anything like a homogeneous social group.

INTERSECTIONALITY, DOMESTIC WORK, AND WOMEN'S MOBILIZATION

In gender studies, intersectionality is a critical method of policy analysis since it asks about hidden forms of inequity and sheds light on mobilizing and organizing around policy debates and policymaking (Bustelo 2009; Kantola and Nousiainen 2009). Intersectionality relates to the observation that power structures based on categories such as gender, race, sexuality, functionality, and class interact with each other in various ways and create inequalities, discrimination, and oppression. It aims to make visible not only similarities and differences between the sexes but also to recognize how the diversity that stems from other social categories affects women in different ways.

Domestic work is a particularly complex site of intersectional analysis and activism because of the ways in which it creates power imbalances between some women and others. Today, Sweden can be said to form part of a developing global division of labor, the so-called global care chain, whereby cheap labor from poorer countries is increasingly demanded by, and supplied for, average and highly paid European households trying to combine family and work (Anderson 2000; Ehrenreich and Hochschild 2003). The availability of foreign women workers in Sweden had never been higher than at the time the RUT reform bill was passed in 2007 (Shmulyar Gréen and Spehar 2014). This was primarily a result of the new European Union rules on free movement of labor and the recent extension of EU membership to several central and eastern European countries. In both 2004 and 2007, when a total of twelve new member states joined the Union, Sweden was one of the few old member states opting not to use its right to temporarily restrict the free movement of labor for new states (see, e.g., Berg and Spehar 2013). In addition, the new Swedish immigration law of 2008 dramatically liberalized the country's labor migration policy for people from outside the EU and made the policy more employer-driven (Murhem and Dahlkvist 2011).

Notwithstanding the increasing tendency toward commodification of domestic and care work, paid work performed by migrant women, like the unpaid care work of all women, remains undervalued and deprived of social and economic recognition. The pitfalls of low-work status arise in the field of paid domestic and care work because the economic logic of this work coexists and overlaps with the opposing logic of the family. As Kontos convincingly argues, the logic of satisfying human needs is opposed to the economic logic of work standardization, which involves issues of formalization, productivity, and profit (Kontos 2013). Moreover, the lack of formal regulations for work in private households contributes to working conditions characterized by flexibility, low pay, and a lack of safety and protection, all of which make the workers' situation precarious. As Anderson asserts, this precarious situation "captures both atypical and insecure employment and has implications beyond employment pointing to an associated weakening of social relations" (Anderson 2010, 303).

Feminist and Women's Mobilization

Employing an intersectional approach can help explain the development, formulation, and limitations of specific gender dynamics of organizing related to policymaking processes. Feminist and women's movements are not unitary actors; they encompass myriad perspectives including liberal, Marxist, radical, socialist, cultural, postmodern, and post-structural, to name a few. They are composed of coalitions of actors acting on some element of shared goals and competing for prominence in defining claims and tactics (Alvarez 1990; Beckwith 2000; Mazur 2002). Actors in feminist and women's movements promote what they consider to be gender equality and to advance women's interest in different spheres of social life. Since a unified women's movement does not exist, it is an open question as to what can be considered "good" for women or to which women any given "good" will apply. The classical ideological divide between liberal (focus on individual choice) and leftist (focus on structural disadvantages) feminism was very prominent in the Swedish policy debates on RUT.

Feminist and women's activism has also expressed itself in different ways in different contexts, and in Scandinavian countries equality policies have been a crucial part of so-called "state feminism." This concept refers to the "activities of government structures that are formally charged with furthering women's status and rights" (Stetson and Mazur 1995, 1–2). State feminism is particularly robust in Sweden, where the welfare state is often described as "woman-friendly," with women's strong representation in political office and their high levels of participation in education and the labor market (Nyberg 2012). Feminism in Sweden is not politically contested as it is in some other European countries or in the United States. In the past two decades, gender equality has become central to the government's priorities, and leading female as well as male politicians are not hesitant to proclaim that they are feminists (Aftonbladet 2013). Only one political party does not include feminism in its program—the far-right Sweden Democrats. Today's left-green government describes itself as the "first feminist government in the world" (Swedish Government 2018).

State feminism was the dominant form of feminist mobilization in the process of formulating and adopting RUT, with government bodies and female and male MPs playing the main role. In several European countries, migrant domestic workers have developed different strategies to improve their working conditions over the past few decades; however, this is not the case in Sweden (Lutz 2011). The only mobilization around RUT associated with the civil society sector was the Feminist Initiative (Fi). Fi was formed in 2005 and represents the biggest and perhaps most important form of resistance to mainstream state gender equality policies that has emerged in Sweden in recent times. In contrast to mainstream feminist political initiatives at the state level, Fi demands intersectional politics and policymaking, advocating for fundamental changes in the power structures surrounding gender (Filimonov and Svensson 2016). For example, during the 2014 election campaign, Fi focused on both feminism and anti-racism, actively engaging the LGBTQ (lesbian,

gay, bisexual, transsexual, and queer) and immigrant communities (Feministiskt initiativ 2014, 204). Even in the case of Fi, there are strong state feminist
elements in organizing since the Fi mobilization is partly articulated through
the political party structure.[1] Its supporters are primarily highly educated
women from large urban areas and the party is generally perceived to be left-
wing (Blombäck and de Fine Licht 2017).

INTERSECTIONAL FRAMING ANALYSIS

As a growing body of theoretically informed case studies has shown, close
attention to ideas, agendas, frames, and policy paradigms is necessary for
a fuller understanding of policy adoption and policy change, what in the
framework of this volume is called the process of finding voice (Bacchi 2012;
Béland 2009). Some of the key concepts and ideas of such framing analysis
have already been put to use in policy research addressing women's and
gender-related issues, to help understand the development, formulation, and
limitations of specific gender policies (see, e.g., Bacchi 1999; Lombardo
and Agustín, 2011). The focus in this chapter will be on how, when, and why
activists identified policy limitations related to RUT and their intersectional
implications.

The center-right "Alliance for Sweden" government presented the RUT
reform domestically as a "women's issue." Domestic services were depicted
as a key to gender equality in today's Swedish society. However, women,
whether as a category or a social group, are not homogeneous but find themselves in a number of different structural and individual positions in society
and social life. The provision of domestic and household services can, in
other words, be said to either contribute to or undermine their equality,
depending on their social location. Some observers argue that introducing
tax relief for domestic services encourages and even directly enables men
to focus on work outside the home instead of taking increased responsibility
for unpaid domestic work. Where gender equality policies fail to specifically
induce men to share in caring work and housework, there is a risk that the
vision of the dual-earner/dual-career model will lack the necessary precondi-
tions required for its full realization (e.g., Duvander, Ferrarini, and Thalberg
2006; Morgan 2008). In addition, in making it possible for domestic services
to be purchased at a low price, the RUT reform may well have contributed
to the devaluation of tasks associated with the home and family care in the
country (Lutz 2011).

In what follows, I look at the various ideas and notions put forward in the
Swedish RUT policy debates, considering them as frames, or normative or
cognitive beliefs, promoted by the advocates and opponents of the reform.

In particular, I assess how actors involved in the RUT debate differed in the degree to which their political framing reflected *intersectional consciousness* (focus on sensitivity to differences among women arising from intersections of social identities, such as class and ethnicity with gender) and/or *intersectional blindness* (focus on only one shared social identity, such as gender). The research questions guiding the intersectional analysis of the RUT reform were the following: What are the main "problems" the tax deduction has claimed to solve, and what alternative solutions are excluded from consideration as a result of this formulation of the problem? Which categories of citizens are expected to benefit from the reform and based on what expectations? What were the major lines of agreement (and disagreement) among feminist actors involved in the debates and the policy process? What kind of notions of gender equality did the proponents of the reform put forward in the various documents in which the tax deduction is discussed? To what extent is the emphasis in these discussions on women, on men, and/or on the relationship between them concerning their respective involvement in household and caring work? Are the traditional gender roles (standards, norms, and actual behavior) of men as well as women called into question and, if so, to what extent? Is the tax deduction ever problematized from a class and/or ethnicity perspective?

Liberal Feminist Frame:
Domestic Workers as Family-Work Reconciliations

All actors involved in the RUT reform debate over the years held a common view that the issues of gender equality and paid domestic labor were somehow intertwined. The Swedish debate on tax relief for domestic and household services first gained momentum in the early 1990s. Liberal female politicians played a leading role in setting the agenda. A chief advocate of the reform, the economist and Moderate Party member Anne-Marie Pålsson, argued that a tax deduction of this kind would help enable well-educated women to compete with men in the labor market on more equal terms (Pålsson and Norrman 1994). However, between 1994 and 2006, Sweden was ruled by Social Democratic governments, with the center-right lacking the majority it needed in the parliament (Riksdag) to pass the tax reform. In the period leading up to the country's 2006 general elections, the newly formed center-right Alliance for Sweden, as one of its campaign promises, took up the issue of tax relief for domestic and household services anew (Allians för Sverige 2006).[2] After winning the elections, the Alliance announced its plan to submit a law to fulfill its promise. The RUT law was passed by the Riksdag in May 2007 (Government Bill 2006).

The center-right government considered the tax deduction on domestic and household services to provide men and women with improved opportunities to combine paid work with family life. Moreover, the stated intent of the reform was to equalize conditions so that women would no longer need to "forgo their paid professional life to manage their unpaid work in the home" (Government Bill 2006, 55). To support its claim, the government referred to studies showing that women and men use their time differently in Sweden, with women to a greater extent than men taking on the responsibility for unpaid household work such as cleaning and caring for children and relatives. The tax deduction, according to the government, would provide "an opportunity for more women with longer education and more qualified positions to work more" (Riksdag Records 2007, 116). In addition, "if working women are provided with opportunities to allocate more time to labor market activities and less time to housework, their chances of earning a higher income will increase" (Government Bill 2006, 56).[3]

The liberal proponents of the RUT reform habitually resorted to bringing up its benefits from a gender equality standpoint. In the Riksdag, the parliamentary debates had started in 2003 with a motion introduced by two female Center Party MPs, Birgitta Carlsson and Annika Qarlsson. In their motion, the two proposed that "a special tax deduction would likely be highly appreciated by women for whom it would make possible the liberation from the heavy burden that the home in their case entails" (Motion 2003). In other words, since in Sweden as elsewhere it was women who bore the main responsibility for housework, a possibility to purchase domestic and household services from outside providers would diminish their need for working hard on two fronts simultaneously. In the bill it submitted, the government presented the following argument to explain its position on the matter:

> Women and men have different opportunities for combining work and family life. Studies on how women and men spend their time show women to generally bear the larger responsibility for unpaid domestic work such as, for example, the traditional household chores and caring for children and close relatives. In many households, it is typical that women, to a greater extent than men, reduce their paid work to be able to perform unpaid work at home. The proposed tax deduction on domestic services will increase the opportunities for households to purchase these services instead, that way enhancing the ability, first and foremost, of women to free themselves from unpaid housework and involve themselves more in paid work or training and education. In this way, women's career opportunities and economic independence can be strengthened. The implementation of the tax deduction will thus result in more equal opportunities for women and men to combine their family and working lives. (Government Bill 2006, 55)

From this line of reasoning, it becomes obvious that the government construed domestic and caring work as a "women's issue" that would increase gender equality. Expectations of men's involvement in unpaid domestic

caring work were, however, entirely absent or surprisingly low. In the ensu-
ing parliamentary debates, the country's finance minister Anders Borg, for
instance, stated as follows:

> We might of course wish that we could instead have a debate about gender
> equality that would lead to the men in these households taking upon themselves
> more responsibility. And that, I would of course think, would also be very good.
> But that discussion has now been ongoing in Sweden for twenty, thirty, forty,
> fifty, maybe a hundred years, without it having had any major influence on
> things. (Interpellation 2007)

The expected effects of the RUT reform on the division of domestic labor and
the gender equality situation in the homes of the women performing the proposed new services were, moreover, yet another question left entirely unex-
amined by the liberal reform's advocates. Apart from creating more working
opportunities for Swedish women, the proponents of the reform claimed
that the tax deductions would create more jobs for immigrant women, thus
helping the country's integration policy. As the Minister for Migration and
Asylum Policy Tobias Billström argued in an op-ed piece entitled "Immigrants Need Cleaning Jobs," not implementing the RUT reform would have
devastating consequences from the point of view of Swedish immigrant
integration policy:

> Of all those performing the cleaning work in the country, nearly one in two
> are individuals born abroad. What that speaks about is that the house cleaning
> industry is one of the industries where recent immigrants most readily can gain
> a foothold. Many of those finding employment in the sector have for a long time
> been outside the labor force, and thus, thanks to these first jobs of theirs that
> they now can take on it in their new home country, finally get to be able to stand
> on their own feet in the society. (Expressen 2010)

The representations of gender, class, and ethnicity around the issue of domestic services have changed surprisingly little in Sweden, staying more or less
the same throughout the entire postwar period. Correspondingly, the country
has a long history of leaving this type of jobs to immigrant women (Calleman 2011). In the public debates around the reform proposal, its proponents
sought to present those opposing the measure as being against new job creation in a labor market sector dominated by women, including immigrant
women. They succeeded in calling into question the motivations of anyone
resisting the idea of tax deductions on domestic services who at the same time
endorsed the previously enacted, somewhat similar tax relief on home repair
and maintenance (ROT) reform:[4] Why, they asked, would one not be able to
claim a deduction for paying someone cleaning one's house while one could

do the same for having a wooden terrace built in one's garden? In their joint statement published on the website of the Confederation of Swedish Enterprise, an umbrella organization for employer, industry, and business associations in the country, five leading women representatives of Swedish industry and trade associations argued for this standpoint:

> To oppose RUT-related enterprising is to go after a growing industry where both the employees and those running the businesses are predominantly women. . . . Why act against a sector that is women-dominated while leaving a heavily male sector like the one benefiting from the ROT deductions alone? The question of why it should be right to be able to purchase services to install a new window but not to clean the same window may sound like a rhetorical one, but is fully relevant. It is a question that the politicians opposing the RUT deduction need to be demanded to answer. (Svenskt Näringsliv 2010)

Leftist Feminist Frame:
Domestic Workers as "Precarious Workers"

The criticism put forward by the left-oriented feminist opposition was centered on the claim that the RUT reform would lead to luxury for the few, given that the majority of the families in the country, even with the help of the tax deduction, would still not be in a financial position to make use of the services (Riksdag Records 2006). The critics of the reform initiative, in particular those from the Left Party, the Social Democratic Party, the Green Party and the Fi, argued that the creation of a domestic and household service sector would imply a return to a class system. According to them, those already disadvantaged in society, such as women with low levels of education and people from foreign backgrounds, would only get stuck in their jobs, ensuring their marginalization and condemnation to poverty. The main question that left-leaning feminists from the Left Party and Fi insisted on asking during the debates was "Who will clean in the cleaning lady's home?" Moreover, in its official comments on the new proposed law, the Swedish Trade Union Confederation (LO) also dismissed it as having only negative income distribution effects by benefiting households that already were well off (Promemorian 2007).

Another objection raised by the center-left bloc was that the implementation of the reform would result in a low-paid, women-dominated labor market sector. According to this block, the cure for gender inequalities was to be found in universal social rights and effective welfare policy. The critics of the proposal also pointed to the lopsided division of labor between women and men in families, claiming that "the RUT deduction offers men in unequal family relationships a possibility to buy their freedom from their housework and childcare obligations" (Dagens Arena 2011). Others noted that the reform would also confirm the notion that taking care of household chores and care work was a low-cost affair: "The tax deduction offers no solution to the gender equality dilemma. This kind of deductions only confirms the notion that one does not need to pay that much for typical women's work" (SVT Nyheter 2010).

Split within Left Feminism

Not all leading politicians from the Social Democratic and the Green Party, however, were against the proposal. It had both its opponents and supporters in the two parties and gave rise to major ideological disagreements within them. In their much-discussed op-ed piece published in a major Swedish daily morning newspaper, Mikael Damberg, chair of the Social Democrats in Stockholm, and Even Nordmark, chair of the Swedish Union of Local Government Officers (SKTF), stressed that the unequal domestic division of labor between women and men in the country had remained virtually unchanged, suggesting that government-sponsored household-related services, especially for families with children, had a clear gender-equality rationale:

> Those supporting the proposal for the government to subsidize the cost of household-related services through tax deductions have pointed to the fact that there is an increasing need, felt in particular among single parents and working parents, to lower the stress levels experienced and find ways to manage better the pressures of modern working life. In our opinion, there is much to be said about this and it is important to understand that the question here is of an entirely new area for welfare policy—not least in our big cities. . . . It is sometimes claimed that making the purchase of household-related services an option allows men to not take on their share of housework. But why should women's prospects at work be made wholly dependent on whether men can change their behavior? (Svenska Dagbladet 2009)

Jens Orback, the Social Democratic minister for gender equality in the country's previous government, reflected a similar view in a newspaper article as follows: "What we need is a growing service sector. I am in particular thinking about those who come here as refugees and who can bake bread, sew, look after children, and clean" (Dagens Nyheter 2004a). His statement, awkward as it might sound at best, represents a rather typical viewpoint in Sweden in that it associated immigrant women with traditional low-paid work. Indeed, no other sector in Sweden is so overwhelmingly dominated by foreign-born labor as home cleaning (Abbasian and Bildt 2007).

Several notable Social Democratic politicians felt forced, to some extent, to go along with the point, emphasized by the liberal proponents of the reform, that the ROT and RUT reforms could in fact be seen as comparable.

Already in 2004, the Social Democratic Party cabinet minister, Ulrica Messing, had conceded that "today we subsidize people's ability to have carpenters come to their home to lay a new floor, so why would it then not be OK to do the same to help them get someone to wax and polish that floor?" (Dagens Nyheter 2004b). Even earlier, in her 1996 book *Med mina ord* (Sahlin 1996, 204), Mona Sahlin, the prominent state feminist and a future leader of the Social Democratic Party (from 2007 to 2011), had discussed the issue in similar terms:

> Whatever can turn at least some of these black market jobs into official ones is good. The more there are people no longer exploited by those not paying for their workers' insurance or employer's social security contributions, the better. Besides, there is a seldom-noted gender dimension to this debate: to tax subsidize construction workers renovating one's kitchen is perfectly fine, but to subsidize (help) a company employing a cleaning woman who cleans up that same kitchen is objectionable.

Once the RUT reform was passed by the Riksdag in May 2007, it became even more difficult for the opposition to wage a coherent, clearly articulated campaign against it. Currently, of all political parties active in the country, only the Left Party and the Fi continue to express their unambiguous opposition to the RUT reform, demanding its repeal.

CONCLUSION

In its 1975 report to the country's then Social Democratic government, a special state-appointed committee on gender equality described the fundamental problem as follows:

> The efforts to achieve equality of opportunity between men and women must form an elemental part of the overall quest for economic and social equality for all groups and individuals in society. Those hit hardest by the disadvantages of their woman's role are the women with lowest pay, the women with least education, the women most worn down by work, the women with least influence in society. When these women's legitimate demands for justice and equity are satisfied, one at the same time attains greater economic and social equality and greater equality of opportunity between the sexes. (Swedish Government 1975, 9)

In this conception, equal opportunity for women and men (*jämställdhet*) and broader (economic and social) equality in society (*jämlikhet*) are presented as two interconnected projects. The present-day gender equality policy in Sweden, however, has come to increasingly differentiate between the two aspects in practice, compartmentalizing them into their own, separate spheres. In the debates around the tax deduction for domestic and household service, the liberal feminist proponents of the RUT reform elected to decouple the discourse on gender equality from the discourse on equality in society more broadly. The Swedish RUT reform bringing a tax deduction on domestic and household services represents, in other words, a fundamental reluctance of its proponents to address more broadly existing forms of (class, ethnicity, and gender-based) structural inequality. Even though the liberal feminist proposal provoked considerable national debate and clear rhetorical opposition to the RUT policy, those against the idea nevertheless failed to present competing frames to challenge the reform proponents' arguments about why RUT was "necessary."

The liberal arguments regarding the introduction of the tax deduction were focused on the women in the country who had trouble finding time to attend to both their professional careers and their responsibilities at home. For them, the RUT deduction would enhance the ability to compete in the labor market on equal terms with men. Apart from creating more working opportunities for Swedish women, the reform advocates claimed the tax deduction would create more jobs for immigrant women, thus helping the country's integration policy to achieve its goals. The fact that an entire new branch of "women's work" would be created in the labor market was, however, something never explicitly addressed by the reform supporters nor was the question of the working conditions of the women to be employed within this branch ever addressed in the debates. This omission is problematic in the light of the country's stated overall gender-equality policy goals, one of which is to reduce gender segregation in the labor market with its negative effects on women's pay levels.

The question is whether securing for a limited number of Swedish women, with relatively high income but little spare time, the option of purchasing domestic services for themselves ought to be seen as a step toward women's emancipation in general or whether the RUT simply buttresses privileged class positions and ethnic hierarchies in society (Tronto 2002, 2011). The entire reform agenda was promoted under the banner of every Swedish citizen's right to freely choose where they want to work and what they want to do for a living. What this shared assumption concealed was the existence in society of barriers to exercising this right for those who deviate from the norm due to their economic position or immigrant status. The declared rationale for the RUT reform in Sweden was that it would help advance the cause of equality for all Swedish women. Nevertheless, there is much to suggest that, when implemented, the reform first and foremost benefited women who are middle class, and that it has served to reinforce inherited stereotypical notions about gender roles in caring and household work.

In the evaluations of the overall gender-equality outcomes of the RUT reform in Sweden, certain tendencies can be discerned (Statistics Sweden 2017). To begin with, the buyers of the domestic and household services qualifying for the tax deduction have come primarily from ethnic Swedish middle- and upper-class families, while those who perform the actual services have been largely people born outside the country. Indeed, here we might speak of a "new gender order" being created in Sweden, one which, just like in many other European countries, increasingly enables certain groups of (well-to-do European) women to simultaneously pursue both career and family commitments. This ability relies on the presence of immigrant women from poorer regions of Eastern Europe and beyond to whom they can delegate their family- and household-related caring work. The Swedish working women's right to be spared of their double burden of market and household work, and from having to compete in the labor market on terms set by men, thus needs to be considered against the background of socioeconomic, ethnicized, and racialized inequality among women themselves. The Swedish RUT reform should, in other words, be looked upon not just as something resulting from a fundamental reluctance of its proponents to address existing forms of (class-, ethnicity-, and gender-based) structural inequality but also as something that may contribute to the perpetuation and even reinforcement of that inequality.

An explanation for why the organized opposition to the RUT reform remained so weak has to do with a conflict of values that women, with their differing ideological backgrounds and societal positions, found themselves involved in when debating the issue. In the debates around the RUT reform, women politicians and women representatives of the industry and service-sector employees were allowed a major role among those speaking in favor of the initiative. The women who were expected to perform the services in question, in contrast, had no voice in the debate. Furthermore, the Swedish feminist and women's movement was lacking a *common identity strategy* around the RUT reform. Women's political agency differed in the degree to which their political consciousness reflected intersectionality. In particular, the liberal Swedish feminism was characterized by a particular type of singular consciousness, in which sex was seen as the most fundamental axis of social structure and the most fundamental source of oppression.

Sweden is often cited as providing examples of far-sighted gender equality policy that can serve as a model for other European Union member countries. The Swedish RUT reform case, however, points to social contradictions and problems in gender-equality policy that the government as of yet is incapable of resolving. In this sense, the RUT debate underscores the need for a new, revamped gender-equality discourse and new gender-equality institutions that, by fostering intersectional consciousness and activism, can help bring about the conditions necessary for a more egalitarian Europe to emerge, irrespective of class and ethnicity.

NOTES

1. The party was formed (from a previous civil society group of the same name) in 2005 and announced that it would put up candidates for the 2006 parliamentary elections. In 2006, Fi received 0.68 percent of the vote and in 2010 0.4 percent of the vote. In the 2014 European parliament elections, Fi became the first feminist party to get a seat in the European parliament when it attracted 5.3 percent of the vote. The same year, Fi received 3.1 percent of the vote in the general elections. While not meeting the 4.0 percent threshold for getting seats in parliament, the party was elected into thirteen municipalities, including in Sweden's largest cities of Gothenburg and Stockholm where it became part of governing "red-green-pink" coalitions.

2. Historically, Swedish political parties have tended to coalesce into two main blocs, uniting, on the one hand, the liberal and conservative parties of the center and right (the Moderate Party, the Liberal People's Party, the Centre Party, the Christian Democrats) and, on the other hand, the left and left-leaning parties (the Social Democratic Party, the Left Party, the Green Party).

3. All translations from the original Swedish are by the author.

4. The tax relief on home repair and maintenance (ROT) was originally introduced in the 1990s as a temporary measure to boost employment in the construction sector. Since then, the measure has been implemented periodically, most recently on December 8, 2008 (remaining in effect to this day). The joint term for ROT and RUT is "tax deduction for domestic services." Domestic work or "housework" (*husarbete* in Swedish) is, hence, a general term for household work and renovation work.

Chapter 3

The Politics of Intersectionality in Activism against Domestic Violence in Hungary and Romania

Raluca Maria Popa and Andrea Krizsán

Feminist projects have become increasingly embedded within larger, inter-sectional movements, coalitions, and networks (Conway 2012; Walby 2011), "sidestreaming" into other social movement organizations (Alvarez 2009). The field of domestic violence activism is particularly fruitful for studying intersectionality for two main reasons. First, domestic violence as a form of violence against women came to the international agenda as a unifying issue, which brought together women from North and South, East and West in a common struggle (Keck and Sikkink 1998; Weldon 2006b). Violence against women was seen as a gender inequality problem that affects women uni-versally regardless of ethnicity, religion, class, or age, thus requiring global action. The universality claim was key to the initial movement agenda on violence against women, more so than in any other gender equality field. Intersectionality comes as a challenge to this claim, complicating the narra-tive and showing that women of diverse backgrounds experience violence in diverse ways and thus that universality needs to be qualified. The tensions within and among women's movements that result from this challenge make domestic violence activism an ideal site for investigating intersectionality.

Second, multiple groups stake claims in activism and mobilization on domestic violence. A variety of other inequality groups, such as movements against racism or ethnic discrimination, for the rights of people with dis-abilities, for elderly or children's rights, LGBT groups, or migrants, join the mobilization processes against domestic violence, thus creating further potential for intersectionality praxis across movements. Additionally, domes-tic violence is a field of gender equality policy with high mainstreaming potential, mainly due to its resonance with elements of human rights agen-das (Htun and Weldon 2012; Keck and Sikkink 1998; Kelly 2005; Mazur 2002). Such resonance may result in the involvement of mainstream human rights organizations in anti-domestic violence activism with the potential for strengthening inter-sectoral and potentially intersectional attention in domestic violence debates.

This chapter conducts an actor-centered analysis of political arenas where political intersectionality can play out in relation to domestic violence. It investigates meeting points between different inequality claims within mobilization processes with the aim of assessing their potential for intersectionality. We look at political intersectionality through actor interaction, coalition building, and alliance seeking in processes of developing domestic violence policy in two relatively under-researched countries: Hungary and Romania. Both countries have witnessed intensive women's movement mobilization around domestic violence in the past two decades, with increasing awareness of intersectionality. At the same time, both countries passed domestic violence policies, which show little sensitivity to intersectional disadvantages and in some cases even to gender inequality (Krizsán and Popa 2014). Our aim in this chapter is to trace intersectional practices in the processes around these policy outputs. We attempt to understand what factors are favorable to intersectionality praxis and claim making in domestic violence activism and what factors are inhibiting meaningful integration of multiple inequalities.

The first section of the chapter discusses theoretical considerations on intersectionality in movements against domestic violence. The subsequent empirical sections describe dynamics of intersectionality in alliances against domestic violence in the two countries. The analysis employs a qualitative approach to compare intersectional practices in movements and mobilization processes against domestic violence. The data come from a multiyear comparative project on domestic violence policy processes in Central and Eastern Europe (Krizsán and Roggeband with contributions from Popa 2018) including analysis of reports by international human rights bodies, and international and local NGOs, as well as interviews with activists and experts.[1] The final section provides a comparative analysis of the main findings for the two countries, in which we discuss several factors explaining divergence in practices of political intersectionality, in particular the intersectional capacity of movements against domestic violence and organizational dynamics.

POLITICAL INTERSECTIONALITY IN MOVEMENTS AGAINST DOMESTIC VIOLENCE

In this chapter, we focus on "political intersectionality" (Crenshaw 1991) and we ask how intersecting inequalities influence the politics, strategies, and claims of anti-domestic violence activists. Political intersectionality provides a framework for contesting power and "for reshaping modes of resistance beyond allegedly universal, single-axis approaches" (Cho, Crenshaw, and McCall 2013, 800). A variety of manifestations of political intersectionality can be expected in the interactions among actors mobilizing for women's rights in general and against domestic violence in particular (Cole 2008). Literature shows how the awareness of intersecting inequalities alters struggles for progressive change by providing movements with opportunities to enlarge mobilization but also with a host of organizational, representational, and framing dilemmas (Lépinard 2014). Some practices of political intersectionality bring complexity and enriched understanding for domestic violence politics and are more compatible with social transformation objectives; others are reductionist, resulting in exclusionary objectives and policies.

As laid out in the introduction to this volume, scholars have debated whether separate organizing around social positions weakens movements and reduces their political effectiveness (Tarrow 1998) or whether coalition making and common political work across more diverse groups may lead to more inclusiveness (Weldon 2011). Alliances can put pressure toward homogenizing claims (Strolovitch 2006) but can also facilitate a goal-oriented strategy (Townsend-Bell 2011). Previous research points to a number of internal and external factors that determine whether or not feminist coalitions are successful in integrating intersectionally disadvantaged groups including (a) how they define common interests (Cole 2008) and shared framing (Verloo 2013) (finding voice); (b) the organizational dynamics of forming alliances (Staggenborg 2010) including the role of bridge-building actors (Borland 2010) or "movement crossovers" (Reese, Petit, and Meyer 2010); and (c) the response to power differentials, which may skew coalitions of minority and mainstream women's organizations toward the benefit of the more powerful and the marginalization of the less powerful (Cole 2008; Strolovitch 2006). The political opportunity structures, whether favorable, such as the European Union accession process, the CEDAW or Universal Periodic Review monitoring process, or unfavorable, such as weak gender equality institutions opposed by strongly embedded institutions for competing inequalities, as well as the structure of privilege may also factor into the intersectional content of coalition work (Cole 2008; Verloo 2013).

Building on this literature, in our empirical analysis we look at the extent to which forming alliances across groups—be those diverse women's groups or other inequality and human rights groups—results in more intersectional claims and practices. Further, we examine whether the preference for mainstream claims that resonate better with dominant social and political approaches diverts the intersectionality potential of activist groups. We bring into focus the factors that enable intersectional praxis in some coalitions and constrain it in others, with special attention paid to the role of intersectionally disadvantaged movements actors, in particular minority women. Following

McCall's (2005) distinction, we look at two arenas for practicing intersectionality: *intra-categorical arenas*, where diverse women's groups form coalitions to promote domestic violence policy change, and *inter-categorical arenas*, where women's groups enter alliances with other inequality groups or mainstream human rights groups that might bring diverse inequality rationales beyond gender.

Our analysis is focused on two Central and Eastern European postcommunist democratizing countries. This context implies relatively weak women's movement capacities that emerged in some cooperation with transnational actors and often supported by international resources. Violence against women is a field where the development of women's movement capacities was particularly embedded in transnational networks such as WAVE (Montoya 2013). Thus, international and transnational inspiration and resources also should be assessed in mobilization processes against domestic violence.

POLITICAL INTERSECTIONALITY INSIDE THE WOMEN'S MOVEMENT AGAINST DOMESTIC VIOLENCE

In this section, we map out intersectionality practices within domestic violence activism in Hungary and Romania. We first look at whether and how intersectionality is articulated in coalitions of women's groups. We are interested in whether the meeting points between various approaches open up possibilities to complicate the gender equality rationale behind domestic violence advocacy or rather lead to exclusionary logics that may even challenge gender equality approaches.

Distinct moments of mobilization for domestic violence reforms can be discerned in both Hungary (2003–2004 and 2012–2013) and Romania (2003–2004 and 2010–2012), with cooperation and various interactions among women's groups sustained also in between these moments. The more recent mobilization events differ from the first cycle precisely in the emergence of arenas of political intersectionality within women's activism that did not exist previously. In this second cycle of mobilization, more women's organizations and activists representing multiple social locations, such as Roma women, disabled women, or lesbian women emerged, and some joined activism to challenge the state's lack of responsiveness to domestic violence. The advocates representing intersectionally disadvantaged groups have significantly altered the landscape of domestic violence activism and the women's movement context in which such activism takes place. Minority women activists in the fields of Roma rights, sexual orientation and gender identity equality, or disability and their organizations have prompted an examination of practices and political positions in women's rights organizations, while at the same time helping them to bridge alliances with new actors. These processes have been enabled by the development of intersectional capacities within civil society, particularly women's NGOs.

Intersectional Capacity of Women's Movement Organizations

Women's activism against domestic violence emerged in both countries in the early and mid-1990s. In these early stages of organizing, there was little awareness of and attention paid to differences among women or other victims. Activists struggled to name the issue and place it on the public and policy agendas as an issue of gender inequality, using a unitary category of gender. As women's movements grew stronger in the two countries, they became more prone to specify and recognize differences among women as well as work politically across other axes of inequality; in effect, they created stronger intersectional capacities. This happened differently, however, in the two countries.

In Hungary, organizations of intersectionally disadvantaged women emerged from the late 1990s. While Roma women and lesbian organizations existed in the late 1990s, wider awareness of diversity within the women's movement and cooperation across diverse groups emerged and became problematized in the mid-2000s with the creation of the Hungarian Women's Lobby, the organization representing the Hungarian women's movement to the European Women's Lobby (EWL).

In Romania, very few separate organizations established around inter-sectional social positions existed in the mid-1990s. The few examples were mostly community-based organizations of Roma women, such as the Asso-ciation of Roma Women in Bucharest or the Association of Gypsy Women in Timisoara, which rarely engaged in national-level advocacy. Issues of differences and inequalities were addressed, however, in dialogues between women's rights organizations and Romani women's activists from general Roma organizations, such as Romani CRISS, Agency "Împreună" (Together), or Civic Alliance of Roma as well as the specific Roma women's organiza-tions. As a result of open challenges and processes of mutual sensitization between women's organizations and minority women activists, women's organizations became more inclusive. As one longtime activist and founder of the first feminist organization in the capital, Bucharest, explains, "Inter-sectionality as a strategic approach is present, gender being often treated (at least at the level of discourses) as a multidimensional category of analysis" (Grünberg 2014, 253–4).

In both countries, the development of intersectional capacities in women's movement organizations was supported in various ways by international and transnational resources, networks, and frameworks. International and regional human rights norms, coming from the United Nations or the Council of Europe, transnational organizations, and funders as well as the European Union, encouraged the affirmation of diversity among women and the articulation of specific interests by minoritized women's groups. Importantly, intergovernmental organizations and several funders including the Council of Europe, the European Commission, or the Open Society Institute (OSI)[2] strongly supported the participation of Roma women in international anti-racist and women's rights fora as well as Roma women's own transnational organizing.[3] The adoption of the UN Convention on the Rights of Persons with Disability, which includes several references to intersectionality, gave impetus to an intersectional sensitization of the long-developed disability movements. In Hungary, the main, national-level mental disability advocacy organization (*Ertelmi Fogyatekosok Orszagos Szovetsege*, EFOESZ) became increasingly aware of the special interests of disabled women.

Favorable opportunities encouraged not only specific organizing around intersectional social positions but also the forging of alliances across identity-based differences in the women's movements. As the countries gained membership in the European Union, there were more incentives to seek membership in European umbrella organizations for civil society organizations along axes of gender (EWL), sexual orientation (ILGA Europe), gender identity (Transgender Europe, TGEU), and others.

The umbrella-type coalitions, however, function differently in the two countries. Setting up the national chapter of the EWL proved to be a platform for cooperation in Hungary, where the creation of the Hungarian Women's Lobby formalized the existing, weakly coordinated women's movement network and also institutionalized diversity within the movement by including several intersectional women's groups in the network. The lesbian organization Labrisz was among the founding members of the Hungarian Women's Lobby, while Roma women's organizations and smaller organizations that represented disabled women became members at a later stage. Cooperation within the Hungarian Women's Lobby also led to development of specific intersectional analysis. For example, in 2003, the Hungarian Women's Lobby issued a commentary to the Equal Treatment Bill discussed at that time.[4] The commentary had a distinct chapter on intersectionality that discussed the need to regulate multiple discrimination in the law and also to address the specific needs of Roma, disabled, lesbian, and rural women.

At the same time, in Romania, we witness a relative failure of the more institutionalized women's movement coalition in its early years. Establishing the national chapter of the EWL became instead a source of tension and conflict. The Romanian Women's Lobby (RoWL) was set up as a national coalition in 2007 to be the representative structure of the EWL at country level. Issues of resources and leadership, however, marred the coalition's potential to bring together the otherwise fragmented women's organizations in Romania (Vlad 2013). More recently, the RoWL has widened its membership and three organizations working on Roma women's rights were included in its seventeen-member network. Roma women are also represented among the leadership of the RoWL.

We can conclude that intersectional capacities of women's movement organizations in Hungary developed earlier and intersectionality was institutionalized in the coordination structures of the movement, while in Romania, this happened later and was less institutionalized. This can partly be explained by the fact that Romania is a much larger and more decentralized country. Surprisingly, the reverse dynamics of intersectionality play out in the issue-specific arena of domestic violence advocacy. Intersectional groups are conspicuously missing from the mobilization on the issue in Hungary, while they are included throughout the mobilization process in Romania.

Forging Women's Movement Coalitions against Domestic Violence

Domestic violence policy advocacy emerged as one of the key fields of action for women's groups in both countries. With the diversity in the women's movement and gender equality advocacy more generally becoming more pronounced throughout the years, two particular axes of political intersectionality became especially relevant to the women's movements in Hungary and Romania: ethnicity (especially Roma) and sexual orientation and gender identity. The relationship of these two axes of intersectionality for women's movement mobilization in the specific issue of domestic violence, however, is markedly different in the two countries.

In Hungary, while gender equality advocates showed quite remarkable sensitivity to intersectionality, this did not trickle down to the practice of domestic violence activism. Intersectional organizations remained largely silent on domestic violence and mobilization campaigns around the issue did not formally include minority women's groups. In the first wave of mobilization, in 2002–2003, a coalition of organizations working on women's and children's rights came together to demand progress in domestic violence policy. No intersectional women's groups joined at that point, and the agenda of the mobilization revolved around the tension between women's rights and children's rights rather than diversity of women's interests (Krizsán and Roggeband 2018). Anti-domestic violence activism continued throughout the following years and brought moments of cooperation between women's groups working on domestic violence and organizations working on Roma rights, such as the ERRC. Nevertheless, the minority women's groups that emerged on the women's rights scene in Hungary showed limited interest in domestic violence. Although a high-profile litigation case under the Optional Protocol to CEDAW on forced sterilization of a Roma woman (A.S. v. Hungary, Communication No. 4/2004, CEDAW/C/36/D/4/2004) brought a celebrated success of cooperation across group boundaries, the discussion of the issue did not connect to the domestic violence debates.

The next major period of mobilization, between 2012 and 2013, had yet again no intersectional voices speaking. The *Keret* (Framework) Coalition that brought together all key actors in the domestic violence against women advocacy campaign included MONA, NANE, Patent, Hungarian Women's Lobby, and Amnesty International Hungary. No minority women's groups formally became members of the coalition, mainly because no such organizations were dealing with the issue of domestic violence in Hungary.

In Romania, despite little formalized networking and diversity at the level of the general women's movement, the issue-specific organizing in the field of domestic violence became a fruitful avenue for intra-movement political intersectionality. This happened gradually with the consolidation of intersectional capacities in the women's movement and the sensitization of minority women advocates to the issue of domestic violence. In the first wave of mobilization, in 2003, while women's organizations actively pursued a coalition strategy and thirty of them came together to support the passing of a law against domestic violence, no organizations of intersectional groups joined and intersecting inequalities were not problematized in the work of the coalition.

In the years between 2008 and 2010, however, mostly as a reaction to the economic crisis and the heavy austerity measures imposed by the government, the need to amend the domestic violence legislation became more pressing. New actors came to the field of domestic violence activism, including Roma women's advocates. Particularly influential in the mobilization efforts against domestic violence was a research report published by the feminist organization FILIA in Bucharest, which showed that the economic crisis had a disproportionate impact on women victims of domestic violence (Băluță, Bragă, and Iancu 2011).

When the mobilization efforts to change the domestic violence legislation swelled in 2011, Roma women's advocates joined, and one of them actually co-organized the largest protest, along with sexual orientation equality organizations.[5] The organizations that supported the 2011 protest had a practice of working together from an anti-discrimination coalition that existed in Romania. They were brought into the domestic violence field, however, by the organizing efforts of women's rights activists and specifically those representing minority women. The Roma women's advocates who joined the anti-domestic violence mobilization not only strengthened the ranks of the protesters, they were also instrumental in forging new alliances with the Roma rights groups, such as *Împreună* (Together) and Romani CRISS. Later on, in 2012, the same Roma feminists that co-organized the domestic violence protest founded a separate Roma women's organization, *E-Romnja*, which continues to be active in the violence against women field. The 2011 coalition was successful in pushing for the desired amendments of the domestic violence legislation. A new law was passed in 2012, which introduced a civil protection order for victims of domestic violence. The obligation to support shelters was included for the local administration, and later a methodology and standards for setting up shelters were developed.

In the 2011 story of mobilization against domestic violence in Romania, it is apparent that *intersectional capacity*, in the sense of inclusion of more diverse groups of women, strengthened the anti-domestic violence advocacy alliance and its ability to influence policy. Organizations or programs of minority women as well as individual women activists consolidated the coalition and its advocacy by increasing the number of participants and their resources. Importantly, participation of intersectional groups acted as bridge builders (Cole 2008) to enable the formation of new alliances, in this case with Roma rights organizations. Alliances, in turn, may have contributed to strengthening the intersectional capacity even further by providing the impetus for some of the activists involved to set up their own separate organizations for Roma women.

At the same time, the coalition did not result in gaining specific intersectional benefits for its members. Intersectional claims were initially recognized as the heightened vulnerability of specific groups of women. The report on the impact of the economic crisis on women (Băluță, Bragă, and Iancu 2011, 84) explained that the narrowness of the definition of family members created gaps in protection from violent intimate partners especially for Roma women, Turkish-Romanian women, and same-sex couples, who were all much more likely to live in consensual unions.[6] These dimensions did not feature, however, in the messages of the 2011 coalition that advocated for the amendment of the domestic violence legislation. The manifesto that the organizations agreed on in 2011 was based on a universal gender inequality frame, accepted by all members of the coalition for strategic reasons. It called for introducing a protection order in the Romanian legislation and for state funding for shelters.

We had Roma women activists . . . who are supporting Roma women's rights for a long time, who participated in the protest and supported the claims. We really thought our claim to set up a protection order was cross-cutting, and we could find a common basis on gender and we did not go into further discussions about specific interests or identities. The protection order should be there as a measure for protection no matter who you are: elderly, lesbian, disabled. The manifesto that we agreed on was one that looked for the common interest.[7]

The legal process offered little amenability to intersectionality claims. Although the coalition did not ask for specific measures for intersectionally disadvantaged groups of women, there were efforts to ask for the inclusion of the notion of "multiple discrimination" in the new law on domestic violence and the subsequent strategy. This met, however, the opposition of MPs.[8]

This example shows particular dynamics at play that exclude intersectional claims from movement demands in the context of domestic violence activism. The tension between efficiency in seeking the achievable goal and inclusiveness in the representation of diverse interests is resolved in favor of movement efficiency. More specific benefits for intersectionally disadvantaged groups, however, may be obtained in the implementation stages, where intersectionality practices are more present through participation in implementation processes, in monitoring, and availability of special nondiscrimination measures in service provision. The longer-term benefits are secured through the continuous participation of intersectional groups in the civil society coalition. The newly formed Roma women's organization (E-Romnja) remained involved in the smaller coalition of nine NGOs that has continued to monitor the implementation of the law. This also implies sharing of resources between the larger coalition of women's rights groups and the Roma women's organization, as the monitoring process receives funding from the Open Society Foundation in Budapest. The participation of Roma women's organizations may also alter the agenda of the larger coalition. In 2013, for example, the larger coalition issued a statement against the forced sterilization of Roma women.[9] E-Romnja remains engaged in the Romanian Network for Preventing and Combating Violence against Women, which currently has twenty-four members and continues to monitor and advocate for improved responses to gender-based violence in Romania.

Political Intersectionality in Alliances with Nonfeminist Groups

Women's groups in the region appealed to coalitions with nonfeminist actors from relatively early on, using it as an important strategy to strengthen advocacy, gain access to the state, and instigate reforms. The relatively wide appeal of addressing domestic violence among civil society, and particularly rights groups, has the potential to rally three different kinds of allies, all rights groups, but with divergent agendas and approaches to domestic violence. First, alliances with rights groups, such as those advocating for equality for ethnic minorities, the elderly, the disabled, or LGBTQ people seem feasible, based on the *shared* equality *framing*. Importantly, alliances with these groups can highlight the differential experiences of violence suffered by women along these axes of inequality (elderly women, lesbian, disabled women, or ethnic minority women). Second, groups representing the rights of children as victims of domestic violence can be further allies, with potential for attention to intersecting inequalities (the girl child). Finally, mainstream human rights groups in the region also engage increasingly with domestic violence and thus might contribute intersectional sensitivity to these alliances. While none of these groups bring an explicit intersectional agenda to domestic violence alliances, the integration of their priorities and the proactive attempts to bridge interests show potential for intersectionality. We look at these alliances separately in the two country cases.

Alliances with single-focus inequality groups, particularly Roma and LGBT groups, emerged in both countries. Beginning in the mid-2000s, the European Roma Rights Center (ERRC), which is a transnational advocacy organization working on Roma rights, has become increasingly active in the arena of violence against Roma women. ERRC wrote a CEDAW shadow report on violations of Roma women's rights for Hungary for the first time in 2007,[10] in parallel to the shadow report written by an alliance of mainstream women's organizations. Prolonged negotiations between ERRC and mainstream women's groups resulted in parallel reporting and the absence of an agreement on terms of cooperation. The report included a chapter on violence against women with specific assessment and recommendations concerning domestic violence against Romani women. After years of developing intersectional capacities, the 2013[11] shadow report marked a move forward in coalition building. The report was a joint one, written in coalition between the Hungarian Women's Lobby and ERRC. The impact of the coalition on how claims are articulated, however, was mixed. The chapter on violence against women failed altogether to acknowledge intersectionality on any grounds. At the same time, another chapter was devoted to violence against Roma women, as a specific and separate problem. Importantly, though, that chapter did not discuss domestic violence to any extent. Specific experiences of Roma women with domestic violence are absent from the report. The domestic violence agenda, one of the most important fields of activism for Hungarian feminists, continued to operate with a homogenous understanding of women.

In Romania, the ERRC and the Roma rights NGO Romani CRISS in Bucharest jointly submitted a shadow report to the CEDAW Committee in 2006[12]. This marked the first intervention of Roma women's advocates in the violence against women field. A few transnational Roma women advocates, using funding mostly from the OSI, were behind the production of the report and acted as its spokespersons. The report did not go into details about domestic violence, but it did acknowledge that perpetrators of violence against Roma women included "public officials, members of other ethnic groups, Roma and indeed close family" (ERRC and Romani CRISS 2006, 13–4).

In the case of the above-discussed 2011 domestic violence protest in Romania, intersectionality was consciously used as a strategy for cross-movement mobilization. As one of the organizers of that protest recalls,

> We realized that we needed to form alliances, to build coalitions, so that we could show politicians that there are numerous civil society organizations . . . that are not content with the government's response to violence against women. . . . the list of organizations supporting our protest shows diversity, which was beneficial for our organizing. . . . We had ACCEPT [leading organization on sexual orientation rights], we had "Împreună" [Roma organization], and we had organizations that are working on human rights.[13]

The acceptance of a particular diagnosis of the problem of domestic violence, which sees women as the main group of victims and accepts that gender inequality is its root cause, contributed to the success of this alliance between women's groups and other inequality groups, in particular ethnicity and LGBTQ equality organizations.

A similar example is the Hungarian civil society participation in the United Nations Universal Periodic Review (UNUPR) in 2010,[14] which generated cooperation between inequality groups, including mainstream human rights groups. This cooperation resulted in an exemplary inclusion of intersectional disadvantages in the context of gender violence and particularly domestic violence in the issued report and recommendations. The cooperation included MONA (Foundation for the Women of Hungary) and Patent (People Opposing Patriarchy) both mainstream women's groups that engage with domestic violence along with EFOESZ (the main mental disability organization in Hungary), ERRC, and other Roma rights organizations such as NEKI, Chance for Children Foundation, and others. The report discussed gender equality as a horizontal principle that cuts across all fields and paid particular attention to multiple discrimination and particularly discrimination of Roma women. Domestic violence and human trafficking were discussed in intersectional terms and not only in the diagnosis of the report but also in its recommendations for further state action. It recommended that

> Hungary recognizes multiple discrimination in current and future policies and take concrete and effective steps to prevent and counter the effects of multiple discrimination faced by Roma women and provides law enforcement officials and other state actors which assist victims of violence with anti-racism and anti-discrimination training in order to effectively assist Roma women, and other women from disadvantaged groups who are experiencing violence.

In contrast, the Romanian UPR took place in 2008 and gathered separate reports from different stakeholders, none of which were specifically women's organizations or intersectional women's groups. The few references to women's rights are brought in by a general human rights organization SIRDO (Romanian Independent Society for Human Rights), but these references largely disregard intersectional priorities.

These examples from the two countries show that alliances between women's groups and groups advocating against other inequalities worked when there were intersectional minority groups that actively engaged in the bridging work that is needed to agree on commonalities and affirm a common cause (Beamish and Luebbers 2009). Indeed, in the case of the participation of ERRC in the CEDAW Shadow reporting on Hungary, it was a group of transnational Roma women activists that spearheaded the process and practiced intersectionality, both in voice and in content. Along with the shadow reporting, ERRC was also increasingly active in opposing the trafficking of Roma women and forced sterilization, where they were among the initiators of the related A.S. v. Hungary (2006) CEDAW case. In a similar manner, the participation of Roma rights organizations in the 2011 Romanian protest and petition to reform the domestic violence legislation in Romania was the result of feminist networking prior to the forming of the alliance as well as the organizations' practice of working together as part of a coalition against discrimination. Importantly though, in Hungary these processes of cooperation remained limited to international advocacy stages and did not impact domestic mobilization objectives. Hungarian domestic violence advocacy groups remained remarkably closed to integrating intersectional approaches into their activities in the country (Mihálovics 2013). The praxis of inclusion was much more continuous in Romania where the involved actors included domestic Roma organizations, and domestic advocacy campaigns also featured Roma women's rights advocates as well as LGBT groups.

A different logic, which is less friendly to intersectionality, is at play in alliances with children's rights groups in both countries. In Romania, children's rights groups are not involved in alliance building with women's rights groups on the issue of domestic violence. In Hungary, children's rights groups were allies in the initial advocacy campaign for domestic violence policy reforms in 2003. While women's organizations (NANE, Habeas Corpus, and Center for the Rights of Women and Children) initiated the advocacy effort, children's rights groups also ran their parallel campaigns to support policy progress and awareness raising, although not formally within the advocacy alliance. Claims made in this mobilization campaign did not bring intersectionality to the forefront. Violence cases used for campaign purposes on both sides had in their focus children victims, in one case a girl child victim (Sáfrány 2003; Ványa 2006). Women's groups also used a cautious framing, which made their claims applicable to children as well as women victims, and avoided spelling out the gender inequality logic of domestic violence even in the major petitions (Fábian 2009, 316; Leaflet for the Signature Collection Campaign for Domestic Violence Legislation in Hungary 2002).

While the initial commonality of interest between women's rights and children's right groups in advocating for policy change was present, divergence in ideas and claims emerged in the policy development process. The informal alliance lasted shortly, and its intersectional potential was not realized. Rather than pursuing common action in which women and children victims were discussed together, and intersectional specifics of girl child's victimization spelled out, competing frames took over in which children's interests were pitted against women's interests. In the context of competing frames, it was the framing that resonated better with the mainstream, that is child protection, that ultimately was used by state officials in implementation practices and services. This dynamic supports the argument that the groups whose messaging resonates most with mainstream master frames are the ones to benefit from such coalitions (Strolovitch 2006). The potential of a co-supportive relationship between women's rights groups and children's rights groups was never realized; instead, gender equality and child protection rationales became competing goals. As intersecting inequality claims met in this arena, a logic of co-optation of gender rather than of intersectionality prevailed.

In addition to other, single-focus inequality groups and children's rights groups, mainstream human rights organizations can also be seen as potential allies for women's groups in domestic violence advocacy coalitions. These include transnational organizations, such as Amnesty International or Human Rights Watch, or domestic civil rights advocacy groups such as the Center for Legal Resources in Romania. Transnational human rights groups, such as Amnesty International and Human Rights Watch in Hungary or the Minnesota Advocates for Human Rights (MAHR, currently the Advocates for Human Rights) in Romania, engaged significantly with the issue of violence against women. They issued reports, such as 2007 AIHU report, *Cries Unheard*.[15] These organizations have a variety of rights issues on their agenda and engage in the protection of different vulnerable groups in their various projects. Involvement with domestic violence for them is short-term, campaign-based, and more or less engaged with local women's rights activism. Yet, their multisectoral activities might bring an intersectional approach to the claims made.

CONCLUSION

The two cases of anti-domestic violence activism in Hungary and Romania over a period of fifteen years present some similarities in terms of the dynamics of political intersectionality as well as marked differences. In both countries, a gradual openness to diversity took place within women's activism that led to more inclusiveness of minority women's groups. Intersectional capacities gradually increased in both countries, as evidenced by the emergence of more organizations and activists representing multiple social locations, in particular Roma women, lesbian women, and disabled women. In both countries, the development of intersectional capacities was supported by similar funders and favorable opportunities in the European Union accession process as well as the monitoring processes under CEDAW and facilitated by various transnational actors and platforms such as EWL or ERRC. The two countries, however, are markedly different in the type of political intersectionality dynamics that emerged in domestic violence activism.

Opposite dynamics of intersectionality play out in the two countries in the development of intersectional praxis within the women's movements against domestic violence, on the one hand, and the development of women's movement organizations and their coordination structures, on the other hand. Intersectional groups are conspicuously missing from the mobilization against domestic violence in Hungary, while they are included throughout the mobilization process in Romania from 2010 onward. This is in contrast to the dynamics taking place in the development of women's movement organizations in the two countries. There, we witness formal acceptance of diversity at the level of the women's movement organizations in Hungary and the development of coordination and cooperative mechanisms that include intersectional women's groups, particularly through the Hungarian Women's Lobby. The same mechanisms fail to appear in Romania at the level of the coordination of women's movement organizations, but intersectional cooperation emerges in domestic violence advocacy and other specific issue-based coalitions that are not discussed here.

These differences highlight the centrality of the agenda and capacities of intersectional women's groups for shaping the politics of intersectionality. In Romania, where strong Roma women's movement actors engaged in activism against domestic violence, a common agenda developed between them and mainstream women's groups. In Hungary, where individuals or groups of intersectionally marginalized women did not become involved in domestic violence activism, women's mobilization in this field has remained single-axis focused and arguably exclusionary. These findings point to the importance of empowering intersectional voices in anti-domestic violence activism.

The second significant difference relates to *organizational dynamics* in the women's movements in the two countries. In Hungary, the coalition that sustained cooperation and coordination among diverse women's groups, namely the Hungarian Women's Lobby, is arguably hierarchical and centralized. Political intersectionality, thus, has emerged in a top-down manner and takes its cue from international frameworks without discussion and debates in local struggles. In Romania, the women's coalition that came together to support domestic violence activism in the second period of mobilization is open, fluid, and decentralized, emerging from exchanges and networking in spaces such as universities, cafes, and cultural festivals. The advocacy coalition in Romania, moreover, is not attached to any transnational structure that would impose organizational requirements, as the European Women's Lobby does in Hungary. The two cases also illustrate the importance of resource pulling in building intersectional alliances. In Romania, where local Roma and LGBT organizations present key advocacy capacities at the domestic level, resources are pooled, and the alliance works together against domestic violence. In Hungary, the resources of intersectional groups are very weak at the domestic level and weaker than similar organizations in Romania; thus, they could not bring significant resources to the anti-domestic violence campaign. In the absence of resources, no alliance is created.

Importantly, though, the intersectional content of domestic violence claims remains weak in both cases. *Framing intersectionality* at the level of policy advocacy claims is problematic in both the top-down intersectional model apparent in Hungary and the bottom-up model in Romania. In Hungary, intersectional claims emerge as part of general gender equality claims, but they do not translate to the domestic violence project. This happens partly because there is no intersectional participation in the project at the domestic level and partly presumably because of strategic considerations. In Romania, where the domestic violence project has intersectional participation, the reasons are strategic and driven by prioritizing the efficiency of the coalition.

In the *cross-movement arenas* of political intersectionality, we find that existence of alliances across concerned inequality groups does not necessarily confirm intersectional potential. In Romania, the successful coalition that comes together to support reform of the domestic violence legislation in 2011 brings together Roma rights, LGBT, and human rights organizations. The coalition endorses the gender equality framing of domestic violence and accepts the underlying logic of gender inequality, while making intersectional differences explicit. Yet, the claims made are adjusted for strategic reasons to reflect the commonality and common interest rather than the specific intersectional claims of particular groups.

The comparison suggests that, in the domestic violence arena, different inequality axes interact differently from the perspective of political intersectionality. The intersection of gender and ethnicity, as well as gender and sexual orientation, follows the intersectional logic more easily than gender and age (as manifested in children's rights). This is a reflection of several factors. First, the groups that mobilize on each specific axis are varyingly sensitized to diversity and intersectionality. Roma rights groups and sexual orientation equality organizations are more sensitive to intersectionality than children's

rights groups in the two countries. Second, the ways in which the inequalities have been institutionalized in the larger context, at the global, regional,
and domestic level, constrain the possibilities of overlaps in the framing. The
children's rights frame is a difficult fit for the women's rights frame, because
one has a protection logic and the other has an inequality logic. As such, the
search for common ground in terms of intersectionality has little chance to
produce working alliances. Overall, the findings confirm that the overlapping
and compatibility or lack thereof in the framing determines in important ways
the limits of intersectional praxis in anti-domestic violence activism.

We can also observe important dynamics between the two arenas of intra-
categorical and inter-categorical political intersectionality and ways in which
they support each other. In Romania, we see first a mobilization of various
women's groups, which then supports an expanded mobilization that includes
other equality movements. In Hungary, we see how the lack of intra-categorical
intersectionality contributes to the failure of the inter-categorical coalition
to realize its potential for political intersectionality. Cross-movement intersectionality seems to work if the inequality groups that enter coalitions are
already internally sensitive to intersectionality, which allows for a common
frame to be found and agreed upon.

We find that alliances in the field of domestic violence enable or constrain
intersectional praxis in several specific ways. Resource pulling and identification of common interests between domestically organized intersectional
women's groups prove successful in terms of gendered policy advocacy
as well as intersectionally sensitive coalition work; yet, claim making that
is sensitive to intersectional interests proves more difficult. Availability of
intersectional resources committed to anti-domestic violence advocacy and
long-term participation in feminist coalition work, however, is a key element of intersectional practice. Transnational actors importantly complement
local-level intersectional capacities, and this contributes to intersectional
practice particularly where local capacities are more limited. International
platforms can also facilitate intersectional practice, particularly when it is not
emerging from local capacities. Finally, as the comparison between Romania
and Hungary shows, intersectional praxis might emerge more easily from
within the gender equality mobilization and framing than from interaction
with other equality movements.

NOTES

1. The initial dataset for this chapter was collected within the framework of the
European comparative project *Quality in Gender+ Equality Policies* (QUING, www.
quing.eu). Data collected within QUING included the history of domestic violence

policy development until 2007, contextual data, and frame analysis of one key domestic violence policy debate for each country. This was complemented by interviews with activists and experts (*n*=7) and extensive document analysis in the framework of a multiyear comparative project on domestic violence policy processes in five countries of Central and Eastern Europe.

2. OSI (now OSF) is a transnational donor that is particularly important in the region and in funding Roma rights-related initiatives (www.soros.org).

3. As early as 1994, the First Congress of Roma in Seville, Spain, sponsored by the Council of Europe resulted in the Manifesto of Roma/Gypsy Women, which, *inter alia*, discussed violence against Roma women (Bițu 1999). The manifesto primarily addressed external discrimination, but it also challenged the internal discrimination of Roma women. In 1999, the Open Society Institute established the Roma Women's Initiative (now discontinued) and the Council of Europe granted its sponsorship to the International Roma Women's Network. The latter initiative is partly continuing to this day.

4. A Magyar Női Érdekérvényesítő Szövetség bírálata és javaslatai az egyenlő bánásmódról és az esélyegyenlőség előmozdításáról szóló törvényjavaslathoz" [Hungarian Women's Lobby: Commentary and recommendations on the Hungarian Equal Treatment and Equal Opportunities Bill]. November 28, 2003.

5. Author's interview with Oana Băluță, October 6, 2012. The Roma activist who co-organized the protest is Carmen Gheorghe, who around the same time also founded a Roma women's organization, E-Romnja: e-romnja.org.

6. According to census data, 19.14 percent of Roma women lived in consensual unions compared to 3.73 percent in the general population. Furthermore, research on domestic violence in Romania (VIODOM Study 2009, quoted in Băluță, Bragă, and Iancu 2011, 84) found that people living in consensual unions were in fact more likely to suffer violence from their partners than others.

7. Raluca Popa's interview with Andreea Braga on October 5, 2012.

8. Raluca Popa's interview with Andreea Braga on October 5, 2012.

9. See Sterilizarea femeilor rome—expresia urii sistematice și instituționale (*The sterilization of Roma women—expression of systematic and institutionalized hatred*) 2013, signed by nineteen women's, Roma, and human rights organizations. https://fia.pimienta.org/weblog/uploads/ladyfest-ro/2013/11/sterilizarea_femeilor_rome.pdf.

10. http://www.errc.org/reports-and-submissions/errc-submission-to-un-cedaw-on-hungary-july-2007

11. http://www.errc.org/uploads/upload_en/file/03/82/m00000382.pdf.

12. http://www.errc.org/uploads/upload_en/file/03/82/m00000382.pdf.

13. Raluca Popa's interview with Oana Băluță, October 6, 2012.

14. http://www.errc.org/cms/upload/file/hungary-upr-08112010.pdf.

15. https://www.amnesty.org/download/Documents/64000/eur270022007en.pdf.

Chapter 4

Counter-Intersectionality

The Politics of Conservative Women's NGOs in Turkey

Ayşe Dursun

An increasing number of studies document that intersectional approaches to social inequality, which acknowledge the interrelatedness of inequality structures, enhance prospects for solidarities and coalitions within and across movements (Bassel and Emejulu 2014; Chun, Lipsitz, and Shin 2013; Dursun 2018b). As argued in this volume, intersectional activism helps create collective identities around shared interests and alliances across groups and movements. Intersectionality, however, is a particular orientation, one focused on inclusion and aimed at combating oppression in its multiple and intersecting forms. This chapter explores the other side of the same coin. It introduces the term of "counter-intersectionality" to describe and analyze a mode of politics that seeks to dismantle intersectional discourses and practices by misrepresenting inequality structures and mechanisms as isolated and unidimensional, resulting in shrinking inequality discourses and dissolving political solidarities between multiply marginalized groups.

In this chapter, I examine counter-intersectionality as a mode of politics exercised by conservative women in Turkey. It is an approach developed and favored by the contemporary Turkish political environment, as ruled by the neoliberal, pro-Islamic *Adalet ve Kalkınma Partisi* (Justice and Development Party, AKP). AKP has actively promoted the expansion of Islamic-conservative civil society, while suppressing oppositional movements.[1] In this political context, Islamic-oriented humanitarian organizations have proliferated, providing aid to countries in the former Ottoman lands, including the Middle East and Africa (Çelik and İşeri 2016). Charity organizations also play an increasing role in service and welfare provisions within Turkey (Atalay 2017). Along with humanitarian and charity organizations, pro-family organizations have flourished under the current government and have come to represent a countermovement to the feminist movement in Turkey (Negrón-Gonzales

2016, 208). Conservative women's NGOs have proliferated, while feminist, Kurdish, and LGBTQ movements have experienced serious backlashes. These conservative organizations make claims of representation as the "new women's movement of the new Turkey"[2] and work toward the erosion of feminist ideas, achievements, and strategies (Dursun 2018a; Dursun and Kovar 2018). This includes pursuing strategies and discourse antithetical to intersectionality.

While this volume focuses primarily on socially progressive organizing (by feminists, LGBTQ rights, and anti-racist activists), assessing the manner in which they pursue intersectional mobilization, this chapter focuses on one set of actors aiming to do the opposite. An investigation of conservative women's NGOs operating in Turkey expands our knowledge on the politics of counter-intersectionality, throwing light on the hitherto unstudied impact of politics aimed against and toward undoing intersectional discourses and strategies. I start this chapter by first sketching a theoretical framework for the analysis. Next, I reflect on case selection and methods. I then provide a political and institutional context in which this study is embedded before moving on to analyze the selected cases. I conclude with a discussion of the findings.

POLITICS OF COUNTER-INTERSECTIONALITY

As discussed in the introduction of this volume, intersectionality is a political and analytical approach that centers multiply marginalized groups and communities, drawing attention to their everyday experiences with inequality, the politics which target these inequalities, and to structures of inequality themselves (e.g., Chun, Lipsitz, and Shin 2013; Collins 2000; Crenshaw 1989; Harris 1990; Yuval-Davis 2007). In this chapter, I focus on the historically constructed nature of inequalities and their sedimentation in social institutions (Walby, Armstrong, and Strid 2012, 231) as a point of departure for a structural analysis. Among these institutions, I attribute key significance to statehood as an intersectional arena where interacting structures of difference and injustice are condensed and where forms of injustice are combined with each other and are linked, often hierarchically, with state norms and institutions (Sauer 2012).

In the past four decades, the state has been dramatically transformed by neoliberalism, which denotes in its narrow sense "a mode of political and economic rationality characterized by privatization, deregulation and rolling back and withdrawal of the state from many areas of social provision" (Gill and Scharff 2011, 5). Likewise, Turkey has undergone neoliberal consolidation under the AKP government (Coşar and Özkan-Kerestecioğlu 2017) through an aggressive privatization program, flexibilization of labor, commodification of health and education services, and reduction in public spending (Atalay 2017, 4). A synthesis of Turkish nationalism and cultural conservatism based on Islam, the "Turkish-Islamic synthesis" (Coşar and Yeğenoğlu 2011, 559), has been constitutive of the neoliberal project in Turkey from the beginning. The current government has further cemented this ideological basis by advocating "a moral framework built upon a thick notion of Islamic solidarity, tradition, family values, and gender complementarity" (Atalay 2017, 4).

Islamic and conservative NGOs have become key instruments to reinforce this moral framework against the neoliberal background. In the early 2000s, the AKP increased associations' and foundations' sociopolitical influence by giving them the status of "public-service associations," which grants them tax exemption and permission to collect money without authorization (Atalay 2013, 167; Çelik and İşeri 2016, 435), contributing to the proliferation of faith-based charity and philanthropic associations (Atalay 2017; Buğra and Candaş 2011, 522; Eder 2010; Kaya 2014). Similarly, pro-family associations have not only grown in numbers but have also improved their organizing skills under the current government and have come to represent a countermovement to the feminist movement (Negrón-Gonzales 2016, 208). Not least, conservative women's NGOs with close ties to ruling elite have served as the government's Trojan horse to hijack the feminist movements in Turkey (Dursun and Kovar 2018), sometimes co-opting feminist initiatives and shifting them in more conservative directions. These organizations have worked to reinforce notions of Islamic solidarity, tradition, family values, and gender complementarity, thereby threatening to erode feminist ideas and achievements (Dursun 2018a).

A hitherto unstudied aspect of these organizations and their politics is their impact on intersectional discourses, practices, and strategies. Hegemonic images and narratives of *the* woman, *the* family, and *the* society tend to privilege the demographically and/or politically dominant groups (i.e., Turkish, Sunni, heterosexual, cisgender), whereas the stories of ethnic, religious, and sexual minorities are further pushed to the discursive periphery. When the discursive peripheralization of multiply marginalized groups is promoted through collective action by a movement or organization, we deal with politics of counter-intersectionality.

For purposes of clarity, we should briefly address what counter-intersectionality does *not* suggest. First, it does not suggest that intersectionality is *per se* immune to stereotyping. On the contrary, a depoliticized intersectionality may serve to reinforce "status-quo stories of identities" (Keating 2009) without tackling the power differentials that (re)produce these identities in the first place. Despite these risks, intersectionality continues to inspire and inform emancipatory social theory and practice in Turkey as observed among feminists, Kurdish women, and the LGBTI community. Second, it does not suggest that the bearers of counter-intersectional politics (conservative women in this chapter) are not affected by intersectional structures of inequality; they can themselves be multiply marginalized subjects. It should be noted that counter-intersectionality refers to a mode of politics rather than to an identity. Third, "counter-intersectionality" does not denote an outspoken, well-defined, or coordinated strategy against intersectional discourses. On the contrary, it refers to a series of diffuse and at times contradictory discourses that promote single-axis definitions of inequality and politics of social change. Here, I deliberately refrain from using "single-axis" to describe this particular mode of politics because I wish to underline the political efforts—diffuse and contradictory as they may be—to dismantle discourses and practices that are *already* intersectionalized. While the critique of single-axis approaches is often aimed at socially progressive strategies that neglect to address the complexity of multiple and interlocking forms of oppression (focusing on gender-only or race-only approaches), counter-intersectionality is more deliberately aimed at undoing intersectional discourses.

Socially progressive, gendered mobilizations have increasingly attempted to find a collective voice by expanding inequality perspectives to include politically salient racial, ethnic, and other socially constructed "differences" between women (see Introduction to this volume). The recognition and articulation of power differentials that account for women's intersectional experiences of inequality is integral to this strategy. Counter-intersectionality, on the other hand, seeks to shrink inclusive discourses and dissolve the solidarities and alliances built on the acknowledgment of these "differences." As such, counter-intersectionality represents an assault on the knowledge and practices produced by multiply marginalized communities.

In the case of conservative women's NGOs operating in Turkey, their prospects for successfully dismantling intersectional discourses and practices lie first and foremost in their conformity with the AKP government's general "patchwork politics," which describes the "pursuit of policies by disentangling the political sphere into disconnected spheres of issue and disregarding the axes of junction among these spheres" (Coşar and Özman 2009 as quoted in Coşar and Yeğenoğlu 2011, 556). Similar to the government's patchwork politics, conservative women's NGOs' politics of counter-intersectionality dissociates distinct yet interrelated structures of inequality from each other.

DATA COLLECTION AND OPERATIONALIZATION

This chapter builds on data collected between January and March 2018 on the websites of three selected conservative women's NGOs based in Turkey,

namely *Kadın ve Demokrası Derneği* (Women and Democracy Associa-
tion, KADEM), *Ayrımcılığa Karşı Kadın Hakları Derneği* (Women's Rights
Association against Discrimination, AKDER), and *Hazar*[3] *Eğitim, Kültür ve
Dayanışma Derneği* (Hazar Association Education, Culture and Solidarity).
I have also consulted news articles to trace certain events as well as numbers
and dates. Turkish citations from the online materials of the NGOs were
translated by the author of this chapter. The selection of the associations
KADEM, AKDER, and Hazar for the current study is justified by the fact that
these organizations represent important hubs for conservative women's politics in contemporary Turkey. At the same time, they differ from each other in
their political origins and development. AKDER was established in the midst
of a phase of intensified prohibitions against wearing Islamic headscarves
at universities in the 1990s to lobby for the lift of the ban and keep track of
(and publicize) rights violations faced by headscarved women who were dis-
charged from the public sector and universities. Unlike AKDER that operated
under secularist prohibitions against the Islamic headscarf and had a narrow
focus on the headscarf ban, KADEM was established under more favorable
conditions during the pro-Islamic AKP government in 2013 and understands
itself as carrying out advocacy for women in a broad sense. Hazar has been
active since the 1990s and pursues educational and cultural, rather than
rights-based, activities. All three associations are well institutionalized and
professionalized, follow a religious conservative gender agenda, and display
ideological and, as in case of KADEM, organic proximity to the ruling elite.

As the politics of counter-intersectionality is embedded in discourse, one
convenient way to assess its concrete workings, given the admittedly limited
scope of this chapter, is through the examination of online materials produced by these NGOs. I examine the contents (e.g., statements, campaigns,
conferences and workshops, publications) produced by these organizations.
Based on common definitions of intersectionality, I put forward three crite-
ria for counter-intersectionality. First, a discourse is counter-intersectional
when it obscures the intersectional character of historically constructed and
institutionalized mechanisms of oppression (e.g., sexism, racism, classism).
Second, it is counter-intersectional when its universal subject (e.g., woman,
family) is stereotypically represented *within* the scope of hegemonic narratives of inequality. Third, counter-intersectionality systematically miscon-
strues intersectional debates and achievements or selectively recognizes only
some aspects of it, thus eroding the concept.

I limit my inquiry to the much-contested discourses on gender equality
and violence against women. Since the intersectional turn, the idea of gender equality has been expanded to accommodate and include other forms of
inequality. The discourse on violence against women has also been expanded
by the intersectional turn (see Crenshaw 1991). In Turkey, too, cleavages

emerged within the feminist movement in the 1990s due to the challenges posed by Islamist, Kurdish, and LGBTI movements to core feminist assumptions on the roots of and solutions for women's problems (Diner and Toktaş 2010, 42). Today, women's movements are under growing pressure to defend the notions of gender equality and gender-based violence vis-à-vis the religious-informed, family-centered approaches of the ruling elite and their allies within the civil society.

THE CONTEXT OF COUNTER-INTERSECTIONALITY IN TURKEY

As with all politics, counter-intersectionality is contextual and can best be grasped against the background of the political developments in Turkey of the 1990s and 2000s. The political turbulences of the 1990s were crowned by a devastating economic crisis in 2001, which, given the electorate's disappointment with old parties, facilitated the rise of the newly established AKP to power in the elections of 2002. Originally an offshoot of the Islamist National Outlook (*Milli Görüş*) movement, the AKP rebranded itself as a "conservative democrat" party to obscure its Islamist roots (Negrón-Gonzales 2016, 201) and thereby to avoid the fate of earlier political parties from the same tradition that were abolished by the constitutional court based on their anti-secularist agenda. The new government was determined to proceed with Turkey's EU accession process and to implement the postcrisis measures imposed on Turkey by international financial institutions, a position it used to distinguish itself from its Islamist forerunners that supported a break from the hegemonic institutions of the West. In this sense, the AKP represented a unique synthesis of reformism and conservatism, which helped consolidate its popularity in national and international circles (Öniş 2006). This ideological flexibility further enabled the AKP to incorporate diverse community interests into its pragmatic program and to gain a broad cross-class constituency (Axiarlis 2014, 77–8).

Throughout the 1990s, social movements, including feminist and other women's movements, underwent a process of NGO-ization "by which social movements professionalize, institutionalize, and bureaucratize in vertically structured, policy-outcome-oriented organizations that focus on generating issue-specific and, to some degree, marketable expert knowledge or services" (Lang 2013, 63–64). Despite initially giving rise to feminist grassroots organizations such as *Mor Çatı Kadın Sığınağı Vakfı* (Purple Roof Women's Shelter Foundation), feminism's institutionalization also coincided with "the marketization-cum-civil societalization, which brought in project-feminism—the traverse of the loose structuring through neoliberal political dynamics"

(Coşar and Özkan-Kerestecioğlu 2017, 157). Nevertheless, through institutionalization, feminist discourses reached an increasing number of women and women's organizations emerged in cities beyond Istanbul and Ankara (Özkan-Kerestecioğlu 2004). Turkey's acceptance as a candidate country to the EU in 1999 affected NGO-ization positively (Diner and Toktaş 2010), offering a political opportunity for rights activists in the country (Negrón-Gonzales 2016). The EU Commission released annual reports on the development of human rights and women's status, and the EU set up an accession partnership, thus enabling Turkey to participate in EU programs and agencies and access pre-accession assistance (Diner and Toktaş 2010). Women's movements encountered new political opportunities in the reform-friendly atmosphere under the new government in the early 2000s when hopes for a full membership into the EU were high. Muslim women worked with feminist and Kemalist women to push forward and monitor the implementation of legal reform (Aksoy 2015, 158), which marked significant achievements on behalf of women. The new penal code (2004) included more than thirty amendments recommend by the women's coalitions (Negrón-Gonzales 2016, 202). Among others, the new penal code (2004) classified crimes committed against women for the first time as "crimes against the individual" rather than "crimes against the family or social order" (Negrón-Gonzales 2016, 202).

Despite reforms that brought about formal improvement for women's rights in the early 2000s, the women-friendly version of neoliberalism soon came to an end (Coşar and Özkan-Kerestecioğlu 2017, 159). In the meantime, former prime minister and current president Recep Tayyip Erdoğan publicly voiced disbelief in equality between genders and compared abortion to massacre. These religiously informed discourses serve to ideologically buttress the neoliberal welfare system in the country that assigns the "task of social reproduction to families and traditional support networks" (Atalay 2017, 10), thus promoting Islamic-oriented organizations.

AKP's rise to power has been a gamechanger for organized conservative women, too. Conservative or "Islamist"[4] women were commonly associated with the pro-headscarf movement of the 1980s and 1990s under the former secularist regime (Arat 1998; Çakır 2000; Göle 1998, 2000). Historically, women who organized around the "headscarf issue," along with the Kurdish and LGBT movements, challenged Turkish feminism with different conceptualizations of the "women question" and politics of identity and "difference" (Diner and Toktaş 2010, 42), thus contributing to the intersectional turn. Kurdish women who were part of the feminist movement during the 1980s pioneered an ethnic feminism in the 1990s (Çaha 2011). They pointed to the dual exploitation faced by Kurdish women both due to the patriarchal system and the imperialism of the centralist Turkish state (Diner and Toktaş 2010). Islamist women, who had become politicized in the broader homegrown

Islamist movement and became the center of public (and scholarly) attention due to their controversial headscarves, both protested the secularist ban and objected to the masculinist interpretations of Quran (Diner and Toktaş 2010). Since the final lift of the bans in 2013[5] after being gradually loosened through the 2000s, conservative women have largely dropped the decades-old "headscarf issue." The vacuum created by the lift of the headscarf bans, which had inspired collective political action among conservative women for the past three decades, is currently being filled by conservative women who pursue pro-Islamic, family-centered women's politics (Dursun 2018b). While a small number of Muslim women pursuing pro-feminist politics such as the Ankara-based *Başkent Kadın Platformu Derneği* (Capital City Women's Platform) are marginalized within their own ranks, conservative women's NGOs are expanding (Dursun 2018b).

POLITICS OF COUNTER-INTERSECTIONALITY IN CONSERVATIVE WOMEN'S NGOS

Characterizing Conservative Women's NGOs

KADEM was established in 2013 in Istanbul and is the youngest and largest of the three NGOs. It currently has over thirty branches (as of March 2018) across Turkey. In 2015, the association established a foundation under the same name that runs student dormitories in various cities in Turkey. The board members are composed exclusively of women, many of them wearing a headscarf. KADEM does not openly identify as an Islamic organization, not necessarily due to concerns of secularism or impartiality but because, as I argue, in a context where Islam has become hegemonic, its omnipresence lies in its latency.

A fine-tuned blend of Islamic notions of complementarity of sexes and universal women's rights runs through the entire discourses and practices of the association. Its announced mission includes promoting women's potential to contribute to political, social, and economic progress, helping balance women's roles within the family and in social life, contributing to the advancement of democracy, rule of law, and human rights by protecting women's rights and supporting women to become productive individuals in economic, social, and cultural life. Among the main activities of KADEM are campaigns, trainings, workshops, international conferences, and publications. KADEM has hosted the International Gender Justice Congress (*Toplumsal Cinsiyet Adaleti Kongresi*), held since 2015, and the International Women and Justice Summit (*Uluslararası Kadın ve Adalet Zirvesi*), held in 2014 and 2016. The association is well networked with other conservative women's and pro-family NGOs and has close ties, both ideological and organic, to the ruling elite (Dursun 2018a). The unique magnitude of its financial, human, and political resources has turned the association into a gravitational force for smaller organizations. KADEM's attitude toward feminists, Kurdish women, and the LGBTI community is characterized by nonrecognition to hostility.

AKDER was established in 1999 by a group of women who were affected by the headscarf bans. The association is an all-women organization whose executive board is predominantly composed of medical doctors. Its stated goal is to identify and eliminate all legal and social obstacles to women's access to their rights and to enable individuals to receive education and work without having to compromise their religious convictions. The organization convened seminars and meetings and launched press statements for the lift of the ban and released a few publications on the issue. Contrary to KADEM, AKDER was established during times of strict state scrutiny over political Islam that resulted in the dismissal of headscarved women from the universities and the public sector. Since the ban was gradually loosened and finally lifted by the AKP government, the association has lost political ground and currently seems to be reorienting in terms of shifting its focus away from "the headscarf issue" in search of a new focus.

The third association was initially organized as Hazar Group and was later turned into the Hazar Association of Education, Culture and Solidarity. Like KADEM and AKDER, Hazar is an all-women association and synthesizes modern, secular values with Islamic ideas in its self-description and goals. Besides educational symposiums, the association engages in charity activities for the people of war-torn Muslim countries and organizes touristic-cultural trips abroad and in Turkey for women. Activities include education on topics such as religion, sociology, psychology, health, history, and women. In recent years, Hazar has taken up the issue of forced migration, organized Turkish lessons for refugee women, and paid occasional visits to refugee camps. Similar to KADEM, Hazar's relation to its target groups—whether women, children, or refugees—is hierarchical. Hazar engages experts and opinion leaders to achieve social change and institutes itself therein as the provider of such services. This is a fundamentally different mode of politics than initially pursued by AKDER where women who were affected by the headscarf ban pursued grassroots mobilization for the lift of the ban.

Gender Equality

Islamist women generally defended the complementarity, rather than equality, between men and women while submitting that hierarchies between genders are human-induced (Arat 1998). Accordingly, they accused feminists of seeking to nullify the ontological differences between men and women as they were intended by God. Currently, conservative women seek to mainstream the concept of "gender justice" as a counterweight to the feminist gender equality. KADEM stands out as a major driving force behind the notion of "gender justice." The association contributes significantly to the development and dissemination of the notion by means of publications and conferences on national and international platforms and in close cooperation with the political elite. In an article published in *Turkish Policy Quarterly* in 2015, the former president of KADEM notes that gender justice "highlights the different features and characteristics of men and women by nature, and acknowledges different liabilities between men and women attributed by society and culture, but also notes that there is no hierarchical superiority or inferiority between sexes" (Aydın-Yılmaz 2015, 113), and she underpins her argument by providing verses from the Quran. In a more recent publication, KADEM's former president notes that "instead of positioning women and men as opposites [something feminism and gender equality are accused of doing], they must be regarded as the arms of a scale to establish balance; as 'humans' with different qualities and characters but with the same weight on the scale."[6] Here, "human" is constructed as a universal subject who is sex-less, class-less, and race-less.

KADEM's annual Gender Justice Congress offers a platform with national and international outreach through which the concept of gender justice is promoted. The first congress in 2015 was dedicated to discussing the concept of gender justice as an alternative to the allegedly failed concept of gender equality. In there, KADEM placed emphasis on the role of the institution of family in eliminating established stereotypes through educational, social, and cultural public policies[7] without critically reflecting on the family's key role in reproducing these stereotypes. The association picked up the topics "women and family" and "divorce" for its third and fourth congress on gender justice[8]—symbolically held around or on the International Women's Day—and discussed the conclusions drawn from the congress' final declarations.[9] The core ideas put forth construct the family as the cornerstone of Turkish society where, the argument goes, religion plays a crucial role in shaping social norms and values. The declaration suggests that religion's diminishing social role should be revaluated for the sake of families that are currently under threat, as purportedly evidenced by rising divorce rates worldwide. The gender justice framework, against which these and other related topics are discussed, constructs spouses as gender-less humans, thus depoliticizing gender equality concerns. Furthermore, the gender justice framework helps disguise the fact that gender inequality intersects with other forms of inequality within and across families. Normatively loaded terms such as society, family, religion, culture, and values are used as self-evident, universal categories, even though they indeed narrowly refer to the Turkish, Sunni, heterosexual family. Families that do not conform to these hegemonic images such as single mothers and their children and ethnically and religiously minoritized families fall out of the scheme.

Although AKDER and Hazar do not enjoy as much public attention as KADEM which has become the engine of the conservative women's movement in Turkey, the same the conservative gender ideology is evident in AKDER's and Hazar's work as well. Similar to KADEM, AKDER and Hazar's approach to gender relations is informed by Islamic teachings on the ontological differences between and complementarity of the sexes. Notes from a 2007 workshop held at Hazar and organized by numerous Muslim women—including the anti-abortion gynecologist and wife of former prime minister, Sare Davutoğlu—are illustrative.[10] In these notes, policy makers and the public are warned against the ambitious concept of gender equality that, the argument goes, does not only seek to achieve equality between men and women but also seeks to eliminate all differences between them for a sex-less society. Furthermore, it is argued that the idea that gender is a matter of "choice" (read, social construction) rather than *fitri*, that is, related to the primordial human nature, runs the risk of legitimizing homosexuality. Here, homosexuality is considered an undesirable outcome of feminist advocacy for equality, while the LGBTI movements' struggle against heteronormativity is disregarded.

In contrast to KADEM, Hazar formerly displayed heterogeneity regarding its discourses and interlocutors. This may have to do with the fact that, throughout its existence, which stretches over two decades, Hazar has experienced and adjusted to political opportunities and threats ranging from the reform-friendly 2000s to increasing authoritarianism in the following decade. KADEM, by contrast, operates under the impressions of the most recent political developments such as the mass mobilization against the government during the Gezi Park protests in 2013, the recommencement of armed struggle after the peace talks between Turkey and *Partiya Karkerên Kurdistanê* (Kurdistan Workers' Party, PKK) came to a sudden end in 2015, and the declaration of state of emergency in the immediate aftermath of the failed coup attempt of 2016 assumed to be plotted by the US-based cleric and former AKP ally Fetullah Gülen. Hazar previously organized, together with other NGOs, eleven *Kadın Buluşmaları* (Women's Gatherings) between 2003 and 2013, which hosted a large number of Muslim, Kurdish, and feminist women as well as men to discuss various topics related to gender.[11] It also organized a series of events where feminist ideas and works as well as the history of Ottoman and contemporary women's movements were discussed.[12] Since that time, Hazar has increasingly engaged with the Islamic-oriented, conservative, pro-government civil society while communication with former interlocutors seems to have largely, if not completely, disappeared. Hazar's politics of counter-intersectionality where it abstains from alliances with women other than conservative women is closely linked to the policy change of the government, which followed a moderate and reform-friendly course through the 2000s but grew increasingly hostile toward the claims of feminists, the broader Kurdish movement, and the LGBT movement in the 2010s.

AKDER may be the least vocal of the three associations when it comes to gender equality or gender justice. Despite its ambitious name, the Women's Rights Association against Discrimination (AKDER) was formed in response to and narrowly focused on the headscarf bans during the *28 Şubat süreci* ("28 February process"), which marked an intensified phase of state scrutiny over political Islam after the military pressured the Islamist prime minister Necmettin Erbakan to resign during a National Security Council meeting on February 28, 1997. Between 1998 and 2002, 5,000 female public servants were fired for violating the dress code and some 10,000 were forced to resign (Cindoğlu 2011, 36). During this time, AKDER served as a hub for solidarity among women affected by the bans, provided them with legal assistance, and gave scholarships to female students to continue their education in European countries (Çaha 2016, 134). One can observe that since the official removal of the headscarf, the association has reduced its activities in this area to passing on their collective memory of the "28 February process" to younger generations and the broader public through online statements, interviews, and involvement in the lawsuit against the protagonists of the "28 February process." In the absence of the previous headscarf ban, AKDER is urged to reorient and find new political ground. The fact that the association recently established a foundation (*Ayrımcılığa Karşı Kadın Hakları Eğitim ve Yardımlaşma Vakfı*, Women's Rights Education and Cooperation Foundation against Discrimination) suggests that it may increasingly engage with the Islamic charitable efforts that have proliferated under the current government. Similar to KADEM and Hazar, AKDER's understanding of gender-based discrimination builds on a female subject that is Turkish, Muslim, and heterosexual. AKDER homogenizes Muslim women's narratives of gender inequality irrespective of their class and ethnicity and thus serves to de-intersectionalize gender-based discrimination.

All three associations have in common the assumption that gender (in)-equality is extractable from other forms of social (in)equality. The isolated treatment of gender inequality—disjointed from class, racial/ethnic, and other forms of inequality—is enabled through the imposition of universal Sunni, Turkish, and heterosexual subjects who only "differ" based on their sex (women/men). Although all three acknowledge that gender inequality exists, their disregard of the intersections of different structures of inequality only serves to silence the voices of multiply marginalized women. With regard to the gender equality discourse, conservative women's NGOs' politics of counter-intersectionality is latent in that it does not involve an explicit assault on intersectionality but it is thorough in that it runs through all discourses.

Violence against Women

Violence against women has been among the top priorities of the feminist movement since 3,000 women attended a march in May 1987 in Istanbul to mobilize against domestic violence (Sirman 1989). The Kurdish women's movement and the LGBTI movement have worked to expand the scope of what violence against women entails beyond most feminist conceptualizations. Kurdish women have pointed to the impact of ongoing armed conflict between Turkey and the PKK in Kurdish provinces, which has caused massive human rights violations and increased the vulnerability of Kurdish women (Diner and Toktaş 2010, 47ff.). Similarly, the LGBTI movement has given priority to reporting and scandalizing homophobic and transphobic hate crimes.[13] Rising numbers of killings against transwomen have been politicized under the slogan "Trans murders are political,"[14] pointing to the aggravated inequality endured by transwomen who may be sex workers.

Compared to feminist, LGBTI, and Kurdish women's movements, Muslim women's interest in the topic is fairly recent. All three associations acknowledge that violence against women exists—itself a much-contested fact among Islamic NGOs—and engage in broaching the issue of violence, interacting with policy makers, and supervising the implementation of existing legislation. It is mainly feminist activists who work to keep the issue high on the political agenda to the point that even conservative women's NGOs cannot ignore it. At the same time, however, conservative women's NGOs contest that violence against women is systemic and intersectional.

Anti-violence discourse pursued by KADEM represents a textbook example of counter-intersectional politics. Some of KADEM's anti-violence campaigns are titled "If you are a man, defeat your anger!" and "First, be a man!"[15] In there, KADEM defines the perpetrators of sexualized violence against children as "perverts" and children and women as "the most vulnerable segment of the society."[16] The association consistently refrains from employing the term "patriarchy" or "gender (in-)equality" to explain violence against women and does not make reference to differences between differently (based on ethnicity and sexuality) situated women regarding their experiences of violence.

Although AKDER's contribution to the anti-violence discourse in Turkey has been rather limited due to its primary focus on the headscarf issue, the following occasion demonstrated AKDER's political proximity to Islamic women's NGOs when it comes to combating violence against women. In late 2014, AKDER was involved in the controversial candidate selection process for an independent expert body (GREVIO) responsible for monitoring the implementation of the Council of Europe Convention on Prevention and Combating Violence against Women, shortly known as the Istanbul

Convention, in Turkey (Dursun 2018a). The Ministry of Family and Social Policy sought to exclude independent women's and LGBTI organizations from the selection procedure by announcing the meeting on short notice and requiring additional documents from organizations that planned to attend the meeting. In the face of the undemocratic methods pursued by the ministry, the members of the Istanbul Convention Monitoring Platform—a civil initiative composed of eighty-five women and LGBTI organizations—left the meeting early. Despite the fact that an overwhelming majority of participants had exited the meeting, KADEM, AKDER, and KASAD-D, another conservative women's NGOs associated with anti-abortion gynecologist Sare Davutoğlu, were selected to the committee to nominate GREVIO candidates for Turkey. Although feminist scholar Feride Acar was eventually elected to GREVIO thanks to the pressure from women's and LGBTI organizations, the selection process illustrated the government's preference for conservative women as collaborators in addressing gender-based violence despite their lack of experience and expertise (Altınok and Somersan 2015). In its statement, the Istanbul Convention Monitoring Platform pointed out that the NGOs the government chooses to cooperate with are known to mobilize against some provisions of the Istanbul Convention, which they believe will damage "the structure of the family" and against its prohibition of discrimination against LGBTI individuals, which they consider a threat to "society's structure."[17]

Hazar approaches violence against women from a similar perspective. Hazar's activities include attending consultation meetings with government officials, participating in the Violence against Women Monitoring Committee meeting organized by the Ministry of Family and Social Policy, and visiting a Violence Prevention and Monitoring Center (*Şiddet Önleme ve İzleme Merkezi*), an institution established by the 2012 Law to Protect the Family and Prevent Violence against Women. The association's major contribution to the public debate on violence against women in recent years has been through an EU-funded project on violence against women. The project "Wo/men for women" was carried out by Hazar in cooperation with Küçükçekmece Municipality (Istanbul) and the Ella Social Gender and Ethnicity Information Centre in Brussels between 2014 and 2015 and involved field research with and trainings for women, workshops, a final meeting, and a report. The project description on the website of Hazar begins with reference to a surah, a chapter of Quran, that men and women were created from one soul, that women and men were created as different forms of the same species with shared rights and responsibilities and were assigned the task to institute justice, compassion, and respect in the world as "each other's friend and helper."[18] The family is identified as the primary and most significant institution where this task shall be realized. Similarly, the final meeting or session for "Wo/men for women" opened with a surah, which pointed out that "faithful men and faithful women are each other's friends and helpers."[19]

In her opening speech, the former president of Hazar underlined that, within the scope of the project, they approached the issue of violence against women as a social problem that affects—beyond women—children, families, the society, and its future. Suggestions made during a workshop organized by Hazar, and attended by numerous NGOs, included the prevention of unemployment and female poverty as well as the revision of the penal system and training judges and prosecutors on the issue of violence.[20] Suggestions furthermore included educating all parties, preventing drugs consumption, creating early prevention mechanisms in the family and rehabilitation for men with anger management problems, a stricter state control of media content, psychological rehabilitation for persons convicted of violence and the introduction of a legal obligation for psychological examination prior to marriage, intervention by the Directorate of Religious Affairs (*Diyanet İşleri Başkanlığı*) to eliminate patriarchal interpretations of Islam, and increased cooperation between public institutions and NGOs on the issue. Despite Hazar's attention to some important structural factors in violence prevention such as female poverty alleviation and sensibilization of the judiciary, its simultaneous emphasis on "anger management problems" and "psychological examination and rehabilitation" of perpetrators shows parallels to KADEM's anti-violence campaigns ("If you are a man, defeat your anger!"), which similarly misrepresent a patriarchal practice as an individual issue of anger management. Hazar's mention of the economic dimension of gender-based violence remains merely lip service given the association's general disregard of systemic poverty among transwomen and Kurdish women. The logical conclusion here is that Hazar has Turkish, Sunni, and heterosexual/cisgender women in mind when it calls for the alleviation of female poverty to prevent violence.

From a feminist perspective, conservative women's NGOs' position is problematic because it prioritizes the unity of the moralized family over women's well-being and considers cases of violence as incidents of manhood malfunction. This political position mainstreamed by conservative women's NGOs also calls for attention from an intersectional perspective. All three NGOs analyzed in this chapter reinforce hegemonic narratives of violence that render some aspects of the story untellable. They serve to mute the voices of multiply marginalized groups whose experiences of structural violence are (re)produced at the intersection between classism, nationalism-racism, and heterosexism. With regard to anti-violence discourses, counter-intersectionality lies not so much in the denial of gender-based violence but in the imposition of a narrative where the "victims" are only women but not Kurdish or trans. Here, counter-intersectional politics lies in conservative women's NGOs attempt to shrink the scope of the political discourse on violence (what it is and where it comes from), which has been painstakingly intersectionalized by multiply marginalized women in the past decades.

CONCLUSION

While the value of intersectional politics is increasingly appreciated by scholars and activists, this chapter has tackled its political counterpart. Counter-intersectionality is a better fit than the more common terminology of "single-axis politics" because the former recognizes the achievements of scholars and activists who successfully pushed forward intersectional agendas in the past three decades, making it probably the most important theoretical contribution of women's studies so far (McCall 2005, 1771). Counter-intersectionality, then, refers to a phenomenon that historically succeeds decades-long mainstreaming of intersectional ideas and agendas.

I identified conservative women's NGOs that raise claims of becoming the "new women's movement of the new Turkey" as a major driving force behind this mode of politics in AKP's neoliberal-conservative Turkey and studied the discursive workings and political outcomes of counter-intersectionality through the example of three Turkey-based NGOs. All three organizations promote a "gender justice" frame of gender equality that reinforces rather than challenges traditional (and religiously based) gender roles. All three organizations acknowledge that violence against women exists; however, unlike feminist organizations, they narrowly define violence and frame (sexualized) violence as an occasional slip or perversity rather than as the outcome of structural inequality between men and women. Furthermore, all three organizations misrepresent the subjects on the receiving end of inequality and violence. Victims of gendered violence are universalized as Turkish, Sunni, heterosexual and cisgender women. This reinforces hegemonic discourses of inequality and violence while muting the voices of women whose experiences of sexism are shaped and aggravated by nationalism-racism, heteronormativity, and other structures of inequality. While intersectional politics help build alliances within and across movements, counter-intersectionality as pursued by conservative women weakens solidarity among women by compartmentalizing their experiences and disregarding the axes of conjunction.

Although this analysis was embedded in the national context of Turkey, it may serve as a basis to further investigate similar phenomena in different countries. This can serve the purposes of scholars and activists of the field in three ways. First, the vast body of literature on intersectionality research can be further developed by looking at how intersectionality is currently being undone in the context of globalization and rising right-wing movements on a global scale. This can provide data from different contexts and enable comparative analysis of the intricate workings of counter-intersectionality. One issue that can be tackled by future research is that whereas in Muslim-majority Turkey Islamic-oriented discourses are essential to the construction of counter-intersectionality, in the West it is foremost anti-Muslim racism that is used to assault intersectional notions of equality and solidarity. Second, based on detailed comparative analysis, scholars and activists can develop roadmaps and strategies to circumvent counter-intersectional attacks that threaten to marginalize the knowledge on inequality and solidarities based on this knowledge, laboriously produced by generations of multiply marginalized groups. Third, beyond revealing the processes of undoing intersectionality, counter-intersectionality research can inform the broader social inequality research on the strategies to politically manage popular dissent over growing inequality, such as through disentanglement of political spheres and the reprivatization of the social concerns.

NOTES

1. A government decree from November 2016 abolished hundreds of associations, including Kurdish-feminist associations. The Pride Parade was also prohibited.

2. The president of the conservative, pro-government *Kadın ve Demokrasi Derneği* (Association for Woman and Democracy) described her association during the opening ceremony of its twenty-sixth branch as the "new women's movement of the new Turkey." *KADEM Hatay Temsilciliği Açıldı* [KADEM Hatay Branch has been opened]: http://kadem.org.tr/kadem-hatay-temsilciligi-acildi/.

3. *Hazar* means peace and has theological connotations.

4. "Conservative" here describes ideas and politics, which build on traditional images of men, women, family, and society. Although it is neither inherent nor limited to persons and groups who identify as Muslim, in the Muslim-majority Turkish context conservatism is closely linked to the traditional Sunni-Islamic interpretations of gender relations. "Conservative" is historically and politically distinct from "Islamist," which was commonly used to describe activist men and women within the Islamist movement in the 1980s and 1990s, although they share a certain political heritage.

5. The ban for judges, police, and military personnel remained in place. The last ban was lifted in 2017 for the military.

6. Available online at http://digital.tudor-rose.co.uk/a-better-world/files/assets/common/downloads/publication.pdf.

7. *Toplumsal Cinsiyet Adaleti Kongresi sonuç bildirgesi* [International Gender Justice Congress final declaration]: http://kadem.org.tr/toplumsal-cinsiyet-adaleti-kongresi-sonuc-bildirgesi/.

8. For the full programs, see http://kadem.org.tr/3-uluslararasi-toplumsal-cinsiyet-adaleti-kongresi-programi-aciklandi/; http://kadem.org.tr/8-mart-2018-de-gerceklestirilecek-iv-toplumsal-cinsiyet-adaleti-kongresinin-programi-aciklandi/.

9. For the declarations, visit http://kadem.org.tr/3-uluslararasi-toplumsal-cinsiyet-adaleti-kongresi-sonuc-bildirisi-aciklandi/; http://kadem.org.tr/iv-toplumsal-cinsiyet-adaleti-kongresi-sonuc-bildirisi-aciklandi/.

10. *Toplumsal Cinsiyet Eşitliği Çalıştayı Düzenledik* [We convened a gender equality workshop]: http://www.hazardernegi.org/toplumsal-cinsiyet-esitligi/.

11. For more detail see: http://www.hazardernegi.org/kadin-bulusmalari/

12. Series of events were held between March and June 2008 on feminist theory, Turkish modernization and women, and Islam and women (see http://www.hazardernegi.org/turkiye-islam-bati-kadin-okumalari/). Another such event took place between October and December 2010 on women's movements from the Ottoman Empire to the present (see http://www.hazardernegi.org/osmanlida-kadin/).

13. *2016'da en az 169 nefret suçu* [At least 169 hate crimes in 2016]: http://kaosgl.org/sayfa.php?id=24204.

14. *Trans cinayetleri politiktir* [Trans murders are political]: http://kaosgl.org/sayfa.php?id=16450.

15. For the campaigns, see http://kadem.org.tr/erkeksen-ofkeni-yen-medya-kampanyasi/and http://kadem.org.tr/once-adam-ol-kampanyasi-tanitim-filmi/.

16. For KADEM's full statement on a case of child abuse in Izmir, see http://kadem.org.tr/izmir-sapigina-en-agir-ceza/.

17. Turkey's Undemocratic GREVIO Candidacy Process: http://www.wwhr.org/turkeys-undemocratic-grevio-candidacy-process/.

18. *Kadına Yönelik Şiddetle Mücadelenin Yeni Adı: Wo/men for Women* [A new name for the struggle against violence against women: Wo/men for women]: http://www.hazardernegi.org/women-for-women-2/.

19. Wo/men for Women Kapanış Toplantısı Sunumu [Wo/men for Women Final Sitting Presentation]: http://www.hazardernegi.org/wfw-kapanis-sunumu/.

20. Wo/men for Women Projesi STK Çalıştayı [Wo/men for Women Project NGO Workshop]: http://www.hazardernegi.org/wfw-stk-calistayi/.

Chapter 5

Political Opportunities and Intersectional Politics in Croatia

Jill Irvine and Leda Sutlović

Social movement scholars have long been concerned with the impact of political opportunities and strategies on the emergence and success of social movements and mass political mobilization (McAdam 1982, 1996; Tarrow 1983, 1988). While some have seen political opportunities as the driving factor in movement emergence and abeyance, others have cautioned against such structural accounts, pointing to the importance of agency, leadership, and strategic choices in understanding contentious politics (Goldstone 1980; Kitschelt 1986). Most agree, however, on the importance of paying attention to shifting political circumstances including pivotal elections, regime change, and external intervention in explaining the dynamics of social movements and the methods of activism they employ. Scholars of intersectionality, in contrast, have paid less attention to how shifting political environments shape social movement strategies and approaches and how these, in turn, may open or close opportunities for intersectional politics. That is the question we explore in this chapter. In what ways do different women's movement strategies for achieving political change shape the potential for intersectional politics?

Croatia offers a good case for investigating this question for a number of reasons. First, as a post-conflict as well as post-socialist country, issues of identity and collaboration are particularly rich and complex. Moreover, intersectional practices of rooting and shifting as laid out in the introduction to this volume were consciously put into action in Croatia and other post-Yugoslav countries during and after the war. Second, Croatia was subject to seismic shifts in political environment, in significant part due to external actors and forces. The post-conflict political scene in the late 1990s was dominated by an effort to force regime change through an electoral breakthrough, or "color revolution," which was strongly supported and funded by the

US government (Bunce and Wolchik 2011). The period that immediately followed, in contrast, was dominated by the EU accession process and a focus on the legislative and other legal changes required for EU membership. These significant changes in political environment and opportunities resulted in radically different approaches to achieving gender equality, allowing for an examination of how shifts in political strategies affect intersectional politics. Finally, the culmination of the accession process in Croatia coincided with the Europe-wide economic crisis beginning in 2008. This timing provides fruitful opportunities for considering the dynamics of intersectional activism in response to economic uncertainty and crisis.

We begin by reviewing briefly the theoretical literature on political opportunities and social movement strategies and how these might inform questions about intersectional politics. We are particularly interested in considering critiques of legalistic women's movement strategies and the questions they raise for an intersectional praxis of accommodating multiple identities and inequalities. We then turn to an investigation of two different political approaches to achieving gender equality in response to changing political opportunities. During the first period from 1995 to 2000, feminist organizations and activists pursued a disruptive strategy of political opposition aimed at mass mobilization, getting out the vote, and coalitionbuilding across movements. During the second period beginning in 2000, feminist groups and activists adopted a more legalistic approach focused on formulating and passing gender equality policies and legislation and erecting a comprehensive gender equality architecture. We argue that while the first period opened up new inclusionary potential by reaching across the urban-rural divide and facilitating cross-movement coalitional politics, little effort was made to foster intersectional consciousness or to frame and articulate explicit intersectional claims based on multiple axes of identity. These claims became more possible during the second period of EU accession as new channels of influence emerged due to EU formal recognition of intersectional considerations in the policymaking process. At the same time, however, the intra-movement mechanisms for reaching across the rural-urban divide declined, as did cross-movement coalitionbuilding. We conclude by considering emerging forms of feminist protest in response to the economic crisis that may open up new possibilities for intersectional praxis.

The research for this chapter is based on field work conducted by the authors throughout the period under discussion, including active participation in some of the movement activities and events described here. In addition to published material on this subject, we have relied largely on primary sources, participant observation, and interviews for this research. Twenty-three semi-structured interviews were conducted in Croatia with leaders and activists in women's and other nongovernmental organizations in 2002 and 2011. An additional source of information is the material activist organizations and individuals published on websites and other online fora as well as reports by and about women's and other activist organizations. These reports and other secondary literature allowed us to situate our analysis contextually and comparatively and to develop an interpretive analysis of activism in Croatia.

ACTIVIST STRATEGIES AND INTERSECTIONAL POLITICS

Political environments and opportunities have long been recognized by scholars of women's and other social movements as crucial determinants of activist approaches to achieving political change, shaping organizational capacity and leadership, issue framing and claims, and choice of political allies. According to David Meyer, political context is essential to understanding the dynamics of mobilization, claims making, alliance "cultivation," deployment of particular strategies and tactics, and institutional and policy outcomes (2004). In Croatia, the political context of the immediate post-conflict period beginning in 1995 led activists to adopt what Kenneth Andrew has called a "disruptive" political strategy that was "dramatic, disruptive, and threatening to elites" as they worked to remove the ruling party of Franjo Tuđman from power (Andrew 2001, 74). After the defeat of Tuđman's party in the 2000 elections (Tuđman himself died in 1999), the political context shifted abruptly. The governing Social Democratic Party was sympathetic to the goal of legislative gender equality reform and, as the decade progressed, to fulfilling the gender equality requirements of the EU accession process. In response, activists adopted what Andrew has labeled a "routinized" approach to political change, based on "the acquisition of regular access to the polity through institutionalized tactics" (2001, 75). This routinized, legalistic approach, aimed at creating a comprehensive gender machinery, was spearheaded by increasingly professionalized organizations. While the first political strategy falls into what Andrew describes as an action-reaction model of social movement activism, the second can be described as an access-influence model (Andrew 2001, 75).

A key question is how these different political strategies affected the potential for intersectional activism, and the framework of this volume asks us to consider this question in the process of creating capacity, finding voice, forming alliances, and acting politically. The emerging literature on intersectionality and gendered mobilization described in the introduction to this volume offers some important insights in this regard, generating questions for further inquiry. Three main questions are particularly relevant to this study. First, in terms of creating intersectional capacity that can address multiple identities and inequalities, what is the impact of the increasing professionalization of women's and other social movement groups? Second, with respect to finding voice, understood as the articulation of identities, issues, and claims, to what extent and how are rurality and rural identities considered in framing issues and fostering solidarity. Third, when it comes to forming alliances, how is difference accommodated and how are groups and individuals at the intersection of identities included?

With respect to creating intersectional capacity, perhaps the most pressing issue relates to the professionalization of women's organizations and its impact on what Andrew (2001) calls movement infrastructure—organizational structure, resources, and leadership. Over two decades of social movement scholarship suggests that professionalization, while it appears to increase capacity in particular ways, especially in ways that serve donor needs, can reduce the overall effectiveness of feminist organizing (Hemment 2007; Lang 1997; Mendelson and Glenn 2002). Indeed, so much has been written on this topic that is has become almost a truism, in the words of sociologist Paul Stubbs, to denounce the deleterious effects of professionalization, NGO-ization, and the donors who have contributed to this trend (Stubbs 2017). This critique of the professionalization of women's organizing has been extended more recently to its negative impact on intersectional capacity—that is the ability of women's groups and movements to create mechanisms to address intra-movement power differentials and more representative structures of decision making (Bilić 2014; Bilić and Krajinić 2016; Butterfield 2014; Irvine and Halterman 2018). With this in mind, we ask whether and how the increased professionalization associated with a more routinized political strategy shapes the creation of capacity necessary to pursue intersectional politics.

Finding voice, the process of reaching across difference to foster commonalities that can form the basis of issue framing, has been a major focus of research on intersectionality over the past two decades. Much of the literature on intersectionality has centered on the challenges of recognizing difference while seeking common ground in the framing and articulation of identity, issues, and claims (see the introduction to this volume). An aspect of finding voice that has received relatively little attention in the literature on intersectionality is the existence of rural identities and the urban-rural divide that characterizes most societies, particularly when it comes to experiences of gender and its relationship to power. On the one hand, as scholars of queer rurality point out, it is important "to reconceptualize the rural in ways that depart from its traditional characterization as the site of the tragic, the homophobic, the unmodern, and the dismal" (Manalansan et al. 2004, 4). Moreover, it is important to challenge the ways in which urban becomes associated with the cosmopolitan and tolerant, and simultaneously with the European Union, as it has in Croatia, and rural with its opposite of intolerant, bigoted, and backward (Bilić 2014; Irvine and Irvine 2017). On the other hand, there is a need to examine closely the ways in which rurality affects the life paths, experiences, and identities of those who inhabit these spaces. As Sandberg's study of violence against women in rural areas demonstrates, there is a need "to take discussions on intersectionality further by including place and rural/urban geographies as social locations, which impacts on experiences of violence" (Sandberg 2013, 2). Consequently, we consider whether and how different political strategies of the women's movement—disruptive and routinized—affect how rural identities and experiences are included or excluded in the process of finding voice.

Intersectional politics is about forming alliances and building coalitions both within and across movements, the dynamics of which are critically affected by the type of political approach—encompassing particular strategies and tactics—activists employ. As Celeste Montoya's chapter in this volume demonstrates, cross movement movements like Occupy with coalitional movements like Occupy, universal frames may lead to the marginalization of individuals and groups at the intersection of multiple identities if these movements overlook difference. Women's movements have long struggled with the subordination of their interests and claims to other movements with which they have cooperated such as national liberation or labor movements (Beckwith 2000). The democratization movement that emerged in Croatia after 1995 was formed around a universal, pro-democracy frame creating potential challenges for ensuring the inclusion of individuals at intersecting social locations. Legalistic, routinized approaches to achieving political change, however, may be subject to different challenges as the broad coalitions characteristic of mass mobilization are replaced by narrowly constituted, highly professionalized lobbying organizations. As Andrea Krizsán and Raluca Popa's chapter in this volume illustrates, movements employing such access-influence strategies may be more inclined to cooperate with other organizations around limited policy aims rather than seeking to form broad cross-movement alliances on behalf of transformative social and political change. The choice of routinized strategy may also render such movements more subject to co-optation by the state (Alvarez 1999; Naples and Desai 2002). Whether and how disruptive and routinized movement strategies influence alliance formation and address intersectional identities and issues is a question we consider here.

DISRUPTIVE STRATEGIES AND INTERSECTIONAL POLITICS, 1995–2000

After the collapse of state socialism in 1990, gendered mobilization was a "remarkably vibrant element" of the political scene in Croatia with a visible presence in civil society and "strong organizational capacities" (Špehar 2012, 366). Indeed, in the early 1990s women's organizations were central to the first round of peace activism in Croatia and essential in its efforts to address not only the victims of gender-based violence during the war but also the connections between patriarchy and militarism that were seen as an important cause of it (Stubbs 2012). With the end of fighting in 1995, women's groups and organizations turned their attention to the issue of women's political participation and removing the increasingly autocratic government of Franjo Tuđman. As opposition to the Tuđman government grew, women's movement activists joined in the larger pro-democracy mass movement aimed at forcing a "second transition" through an electoral breakthrough (Irvine 2007). This model of electoral breakthrough was executed in several postcommunist countries during this period, with the aim of removing corrupt or authoritarian rulers and to "throw the bums out" through mass mobilization and participation in demonstrations, strikes, and other forms of resistance including, most importantly in this case, elections (Bunce and Wolchik 2011).

The mass politics of this period opened up new opportunities for building political capacity including the capacity for intersectional politics. After nearly a decade of war and government repression, popular opposition to the ruling regime coalesced around the 2000 elections, providing a transformational moment for social, economic, and political change. New organizational forms emerged, which linked women's organizations from all over the county. The two most important were the Ad Hoc Coalition of twenty-three women's groups, formed in 1995 to promote the inclusion of women on political party lists, and the Women's Network, comprising over fifty women's organizations, formed in 1996 to promote gender equality through the electoral process (Deželan et al. 2013, 37; Kajinić 2015). These intra-movement coalitions and networks proved particularly effective in organizing women in rural areas, who had been negatively affected by years of war and dislocation (Irvine 2013). Full-time volunteers were dispatched to various towns and villages where they organized discussion forums highlighting issues important to women such as access to health care and welfare benefits. By 1999, the Women's Network had established regional and local offices that were focused on supporting this work with rural women voters (Irvine 2013). Thus, the intersectional capacity of the women's movement increased during this period by bringing urban and rural women together in the new organizational structures of the Ad Hoc Coalition and the Women's Network dedicated to mobilizing large numbers of women around political issues affecting them and to getting out the vote.

This increase in movement infrastructure and its inclusion of previously marginalized rural women was reinforced by the funding model pursued by the US government, which was a major donor during the last half of the 1990s. During this period, the US government strongly supported electoral efforts to remove President Tuđman from power. Adopting a "social movement" model of funding to bolster a mass opposition movement, it provided significant funding to increase the capacity of the Ad Hoc Coalition and the Women's Network as well as strengthening communication channels and linkages between and among women's organizations and the inclusion of rural women in the political process (Irvine 2018). There were several reasons why the US government saw women's organizations and activists as key players in this oppositional movement including their strength in civil society, their potential for forming donor-local partnerships, and their similar political goals of promoting regime change. While this funding of women's organizations and activists was certainly instrumental, it had the effect of promoting the capacity to act intersectionally through building intra-movement infrastructure that included large numbers of rural women.

Despite these gains in forming organizations and networks that reached across the urban–rural divide, little attention was paid to fostering subgroups within the women's movement, which might increase representation from individuals and groups who found themselves at the intersection of social locations and identities. While the women's movement overlapped with, for example, Roma women's and LGBTQ groups, the primary emphasis of the Network and Coalition was on creating dense networks of women who were understood to share a common interest, identity, and social standing as women rather than as consisting of multiple identities and social locations. There is little evidence that rural women coalesced around their identity as rural women, nor were their particular concerns articulated in the political platform promoted by the Women's Network and the Ad Hoc Coalition. Intra-movement intersectional capacity remained confined to the inclusion of rural women in broad-based networks rather than the incorporation of women and their specific issues arising from different social locations through new organizational or decision-making mechanisms.

As women's organizations coalesced in the Women's Network and Ad Hoc Coalition, they faced considerable challenges in creating a sense of collective identity around which to formulate interests and issues. Gendered mobilization in Croatia during the first wave of peace activism beginning in 1990 was largely framed around issues of gender-based violence. This reflected the way in which these issues were brought to the fore during the wars of the 1990s but also continuity with previous activism during the 1980s (Kajinić 2015; Miškovska Kajevska 2014). Women's mobilization around these issues was essential to the formation of a global campaign against violence toward women and the transnational networks that waged it, and these in turn reinforced the visibility of this issue in Croatia. A focus on violence allowed

Croatian feminist activists to forge strong ties with peace movements and activists and to form common frames and action repertoires throughout the war.

During this period, feminist activists in Croatia struggled, however, with how to frame the issue of violence in relation to other, mostly ethnic identities. While some emphasized the primary importance of gender and patriarchy in wartime violence against women, others focused on ethnic identity and conflict as the primary cause (Korac 1998). Women's activists also contended with the fracturing of their gender solidarity by the rising importance of ethnic identity and nationalist politics (Benderly 1997; Knežević 1994). Transversal politics proved a way to cross these fissures after the war, as activists attempted to find common political ground and a new basis for political solidarity. Throughout this period, violence against women within the larger frame of women's rights as human rights continued to provide a basis of this common ground. Moreover, the adoption of a larger human rights framework opened new pathways for common action with human rights organizations and opportunities for building coalitions across movements (Irvine 2007, 2013).

Women's organizations expanded their common action with a number of groups and issues during the mass political mobilization in the late 1990s, as a variety of actors came together to oppose the Tuđman government. This political approach did not involve a fundamental shift in the previous focus on gendered violence so much as the addition of democratic transformation to the process of finding voice. The universal frame of democratic transformation was embraced by a variety of groups, including, centrally, women's organizations, which shifted their rhetoric to embed women's rights within democratic practices. In this framing of political action, women's rights as human rights required the establishment of more democratic practices, and democracy necessarily involved the recognition of women's human rights. The Ad Hoc Coalition's election slogan demanding that men "share responsibility in the home and power in the state" encapsulated this message.[1] Thus, this disruptive political strategy of the late 1990s based on mass mobilization involved a shift in framing, which allowed the women's movement to find common rhetorical ground within a wider movement for democratic transformation.

This strategy of finding voice reflected what Cole has labeled a common interest approach to intersectional activism (2008). Rather than recognizing or articulating particular claims based on multiple axes of identity, women's activists opted for a broad-based interest in political inclusion, which they assumed would benefit all women. While sporadic reference was made to particular groups of women such as "unemployed women, single mothers, rural women, elderly women, women with disabilities,"[2] little effort was made to afford voice to those whose interests and identities may not be represented equally by a broad platform of women's inclusion in the electoral sphere. Indeed, there was an implicit assumption that elections, both free and fair and including women candidates, would benefit all groups of women since women politicians could be expected to behave radically differently from their male counterparts (Irvine 2013). Moreover, because few subgroups representing the particular identities and social locations of women had been formed within the existing network structures, for example explicitly rural women's groups, there was no mechanism to ensure that these perspectives would be included beyond the occasional rhetorical reference to them.

While the intra-movement mechanisms for recognizing and politicizing multiple identities based on ethnicity, class, and ability were not emphasized in this common interest strategy of finding voice, the platform of political inclusion within a reformed political sphere did allow for the formation of a broad array of inter-movement alliances. For example, the Ad Hoc Coalition and the Croatian Women's Network played a crucial role in Glas (Voice) '99,[3] an organization of 148 NGOs dedicated to getting out the vote, and GONG (Citizens Organized to Monitor Elections), an election monitoring organization (Fisher and Bijelić 2007). They also established close ties with women's sections of the trade unions, which were growing in strength during this period[4] and with opposition political parties, particularly the Social Democratic Party. This was in large part because of their own growing strength but also because of changes in the opposition itself, which united around a similar program of political reform[5] (Knežević and Zaborski-Čunović 2000). The result was that women's organizations were able to articulate women's particular issues and concerns through their strong partnerships with a variety of organizations in civil society and their linkages with media outlets and political parties.[6]

The period of mass mobilization and disruptive politics from 1995 to 2000 thus opened up new opportunities for intersectional activism even as it foreclosed other opportunities for intersectional activism. The campaign to get out the vote was by its very nature aimed at reaching the largest number of people and mobilizing them politically. This resulted in the creation of coalitions and networks that reached into towns and villages around the country, encompassing large numbers of rural women. It also resulted in numerous cross-movement alliances among women's, labor, human rights, and other organizations and political parties, creating a broad-based opposition movement dedicated to disrupting politics as usual. The result of this political approach was successful in terms of political inclusion—the significant jump of almost 20 percent in the percentage of women elected to parliament was the highest among postcommunist countries at that time. In this case, the inclusion of rural women resulted in immediate gains in the electoral sphere.

But with the shift to a more routinized political strategy in the succeeding years, rural women's voices and presence diminished even as other groups at the intersection of social identities became more visible in the policymaking process.

ROUTINIZED APPROACH AND INTERSECTIONAL POLITICS, 2000–2010

The turnover elections of 2000 brought to power a left-centered coalition more sympathetic to gender equality and focused on gaining entry to the European Union by fulfilling the necessary legal requirements, including those related to gender equality. Women's groups and activists responded to this shift in political opportunity provided by the "reconfiguring state" (Banaszak, Beckwith, and Rucht 2003), moving from a previously confrontational and contesting political approach to a cooperative and legalistic approach toward state institutions. Women's organizations, recognized as places of knowledge by the state authorities, strongly contributed to the building of the gender equality institutional structure (Deželan et al. 2013; Kesić 2007; Zore 2013). Nevertheless, while the opening of cooperation with the state and the adoption of a legalistic political approach allowed the women's movement to influence policies more effectively through institutional channels, it also weakened its grassroots connections, especially to those outside the urban areas. During this period of routinized politics, intersectional capacity declined, particularly the capacity to address rural identities and issues. However, it increased in other ways as the recognition of multiple and intersecting marginalities and inequalities became woven into EU discourse and policymaking practices.

The period beginning in 2000 was characterized by a tremendous burst of legislative activity as the newly enfranchised women's organizations sought to translate their electoral gains into legal and policy prescriptions (Irvine and Sutlović 2015). Building upon previous alliances between labor unions, political parties, and other civil society organizations formed in the late 1990s, and working through new consultative bodies established after the 2000 elections, gender equality activists succeeded in erecting a comprehensive gender architecture. The process included the passage in 2000 of Article 3 in the Croatian Constitution, which enshrined gender equality among the highest constitutional values. The first Gender Equality Law was passed in 2003, along with the Law on Protection from Domestic Violence, which provided a legal framework for the protection of victims and their families from perpetrators of domestic violence. Shortly after, in 2004, the Government's Office for Gender Equality was created. In 2008, the new Gender Equality Law and the Anti-Discrimination Law were adopted. Finally, a new Law on Protection from Domestic Violence adopted in 2009 introduced a wider definition of family, including former spouses, people living in cohabitation, and same-sex relationships. By the end of the decade, women's organizations working through institutionalized channels had succeeded in implementing a comprehensive legislative, policy, and institutional framework for gender equality.

While these gains were impressive, the access-influence strategy the women's movement adopted during this period, which was reinforced by EU donors, created new challenges for intersectional politics. As the major regional donor, the EU pursued a "civil society funding model" based on discrete projects, with limited goals and clear deliverables (Irvine 2018). Unlike the "social movement funding model" of the 1990s, this funding model required a higher level of expertise, reinforcing the professionalization of women's organizations and creating a cadre of narrowly focused experts. The "official sanctioning of particular organizational forms and practices among feminist organizations" inscribed into the new funding model favored larger Zagreb-based organizations, leaving organizations in smaller towns and rural areas in a marginalized position (Alvarez 2009, 176). In short, it increased the urban-rural divide, thereby diminishing intra-movement intersectionality. Furthermore, the increasingly competitive conditions of the changing funding environment were partly responsible for causing dissent among larger organizations and fracturing the Women's Network. One of the largest women's organizations, B.a.b.e., left the Network in 2005 and was soon followed by several other organizations (Broz 2013, 154). Thus, the dense network of women's organizations characteristic of the previous period of disruptive politics was replaced by Zagreb-based, lobbying organizations that increasingly focused on the technocratic projects required by the legislative advocacy process (Bagić 2006).

Leadership structures of women's organizations also changed during this period as a result of the more legalistic approach. A possible consequence of creating hierarchical, institutional structures for promoting gender equality is that the leaders of gender equality bodies and agencies, who are often government-appointed, are less accountable to their grassroots constituents (Ruyan and Peterson 2018). Not only are they removed from the base, they also have more power, which can serve to reduce the quality and representativeness of the women's movement leadership. This appears to have happened in Croatia to a certain extent where, as one feminist activist put it, a government-appointed gender equality officer was "killing the movement—we don't know why she is there."[7] Activists expressed frustration with the power these new leaders had to "do what they wanted" and how they "represent[ed] only their own interests."[8] Moreover, even among women's groups the trend was one of increasing inequality as a host of "feminist superstars" became entrenched in their own organizations, ever less willing to address the grow-ing inequality within them (Irvine and Sutlović 2015). Moreover, many organizations were staffed by what Paul Stubbs has called, NGO "flexians," who are "less concerned with direct political goals than their own position" (Stubbs 2012, 22). Organizations that were siloed, with highly personalized forms of leadership, were less able to act intersectionally as they lacked the willingness to address inequality within their own organizations. In short, in the opinion of many interviewed activists, the legalistic and influence-access approach to political change pursued after 2000 ultimately weakened the movement and rendered it far less responsive to "ordinary women" than the disruptive, mass-mobilizing political approach during the previous period.

While intersectional politics were weakened in some organizations during the period of routinized politics, they were strengthened in others, particularly when it came to visibility of intersectional claims, often in the form of anti-discrimination claims, in the policymaking process. Throughout the decade, various Offices of the Ombudsman (for Gender Equality; for Children; for Disability) were established to deal with multiple inequalities, and activist groups were encouraged to press their claims through these bodies. The culmination of efforts to achieve a legal mechanism for intersectional claims was passed with the Law on the Elimination of Discrimination in 2008 that went "beyond the demands of the EU directives" by prohibiting discrimination on the basis of race, ethnic origin and skin color, sex, language, religion, political or other belief, national or social origin, property, membership in trade unions, disability, genetic inheritance, and birth identity—gender, expression, or sexual orientation. The Office of the People's Ombudsperson was formed around this time to address multiple inequalities (Frank 2008, 17). The establishment of these mechanisms emphasized an "individualized, anti-discrimination approach with a tendency to judicialize inequality" (Krizsán 2012, 2–3). At the same time, the established mechanisms, assisted by the EU funding model, resulted in a visible increase in the ways in which intersectional identities were represented in the policymaking process, creating a ripple effect in the number of identity-based subgroups based on ethnicity, age, and ability operating within the women's movement.

These new channels of influence resulted in the formation of new intersec-tional claims in the process of finding voice, although these were highly chan-neled and structured by EU discourse and practices. During this period, the women's movement continued to use the framing and discourse of women's rights as human rights (Frank 2008), which resonated with the prevailing human rights framing and discourse of the EU. Nevertheless, while the EU discourse was one of human rights, it was firmly embedded in the framework of the competitive market and within the limits of liberal individualism, which did little to tackle the broader structural aspects of inequalities (Špehar

2012, 375). Moreover, the EU gender equality discourse was predominately constructed around women as a homogenous category and addressed to white women in paid employment, leaving out of their reach housewives, immigrant women, and ethnic minority women, among others (Hoskyns 1996). With these constraints, addressing issues of marginalized groups based on identities associated with sexuality, class, ethnicity, and ability, particularly in response to growing economic hardship, proved challenging for women's organizations. Although they sometimes attempted to articulate intersectional interests and claims in the policymaking process, the legalistic approach within the EU framework of women's rights as human rights in service of neoliberal economic development made this difficult.

Despite these challenges, however, women's organizations and activists did come together with other groups to form alliances around particular issues and laws. According to the results of the QUING study of the gender equality policymaking process, there was significant engagement in terms of gender and ethnicity among Serb women organized in the Women's Initiative of the Serbian Democratic Forum and the Women's Network Croatia and with organizations of Roma women (Frank 2008, 18). Women's organizations also cooperated closely with LGBTQ organizations, for example, to craft language in the Gender Equality Act that included nondiscrimination on the grounds of sexual orientation as well as gender. They continued to work together over sex education in schools and other anti-LGBTQ initiatives launched by church-affiliated groups (Irvine and Sutlović 2015; Kuhar 2015). Finally, women's/feminist organizations cooperated closely with the Women's Section within the Union of Autonomous Trade Unions of Croatia to address issues in the National Action Plan for Employment such as equal pay, contract work, and child care.

The routinized political approach thus resulted in mixed effects concerning intersectional politics. On the one hand, intersectional capacity increased with the new institutional channels for articulating different social identities and claims in the policymaking process. On the other hand, the grassroots involvement of rural groups declined as did their ability to find voice within the movement. The women's rights as human rights "master frame" appeared to lose its transformative potential and ability to give voice to meaningful intersectional aims as it became tied to particular economic and political priorities of the EU. Focused on legal and policy concerns and dominated by highly professionalized, technocratic organizations, the women's movement failed to respond to the increasingly urgent economic situation and the broad movement for economic justice that emerged in response to it. The economic crisis that began in 2008 would ultimately lead to new, disruptive forms of activism that rejected the intersectional limitations of the legalistic, routinized approach.

TOWARD NEW FORMS OF INTERSECTIONAL
ACTIVISM, 2010–2015

The economic crisis in Croatia followed a similar trajectory as in other East European countries, beginning with economic downturn and austerity measures, which resulted in massive demonstrations and protests (Beissinger and Sasse 2014). In the spring of 2010, "under the pressures of declining output, surging unemployment, and public finances spiraling out of control," the government presented an economic program that called for a host of austerity measures (Bohle and Greskovitz 2012, 254). These measures led to a series of protests, beginning with student strikes in 2009 and widening to massive street demonstrations by the spring of 2011. In contrast to their central role in the disruptive politics of the late 1990s, in the early days of economic protest, women's organizations were, as Paul Stubbs put it, "strangely silent," (Čakardić 2015; Stubbs 2012). Nevertheless, despite their initial lack of response, the deepening economic crisis resulted in the emergence of new forms of activism with a focus on class-gender intersectionality.

The first of the two events that exerted influence on the women's movement began in 2009 when students blocked classes at the Faculty of Humanities and Social Sciences in Zagreb. Within days, student protests spread to around twenty faculties and universities in eight Croatian cities, where protesters replaced the official curriculum with lectures, workshops, film screenings, and other alternative educational programs (Doolan 2014). While the protest was ostensibly in response to a proposed increase in tuition fees, students framed their demands within a much larger critique of neoliberal economic policies and representative democracy. Adopting a neo-Marxist position, they focused on the broader socioeconomic context of attacks on trade unions and particular social institutions and emphasized the importance of "collective solidarity," "social interests," and "a more just society" (Doolan 2014). The student movement did not confine its criticism to the government, however. It was also extremely critical of civil society in Croatia, charging that its conceptions of human rights ignored "the deep structural deficiencies of the form of capitalism developed in Croatia" (Stubbs 2012, 22). Situating the struggle for free education within the context of defending social rights and public goods in the face of rising neoliberal tendencies, the student movement also served as "the catalyst of the piled up discontent" (Horvat and Štiks 2010, 11).

This wider discontent erupted in a series of street demonstrations in the spring of 2011. Organized largely on Facebook, and often referred to as the Facebook Protests, these demonstrations gathered an exceptionally diverse group of participants, from right-wing nationalists, football fan groups, and war veterans, to the individuals and groups close to the student movement, and to a variety of left-leaning civil society organizations (Kunac 2011, 30). Some of the largest feminist organizations, such as B.a.b.e. and CESI, openly endorsed the protests, while other feminist activists participated in the street protests as individuals (Kunac 2011). With the stated goal of removing the government through early elections, the protesters organized marches throughout the capital city that at their peak numbered over 10,000 citizens. As during the 2000 "breakthrough" elections, the message was once again "throw the bums out." In contrast to the 2000 elections, however, the message of the Facebook Protests was also one of deep dissatisfaction with the neoliberal economic policies that had resulted, for many, in increasing economic hardship (Lalić 2011). There was no mistaking this dissatisfaction when "Capitalism, no thanks" became the prevailing slogan of the marches.

In the years that followed, the university blockade and street demonstrations spawned many groups, initiatives, and collectives, including new feminist voices and alliances. The most prominent group, Fem Front (Feministički Front), became visible through different public and educational events and independent media publications that focused on "new" feminist topics and debates. These topics included the revalorization of Yugoslav feminist history, the negative effects of austerity measures, and the impact of diminishing workers' rights on women. Through these activities, Fem Front offered a criticism of liberal feminism and of the legalistic political approach that had prevailed in the Croatian women's movement during the previous decade. This criticism emphasized "the lack of systemic critique and engagement with political economy" (Čakardić 2015, 431). It further charged that the movement had "lost its progressive potential and its focus on the historical relations of gender and class, and . . . was reduced to a theoretical positioning towards dominant liberal feminism and polymorphous 'gender mainstreaming'" (Čakardić 2015, 428). This left-feminist criticism amounted to a rejection of the previous legalistic political approach that, according to it, had been emptied the women's movement of the concepts necessary to provide answers to pressing economic and social issues.

In the process of finding voice, the newly emerging feminist actors reframed gender equality issues, placing class squarely in the center. By reinstating the concept of social reproduction, the left-feminist criticism emphasized the link between austerity measures and social policies as the key source of the deterioration of women's social position. The financial cuts that had produced growing unemployment had also targeted social services and welfare programs, predominately used by women, and decreased the financial support for victims of domestic violence (Roberts 2013). Many of the previously existing regulations that had enabled women to work in paid occupations had been reduced, while the "decisions" on division of care arrangements and participation of women in the labor market had been omitted from policy regulation and left to economic circumstances (Dobrotić, Matković, and Zrinščak 2013, 227). In short, these developments had caused a reprivatization of care work within the family, reinforcing traditional gender roles (Elomäki 2012). According to left feminists, liberal feminists pursuing a legalistic strategy had become preoccupied with recognition rather than with redistribution issues and with a focus on the liberal aspects of human rights (Fraser 2009). The left-feminist initiatives instead called for positioning the "women's issue" within an anti-capitalist and historical materialist context, as the only possible way to discuss gender and class inequalities (Čakardić 2015, 438).

These ideas were given new organizational form with the founding in 2013 of the Women's Front for Labor and Social Rights (Ženska fronta za radna i socijalna prava), which gathered to counteract the announced Labor Acts changes. This group brought together various feminist organizations, women's groups of trade unions, human rights, and workers organizations[9] with the goal of "counteracting the negative tendencies of society's neoliberalization, impoverishment, discrimination and endangering of the direction of social development."[10] The announced changes of Labor Acts among other included atypical, flexible labor forms that rely on the EU work–family "harmonization" policy, making Women's Front to forewarn on the repercussions of these changes that will lead to reprivatization of care and exacerbate women's unfavorable position in the economy. The Women's Front opposed the introduction of labor "flexibility," or part-time work, in the name of work–family balance as these changes, they argued, would lead to lower wages, decrease the possibility of union organizing, increase gender-based discrimination, and generally make family and life planning more difficult.[11] The Women's Front demanded parental leave for fixed-time contract workers, introduction of company quotas for "atypical" labor jobs, better antidiscrimination and sexual harassment protection, clear provisions and regulations regarding outsourcing and agency labor, and pensions for persons that performed unpaid care work.[12]

The new left-feminist activists not only rejected the legalistic political strategy of the previous decade, they also appear to have rejected the previous discourses and practices related to intersectionality. According to them, liberal feminists had adopted a theory of identity and representation "that lacked socio-economic analysis" (Čakardić 2015, 438). Furthermore, they criticized liberal feminists for failing to understand the ways in which identity politics and corresponding ideas about intersectionality had arisen in conjunction with neoliberalism and served its purposes. Although other pressing issues hindered more systematic addressing of intersectional politics among Croatian left feminists, the newer Marxist-feminist theory may indicate their stance. Mainly, this theory understands intersectionality as an incomplete concept with underdeveloped analysis of class as a fundamental axis of oppression, while perceiving it as a "bourgeois ideology" that reinforces specifically capitalist ideas of individuality (Bohrer 2018; Salem 2016, 7). By focusing on the particular, intersectionality ignored the universality of the capitalist mode of production (Bohrer 2018); by multiplying political identities, it had obscured class relations (Mitchell 2013). In sum, intersectional politics had led to a fragmenting of political resistance, limiting the possibilities for intra- and cross-movement coalition building and solidarity.

Although these ideas were not widely accepted within the women's movement in Croatia, left feminist groups were able to shift some of the discourse around women's issues from single legal and policy issues to wider socioeconomic problems. They also pursued a political strategy geared toward building alliances, particularly with labor and union organizations. This, they hoped, would lead to more transformational politics with far-reaching consequences for the lived experiences of working-class women. Nevertheless, although their initial aim was building of class-based solidarity politics, the outcome turned out to be intersectional politics that understood class and gender as inextricably linked. However, understanding of class as the fundamental axis of oppression has also caused the reluctance of left feminist groups to engage with a more complex intersectional politics centered on multiple axes of inequality.

CONCLUSION

An investigation of the Croatian case offers some fruitful opportunities for understanding how shifts in political strategies can affect the dynamics of intersectional politics. The first observation is that different activist strategies undertaken in shifting political environments create different opportunities and obstacles for engaging in intersectional politics. The two different political approaches considered here, the mass-disruptive or action-reaction form of politics and the routinized-legalistic or access-influence political strategy appear to open up different opportunities and challenges for intersectional political action. The first may involve possibilities for building alliances across movements and grassroots activism within movements. Broad universal frames allow a common interest strategy of finding voice that is inclusive and capable of reaching across the urban-rural divide. The challenge for activists engaging in mass-disruptive politics is to create mechanisms for addressing particular identities within the broader movement. If all intersectional politics is understood as coalitional politics, then opportunities for subgroup formation and issue articulation must be fostered, including rural issues and identities. The second routinized and legalistic strategy faces the challenge of relying more heavily on professionalized, technocratic groups that may hinder broad grassroots participation. This political strategy may result in legislative or policymaking gains even as it discourages more inclusionary politics. While it may result in strategic policymaking partnerships, a broader social movement capable of creating transformative political change, which is the ultimate aim of intersectional analysis and action, may prove more difficult to achieve.

The second observation to be drawn is that institutional and funding environments matter. During the first period, as a major donor to women's organizations, the US government pursued a social movement funding model intended to create a broad-based oppositional movement. This funding model helped build women's movement infrastructure and grassroots outreach, but its reliance on universal frames meant that intersecting identities and issues remained unaddressed. The EU, in contrast, pursued a civil society funding model, based on discrete projects, with limited goals and clear deliverables. This funding model reinforced the professionalization of women's organizations and their reliance on urban-based, issue-based, groups. At the same time, however, the EU provided the structure for making more visible claims based on sexuality, ability, ethnicity, and, to a lesser extent, class. This, what might be called "functional intersectionality," opened up new intersectional channels of influence but appears to have come at the expense of grassroots activism.

A final observation that might be drawn from the Croatian case relates to the possibilities and limitations of a progressive, leftist politics that focuses on the relationship between class and gender. Croatian activists are not alone in emphasizing the need "to bring class back in" as a response to the recent economic crisis and the limitations of neoliberal politics. But how to do this in a way that allows for the inclusion of the complexity of individuals' identities and social locations? As the introduction to this volume stresses, where class is foregrounded, often ability and ethnicity are neglected, where ethnicity is foregrounded, gender and class are neglected, foreclosing a truly intersectional politics. As the chapters in this volume richly illustrate, any movement addressing economic inequality will need to accommodate multiple identities and claims, resisting the impulse to see them as distractions. Political activists should think strategically about how best to do this given the opportunities and constraints of the political strategies they embrace for achieving gender equality.

NOTES

1. Election pamphlet.
2. http://www.zenska-mreza.hr/platforma-zenske-mreze/

3. Jill Irvine interview with Suzana Jasić, GONG president, May 5, 2002.

4. Jill Irvine interview with Heidi Ekterović, American Center for International Labor Solidarity, May 8, 2001.

5. Jill Irvine interview with Karen Gainer, director of National Democratic Institute, May 8, 2002.

6. Jill Irvine interview with Sarah Gray, National Democratic Institute staff member, May 8, 2002.

7. Jill Irvine interview with a Croatian activist, June 15, 2011.

8. Jill Irvine interview with a Croatian activist, June 17, 2011.

9. Autonomous Women's House Zagreb, OWID (Organization for Workers' Initiative and Democratization), Centre for Women's Studies, CESI (Centre for Education, Counseling and Research), Initiative Ready to Work (Za rad spremne), Kontra, Women's Coordination of HURS (Croatian Association of Workers' Unions), Women's Committee NHS (Independent Croatians' Unions), Roda (Parents in Action), ROSA (Centre for Women War Victims), Croatian Trade Union, Croatian Pensioners Union, Association for Help and Education of Mobbing Victims, Women's Network Croatia (thirty women's groups), Women's Section of Union of Autonomous Trade Unions of Croatia.

10. http://www.sssh.hr/hr/vise/zenska-sekcija-69/zenska-fronta-za-radna-i-socijalna-prava-748.

11. Ibid.

12. Ibid.

Chapter 6

Intersectional and Transnational Alliances during Times of Crisis

The European LGBTI Movement[1]

Phillip M. Ayoub

This chapter attempts to chart the nature of the understudied European LGBTI movement's alliances and its orientation toward intersectionality. The movement's rhetorical use and attempted implementation of intersectional approaches has been precipitously increasing since 2008, despite a political context fraught with populist resurgence, homonationalism, and financial crisis: one that might typically be a worst-case scenario for the feasibility of furthering intersectionality.[2] After surveying the inclusiveness of the European LGBTI movement (in its claims and its participants), I explore two overarching questions in the wake of the 2008 financial crisis that has come to define much of European politics in recent years: *When and how are cross-organizational and cross-movement alliances facilitated? How has the financial crisis affected such alliance-building work as well as the broader intersectional consciousness of the movement?*

While some social movement literature argues that threat, such as the one posed by the financial crisis, can lead to mobilization, critical scholars in minority politics have questioned its potential for cross-movement alliances. Indeed, there is an active debate about what financial crisis means for intersectional alliance-building work. As Johanna Kantola and Emanuela Lombardo (2017, 6) put it, "Different organizations and movements representing different groups can be pitted against one another in a seeming competition for scarcer resources, or, alternatively it can point to new alliances and solidarity in times of crisis." The tug between these two disparate scenarios—threat or opportunity—has been increasingly explored in relation to activism by women broadly (Bassel and Emejulu 2010). This chapter offers a much-needed, yet often overlooked, exploration of these dynamics in LGBTI activism.

Using the case of the LGBTI movement, I argue that intersectional consciousness and alliances are expanded during times of financial crisis at an organizational level and especially in the transnational sphere. I refer to intersectional consciousness as the awareness of movement organizers to differing inequalities and discrepancies of power and privilege in their surroundings. There remain important caveats to the extent these alliances work and are functional on the ground and especially as it concerns individuals' lived experiences. Nonetheless, the movement's intersectional consciousness has grown in post-financial crisis years in a way that may offer new potentialities to organizers and make more visible the serious shortcomings that exist in the mission of LGBTI groups to address the needs of many of their most vulnerable subjects. Furthermore, while cross-movement alliances are frequent, they are context-specific and predominantly facilitated by international nongovernmental organizations (INGOs) and European institutions— that have been quick to develop an intersectional consciousness. I thus argue that intersectional consciousness is most present at the transnational level, where the potential for creating the capacity to act intersectionally and forge cross-movement alliances is high, and that the financial crisis has heightened that consciousness. Indeed, groups on the ground struggle with realizing the political potential of an intersectional approach to disrupt everyday power dynamics inherent in the movement; and times of scarcity heighten awareness by generating a sense of shared threat and challenging INGOs to think pragmatically about cooperating for access to limited resources. This process also influences domestic organizations, which remain rooted in their local contexts, though they also shift, scaling up and across, in interaction with the transnational sphere in which they operate (Tarrow 2005). I proceed by briefly grounding the above argument in theoretical debates on intersectionality and movement alliances before presenting the methodology and findings in relation to the research questions. My contribution is to shed light on when intersectionality can emerge as a formidable approach for movement alliance-building work.

INTERSECTIONAL CONSCIOUSNESS AND FORMING MOVEMENT ALLIANCES

Intersectionality in Movement

This chapter applies this volume's use of the concept of intersectionality to the social movement concept of alliances—when individuals and groups unite around shared goals (Gamson 1961)—formed by social justice groups, inside and outside of LGBTI advocacy groups. This is an admittedly broad definitional approach to intersectionality, using it as a research paradigm for understanding "social groups, relations, and contexts" (Dhamoon 2011, 230), while acknowledging the importance of it as a social critique emerging out of the struggles of black women in the United States (Collins 2008; Crenshaw 1991). This chapter is primarily concerned with the meso- and macro-level foundations of the approach, as they concern group and institutional organizations, social structures, and power relations and sees alliances across social justice groups as one observable implication—however simplistic it may be—of the application of an intersectional framework.

Even groups that are commonly represented as uniform (e.g., "black men" or "lesbian women") are coalitions (Murib and Soss 2015). This is as true for a conglomerate umbrella identifier such as "LGBTI people," which even in its name encompasses at least five separate identities, let alone the many sub-identities that represent the diverse experiences (at the microlevel) lived by various individuals that identify as LGBTI (Murib and Soss 2015). Indeed, the acronym itself embodies the exclusionary nature of the politics of the movement's earlier classifying labels—such as the "homosexual," "homophile," "gay," or "gay and lesbian"—and an evolution toward recognizing a vast array of experiences dealing with sexual orientation and gender identity (SOGI). While the LGBTI acronym is now commonly employed in research and practice, much scholarship has also noted that intersex, questioning, queer, and asexual people (LGBTIQQA) remain excluded from even this overarching category. Even the contested terrain of terminology highlights the difficulty of uniformly representing the distinct needs of individuals in a diverse constituency as well as the utility of a concept like intersectionality in movement work. While this chapter focuses on cross-movement alliances, it is important to hold these intra-movement alliances in mind, which have similarly manifested in an intersectional framework. Ignoring cross-cutting differences in identity poses serious limits to the project of emancipatory politics at the group level.

Threat and Opportunity in Forming Alliances

Social movement scholars have theorized movement alliances across borders, which can be brought into dialogue with scholarship on political intersectionality that recognizes the nonuniformity across groups. Joe Bandy and Jackie Smith's (2005) volume offers a critical intervention on thinking about alliances across borders as well as the political contexts that facilitate them. In line with theorizing in the political process school, a core claim in this work is that the political environment in which movements operate affects their alliances (Staggenborg 1986). Indeed, alliances and coalitions are likely to form when social justice groups are faced with opportunities or threats—though some studies have privileged one factor over another. For example, Holly McCammon and Karen Campbell (2002) find threat to be the most important determining factor for movement alliances. For Suzanne Staggenborg (1986), whose work on coalition building called our attention to the interaction between political circumstances (in the form of opportunity and threat) and resources, common interests across groups are more salient when financial resources are plentiful.

Yet even in terms of resource abundance or scarcity, findings remain complex. My theorization of the relationship between financial crises and the LGBTI movement follows a line of argumentation that suggests that enhancing efficiency by pooling limited resources can create capacity by incentivizing a certain type of organizing: namely forming alliances. For example, Pauline Cullen (2005) has made such a case in her study of the European Social Platform. Indeed, resource mobilization theory—the idea that external resources strongly affect organizing (McCarthy and Zald 1977b)—also suggests that the availability of funds for certain types of organizing generates that type of organizing. The theory thus interacts in a productive way with the political process school to suggest that the "crisis" of resource strain can open an opportunity for collaborative alliances in some circumstances. While political process theorists often conceptualize external threats as policy threats, I operationalize threats as related to financial crisis here.

Relatedly, an important point that Peter Waterman (2005, 157) makes in reference to the Chinese ideograph for "crisis" is that it entails both opportunity and threat: "a globalized capitalist threat also provides a social movement opportunity." Crisis can thus offer an opportunity for applying an intersectional approach to organizing, in the sense that it puts issues of multiple inequalities on the activist agenda. I thus follow Dara Strolovitch (2013) to also complicate the popular understanding of crisis, a concept that is both political and ideological and overwhelmingly constructed in favor of describing issues affecting dominant groups. If crisis is about dominant groups, we should not expect its effects to be universal, as they may then naturally differ for marginalized groups—many of whom live in "crisis" on a day-to-day basis anyways.

I build on the above by exploring these ideas of threat and opportunity across borders and across group alliances. Looking at ties both within and across understudied LGBTI NGOs, my intention is both to explore these theoretical ideas in a new transnational arena as well as to argue that threat can be good at raising consciousness if organizations and institutions exist to channel it into a compelling intersectional narrative. When threat occurs in the form of an international crisis, transnational organizations are most able to peddle a narrative that defines that threat as shared. Thus, while we rightly expect an environment in which social groups are pitted against each other to potentially limit an intersectional consciousness—for example, homonationalist arguments claiming that migrant ethnic minorities are more threatening to white gay and lesbian people—I argue instead that crisis can also paradoxically create the capacity to act intersectionally and heighten the proclivity of alliances across NGOs.

Hypotheses

Drawing on this theoretical background, three sets of related hypotheses form the core arguments that I outline below. Thereafter, I will further elaborate on the mechanisms and processes behind the general assumptions I make here.

H1: Crisis

- H1(a): Financial crisis leads to resource scarcity, which alters donor requirements at the international level and incentivizes cross-movement alliances.
- H1(b): Financial crisis leads to a more xenophobic political climate, which makes discrimination and a shared sense of threat more visible, generating an intersectional consciousness.

H2: Alliances

- H2(a): The international organizations represented at the European level are more conducive to facilitating cross-movement alliances because of two distinctive characteristics: their ability to broker relationships and supply resources.
- H2(b): Domestic and regional dynamics are at play, with high levels of homo- and transphobia in some European countries and regions hindering external cross-movement alliances at the domestic level but sponsoring intra-LGBTI alliances instead.

H3: Intersectional Consciousness

- H3(a): Acknowledging intersectionality as a political framework for social justice work is clearly desired but not fully developed in practice.
- H3(b): Applying an intersectional framework is context-specific: international LGBTI organizations tend to be more successful at applying an intersectional lens to their campaigns (compared to domestic LGBTI organizations).

There are qualifications to any such hypotheses on intersectionality, which is an undoubtedly complex concept in the case of the LGBTI movement. The sections below also address this complexity, emphasizing that the implementation of a politics that recognizes an intersectional approach can be arduous, even when consciousness is high. Furthermore, alliances across movements and across borders may also be strategic, short-lived, and sometimes they can reify group differences. Finally, the assumptions outlined above are all in relation to social justice NGOs in domestic and transnational spheres, noting that I do not carefully analyze less formal, grassroots groups. In what follows, the chapter's three subsequent sections are structured around each set of hypotheses as it relates to the European LGBTI NGOs.

The analysis proceeds by describing the movement's inclusiveness and consciousness around intersectionality, before analyzing the propensity of such a consciousness to result in alliances across social justice organizations. It addresses both elements, however, by first speaking to the effect of crises—in this case, the financial crisis—on political intersectionality. These dimensions thus elaborate on intersectional consciousness and alliances as well as how these two dynamics interact with resource scarcity.

METHODS

Case Selection

Social justice around European LGBTI rights is an interesting issue for the study of intersectionality and alliances building. The movements that represent LGBTI people have a long history of transnational ties but function in vastly different domestic contexts; for example, European states vary greatly in terms of the resources available to LGBTI populations, the cultural receptiveness they enjoy, and the oppositions they face (Ayoub and Paternotte 2014a). Even within similar country contexts, the LGBTI movement represents individuals and groups with highly varied lived experiences and access to social justice. Not only do LGBTI people represent a group with many cross-cutting identities, but some have also argued that they embody—when compared to the representation of other social categories such as class, race/ethnicity, and gender—the group with the fewest institutional mechanisms for applying pressure at the European level (Verloo 2006). This is said in the sense that LGBTI groups are rarely institutionally recognized as deserving of protection. Such an understanding, which captured the sentiment of many scholarly onlookers a decade ago, reifies the popular notion of a group both "invisible" and "weak" politically. However, this portrayal of a weak and powerless group, while correct some time ago, also mischaracterizes the new paths and institutional mechanisms LGBTI organizations have paved. As Ahrens reports in her chapter in this volume, ILGA Europe currently has more financing per year (2.2 Mio) than other umbrella organizations, such as European Women's Lobby (EWL), European Network against Racism (ENAR), or European Development Fund (EDF). LGBTI groups are now key players in the landscape of European human rights work.

The EU case not only allows for variation in LGBTI recognition and movement across states but also features strong international institutions supportive of LGBTI rights—a most likely case for transnational cooperation and human rights promotion. Finally, it is a region greatly affected by the financial crisis. For these reasons, this study seeks to explore the dimensions of the concept of intersectionality through the lens of the European LGBTI movement.

Method

To gain leverage on this project's questions, I combined insights from a larger project that explores the effect of transnational LGBTI activism on socio-legal change with an expert survey on intersectionality. The larger study (Ayoub 2015, 2016) included twenty-five months of fieldwork in Europe, concluding with over eighty interviews and focus groups, alongside participant observation at dozens of activist meetings and campaigns across the continent. While familiarity with the European LGBTI movement led to a set of theoretical expectations, I collected follow-up data that specifically addressed intersectionality and transnational alliances. The data come from fourteen online survey interviews conducted in February and March of 2015, which centered upon six questions related to this project (overview of questions below in table 6.1). Each question was followed by an open-ended text field (which produced responses that I then coded). I also included two components that asked respondents to rank inclusivity and diversity on a scale.[3] Respondents were selected strategically to elicit a wide range of insights at different levels, including both national and international advocacy organizations. The respondents represent an array of southern, northern, eastern, and western European states as well as countries that experienced the consequences of the 2008 financial crisis quite differently. The survey included experts representing national LGBTI NGOs from Germany, Hungary, Italy, Malta, the Netherlands, Portugal, Poland, Slovenia, Spain, and Sweden as well as LGBTI-focused INGOs based in Brussels and Budapest. Finally, I attended the 2016 annual conference for the European chapter of the International Lesbian, Gay, Bisexual, Trans, and Intersex Association (ILGA-Europe)—the largest umbrella gathering of LGBTI organizations—in Nicosia, Cyprus, to observe the six panels and workshops centered on intersectionality and conduct additional face-to-face interviews with activists and funders on the questions used in the survey. In sum, the results of the analysis offer data that chart the voice of activists and practitioners in response to the guiding questions that motivate the study of intersectional consciousness in the contemporary transnational politics of Europe.

Findings

The results of the survey provide preliminary answers to the overarching questions, which correspond to the three sections in table 6.1. Specifically,

(1) financial crisis has benefited the transnational movement's intersectional consciousness and alliances by generating a sense of shared threat and encouraging cooperation for access to limited resources; (2) on alliances, cross-organizational and cross-movement alliances are frequent, but they are context-specific and they are predominantly facilitated by international organizations and European institutions instead of at the grassroots level; and (3) on consciousness, the movement seeks to be more inclusive and aware of intersectionality than it actually is on the ground, where middle-upper-class gay men still dominate decision-making procedures. I expand on these arguments in detail below, using descriptive data from the expert survey. Table 6.1

Table 6.1.   **LGBTI Movement: Intersectional and Transnational Alliances in Times of Financial Crisis, Average Responses**

	Score	*Scale*
I. Financial Crisis		
How has the *financial crisis* impacted the intersectional consciousness or actions of the movement?	1.33	1 (no negative impact) 2 (some negative impact) 3 (substantial negative impact)
How has the *financial crisis* changed coalitional or alliance-building work (both *within* the LGBTI movement and *with other* groups)?	1.25	1 (no negative impact) 2 (some negative impact) 3 (substantial negative impact)
II. Alliances		
How prevalent are cross-organizational and cross-movement alliances (with social justice groups representing different minorities)?	2.75	1 (not prevalent) 2 (somewhat prevalent) 3 (very prevalent)
What is the role of *transnational organizations* in facilitating these alliances?	2.83	1 (no role) 2 (some role) 3 (substantial role)
What is the role of *European institutions* in facilitating these alliances?	2.61	1 (no role) 2 (some role) 3 (substantial role)
III. Intersectionality		
How inclusive is the movement (in terms of race/ethnicity, class, sexuality, nationality, and ability)?	1.92	1 (not inclusive) 2 (somewhat inclusive) 3 (very inclusive)
How diverse are its participants (in terms of race/ethnicity, class, sexuality, nationality, and ability)?	1.85	1 (not diverse) 2 (somewhat diverse) 3 (very diverse)

Source: Author's survey (2015).

displays simple averages of the survey responses coded on scales of 1 to 3, and its scores are only intended to guide the reader with general descriptive trends and to foreshadow the three arguments that I will make. To make sense of these trends, I use the survey and interview responses of the afore-mentioned experts below alongside other contextual data gleaned from primary organizational documents and an earlier organizational survey to substantiate the three sets of claims.

FINANCIAL CRISIS (AND ITS BENEFITS?)

This section reflects on the financial crisis and how it affects two dimensions of political intersectionality: creating capacity for alliances and conscious-ness. One of the more surprising findings was the common observation that the financial crisis does not rank highly in the factors that LGBTI activ-ists say negatively affect the intersectional work of the movement at the meso- and macrolevels. On the contrary, most interviewees highlighted the benefits of the threat triggered by the crisis for intersectional consciousness and alliance building. To be clear, this is not to say that the financial crisis does not affect the people these groups represent at the individual level. According to the ILGA-Europe report on *Poverty and discrimination based on sexual orientation, gender identity, gender expression and sex* (2014), LGBTI people are at a particularly high risk of poverty based on their high rates of societal isolation; discrimination in access to services, education, housing, and health; decreased likelihood of having access to familial sup-port networks; higher rates of unemployment and pay gaps; and the limited recognition of same-sex unions (i.e., unequal access to rights and benefits linked to such unions).

Yet, with the exception of one respondent, the general consensus was that the financial crisis had little negative effect on the alliance-building work of LGBTI activists. The situation concerning organizational resources only minimally changed, if at all, for many of the organizations in question. It is worth bearing in mind that the LGBTI movement is so accustomed to being underfunded, even in Western Europe, that the crisis had little to no mate-rial impact: "Our specific movement was not funded well enough before the crisis to be hit now that overall funding is less available" (161[4]). Over half of the European movement organizations have one or fewer paid employees (Ayoub 2019). It is also a movement that has gained unparalleled growth and international attention in recent years, especially in the post-crisis years. While the financial crisis seemed for many to have little measurable impact on resources, several said it has had a strong and indirect effect on both inter-sectional consciousness and alliance formation.

Indeed, most respondents noted that having access to fewer resources for social justice organizations in general has a positive effect on alliance formation, in that organizations are more inclined to cooperate to complete projects (166 and 165). An excellent in-depth case study of LGBTI activism in Cyprus by Nayia Kamenou (2018) charts a similar dynamic, as does Petra Ahrens's chapter in this volume on the women's movement. The quotes under H1(a) demonstrate this dynamic.

H1(a): Increased Cross-Movement Alliances

Organisations have considered doing more cross-movement work to appeal to funders, whose resources have become scarcer—especially funders working across different issues, of course. Interestingly, I didn't see the same interest develop [before the financial crisis] when multiple-discrimination was more frequently discussed, roughly in the years 2006–2009. (167)

Competition for resources places tension as groups apply for funding from a shrinking pot of money. However, funders are placing an emphasis on intersectionality and multiple-discrimination, so organizations have incorporated this approach into their work. (165)

Donor organizations have reduced funding as a result of the crisis. Certainly forming coalitions and alliances requires funding in order to advocate for a particular cause, but I don't see it as a major obstacle. On the opposite side, availability of sufficient funds can be a determinant for triggering this kind of cooperation both within the LGBTI movement and with other groups. (166)

There are several examples of this effect in practice. For example, the International Lesbian, Gay, Bisexual, Transgender, Queer and Intersex Youth and Student Organisation (IGLYO) made intersectionality a primary focus since 2008 and they received funding from both the Council of Europe and the European Commission in the post-crisis period, with organizations from other movements listed as primary partners (165). Table 6.2 charts important partners (in 2016) of two prominent LGBTI umbrella INGOs. Below, I will show European-level membership-based organizations like these can play a role in facilitating both cross-organization and cross-movement alliances at the national level.

H1(b): Heightened Intersectional Consciousness

We see a related dynamic around the relationship between crisis and intersectional consciousness. The political shift to the far right and the threat that this has posed has reverberated in activist networks and has made the LGBTI movement more aware of its most marginalized members by further illuminating the struggle that they share with other social justice movements. These two interpretations were prevalent in the survey results. Only one activist

Table 6.2.   Collaboration among INGOs in Europe

ILGA-Europe	*IGLYO*
European Disability Forum	European Disability Forum
European Women's Lobby	European Women's Lobby
ENAR (European Network against Racism)	ENAR (European Network against Racism)
European Youth Forum	European Youth Forum
TGEU (Transgender Europe)	TGEU (Transgender Europe)
OII (Organisation Intersex International)	OII (Organisation Intersex International)
European Anti-Poverty Network	European Network for Independent Living
AGE Platform Europe	World Organization of Girl Guides and Girl Scouts
European Network on Religion and Belief	FEANTSA (European Federation of National Organisations Working with the Homeless)

Source: Author's survey (2015).

argued that the movement itself had taken a conservative turn in response to the crisis. In terms of theoretical novelty, both of these arguments complicate simplistic accounts of resource mobilization and political process theorists, if we shift the dependent variable from mobilization to consciousness and cross-movement cooperation.

> I don't think the economic crisis had a relevant impact. It's more the European democratic crises and the rise of far-right and populist movements that posed a threat to the development of LGBTI/human rights, pushing many organizations within and across the LGBTI movement towards some cooperation. (168)
>
> The crisis has led to a rise in xenophobic and intolerant speech on the part of political leaders in Europe. They have targeted minority groups more frequently, especially people of migrant origin, asylum-seekers, and/or Muslims. I'm under the impression this led . . . the LGBTI movement to become aware of this discrimination, and occasionally stand against it. (167)
>
> It has not impacted our resources or the ones of our partners. The only thing is that we're [now] more inclined to seek alliances with social NGOs. I think internally, we are more aware to better reflect LGBTI people's needs in their daily life: housing, social protection, employment, health, etc., rather than speaking in abstract terms of discrimination. (163)

The discussion within the movements and actors in various organizations has shown how the broader movement's awareness of "threat to equality for *all* minority groups" emerged as a result of populist and nationalist backlash to the economic crisis, like the rise of the far-right parties (165). This notion of "we're in this together" heightened with the feeling that "any *difference in society* became a threat to those on [the] far right," and one that various movements representing *difference in society* had to respond to together (165, emphasis added). I continue by describing further how alliances and heightened intersectional consciousness are facilitated in times of crisis.

Forming Alliances

H2(a): Acting Politically: Europe over the Nation-State

Whether an intersectional consciousness spurred by threat is reflected in the new movement alliances is an important but complex question. In this regard, survey responses suggested that when looking at NGOs, cross-organizational and cross-movement alliances are most pronounced in Brussels and often facilitated by umbrella organizations like ILGA-Europe, IGLYO, Transgender Europe (TGEU), Organisation Intersex International (OII), and their counterparts in other social justice domains. There are several reasons why INGOs are more adept than domestic NGOs at embarking on the cross-organizational/cross-movement relationships that tap into a framework of intersectionality. To explain this, my argument isolates two such primary advantages that the European macrolevel has that support its strong role in creating capacity for the LGBTI movement's intersectional politics: brokerage and facilitating resources.

Brokering Capacity

First, international LGBTI rights organizations have oversight in terms of brokering partnerships around projects that multiple member organizations might be working on in various European regions. Natural constellations of partnerships can emerge from the bird's eye view that these umbrella groups hold. By contrast, national organizations are generally more entrenched in the specifics of their immediate environment and can overlook the potential of convenient alliances in other contexts or with other groups.

There are many ways that international (governmental and nongovernmental) organizations, like the EU and INGOs, can foster cooperation. ILGA-Europe's annual meeting brings together hundreds of LGBTI organizations from across Council of Europe states. The opening thematic panel of the 2016 ILGA-Europe conference, hosted in the ballroom at a time when no other conference events took place, was called *Putting Intersectionality at the Core of Our Thinking* and dealt with a variety of pertinent issues related to the contemporary movement, addressing race, Islamophobia, as well as issues facing Roma, intersex, and trans people within the movement.

I should note that despite those impressive efforts, it was clear at the 2016 meeting that the understanding of the concept of intersectionality—especially how it relates to power—remained muddled among many of the participants from local organizations across the continent, and ILGA-Europe's panelists took on a substantial teaching role. The panel's abstract from the program states,

> So how do we make sure that thinking intersectionally is at the core of all our work? This panel aims at unpacking the very concept of intersectionality and at reflecting on what it means for the European LGBTI movement. This panel will be a place for critical self-reflection, looking at who has power and privilege within the movement and whose voices we are still not hearing loudly enough.

Indeed, the concept "intersectionality" appeared in the conference delegate packet thirty-two times in 2016, compared to just once in 2008. Using NVivo software, figure 6.1 visualizes the upward trend in the crude measure of key terms in the delegate packets that accompanied the annual ILGA-Europe meetings between 2005 and 2016: intersectional/ity, age, disability, race, and migrant/refugee status.[5] Another INGO, IGLYO, has published and maintained an "intersectionality toolkit" with guidelines for activists since 2013.[6] These examples also signal how activism has in recent years been framed as intersectional at the macrolevel, which can bring groups together around a common interest (Tarrow 2005).

Furthermore, the proposal of legislative bills that affect multiple social groups can structurally bring movements together to act politically. For

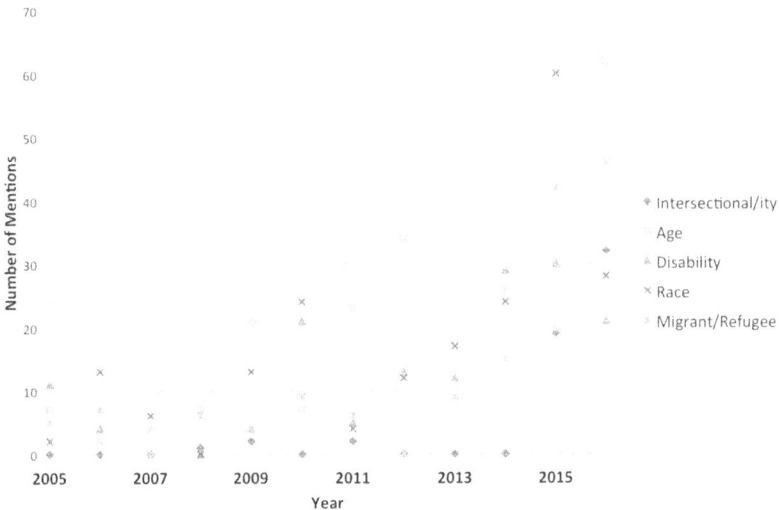

Figure 6.1. Key Terms in Delegate Packets for the Annual ILGA-Europe Meetings, 2005–2016
Source: Delegate packets 2005-2016; Author's calculation; see also Ayoub 2019: 16

example, pieces of legislation concerning anti-discrimination, hate crimes, and hate speech can become EU imperatives that incentivize INGOs representing various social justice groups—all of which are implicated in such legislation—to work together. At the EU level, ILGA-Europe forms part of the Social Platform and has worked with European INGOs on issues of age, disability, religion, and race. ILGA-Europe's recent collaboration with the European Network against Racism (ENAR) is one such example. It involved a campaign monitoring hate speech and discourse by Member of European Parliament (MEP) candidates on grounds of race and sexual orientation and gender identity leading up to the 2014 MEP election (160). According to activists, the European campaign was an "intersectional, cross-grounds campaign in the course of the elections to the European Parliament" (160). ILGA-Europe and ENAR produced a joint campaign, promoting MEP candidates who stood for both the rights of LGBTI people and individuals with a migrant/minority ethnic background.[7] It included a monitoring mechanism to identify and "call-out" candidates who attacked either minority or pitted one against the other (e.g., those stating that Muslims are homophobic).

Second, international organizations, by their very nature, generally encompass more differences and have practice at building consensus around them among their member organizations. Since they are more detached from local and domestic single-issue politics, they may be able to more effectively campaign for projects that have intersectional dimensions. This type of agenda setting can trickle down, with "member organizations often incorporat[ing] the same or similar strategic priorities as the European-level umbrella organization" (165).

A factor that tends to facilitate alliance building is this international aspect. Transnational movements or organizations working internationally are [more likely] to be aware of the intersectionality of certain issues or types of oppression. (167)

At the European level, the notion that LGBTI rights are often at the core of the discussion on human rights has also helped build alliances and coalitions with human rights organizations. (157)

I think ILGA-Europe, at the European level, and ILGA, at the international level, have been useful in focusing the attention of member organizations on diversity within the movement and on the need to take positive steps to be more inclusive and representative of the broader diversity. This has also included capacity building events where the sharing of good practices is facilitated. (160)

Creating Capacity during Resource Scarcity

European institutions and advocacy groups also increasingly play an important material role in creating the capacity to act intersectionally by funding projects that highlight multiple discrimination. Many organizations have incorporated such themes into their work and often prioritize programs and organizations that apply an intersectional framework. Take for example a recent public call by an ILGA-Europe board member: "EU Action Grants to support transnational projects to prevent and combat racism, xenophobia, homophobia and other forms of intolerance."[8] Seeing these struggles as shared, the grants also stipulated transnational collaboration across groups representing organizations from at least five countries. While the national and transnational levels are intertwined, as the execution of such projects often involves domestic organizations, at the national level, alliances are less likely to emerge in the structured fashion of European institutions and INGOs. Instead, domestic activists claimed that these national alliances are most likely to crystallize around current happenings that affect more than one social group, and interviewees noted that these alliances rarely endure beyond the specific campaign. For example, in the Netherlands, LGBTI groups have worked on an HIV-awareness campaign with other affected marginalized groups, such as those representing sex workers and intravenous drug users. Respondents stressed that, while intersectional projects can be facilitated by European INGOs and institutions, they must bring national organizations together to have any effective output.

> I haven't seen much [nationally]. Most of it I've seen in Brussels between high-level networks like ILGA-Europe and other BXL[Brussels]-based advocacy organizations. In most countries I've seen coalitions formed around current events (the necessity to pass an anti-discrimination bill, for example) but little really grassroots level organizing which would effectively bring together the community members. I initiated [a local] effort to bring together the LGBTI and Jewish communities. It was short-lived and didn't result in a long-term collaboration. (169)

H2(b): Domestic and Transnational Variation

The second central argument on cross-movement alliances is related to domestic and regional contexts, which mediate more inclusive transnational efforts to support intersectional alliances. For example, while there is a natural LGBTI affinity toward collaboration with women's groups in many contexts (though the issues of surrogacy and sex work have come between the movements in some cases), alliances with other groups are highly context-specific. Survey respondents noted heightened hierarchies within the acceptance of various marginalized groups at the societal level, which has hindered alliances. In countries where homo- and transphobia remain comparatively high, groups representing other minorities have taken caution against aligning themselves with the LGBTI movement (159 and 166). On this dimension, there was a regional difference between respondents, which respondents working in Central and Eastern European (CEE) countries noted repeatedly. To them, external alliances (beyond LGBTI issues) may be more challenging for CEE organizations. Several natural partners in CEE, such as groups working on issues of disability, have mixed or conservative positions toward LGBTI people, which makes collaboration less likely and subsequently imbalances power away from LGBTI groups when they do cooperate (169). In contexts in which LGBTI people are more stigmatized, however, the LGBTI movement may have an advantage for internal alliances (within LGBTI communities), both in terms of the types of alliances and in their political goals. This "united front" sentiment was captured explicitly in this response: "CEE LGBTI movements are usually less divided (politically) than other equality movements" (159).

Finally, in terms of power structures within these alliances, the most common factor for a privileged position and voice in the movement was the financial strength of certain organizations. Wealthier organizations play a disproportionate role in setting the movement's agenda (Lang 2013), especially in interaction with opportunities offered at the European level. One prominent example in CEE is the rise of Poland's Campaign against Homophobia (KPH), founded in 2001. Its strategies of transnational networking set it apart from those of many other Polish organizations, and its success at wielding funding and recognition from external contexts has created a key role for KPH in Polish LGBTI activism (164; see also Chetaille 2013). While the organization's success has been welcomed by many in the movement, its agenda-setting role naturally engenders some criticism for mainstreaming radical elements of the movement. Relatedly, despite the many benefits international organizations have, the EU's involvement was negatively viewed by one respondent, who noted that the EU can encourage cross-movement networking "at any price" (158), even if that clearly privileges certain advocacy groups and certain types of actors (e.g., large organizations endowed with activists who speak English well).

In sum, institutional mechanisms provided by the European polity often create capacity for cross-movement and cross-border alliances at the transnational level. While still limited on the ground, some practitioners see an intersectional approach as the only sustainable way forward for continued engagement with institutions. The puzzling pattern of the European policy machinery paving a way forward on institutionalizing intersectionality, rather than a bottom-up movement, relates to similar dynamics we see in other gendered mobilizations addressed in this volume.

Intersectional Consciousness

H3(a): A Will in Search of a Way

Two themes emerged around the status of the movement's postcrisis inclusiveness. The first was that the movement was increasingly articulate on the issue of intersectionality. In practice, however, the implementation of intersectional lenses varied greatly, with many activists pointing out that the movement was in fact not as inclusive as it would like to be on the ground. One activist articulated the general sentiment quite clearly: "I might think that the movement is open and tries to be inclusive, but it's not diverse in the end. It's heavily white and middle-upper class" (169). Within the LGBTI categories, trans, intersex, and bisexual people (and their claims) are especially underrepresented. There is awareness of this as a problem and a clear impetus to change it, but it remains a persistent problem nonetheless. Trans advocacy, for example, held an awkward place within many mainstream LGBTI organizations in Europe, which were primarily lesbian and gay organizations that wanted to be inclusive (including in their names), while actually having few competencies on the issues affecting the trans community. TGEU is a transnational organization that was born in response to the oversight of trans issues in other LGBTI organizations (Balzer and Hutta 2014); the same is true for OII, a group focusing on intersex rights. Similarly, lesbian women, despite their central history in a movement with close ties to the women's movement, "are not equal within the [LGBTI] movement in regard to decision-making, leadership, and governance" (158). At the 2016 ILGA-Europe conference, two panels were devoted to increasing the visibility of lesbian issues in the movement, which resulted in organizing the European Lesbian* Conference in October 2017.

Activists also suggested that such lack of representation is apparent even in groups that actively seek to increase diversity. The reason for this (i.e., having the "will" but still in search of a way), they argue, is that being an activist within highly stigmatized organizations requires privilege in and of itself (Newman 2013). This rationale is also well charted in work explaining social movement participation, which has typically found participants to score high on individual resources and biographical availability (Snow and Soule 2009, 109–48). As demonstrated in the survey responses, such privileges are not readily available to individuals whose LGBTI identity intersects with multiple marginalized identities:

> I sense a desire to be inclusive and diverse as a movement. . . . There is however still a lot of bias given where we come from as a movement and [the privileges required to] be active in the movement: higher education, to be able to question heteronormative society, and a level of economical independence to take the risk of working for a group that was so stigmatized. (161)

It strives to be inclusive. . . . But it is still very hard for ethnic minorities, people with disabilities, people from rural areas and people with lower educational backgrounds to participate in the movement. In some countries, gender, trans status, and age are also barriers. (159)

Alongside the systemic reasons for *why* this might be, activists also noted practical and conceptual concerns for implementation. An activist on an ILGA-Europe conference panel in Nicosia gave the example of the financial costs of organizing events that took intersectionality seriously. For example, to include deaf queer people, you need to supply sign language interpreters. Aside from the financial costs, in their context (Moldova, outside the EU) interpreters are often not out and face risks working in a queer space in an official capacity. There are also debates about whether to remove gender quotas, which increase lesbian representation, while reifying gender binaries exclusionary to trans and intersex people. In sum, "the movement is far less diverse than the community itself [and it remains] hard to reach out to people with different backgrounds" (169).

H3(b): Finding Voice as a European Priority

Another trend that conforms to the findings above is that intersectional consciousness has been addressed more clearly at the European level, which has been more successful than states or sub-European regions at inspiring and implementing intersectional strategies (though three activists [162, 168, and 169] singled out Scandinavian SMOs as being experienced in applying an intersectional lens). Transnational umbrella organizations in Brussels, such as ILGA-Europe, are recognized for effectively going beyond rhetoric to implement strategies that lead to diversity and inclusiveness:

[Intersectionality is] more of an imperative at the EU level, but rarely happens in practice on the grassroots level. Although there are a number of LGBTI groups, such as LGBTI Christian, Muslim, lesbian, trans specific or intersex groups, the inclusion at the grassroots level of activists from diverse backgrounds is limited. Many LGBTI events held at the European level have improved in terms of gender, age and nationality being widely represented. I think there is an increasing [top-down] focus to strive to enhance diversity practices within the movement. (160)

Overall, I have the impression the European movement [on the ground] tends to be mostly white, middle-class, and of home nationalities. [At the EU level,] I have the impression sexualities and gender identities tend to be rather diverse however, with LGB and *T* people represented, and intersex people beginning to be represented. (167)

There has been an increased discussion within European organizations over the last five-plus years about intersectionality and about becoming more inclusive. ILGA-Europe has played an important role. (162)

All of the findings above tap into a crucial challenge in finding voice that scholars have highlighted in taking an intersectional approach to movement politics. The issue of underrepresentation in the leadership of transnational organizations is also present and even greater at the domestic level. This is at least partly a result of a lack of opportunities for especially marginalized individuals to attain leadership positions, even if it is precisely the experience of people at the intersections that can help find voice for particularly vulnerable people within LGBTI communities. Activists acknowledge that it remains imperative to improve representation of people targeted by multiple systems of oppression in leadership positions for this to occur. When given a voice, they can serve as the interlocutors that create the capacity to address multiple marginalizations on the ground (Lyshaug 2006). An important way forward, noted on a panel at ILGA-Europe, is to generate positive visibility by further encouraging funders to move away from single-issue campaigns and by diversifying the staff and board of LGBTI organizations—supporting those activists that give new voice to the organization. That latter effort to improve representation can also be achieved in part by "making space": Inclusion can involve people who occupy power, relinquishing some of that power to make room for those at the margins.

CONCLUSION

This chapter has analyzed intersectionality in relation to the European LGBTI movement as well as the consciousness surrounding it in movement alliance-building work. The overarching sentiment, shared by activists and practitioners in various spheres of the movement, is that the movement seeks to be more inclusive than it actually is, suggesting movements must think critically to develop strategies of representation that give particularly marginalized members of LGBTI communities more voice. This connects both to practical concerns—for example, the limited ability of marginalized people to devote additional time to largely unpaid work—and conceptual ones—for example, the ILGA-Europe Board has in recent years faced debates surrounding how to implement intersectionality within its binary gender-quota system.

Yet despite these challenges, there remain important insights to where, and under what conditions, the movement is making headway creating capacity to act intersectionally. The initial analysis explored the relationship between financial crisis and the two dimensions of political intersectionality (intersectional consciousness and alliance formation). Somewhat paradoxically, there are benefits in crisis on these two dimensions. Indeed, collaborative projects that foster alliances have increased in response to the financial crisis. Furthermore, a shared sense of threat provoked by the proliferation of far-right politics and movements has, to some degree, enhanced consciousness surrounding an intersectionally linked fate (Strolovitch 2012). The findings suggest that the movement seeks to be more inclusive in response to crisis at the meso- and macrolevel, an argument I put forth while noting the severe obstacles crises bring in the lives of many individual LGBTI people at the microlevel. Theoretically, this finding is in line with recent work that challenges our thinking around the political construction of crisis (Strolovitch 2013). Acknowledging the socially constructed nature of crisis complicates how we measure its effects, which are far from homogenous. The findings also build on the work in social movement theory, bringing political process and resource mobilization schools together to argue that crisis provides an opportunity for alliances across difference.

The results were complex in terms of how much an intersectional consciousness matters for actual alliances across social justice movements and organizations. INGOs and intergovernmental organizations, like the EU, have clear advantages in terms of facilitating capacity for such cooperation. This, I argued, is mainly due to how brokerage and resource allocation at the transnational level are structured. There are pitfalls to such alliance building, however, including poor or unsustainable implementation, the privileging of large and transnational LGBTI organizations, and occasionally reifying group differences. The findings thus also conform to Staggenborg's (2015, 1) expectation that coalitions "can be hierarchical and exclusionary, imposing strategies and goals on their members and only allowing official representatives to participate." A change in intersectional consciousness, however, may draw new people into movement mobilizations, and it may generate visibility for new narratives of how to understand the broader dimensions to any particular struggle.

My hope is that the hypotheses articulated and substantiated here will spur interest and continued exploration between LGBTI and other social justice movements. Indeed, the results surrounding this multifaceted movement, in contemporary times, remain preliminary and provoke questions that can be tested further. Future research can continue to explore several of the claims, for example, with a content analysis of the development of intersectional frames in organizational policies. It should also look at the effects of cross-movement alliances on policy, as Louise Davidson-Schmich and her collaborators (2017) have carefully explained in the case of Germany. We have more to learn on intersectionality, and LGBTI movements, with all their complexity, provide a fruitful case for analyses that may bring us closer to a more just, and ultimately more inclusive, form of mobilization.

NOTES

1. This work has heavily drawn upon material from Ayoub (2019), published by Oxford University Press and reproduced with permission (license # 4391850999348).

2. Homonationalism is a concept that critically theorizes the incorporation of gay rights into the nation, including projects that reproduce and justify nationalism, imperialism, white supremacy, and war (Puar 2007).

3. The participants were contacted in February 2015 and were offered a $20 Amazon Gift Card for their time. I originally selected twenty expert interviewees from a pool of activists and politicians drawn from the larger project. The survey yielded a 70 percent response rate.

4. Refers to the survey/interview number.

5. Using NVivo software, I performed a discourse analysis in which I tracked the usage of "intersectional/ity" and related terms in ILGA-Europe Conference Delegate Packets. The related terms highlight different forms of multiple discriminations, including age, disability, race, and migrant/refugee status, and these terms made up the other coding categories. Complementary terms and phrases were also coded within these categories; for example, any references to a specific race or ethnicity (black, Latinx, etc.) were coded under the category of race. Each delegate packet was coded in order to find the total number of references to each of the listed and complementary terms. This resulted in raw counts of how often each term/category appeared across the years in the conference delegate packets.

6. http://www.asgi.it/wp-content/uploads/2015/03/Inter-Toolkit1.pdf.

7. http://www.enar-eu.org/NoHateEP2014-campaign-final-hate.

8. http://ec.europa.eu/justice/grants1/calls/2015_action_grants/just_2015_rrac_ag_en.htm.

Part II

INTERSECTIONALITY ACROSS SOCIAL JUSTICE MOVEMENTS

Chapter 7

From Identity Politics to Intersectionality?

Identity-Based Organizing in the Occupy Movements

Celeste Montoya

The US Occupy movement emerged in the fall of 2011, inspired by a global wave of protests that included the Arab Spring and the Spanish encampments of *los Indignados*. Occupy Wall Street started in Zuccotti Park in New York City's financial district, and soon encampments were organized in hundreds of cities across the country. For at least a brief while, the Occupy Wall Street and its corollaries across the country captured the nation's attention, inspiring new and long-standing activists to take the streets in conventional as well as new and creative forms of mobilization. The premise of the mobilization was (and continues to be, albeit in different forms) that the US political system is broken, a democracy captured by the 1 percent that controls a majority of the wealth, marginalizing the remaining 99 percent. The rally cry "We are the 99 percent" echoed across the country, representing both the possibilities and the limitations of Occupy. The universal call brought in diverse populations and interests and has persisted within political discourse long after the evictions ended the encampments. At the same time, it glossed over relevant experiential differences and the work that would be necessary to facilitate and maintain unified mobilization across groups impacted by multiple dimensions of inequality. It did not take long for familiar tensions and debates around race, gender, and sexuality to emerge in most, if not all, of the encampments and mobilizations. Even the name "Occupy" proved to be contentious, raising concern with groups asserting its association with colonialist forms of oppression.[1] As in previous mass movements, identity-based groups began to form around these dimensions of difference, such as Women Occupy Wall Street, People of Color Caucuses, Queering OWS, and so forth.

Identity-based organizing, or identity politics, has long been the subject of debate within the study of social movements and within progressive organizing itself. The critique of identity politics arose in the 1990s when scholars and activists articulated concern for what they perceived as the increasing fragmentation of progressive social movements (Gitlin 1995; Harvey 1996; Hobsbawm 1996; Kauffman 1990; Tarrow 1998). In particular, this critique lamented the rise of "special issues" that shifted the emphasis away from class-based mass mobilization toward what were perceived as the more particularized and fragmented identities of race, ethnicity, gender, and sexuality. To such critics, the conception of the Occupy movement, with both its universalizing discourse and its central emphasis on class, was welcomed as a new era of progressive organizing, one that might resist the segmented predilections that had supposedly weakened movements in the past (Gitlin 2012). As stated by Jodi Dean (2015, 273), "'We are the 99%' also erases the multiplicity of individuated, partial, and divided interests that fragment and weaken the people."

On the other side of the debate, however, are critiques of false universalisms and their hegemonic tendencies. As argued by Clarence Lusane, "Many activists and pundits forget, however, that identity politics is often a matter of necessity . . . struggle or perish . . . an internal fight must be waged inside progressive social change organizations against views and behaviors that serve to perpetuate skin and gender privilege" (quoted in Anner 1996). This view on identity politics emphasizes that such organizing does not simply materialize on its own but emerges out of actual experiences with discrimination and violence. The formation of identity-based factions is the result rather than the cause of movement failures. Such groups might also be the remedy for these failures. Identity-based organizing can provide a place for individuals and groups to develop their politics and establish a more visible place within mass mobilizations such that their concerns are better represented. Moreover, they can replace false narratives of universalism with more meaningful solidarities *if* they can avoid unidimensional approaches that might lead to isolation and fragmentation. The ability of identity-based groups to help create a more inclusive mobilization depends on the development of intersectional consciousness and practices. Intersectionality acknowledges differences not only across groups but also within groups in a way that can avoid the fragmenting of movements into vanishingly small constituencies and instead provide new avenues of cooperation (Bickford 1997; Cole 2008; Collins 1993).

In this chapter, I explore identity-based organizing as a potential site for making intersectional interventions in mass movements. As discussed in this book, intersectionality is an analytical framework and political orientation that emphasizes the complex ways in which multiple axes of difference interact to shape social inequalities. I argue that identity-based groups, like many of those found in the Occupy mobilizations, made intersectional interventions by disrupting single-axis movement frames and practices and by articulating the relevance of other "intersecting" axes of difference. Groups varied, however, in the extent to which they adopted and applied intersectional approaches, with some groups replicating the single-axis approaches they were attempting to disrupt by focusing exclusively on race or gender or sexuality. Such approaches might collectively work to diversify the larger movement but are more limited in their ability to comprehensively address oppression and facilitate coalitional movement building. Collins (1993) characterizes intersectionality as a "matrix of oppression," a conceptualization that simultaneously acknowledges distinct social positions at discrete intersections *and* the connection of these locations along different dimensions of structural inequality. It is this dual awareness, of the differences and the connections, that creates the possible of more meaningful and enduring solidarities.

SOCIAL MOVEMENTS, IDENTITY, AND INTERSECTIONALITY

Despite the negative characterization of identity politics, scholars have long argued for the vital importance of collective identities in social movements. Research demonstrates that collective identity is a significant variable not only in the "new social movements" but also in all social movements and throughout the various phases of protest (Polletta and Jasper 2001; Taylor and Whittier 1999). Collective identity refers to an individual's cognitive, moral, and emotional connection with a broader community, a perception of a shared status or relations (Polletta and Jasper 2001, 285). Social movement actors utilize existing identities to create a movement identity in order to establish a sense of linked fate that can be employed strategically. How these actors frame identities, or "find voice," is critical in the recruiting of participants (Gamson 1988; Polletta and Jasper 2001; Snow and Benford 1988; Snow et al. 1986; Tarrow 1998). Identity work is also crucial to sustaining solidarity and commitment (Taylor and Whittier 1999).

Identity politics do not arise in a vacuum. Experiences of discrimination along particular axes of difference can instigate a sense of group commonality, which might then be mobilized. The critique of identity politics is usually associated with activists' attempts to address race, ethnicity, gender, and sexuality. Critics from the left argue that they detract from a more unified focus on class. Class, however, is only one possible dimension of oppression with an associated identity that can (and has) been mobilized. According to the viewpoint of intersectionality, it cannot and should not be abstracted or prioritized over other dimensions of oppression or identity. To do so would ignore the ways in which class inequality is also raced and gendered, thus defaulting to white cis hetero male experiences with class inequality. Intersectional analysis examines the ways in which individuals might simultaneously experience multiple and *intersecting* forms of discrimination and oppression as well as how one might experience oppression along one dimension of identity and privilege along another. Within this context, individuals might claim membership in more than one group. The interaction of multiple marginalities may result in unique and particular experiences that challenge mobilization along any one axis of identity. At the same time, consciousness is dynamic. Not all identities will necessarily inspire the same meaning (Collins 1993, 23). The meaning given to different axes of identities can shift with political context and issue salience (Bedolla 2007). Furthermore, while individuals might be divided along some dimensions of oppression, they might be connected by others. Thus, while identity politics has a foundation in structural inequalities, individuals (and groups) exercise agency by rooting within or shifting between different collectivities.

The contention around identity politics is less about the use of identity in collective mobilization but rather about which identity (or identities) should be prioritized and which should be overlooked. After all, some critics of identity politics call for an ostensibly broader class identity and analysis in collective organizing. Emphasizing particular identities might play an important initial role in creating a movement, but overlooking (or even actively sidelining) other salient identities can be detrimental. Attempts to define a common identity tend to normalize the experience and perspective of some groups' members while marginalizing or silencing that of others (Young 2000, 89). Assumptions that the fate of all members of a community are similarly linked often work to conceal inequalities within these communities and appeals for a universal interest tend to be framed in a manner that favors the interests of dominant social groups and marginalizes those of others (Chun, Lipsitz, and Shin 2013; Strolovitch 2007, 62). This hurts the movement. A primary reason for movement demobilization is when participants stop believing that the movement represents them (Polletta and Jasper 2001).

Identity-based subgroups are often a response to experiences of marginalization within a movement that may occur via blatant exclusionary practices or subtler (but no less harmful) exclusions that are justified by ostensibly "universal" frames. In this sense, identity-based mobilization that occurs within movements serves as an early symptom of movement failure; it is, however, also an attempt to remedy such failures. Identity-based politics, in general, as well as within the context of identity-based subgroups organizing in larger social movements, is an important means of addressing marginalities. Identity-based groups are a source of strength, empowerment, community, and intellectual development for marginalized groups (Crenshaw 1991; Reagon 1983; Weldon 2012; Young 2000). In the context of a larger movement, identity-based subgroups might then articulate and act on concerns with exclusion, making interventions that can create a more representative and enduring movement. Weldon (2012) argues that separate organizing within movements plays an important role in creating and sustaining strong movements. She stipulates that movements should actually facilitate the self-organization of disadvantaged groups in order to foster ensuring descriptive and substantive representation within them.

While identity-based organizing within social movements can be a result of and potential remedy to marginalization, it has limitations. Such groups can offer a refuge from experiences with marginalization and the prospect for group development, but there may be a temporal component to these functions. Groups that retreat too far or too long may be isolated from the larger movement in a manner that precludes movement transformation toward more inclusivity. Another limitation of identity-based organizing within social movements is that such subgroups might also replicate exclusionary practices. "Group identities are vital for collective mobilizations for rights, resources, and recognition, yet every collective identity expressed through solidarities of sameness runs the risk of occluding differences within the group" (Chun, Lipsitz, and Shin 2013). Critiques of identity politics are not entirely unfounded but should be focused on the more particular manifestations of fragmented, "single-identity politics" that fail to capture complicated and fluid identities (Kurtz 2002, xxix). Identity politics that simplify and essentialize certain identities, failing to recognize the heterogeneity within these identities, may be unable to build and mobilize the necessary and enduring support to facilitate political change.

Iris Marion Young (1990, 2000) argues for the importance of simultaneously acknowledging commonalities and difference. Returning to Collins's (1993) "matrix of oppression" analogy, when groups become overly rooted in particular positions (along one dimension of identity or even one intersection), they may lose sight of the larger picture and all of the potential connections that can (and need to) be made in overcoming systems of oppression. Intersectional consciousness means recognizing the significance of the discrete social locations at the intersection of multiple marginalities but without losing sight of the processes tying all of these unique experiences together. This awareness and normative commitment is a vital part of building and maintaining the connections and coalitions that form a broad and representative movement capable of challenging and changing systems of oppression.

METHODS

In this chapter, I examine different narratives within and outside of identity-based groups in order to interrogate their perceived role, function, and purpose within the Occupy movement. This is not meant to be a definitive analysis of the movement but rather an exploration of how some people experienced the movement and how identity-based organizing fit into those experiences. From 2012 through 2014, I collected data on the Occupy mobilizations from a variety of primary sources (media, social media, online movement documents, published accounts, and interviews). In this chapter, I draw on all of these accounts.[2] For the interview data, I spoke with over thirty activists who participated in various Occupy mobilizations (e.g., Baltimore, Boston, Los Angeles, New York City, Oakland, Portland, San Diego, and San Francisco), with some activists participating in more than one. Most, but not all accounts, come from people who participated in and helped organize groups around issues and identities of gender, race, sexuality, and, in a few cases, age.

The empirical analysis is divided into two sections. The first section focuses on how and why identity-based mobilizations emerged within the Occupy movement. Why were they seen as necessary by founders and participants? What was their intended role or function? Who was included within these groups? What identities were activated and represented? How did participation in identity-based groups influence their connection to the movement? The second section focuses on assessing intersectional awareness and praxis within the various groups. To what extent did groups replicate or resist single-axis understandings of oppression and identity? How did individuals at the intersection of multiple marginalities experience identity-based groups in the Occupy movement?

THE OCCUPY MOBILIZATION AND IDENTITY-BASED ORGANIZING

From the beginning, Occupy was characterized by a "majoritarian populist impulse and organizational logic of massing large numbers of individuals," one that had difficulty recognizing and addressing internal specificity and difference (Juris et al. 2012, 3). One early and poignant account addressing concerns about overly simplistic universal messages was written by Manissa McCleave Maharawal (2012). She describes her reaction to a line in the proposed "Declaration of the Occupation" at the Occupy Wall Street General Assembly in New York City.

> I had heard the "Declaration of the Occupation" read at the General Assembly the night before but I didn't realize that it was going to be finalized as THE declaration of the movement right then and there. When I heard it the night before with Sonny we had looked at each other and noted that the line about "being one race, the human race, formerly divided by race, class . . ." was a weird line,

one that hit me in the stomach with its naivety and the way it made me feel alienated. . . . Now we were realizing that this was actually a really important document and that it was going to be sent into the world and read by thousands of people. And that if we let it go into the world written the way it was then it would mean that people like me would shrug this movement off, it would stop people like me and my friends and my community from joining this movement, one that I already felt a part of (Maharawal 2012, 157).

Manissa, along with a small group of women of color who had just come from a South Asians for Justice meeting (Manissa reports having also attended an anti-patriarchy meeting the night before), intervened by raising an issue with this language, arguing that this phrasing erased a history of oppression. In line with the Occupy norms of consensus, Manissa and her companions initiated a block until their change in wording was accepted: "As one people, united, we acknowledge the reality: that the future of the human race requires the cooperation of its members."

This story is instructive in several ways. First, it speaks to the universalizing impulses of social movements like Occupy and the exclusionary impact it might have when differences are glossed over. Second, it illustrates the need for intervention to incorporate or prevent the erasure of different voices and experiences and the role that separate organizing (directly or indirectly) might play in this. Finally, it shows how interventions might change the movement and the role that identity-based organizing might play in facilitating those interventions.

This section focuses primarily on the formation and purpose of identity-based organizing in the Occupy movements. While a variety of reasons were given for their formation, they generally fell into three categories: (1) the low visibility of particular social groups in general or in leadership positions and the need to improve descriptive representation; (2) the need to create "safe spaces"; and (3) as a means of diversifying movement messages and goals in order to increase substantive representation.

Visibility and Descriptive Representation

If collective identity is an important part of a social movement, then joining a protest where it is hard to find someone from the same social group either on the streets or leading the discussion is a problem. Scholars have argued the importance of descriptive representation in perceptions of democratic legitimacy (Gay 2002; Mansbridge 1999; Williams 1998). It is hard to think of an organization or institution as legitimately representing you when people like you are not visible. The perceived absence or limited visibility of groups was a major impetus to separate organizing in Occupy.

Speaking to general representation were a number of accounts that characterized the movements as being notably different from the cities or neighborhoods in which the encampments were set up. For example, a participant in Baltimore reported this of the local Occupy movement: "It was whiter than Baltimore. Baltimore is approximately 55–65% Black and the General Assemblies weren't that. It was young and it was whiter . . . mostly college educated, most have middle class backgrounds."[3] The issue of lagging racial representation was also noted in other cities such as New York and Boston. In an interview explaining his reasons for starting Occupy the Hood (an offshoot of the Occupy movement), Malik Rahsaan described going down to Zuccotti Park, There were no black people at all (Ross and Lee 2011).

While visibility was an issue raised by a range of identity-based groups, it was particularly salient with those organized around sexuality and gender identity. A participant in Queering OWS explained its formation, "I think it was started because people who initially went down there saw that there was a lack of visibility of LGBT voices and a lack of awareness around LGBT trans issues."[4] This was echoed by a Los Angeles participant, "I think the goals within the group were to make a visible Queer presence, you know, within Occupy. I think that was the first and foremost goal you know was to identify: We are here, we're Queer, we are part of Occupy."[5]

Concerns with representation extended beyond who was participating in the movement to how they were participating. While Occupy was often characterized by the media as a leaderless movement, many participants characterized it as a "leaderful" movement. Yet some leaders had more influence than others. While steps were taken to avoid hierarchical power structures, it was leadership teams (often self-appointed) that set up the structures and mechanisms to facilitate meetings, conversations, and even actions. Such teams often set the agenda for General Assemblies and directed the discussion. These activities provided members of the team with a lot of potential influence. Although most assemblies adopted a progressive stack (a technique used to give marginalized groups a greater chance to speak by prioritizing them in speaking queues), there was still always someone making the decision of how to line up speakers.

Participants in the various identity-based groups raised concern with these dynamics. For example, a founder of the Occupy Boston Women's Caucus described why it was formed with these observations:

> I think a lot of the public faces of Occupy were white men. Like the people that were talking to the media, the people that were facilitating the General Assemblies, the people who were heading up lots of working groups, it was all men, and white men at that. [So one of the goals of the caucus] was getting women more represented within the Occupy movement leadership and the Occupy movement dialogue.[6]

Similar observations were made at other major mobilizations. A woman who ended up participating in the feminist groups at several of the Occupy sites (New York, San Francisco, and Oakland) recounted, "I was concerned that at the General Assemblies it seemed like . . . men, especially white men were really dominating the discussion. . . . So for that and other reasons we were concerned that women's voices needed to be amplified."[7]

The issue with leadership and racial inclusion came up in discussions of Occupy Oakland, one of the more diverse mobilizations. Oakland, like New York, became a destination for activists from other locations. This raised a number of issues, including the critique of outsider activists assuming leadership and the distortion of local messages and initiatives:

> In our experience there were many more people of color in Occupy Oakland. A lot of very radical people of color and people who were interested to take direct action and confront institutions of oppression. . . . There was certainly a high level of attention between sort of not explicitly named leaders who were leading and making decisions in those settings and were white and were not connected to local communities and then folks doing organizing work or participating in small activist collectives that really felt like Occupy belonged to them as well. So there was definitely a lot of tension along those lines on the Oakland side.[8]

After the mass evictions occurred, some of the Occupy initiatives continued in these smaller and more representative activist collectives.

While my study of Occupy found the movement to be much more diverse than it was often characterized, the issue of visibility and representation in leadership structures was ongoing and a major impetus to identity-based organizing. With low visibility also came concerns regarding safety and inclusion.

Seeking or Creating "Safe(r) Spaces"

In many of the interviews I conducted, separate identity-based organizing was initiated as a means of creating a "safe space" for particular groups. Reflecting a now common discourse within the progressive movement, this was fairly prevalent both inside and outside the scope of identity-based organizing. The anti-patriarchy group in OWS was actually renamed "Safe Spaces." What constitutes safety, or threats thereof, however, varied. In my interviews, the discussion of safe spaces might refer to freedom from oppression, broadly conceived. It might also refer to perceptions of more immediate threats of physical violence. To a certain extent, almost all of the identity-based groups I spoke with talked about safe spaces in relation to oppression. While physical violence was discussed in most identity-based groups, those organized around gender (and sometimes sexuality) were more likely to talk and organize around perceived threats of physical violence (sexual violence in particular) coming from within the movement.

Reports of sexual violence in the encampments (in the form of harassment or assault) were a major impetus for the creation of gender-based groups or the organization of gender-based events (e.g., Women Occupy Wall Street, Occupy Patriarchy, the Feminist Assemblies). Within this particular context, the movement's model of around-the-clock encampments served as an obstacle to participation, and identity-based organizing worked to address this. This founding member of Women Occupy Wall Street discussed its creation:

> The formation of it happened . . . one night . . . maybe the third week . . . I didn't sleep there, I was never a camper. . . . But one night I stayed there very late, the latest I ever stayed and there was just this feeling . . . as it started to get crowded, with more and more people, I think there was just this feeling of an instability and a lack of safety. . . . And a whole bunch of girls, young girls actually, got together and wanted to have, wanted to discuss what to do, how to get a safe space going. And I ended up being a part of that conversation and we ended up coming up with the Women Occupy Wall Street working group. That seemed to be the answer. That's what we did.[9]

The concern with safety initiated gender-based organizing elsewhere, something that was not always well received by other members of the Occupy mobilizations. This participant reflected on the issue and its reception in Occupy Los Angeles.

> We had a number of issues come up in terms of sexual assault in the camp. Women, you know, feeling that the encampment especially wasn't a very safe space. So raising those issues was really credible, was really important, and there was a lot of controversy in male feedback on that. . . . A part of what the radical women's caucus attempted to do was raise some of these issues in our general assemblies, talk about how one deals with a sexual predator or someone who is making women feel unsafe, how we deal with that as a community.[10]

While there were not many reported sexual assaults, accounts of sexual harassment were much more numerous and fed into the perceptions of safety. Women's, feminist, and sometimes queer groups organized on these issues in various ways. One response was to create actual physical spaces within the encampment that were supposed to be a "safe" place for women to be protected from sexual violence from other movement members. An activist from the Bay area who participated in several Occupy mobilizations noted several of those spaces. Here she describes the one in Zuccotti Park, "Women there on the ground, so to speak, in the encampment also needed to be protected from sexual harassment and sexual violence. Melanie was one of the women who organized the Women's Safer Space, the very large pink camp that women could sleep in or go to for support, and was involved in many ways in supporting women there in Zuccotti Park."[11]

Groups also organized to raise awareness, education, or even just to express frustration. In Boston, the women's groups disrupted a General Assembly where they read a statement that broadly addressed what they saw as the lack of responsiveness by a majority of movement participants to issues of oppression. They also spoke directly to the issue of violence, "Yeah, we told people what we were doing and we invited women to talk about their experiences. Three or four women basically gave testimonials about harassment and/or violence and experiences in Occupy Boston and beyond and just how it was not to be tolerated."[12] Oakland's feminist and queer bloc hosted an "Occupy Patriarchy" event that included a number of workshops on topics such as the politics of sexual and intimate violence and conflict resolution.

The identity-based groups also served as a refuge from certain forms of oppressive behavior more broadly. Some women reported being interrupted or even aggressively shouted down at General Assemblies. Other participants talked about having their behavior policed.

> More often than not I would get pulled back by lots of times white males, physically like my arm would be pulled back onto the sidewalk and reprimanded that I was disobeying the police and I was unsafe and I was putting other people in jeopardy. And so it was like a pretty constant awareness that your decisions were being scrutinized, criticized, and that it was automatically assumed if you were queer, trans, a POC or ciswoman that you didn't know what you were doing and that you were unknowingly putting yourself in harm's way. So it was a pretty oppressive atmosphere.[13]

There were also reports of homophobic or racist harassment. Separate, identity-based groups offered a place where people might be better able to fully express themselves to people who were more likely to understand. A participant in Queering OWS explains this, "Very literally it was [formed] to give the LGBT voices a safe space to express themselves in all forms of gender identity."[14] To some, it was a place of consciousness raising or even healing, as described by this participant in the People of Color Caucus, "A corollary goal was to create a space for people of color to convene and have their voices heard and also have it be sort of a healing space within the movement."[15]

Separate identity-based organizing also served to create spaces for those who otherwise felt lost within the movement. For example, a participant in Occupy San Diego discussed the Women Occupy group there, which consisted primarily of older, middle-class, straight, white women, many of whom had ties to each other prior to Occupy. While they engaged in a number of Occupy efforts, gender-focused and not, the formation of the group was primarily about creating a *comfortable* space, "I would say that it was partly because the culture of the movement wasn't the culture of these middle age women and so they created a culture they were more comfortable with and they fully supported the culture of Occupy but they participated in a way that gave them a space that was more familiar to them."[16] While many accounts focus on the youth of the Occupy movement, "Elder Caucuses" were formed in several cities, often with similar concerns raised by the other identity-based groups.

The separate identity-based organizations helped facilitate a sense of belonging, a means of allowing people to find or make their place within the larger movement. Many of the people I spoke with suggested that forming and participating in these groups played a vital role in their engagement with the Occupy movement. It is important to note that many of the people I interviewed who engaged in such organizing also expressed a sense of disillusionment or disappointment in finding discriminatory behavior in the Occupy encampments. Such behavior was seen at odds with ostensibly progressive aims of the movement. A participant in Occupy Boston reflected, "To me it [the Occupy movement] was this incredible opportunity to be part of something that was important but then I discovered that essentially the encampment was kind of a microcosm of the broader society in that all of the 'isms' that exist outside were kind of manifesting as well in the encampment."[17] A similar sentiment was expressed by this participant of Occupy Philly, "It's hard to admit that any of the encampments aren't really a utopia just because we are all really excited about social change . . . but Occupy encampments are sort of a microcosm of larger societies so all of the issues that we face . . . it's easier to talk at least about how to address these issues of sexism and oppression against women in what we call 'safer spaces.'"[18]

While the people I interviewed and some of the written accounts referenced people who ultimately left the movement because of this frustration and disillusionment, for others (including most of those I interviewed) forming identity-based groups allowed people an opportunity not only to express these emotions but also to do something about them. These groups are where many found their place and voice within the larger movement, some of which even seemed to be gaining traction before the evictions prematurely ended the mobilizations, at least in the larger mass manifestations.

Diversifying Movement Goals and Messages

Beyond increasing participation, representation, and visibility of certain groups, the identity-based groups were also concerned with having a substantive impact on the movement in regard to the way messages were framed and what issues were addressed. Many mobilizations adopted practices aimed at diversifying the voices being heard. As discussed earlier, in many general assemblies, facilitators used progressive stacks, a process that allowed facilitators to move underrepresented voices to the front of the speaking queue. These processes were important, but identity-based organizing within the movement became a means of collectively amplifying underrepresented voices in a way that was more likely to garner attention and response. One participant in OWS, who works professionally as a social justice trainer, described it in the following way:

> I think that the goal was to create a space for people of color voices to be integrated into the General Assembly with more clarity and more cohesion. . . . We had to get representation from not just people of color on Facilitation but people of color that were part of the Caucus that were able to collectivize the challenges and struggles that were coming up in the Caucus and feed that into the facilitation of the GA somehow. So that was one way that we were trying to deal with the strategies to insert our voices into the General Assembly and that was definitely a goal.[19]

Engagement with substantive issues tended to be one means of making intersectional interventions. Here groups were more likely to take the broader message of the movement regarding economic inequality and nonresponsive/oppressive state institutions and tie it to the issues experienced within their particular communities. Often the intersectional intervention was limited to adding one intersectional dimension to the discussion. For example, women's groups tended to combine the universal emphasis on economic/class issues with gender: "We were talking about economic issues and [how] they are hitting women the hardest, and so it needs to be, our voices need to be, very much so, heard within the movement."[20]

Occupy the Hood and the People of Color caucuses and working groups tended to focus on racial dimensions of the economic downturn.

> [In the POC caucus in OWS] people were having conversations about the racial underpinnings of the economic disparity conversation, [while] a lot of other folks in Occupy Wall Street who weren't really approaching it from the injustice of the economic disparity with the 99 or the one percent conversations. [They were] not having a conversation about how a racist economic structure actually rigs this type of disparity so all of the racist predatory practices that started in communities of color, anything from predatory loans and mortgages to the legacy . . . how those things have actually contributed to the 99 versus one percent dichotomy. Those conversations were completely invisible in Occupy Wall Street for a large portion.[21]

These interventions also focused on expanding the movement agenda to address a broader range of issues: "The POC Caucus wanted to make sure that all of those issues were connected in so that it could become a conversation about the 99% rallying in solidarity around all of these other issue areas where . . . racial disparities are significant . . . everything from criminal justice to education to healthcare."[22]

Stances on the issues or on how to prioritize them were not always grounds for consensus within or across identity-based groups, as is illustrated by this participant of OWS, "Listen. I graduated from college with a lot of student debt. I'm all for addressing student debt and lack of access or lack of access to a quality education and from the start all the way to PhD, but I cannot put that on the same plane as not allowing brown and black people to walk down the street without being harassed by the cops. I just can't do that."[23] The critique of the criminal justice system was discussed in many of the Occupy groups organized around issues of race and racism, representing ongoing efforts to address the institutionalized racism within policing and the legal system. Within the Occupy movement, it was a divisive issue. The question of whether or not the police were a part of the 99 percent became extremely contentious and often represented the racial dynamics of the movement. The claim that police were somehow part of the movement was more prevalent in the whiter Occupy mobilizations, like Occupy Portland, although identity-based groups helped to contest this. It was less likely in places like Oakland, where the movement was more racially diverse and the critique against law enforcement was more prevalent. In Occupy Baltimore, activists combined efforts with local groups of activists (primarily young black men) to stop the building of a new youth prison.

Identity-based groups were often responsible for raising issues related to race, class, and sexuality in General Assemblies. Sometimes they did this by organizing action that disrupted General Assemblies, via blocks or speak outs. They also organized events centrally about these issues. The People of Color Caucus in OWS hosted a racial economic justice educational session. Queering OWS had a special assembly on transgender issues. Feminist assemblies and anti-oppression workshops were organized in various locations. Sometimes, these special sessions replaced a scheduled General Assembly; other times, they were held as separate events. Attendance varied due to self-selection, which often meant that the message was not spread as well as intended.

These interventions served an educational purpose that broadened the way that the movement addressed issues or even the issues it addressed. This broadening made space for marginalized groups to have their concerns addressed, while laying the groundwork for future solidarities. While the encampments did not last long enough to have these intersectional interventions fully realized, they played a role in facilitating the social learning and networking that could be utilized in later movements such as #BlackLivesMatter.

PARTIAL OR INCOMPLETE INTERSECTIONALITY

The impetus and purpose behind separate organizing offers important insight into their intersectional contribution to the Occupy movement, but groups varied in the degree to which they embraced and enacted intersectionality internally. Some groups were more intersectional from their inception. For example, the feminist queer bloc in Oakland was organized primarily around gender and sexuality but with strong attention to other intersectional positions. Their "Points of Unity" document starts by articulating the need for a separate space and an internal coalitional politics:

> Women, Trans people, Queers, Fags, Dykes, need a space that is OURS. We are marginalized, harassed, and attacked in other spaces all the time. We do not have the same needs and desires; our relationships with one another are structured by the intensified oppression of people of color, trans people and poor folk. However, we think we can support each other and increase our power by working together.

Most of the groups, however, tended to be more single-identity focused (race, gender, or sexuality) and therefore sometimes fell into single-axis organizing. Within the identity-based groups, single-axis representation sometimes precluded the participation and representation of certain intersectional identities. Race groups might not address issues of gender or sexuality. Women's groups might become the site of predominantly white cisgender, middle-class women. LGBTQ groups might become sites for the white, middle class, male-bodied. That these dynamics occurred was not necessarily an issue of intent but a problem in practice. Single-axis organizing might then recreate or at least make it more difficult to address intersectional forms of oppression within and outside of the group. It proved exclusionary for those located at intersections, unable to find the type of retreat accorded to those more advantaged members of subgroups. Sometimes, the messages that drove groups to form in the first place, such as "stay on task" or "don't be so divisive," were echoed within single-identity groups. If these groups were formed to provide representation or "safe spaces," then it becomes important to ask who is actually being represented. Whom is the space safer for?

Oppressive behavior within identity-based groups was one blatant means of exclusion. Others were subtle. For example, participating in single-identity-based organizing can be a logistical challenge for people located at multiple marginalities. A person might have to make difficult choices regarding which identity to prioritize when choosing where to participate. Not only might a person have a limited amount of time and energy to devote to a movement, but participation in multiple groups might not even be possible. This was the case for a participant of Occupy OWS who, as a queer Latino, identified with several different and overlapping marginalized groups:

> The problem even from the very beginning was that the Spanish group ran at the same time as the POC group. So if you had an interest or if you aligned with both . . . you had a conflict. So we would have both meetings side by side and there would be like five or ten of us who would stand right in the middle and be walking back and forth trying to hear everything. . . . Then after that it was just kind of attending meetings. And so everyday there were lots of meetings, every day there were so many meetings. You know you couldn't keep up.[24]

This participant also spoke to an issue that was echoed by other participants in different types of identity-based groups. Even when groups were cognizant of the lack of internal diversity, they were unsure of how to correct it.

> I found out that there was a queer group and it just started. So I went to a meeting . . . And as I was sitting down they're saying, how do we get more people of color to come to this meeting. And I hear folks, and it's a group of mostly male presenting, white men . . . And they were saying something like . . . the LGBT community center has a pamphlet in the back there are POC groups and we can just call them and tell them to come to our meetings. And I thought, oh wow. I mean it's what typically happens, right? We'll just tell you to come to our meeting and then we'll just show up and say like participate. Like now that you are here, you legitimize our presence and with no real analysis or like effort to work together. It's just kind of like come to our meeting. If a group already exists, you can't just invite people after the fact because there are so many implicit and subconscious things already happening that like. The culture has already been set. So then you're asking people to come into an unsafe space because they are not represented there and they don't have a say on how it came together.

This point about a group's culture raises important but difficult questions. If a group is not intersectionally inclusive from the beginning, can it change? And who is responsible for doing the work of recruitment and coalition building? As suggested by this participant, the risky work of building bridges often falls on people at the intersection of multiple marginalities (those doing the rooting and shifting between different positions). When asked about coalition work, many of the [white] women in feminist Occupy groups referenced Latina or African American women who took the initiative, had volunteered, or were asked and thus ultimately expected to do this work.

These examples demonstrate the difficulty of putting intersectionality into practice. Even when groups expressed a desire to be inclusive, it was hard to change the trajectory of single-axis organizing. Some of the identity-based groups ended up alienating people in a manner that replicated their exclusion from the broader movement, "There were people who showed up and got really frustrated by those issues of diversity and never came back to the meeting, or got turned off the movement. Any time you have people storming away or who don't want to come back, that ends up being divisive."[25]

Single-identity organizing that does not engage in intersectionality and transversal politics can also result in the isolation and movement fragmentation that "identity politics" detractors lament. In this interview, the participant talks about the challenge of balancing this with the other goals of identity-based groups:

> We think of caucuses as very strategic spaces that should be used for doing specific things . . . you know so using a caucus for dealing with dynamics of internalized oppression and doing healing work and mentorship work and education work makes a lot of sense . . . but in the context of OWS what was happening was that the POC Caucus was that space as well as a strategy space for the whole movement . . . so it was trying to do two things that were pretty different from each other and people were struggling with how to make both of those things work. You know how can the movement have space for both internal oppression as well as multi-racial organizing?[26]

In the course of a longer mobilization, a group might address these different goals in turn. Emphasized indefinitely, however, "safe spaces" can impede internal and external coalition building and stagnate political action. Building intersectional awareness becomes a means of recognizing difference in a manner that keeps open opportunities for building and maintaining collectivities. It is hard work, however, and the time horizon often extended beyond the duration of the encampments.

CONCLUSION

The Occupy mobilizations offered many examples of the benefits as well as the limitations of identity-based organizing. Groups organized around race, gender, and sexuality arose, not out of nowhere but from actual experiences with oppression and exclusion. Identity-based organizing offered marginalized groups a different avenue for inclusion, one often aimed at finding voice, building capacity, and to some extent acting politically. Within the movement, identity-based groups varied, in their ability to address difference within their groups and maintain connection to and facilitate representation in the movement. Some groups, like the Occupy Patriarchy in Oakland, exhibited a stronger and more extensive intersectional consciousness, via its more coalitional structure and explicit addressing of gender, sexuality, and race. Other groups made limited intersectional interventions, emphasizing a single dimension to complicate the predominant class analysis. Competing purposes limited the ability of groups to translate consciousness into action, at least in the short time period of the mobilizations. The boundary building that sometimes accompanies building safe spaces hindered transversal and coalitional politics, and the burden of such work was often placed on those at the intersection of multiple marginalities.

Although the short timeline of the encampments may have limited the transformation of intersectional interventions into political action, such interventions likely laid some of the groundwork for the mobilizations that have followed, particularly in the oppositional movements arising to protest the 2016 election of Donald Trump and the reactionary policy direction of his administration. Vivian May (2015) describes intersectionality as a resistant imaginary concerned with identifying omissions, approaching them as meaningful, and engaging with them politically. This is an ongoing process. Identity-based groups can help movements to do this. Not only do they facilitate and maintain ongoing participation, but they make interventions that improve and strengthen the movement's understanding of the systems they seek to challenge and provide additional tools for resistance. At the same time, they run the risk of excluding those at the intersection of multiple marginalities. A tendency to focus exclusively on a single dimension or intersection of oppression creates new internal exclusions and inhibits cross-group connection. Intersectionality provides an alternative means for addressing difference in a way that can simultaneously identify the complexities of a system characterized by multiple and interlocking forms of oppression, while building and maintaining the solidarity needed to successfully challenge and overcome this system.

NOTES

1. Such groups proposed renaming the movement "Decolonize," a moniker that was adopted by some groups and local mobilizations.

2. For public accounts, I use full names when reported and cite the publication source. For interviews, I provide the date of the interview and a brief description of the person's participation (geographical and group).

3. Interview, February 13, 2013.

4. Interview, December 20, 2012.

5. Interview, June 26, 2013.

6. Interview, December 20, 2012.

7. Interview, March 8, 2013.

8. Interview, August 8, 2013.

9. Interview, June 18, 2013.
10. Interview, June 3, 2013.
11. Interview, March 8, 2013.
12. Interview, December 20, 2012.
13. Interview, June 24, 2014.
14. Interview, December 20, 2012.
15. Interview, August 9, 2013.
16. Interview, January 20, 2013.
17. Interview, December 20, 2012.
18. Interview, March 13, 2013.
19. Interview, August 9, 2013.
20. Interview, December 20, 2012.
21. Interview, August 9, 2013.
22. Interview, August 9, 2013.
23. Interview, March 6, 2013.
24. Interview, March 6, 2013.
25. Interview, December 20, 2012.
26. Interview, August 9, 2013.

Chapter 8

Navigating Transnational Complicities:

Expanding Frameworks of Intersectionality in the Deadly Exchange Campaign

Rachel H. Brown

Since its first usage by Kimberlé Crenshaw (1989) and its genealogy within women-of-color scholarship and activism, the concept of intersectionality has "traveled" across social media, political campaigns, social movement spaces, and the university. On the one hand, popularization of the term has encouraged activists, allies, and accomplices to find voice and disrupt the multiple complicities in systems of oppression from which they benefit.[1] Through this raising of intersectional consciousness, popularization of the term has and can continue to enable allies/accomplices to find voice and forge new political alliances and mobilizations (Davis 2008, 70). On the other hand, intersectionality's diffuse application and its "capacity to travel" have often deracinated it from its original structural critique (Falcón and Nash 2015; Lewis 2013, 871; Mohanty 2013).[2] In contrast to its application as a "diversity management" strategy in the corporate board room and university, its original conceptualization by Crenshaw enables engagement with the structural inequalities producing and differently impacting multiple, mutually nonexclusive, mobile identity categories such that social movement actors can envision identity groups "as potential coalitions waiting to be formed" (Cho, Crenshaw, and McCall 2013; Carastathis 2013; Crenshaw 1991, 1299). It is out of this understanding of social categories as never uniform and always heterogeneous that new alliances are formed. Indeed, as developed and elaborated within black feminist, Chicana feminist, queer-of-color, and woman-of-color feminist scholarship and activism, intersectional methodologies foster deep engagement with the coalitional politics of solidarity within and across social movements (Anzaldúa 1987; Combahee River Collective 1977; Crenshaw 1991).

Taking stock of the insurrectionary power of intersectionality and its multiple redeployments, I explore how the concept can be an analytic tool for allies/accomplices to raise consciousness about intersecting complicities beyond single-issue thinking, as part of the process of finding voice and, ultimately, creating new feminist mobilizations. I address how use of the term alongside the analytic frameworks already being deployed by social movements can help allies/accomplices (re)frame their intersecting complicities in ways that build upon the messages of extant resistance movements. In doing so, I draw from my experiences as a white, cisgender Jewish American woman involved with Jewish Voice for Peace (JVP), a US-based national organization campaigning for justice in Palestine.

Examining JVP's Deadly Exchange campaign, which calls for an end to the training of US police officers, ICE officials and homeland security personnel in Israel, I highlight how the frameworks of abolition, critiques of anti-blackness, and settler colonialism can build upon the movement language already being deployed within racial justice and indigenous struggles, while revealing the "racialized-gendered systems that operate under the pretense of neutrality" (Spade 2013, 1033). I suggest how allies'/accomplices' simultaneous deployment of these frameworks can pave the way for a more robust, gendered critique of police brutality, anti-black violence, and militarization and land colonization in the United States and Palestine. This reframing may help allies/accomplices find voice to (re)frame campaigns more intersectionally so as to forge stronger alliances with actors and organizations addressing gender and racial liberation. It can also guide allies/accomplices to incorporate multiple perspectives into campaign framing and mobilization, a necessary precursor to creating unlikely alliances and acting politically. While an abolitionist framework and critiques of anti-blackness help social movement actors locate gendered racisms within the longer historical trajectory of slavery and racial violence foundational to the consolidation of the nation, a settler colonial framework highlights how gender violence against communities of color is intertwined with the quest for territorial expansion and a concomitant "logic of elimination" of the native population (Pappé 2012; Piterberg 2008; Wolfe 2006, 387). Ultimately, this expanded intersectional consciousness can increase allies'/accomplices' ability to mobilize alongside social movement actors and collectives, some of whom may overtly identify their interventions as feminist, and others who may not. The incorporation of a greater number of perspectives that intersectional consciousness raising facilitates can also inform the reforming of organizational leadership structures of groups such as JVP, thereby creating greater capacity for intersectional action.

I begin by highlighting my methodologies for analyzing the Deadly Exchange campaign and then address the relevance of intersectionality to the work of consciousness raising, framing, solidarity building, and political mobilization among allies/accomplices. I then highlight how the deployment of intersectionality alongside the frameworks of abolition, critiques of anti-blackness, and settler colonialism allow allies/accomplices to find voice by incorporating a gendered analysis of racialized violence and the many concomitant forms of resistance. In conclusion I suggest how intersectionality can be a "nodal point," rather than a "closed system" of political analysis, allowing researchers to understand when social movement actors choose to frame campaigns in explicitly gendered terms and when they may not (Cho, Crenshaw, and McCall 2013, 788).

METHODOLOGY AND POSITIONALITY

Throughout my analysis, I engage with intersectionality as a method for situating my own political involvement in social movement spaces and an analytic for exploring how white Jewish American allies/accomplices might form new alliances, strategically leverage our identity, and forge solidarity. Intersectionality is thus the object of my analysis and the structuring principle for my method of inquiry. I take cue from autoethnographic methodologies that center the researcher's subject position and experiences within the knowledge-production process rather than treating sites of inquiry as objectively knowable (Behl 2017). In my discussion of JVP, I draw solely from publicly available resources rather than information relayed to me through my own involvement. In this way, I do not represent the views of other JVP activists nor the political positions of JVP as a national organization. Instead of generating universal knowledge claims, I use my personal experiences to think through the role of white Jewish allyship and intersectional consciousness raising. In doing so, I follow feminist critiques of the knowledge-production process that reject the possibility of pure objectivity and the impartial "view from above" (Alcoff and Potter 1993; Anzaldúa 1987, 2015; Collins 1990; Haraway 1988, 589) and feminist social science methodologies that attend to the power dynamics inhering in the knowledge-production process (Hawkesworth 2006; Naples 2003).

As such, I consider how my subject position as a cisgender, white, middle-class Jewish American whose research and political involvement addresses issues of migration, colonization, gender, and labor in Palestine at times reinforces particular hierarchical power relations. Accordingly, throughout the chapter, I therefore use both the terms "our" and "their" in reference to allies/accomplices. When adopting the former, I refer to a specific group of allies/accomplices of which I am a part—that of white Jewish Americans; when using "their," I refer more broadly to allies/accomplices in social movement spaces. In my own political involvement and research, questions of when and how to engage as an ally/accomplice arise as a white settler living permanently within the United States and as a Jew who holds the legal right to become a permanent settler in Palestine under the Israeli Law of Return.

My status as the latter was especially salient while living for short periods in Jerusalem and Tel Aviv when I was conducting research on migrant caregivers who work for Jewish-Israeli citizens. My analyses are also shaped by my experiences growing up in a middle-class, predominantly white suburb and attending a Hebrew school where Israeli history and politics were taught through Zionist discourses of Jewish nationalism, exceptionalism, and self-determination.

Finally, my analysis of Deadly Exchange is informed by feminist scholarship analyzing how nation building and demographic control are inherently gendered and sexualized processes, even as movements resisting them may not overtly use the language of feminism. I also draw from Carastathis' (2013) insight, drawing on Crenshaw's work (1991), that identities are ontologically and politically coalitional in nature, able to be strategically deployed at key moments.

INTERSECTIONALITY AND THE DEADLY EXCHANGE CAMPAIGN

The cross-cutting connections that Deadly Exchange draws between police brutality in the United States and the securitizing of Palestinians by the Israeli state are the source of its strength and its challenges. For white and white *Ashkenazi* (European-descended) American Jews, this tension requires thinking contextually about our rhetorical strategies and framing as well as the form, content, and timing of our direct actions. Founded in Oakland, California, in 1996, JVP is a nonprofit organization "inspired by Jewish values and traditions" organizing for justice in Palestine and pushing for a more progressive US foreign policy (JVP 2016a). As a nascent organization, JVP exclusively targeted Israel's ongoing occupation of Palestine, calling upon Jewish Americans to strategically leverage their identities to critique oppressive policies carried out in our name. At its inception, the racial, gender, and class politics of American and Israeli Jewry was not central to the organizing mission, nor was the interconnection between the historic oppression of Palestinians and the marginalization of *Mizrahi* (Middle Eastern and North African) Jews, Ethiopian Jews, and Jews of Color.

Although the organization has begun to increase its intersectional capacity by addressing intragroup inequalities, largely through its partnership with the Jews of Color and Sephardi/Mizrahi (JOCSM) Caucus, JVP leadership is still disproportionately comprised of white *Askhenazi* Jews (2016b). Refiguring organizational leadership to center the perspectives of nonwhite Jews will be central to building the organization's intersectional capacity and to helping its members find voice through a reframing of the core organizational issues. Acknowledgment of its members' multiple lived realities can create, in turn, the forming of new alliances across intracategorial identity categories.

Today, JVP consists of over 200,000 online supporters and at least sixty chapters, and its mission and priority areas have expanded to include racial, gender, and economic justice issues, and its guiding principles invoke inter-sectionality (JVP 2016a). Current JVP initiatives center the ongoing occupa-tion and colonization of Palestinian land; US racism, police brutality, and anti-Semitism; and white *Ashkenazi* supremacy toward Jews of Color and *Mizrahi* Jews. Its stated priority areas include fighting the Trump agenda; undertaking legislative advocacy to support Palestinian human rights and the Boycott, Divestment, Sanctions (BDS) Movement; and through its Net-work Against Islamophobia, advocacy for the right of refugees to settle in the United States (2017a). JOCSM (2016, 2017, 2018) has led the charge in articulating the connection between settler colonialism and anti-black violence in the United States and the oppression of Palestinians and African refugees in Israel and in pushing the organization to address intragroup inequality, beginning the long process of deconstructing its own representations of Juda-ism as necessarily white.

To this end, Deadly Exchange intervenes in JVP's recent attempts to connect settler colonialism and anti-blackness in the United States to the Israeli occupation of Palestine. The campaign highlights the "extrajudicial executions, shoot-to-kill policies, police murders, racial profiling, massive spying and surveillance, deportation and detention, and attacks on human rights defenders" that characterize training trips to Israel taken by US law enforcement, homeland security, and Immigration and Customs Enforcement (ICE) officials (JVP 2017b). Nationally, the campaign provides resources and information on these trainings so that chapters can mobilize within the context of local city and state politics. The campaign has targeted Jewish institutions that financially support law enforcement trainings, including the Anti-Defamation League (ADL), an organization whose mission is to "protect the Jewish people and secure justice and fair treatment to all" (ADL 2017). Deadly Exchange thus positions white *Ashkenazi* JVP members in a relationship of potential allyship/accompliceship with not only Palestinians but also communities of color in both Palestine and the United States who are disproportionately impacted by police brutality and militarization.

In my engagement with and reflections upon Deadly Exchange, I identify three formulations of intersectionality that are particularly relevant to the process of white Jewish Americans finding voice, forming alliances, and act-ing politically. Each of these iterations can facilitate—and have in particular instances enabled—the building of intersectional capacity, first and foremost by allowing allies/accomplices to raise intersectional consciousness and understand seemingly isolated instances of oppression as multi-axis structural injustices. The first formulation is that of intersectionality as an analytic for understanding our intersecting complicities with, rather than the "experiential dimensions" of structures of oppression (Allen 2018, 112). Through this formulation, allies/accomplices can more deeply understand how it is that those with race/gender/class privilege become the unspoken referent protected under US law and the implied ideal citizens benefiting from Israeli immigration laws and colonial displacements. In the second formulation, intersectionality is a tool of critical self-reflection that can mitigate attempts by white allies/accomplices to transcend whiteness through what Crenshaw terms "vulgar constructionism," a practice that assumes the social constructedness of identity categories renders them materially inconsequential (Crenshaw 1991, 1297). In both formulations, intersectionality helps allies/accomplices find voice by first understanding how various gendered oppressions are multiaxis injustices. This increased awareness allows allies/accomplices to reframe campaign messaging more intersectionally, creating opportunities for new, unlikely alliances. The third conceptualization is that of intersectionality as a method of political mobilization that requires deep engagement with the long histories of resistance among and between "intersecting struggles" (Davis 2016, 19). In this formulation, intersectionality becomes an analytic for understanding how the social movement actors most impacted by interlocking oppressions have historically formed alliances, so as to amplify and support the ways they are already acting politically.

In the first conceptualization, intersectionality is an analytic for allies/accomplices to understand our own transnational imbrication in multiple systems of oppression. This iteration provides a methodology for understanding and naming structures, rather than finding voice to name our own experiences, of oppression (Allen 2018, 124). For allies/accomplices engaging in solidarity work that has long existed between black and Palestinian individuals and collectivities, effective local implementation of Deadly Exchange requires an in-depth understanding of how we are constructed by government, corporate, and civil society actors as the unspoken beneficiaries of public safety discourses in the United States and Zionist-nationalist policies of land dispossession in Israel. By beginning to see our white Jewish American identities as constructed yet materially significant, intersectionality thus provides a tool for destabilizing the very categories of gender, race, and class (Crenshaw 1991). This understanding also enables white Jewish allies/accomplices to question how it is that Jewishness and whiteness become synonymous in ways that erase the existence of Jews of Color and *Mizrahi* Jews.

Serving as a "diagnostic" of structural domination that increases consciousness among allies/accomplices, intersectionality can also reveal how the very texture of racialized and gendered violence changes across national contexts (Falcón and Nash 2015, 3). In helping (re)define the problem, intersectionality as a diagnostic can mitigate the tendency to universally frame gendered and racialized oppressions in a manner that flattens difference, erases the specificity of particular political contexts, and overlooks forms of resistance. At the same time, by finding voice to name our own intersecting complicities, allies/accomplices can disrupt the real material exchanges that uphold our status as ideal settler citizens in the United States and Israel. Publicly invoking concrete examples of these exchanges that serve as common targets of resistance can be a focal strategy for creating intersectional alliances. As a member of the "Demilitarize! Durham2Palestine Coalition," for example, JVP worked with a range of Durham-based social justice organizations to draw public attention to former Durham Police chief Jose Lopez's participation in a week-long training seminar in Israel. Mobilizing around this concrete example, JVP, in coalition with Black Youth Project 100, Duke Students for Justice in Palestine, Muslims for Social Justice, and other organizations, successfully lobbied Durham city council to pass a resolution banning police exchanges with Israel (Haaretz 2018; Vaughan 2018). Within St. Louis JVP, we hosted a teach-in about city and county law enforcement officers participating in training trips to Israel. Cosponsored by the St. Louis Palestine Solidarity Committee (PSC) and the St. Louis Coalition Against Police Crimes and Repression (CAPCAR), this event provided specific examples of the benefits corporations receive from police exchanges and how the swapping of repression tactics has facilitated police repression against brown and black communities in the wake of Ferguson. This event ended with a discussion of police abolition and the ways in which social policing occurs far beyond law enforcement institutions.

Importantly, intersectionality as a diagnostic of multiple complicities has also helped us navigate when to strategically leverage different aspects of our identities, choosing when to "root" within our shared identity as Jews who oppose the colonization of Palestine and when to "shift" to align with the mission and views of other groups (Yuval-Davis 1997). In a recent action targeting the ADL, for example, St. Louis JVP elected to publicly "root" within our political values so as to strategically differentiate ourselves from Jews supporting the ADL. The goal of this approach was to destigmatize the conversation around Palestine within the Jewish community, publicly underscoring the ADL's contradictory logic of championing civil rights causes while actively sponsoring police trainings that perpetuate the militarization of US police forces. Another goal of this "rooting" has been to illustrate to lawmakers and lobbyists that Jewish Americans are not a political monolith. In this way, we have aimed to strategically redefine what it means to be a Jewish American.[3]

At the same time, intersectionality has been and can increasingly be a tool of critical self-reflection mitigating tendencies among allies/accomplices to disregard, disown, or transcend the privileges of whiteness and Jewishness. As Moon and Flores suggest, intersectionality can help white allies examine the "repressive strains" within abolitionist discourses that call for the eradication of whiteness. As a tool for self-reflexivity, intersectionality can help in thinking through the pitfalls of a deconstructive, anti-categorical approach that leads to a denial of our own material privileges (McCall 2005; Moon and Flores 2000). In this way, intersectionality highlights how whiteness is a "fluid sociohistorical process" that generates real, material effects shaped by gender, sexuality, ability, class, and citizenship status within and outside of JVP (Moon and Flores 2000, 98). In the process of finding voice, it enables white American Jews to strategically navigate when to "root" in our identities with the purpose of naming and dismantling privilege and when to "shift" toward broader, interest-based strategies that foreground, for example, the common interests social groups share in working toward ending occupation and land colonization.

Finally, interpreted as "intersecting struggles," intersectionality can help allies/accomplices learn from and center the many social movements and forms of resistance that have long articulated the connections between racial violence in the United States and Palestinian liberation (Davis 2016, 19). As Allen highlights, the historical forging of Black-Palestinian solidarity has highlighted the connections between apartheid regimes in South Africa and Israel; racial violence in the United States and Israel; the operations of the military and prison-industrial complex across borders; shared colonial ideologies that undergird land expropriation; and the role of the settler-citizen, the corporation, and the tax payer in maintaining circuits of oppression through silence (Allen 2018; JVP 2015). As I discuss in the subsequent section, making use of the language and framing employed by "intersecting struggles" allows allies/accomplices to disrupt and de-normalize racialized and gendered violence transnationally.

ABOLITION, ANTI-BLACKNESS, AND INTERSECTIONALITY

As Crenshaw remarks, rather than being a "grand theory of everything," intersectionality is an analytic tool and method that can coexist alongside many other frameworks (2017). The simultaneous use of intersectionality and other analytics is neither a consequence of shortcomings necessarily inhering in the concept nor a result of single-axis thinking within these other frameworks. Rather, using multiple frameworks that are "mutually constructive or overlapping" can enable a "contextualized intersectionality" that mitigates tendencies by allies/accomplices to deploy the concept as a synonym for diversity or additive notions of identity, instead rooting its meaning within particular movements and national contexts (Falcón 2012; Falcón and Nash 2015, 7). This contextualization is especially important when applying

intersectionality transnationally, as racial, gender, class, and national categories carry disparate meanings and intersect in unique ways across national
contexts (Falcón 2012). Using intersectionality alongside the analytic and
rhetorical frameworks taken up by multiple oppressed groups can also help
allies/accomplices find voice to articulate the gendered nature of various
oppressions and forms of resistance that may not overtly invoke feminist language. Raising intersectional consciousness can thus help allies/accomplices
understand how various movements have long responded to gendered racisms, even if these actors do not necessarily adopt the language of feminism
or gender equality. This heightened intersectional consciousness can inform,
in turn, the alliances allies/accomplices forge and their ability to "shift" their
own messaging in solidarity with multiple marginalized groups.

Scholars studying how the concept of intersectionality has "traveled" over
time have highlighted its incorporation into the neoliberal university, its
deployment as a stand-in for diversity, and its deracination from its origins
as a theory born out of the material experiences of women of color (Falcón
and Nash 2015; Jibrin and Salem 2015; Mohanty 2013). Given the many
misappropriations of intersectionality and the ways its popularization has
sometimes dulled its analytic potential, its use alongside an abolitionist lens
can help ensure its capacity for structural analysis. In contrast to a reformist
framework, an abolitionist lens understands high instances of police brutality against communities of color and incarceration more broadly not as an
"aberrational malfunction" of otherwise just legal processes but rather, as the
intended outcome of inherently racist institutions (Davis 2003; Roberts 2008,
263). It situates the carceral system within a broader genealogy of slavery and
racial oppression, calling for an end to incarceration and policing altogether,
rather than an improvement in the functioning of prisons. As Russell and
Carlton assert (2013), an "abolitionist intersectional approach" allows the
researcher and activist to understand the oppression of women of color within
the criminal justice system as rooted in racialized and gendered ideologies
that give identity categories their social meaning. Together, intersectionality
and abolition can raise consciousness among allies/accomplices about the
setbacks of backing narrowly defined reforms that, in Spade's words, "(neutralize) resistance and (perpetuate) intersectional violence" (Spade 2013,
1047–8).

By engaging critiques of anti-blackness, white Jewish American allies can
engage with intersectionality in its anti-categorical, structural, and deconstructive capacity, locating our own social statuses as socially constructed
and yet materially and historically significant (McCall 2005). Drawing from
the Afro-pessimist tradition and the work of Jared Sexton (2010), Bassichis
and Spade (2014) highlight the shortcomings of LGBTQ movements that
fail to assess how particular reformist initiatives reinscribe power in state

institutions that are premised upon the oppression of black Americans. They show how measures seeking punitive redress for hate crimes against LGBTQ communities reinforce the centrality of the police state in perpetuating the myth of black criminality, while reinvesting whites' "membership in racial national norms" (2014: 194, 199). Alongside intersectionality, the lens of abolition and critiques of anti-blackness can thus deepen allies'/accomplices' understanding of the root causes of police violence, guiding them in navigating the tensions between short-term policy wins and the longer-term goal of abolition.

Significantly, although JVP is indeed supportive of abolition, there nevertheless exists a tension in the language framing the Deadly Exchange campaign between short-term "wins" and long-term abolitionist futurities. According to the campaign website, Deadly Exchange allows movement actors to

> (see) where we can slow, stall, or chip away at the big systems hurting us, our communities, and our neighbors. Although we know that ending these exchanges will not end police violence or deportations in the U.S., abolish Israel's violations of Palestinian rights, or terminate all security collusion between the U.S. and Israel, we must start somewhere. (JVP 2017b)

Employing intersectionality as a tool of self-reflexivity, allies/accomplices could locate their multiple, shifting identities and complicities, contextually negotiating when and how to support efforts to pass particular reforms. A debate among JVP members across chapters concerns the call to end the "exchange of 'worst practices'" between US law enforcement officials and Israel, and whether this framing implies there are ever "better" practices for training police (JVP 2017b). While an abolitionist lens and a critique of anti-blackness allow allies/accomplices to ask if and how "draw(ing) the line at (police) exchanges" might obscure the everyday violence practiced by US and Israeli institutions, the self-reflexive capacity of intersectionality could help determine how, if, and when to call for more radical reforms in light of this structural critique. As a means of locating one's own shifting social position in relation to other social movement actors, intersectionality can thus help allies/accomplices navigate when to refrain from supporting reformist efforts that may reinforce anti-blackness. Intersectionality in this context becomes a method for determining when to "root" in political beliefs and demands and when to broaden framing to build intersectional alliances that further strategic reforms. At the same time, intersectionality can help reveal how this "rooting" might look different across lines of gender, sexuality, race, and class *within* JVP.

An abolitionist framework and a critique of anti-blackness also offer methodological guidance in considering how white Jewish Americans might strategically critique the structural roots of military occupation in Palestine. A prominent point of political departure among Jewish Americans arises in regard to Zionism as a modern political project. While some Jews active on the political left critique Israeli human rights violations and leave unaddressed Israel's right to exist as an exclusively Jewish state, others call for an end to race- and ethnicity-based exclusions. An abolitionist lens broadens the scope of critique in ways that do not reinforce the constitutive anti-Arab and anti-Palestinian nature of the Israeli state, calling for a prefigurative envisioning of a new state that exists for all its citizens or a form of community beyond any state at all.

Crucially, deploying an abolitionist lens and a critique of anti-blackness alongside intersectionality helps white Jewish American allies/accomplices find voice to articulate the gendered nature of police brutality and military violence, using the language already being deployed by organizations such as Black-LivesMatter and Critical Resistance, a national organization dedicated to prison abolition. This is not to suggest that an intersectional lens does not lend itself to a critique of anti-blackness, nor that an abolitionist framework cannot attend to gender. Rather, *deliberately* thinking these frameworks together allows allies/accomplices to systematically engage in the practice of understanding the prison-industrial complex, police brutality, and the history of racialized violence through "an analysis of population-level state violence (as opposed to individual discrimination)" (Spade 2013, 1031). The intentional use of both frameworks can guard against a reformist use of intersectionality aimed only at legal equality that "extends (the prison-industrial complex's) life or scope" (Critical Resistance, 2018; Spade 2013). Using multiple frameworks also allows allies/accomplices to understand how instances of racial or class violence might be gendered, even if this language is not deployed, allowing allies/accomplices to (re)frame Deadly Exchange as a feminist campaign. By providing a historical contextualization of "racialized-gendered control and exploitation," an abolitionist framework, critiques of anti-blackness, and intersectionality enable a *long durée* understanding of police brutality, demonstrating how the disproportionate harassing of women of color by police, their hindered access to legal recourse in the event of sexual harassment, and the use of their labor in prisons are contiguous with the sexual violence and labor exploitation enacted against enslaved women in the American South, facilitating the accumulation of capital (Davis 1972, 2003; Morgan 2004; Spade 2013, 1044).

This increased consciousness is necessary to build broad-based, intersectional alliances premised upon concrete, embodied, and specific forms of oppression rather than a universalized black or Palestinian subject within the white or Jewish imagination.

To date, JVP has engaged with abolition and critiques of anti-blackness alongside an intersectional perspective at the national and local levels. Following the lead of JOCSM, JVP endorsed the Movement for Black Lives policy platform in 2016, which explicitly supports the Palestinian BDS movement, drawing connections between US anti-blackness, military aid to Israel, and the diversion of money away from health care, education, and reparations. Significantly, the platform also calls attention to the disproportionate impact of anti-blackness on queer, transgender, and gender nonconforming populations. At the local level, JVP Chicago worked with Critical Resistance and the Chicago Community Bond Fund to cohost a workshop on prison abolition and the creation of alternatives to policing (JVP 2017d). Similarly, in a recently launched online project entitled "Imagining the World to Come," JVP has begun collecting written submissions that explore the topic of "Jewish abolitionist communities," asking participants to reflect on the "kinds of investments (that) we, as Jewish people, have in security and safety." This initiative draws explicitly upon the definition of abolition offered by Critical Resistance, asking Jewish participants to think about abolition in relation to immigration, the scapegoating of Muslims, and "the struggle for Palestinian self-determination, Black Lives Matter, (and) Native sovereignty struggles like NoDAPL" so that Jews can "join in co-resistance" (JVP 2018).

At the same time, there is room within this initiative and others to more explicitly follow the intersectional analyses of women-of-color feminists engaged in abolitionist politics. Incorporating such analyses could also illuminate how white cisgender American women are the unspoken referent against whom "threats" to safety have historically been imagined. To this end, Deadly Exchange could highlight how white femininities and sexualities have been comparatively constructed against the hypersexualizing of nonwhite bodies, impacting nonwhite women's access to legal redress when they have faced sexual violence (Crenshaw 1989; Davis 1972; Ritchie 2017). At a national level, the campaign could highlight the particular impact of deportation on men, women, transgender, and gender nonconforming individuals and ways the training of ICE officials in Israel facilitates the differential criminalization of immigrant men, women, and gender non-conforming individuals. Deploying intersectionality alongside an abolitionist framework and a critique of anti-blackness could elucidate how the call for police or prison reform could exacerbate the conditions of women in prisons, disproportionately so for women of color and transgender women of color (Davis 2003; Lambda Legal 2015; Ritchie 2017). It could also help develop a more capacious understanding of the connection between state search and seizure laws, protesters' rights laws and incarceration rates, and the differential access women, men, gender nonconforming and transgender individuals have to legal services when held in detention. By centering the impact of police brutality and incarceration on transgender women of color, JVP also creates an opportunity to forge connections between LGBTQ collectivities *within* and beyond JVP.

Using these frameworks alongside intersectionality would also build upon the messaging already being deployed by prison abolition, feminist, and transgender rights advocates and by social service organizations providing resources in each of these areas.

INDIGENOUS FEMINISMS, SETTLER COLONIALISM, AND INTERSECTIONALITY

A settler colonial framework can situate the Deadly Exchange campaign within the language already being deployed by resistance movements, linking contemporary struggles against state violence to decolonial liberation movements. In addition to highlighting the "logic of elimination" inhering in settler societies, this framework draws attention to the permanent settlement of the colonizing population, land expropriation, narratives of settler exceptionalism, and racial discourses that "indigenize" non-natives and "racialize natives" (Rohrer 2016, 79; Wolfe 2006, 387). As Patrick Wolfe famously asserts, settler colonialism is a "structure rather than an event," a "complex social formation" persisting over time rather than a historical moment that establishes control over a territory (Wolfe 2006, 390). While a settler colonial perspective provides a *long durée* perspective of the genocidal history of European colonization and land expropriation, intersectionality allows white Jewish Americans to understand the ways in which our intersecting identities are differentially constructed as settler citizens in the United States and Israel (Morgensen 2012; Pappé 2012).

Alongside intersectionality, the lens of settler colonialism can highlight how both the Israeli Law of Return granting Jews of any nationality citizenship right and discourses portraying DREAMers as invaders of an imagined white America work to portray European-descending citizens as indigenous. This self-indigenizing by white settlers obscures the ongoing displacing of Palestinians, Bedouin, and Native Americans as well as the US military interventions in Latin America responsible for the out-migration of Salvadorans, Nicaraguans, and Hondurans. To date, JVP, and the JOCSM caucus in particular, has used these frameworks to underscore the violence committed against migrants and refugees whose construction as "foreigners" works to represent European-descending Americans as indigenous. The connections JOCSM has drawn between mass incarceration, anti-black racism and police brutality in the United States and Israel's human rights violations of African refugees fleeing persecution also underscore how xenophobia works to construct settler society as indigenous while criminalizing indigenous populations (JOCSM

2017). Similarly, local JVP chapters have organized actions against Trump's plans to build a wall between the US/Mexico border and the wall separating Israel and the West Bank, highlighting how land colonization underlies both cases, creating populations of migrants and refugees. JVP-Tucson, for example, worked with School of the Americas Watch (SOAW) and migrant justice activists to highlight the militarization of borders in the United States and Israel (JVP 2016d). Similarly, JVP cosponsored the organizing of a "US-Mexico anti-wall delegation to Palestine," a trip intended to facilitate learning between activists resisting walls in both places (Baltzer 2017).

In turning this heightened intersectional consciousness into political action, future St. Louis JVP campaigns could use these frameworks to highlight how the militarization of US police officers through trainings in Israel might impact Native Americans, who are over three times more likely to be killed by police than white Americans (Hansen 2017). A future teach-in could explore how the policing and repression of black communities in St. Louis and the use of corporate security firms in the repression of protests at Standing Rock each work to reconfigure white Americans as the ideal citizens for whom land and law are intended, just as the militarization and expropriation of Palestinian and Bedouin land and the deportation of African asylum seekers in Israel work to reconfigure *Ashkenazi* Jews as the taken-for-granted bearers of citizenship. Indeed, JVP has called for solidarity with the Standing Rock water protectors, drawing parallels between "stolen and expropriated resources and land: from the path of the apartheid wall over Palestinian aquifers to the route (the Dakota Access Pipeline) took" (JVP 2016c). Future campaign messaging could connect police trainings in Israel to the broader US history of importing military tactics that have been used against populations abroad, such as those in Vietnam and the Philippines (RAIA and JVP 2018, as referencing McCoy 2009 and Tullis 1999).

In our future work, these dual frameworks can also help us understand and articulate how occupation and colonial conquest are inherently gendered processes (Arvin, Tuck, and Morrill 2013; Kahaleole 2009; Morgensen 2012). As feminist and queer scholars have demonstrated, a comparative settler colonial framework illuminates not only the transnational continuities in gendered violence but also the ways these forms of repression rely upon sexualized constructions of the ideal settler and concomitant constructions of indigenous populations who are racialized as sexually backward and in need of colonial intervention (Fobear 2014; Morgensen 2012). A settler colonial framework centers how heteropatriarchy, colonial imposition of the nuclear family, and the regulation of nonheteronormative sexual practices were strategically deployed by European settlers to create hierarchies and divisions within indigenous communities (Arvin, Tuck, and Morrill 2013; Lugones 2007; Morgensen 2011). Likewise, the forced sterilization and contraception practices enacted upon Native, black, Puerto Rican, and Chicana women in the United States, and Ethiopian Jewish women in Israel, underscore how women's reproductivity figures in the demographic regulation of the nation in ways that differentially impact Jews across racial lines (Nesher 2013; Torpy 2000). Further, as Abdo asserts, the confiscation of indigenous land by the Israeli government uniquely impacts Palestinian women, whose livelihoods often depend upon family inheritance of land (Abdo 2011). The reliance of the settler colonial state upon fluid, unfixed borders that continually expand and shift also uniquely impacts the mobility of women, who must navigate militarized spaces and checkpoints while facing the threat of sexual harassment (Shalhoub-Kevorkian 2009).

Using intersectionality alongside a settler colonial framework also underscores the perils of universalist claims to feminist and queer solidarity that fail to interrogate the complicities of queer settlers in ongoing violence against indigenous populations. As Morgensen articulates, universalizing claims to feminist or queer solidarity by individuals who do not acknowledge their own status as settler citizens obscure how different settler societies enable each other's existence through the normalization of various "myths of origin" (Stasiulis and Yuval-Davis 1995, 8). Failure to acknowledge queer settler complicity also risks reinforcing the idea that settler states such as the United States, Canada, and Israel are more gender progressive and tolerant of queer identities, thereby justifying the enactment of interventionist policies impacting indigenous communities (Morgensen 2012; Ritchie 2014). An analysis of the perils of uncritical feminist and queer solidarity across settler societies is therefore crucial for building effective campaigns that resist the pinkwashing of colonial governing structures.

Finally, adopting intersectionality alongside a settler colonial framework can guide white Jewish Americans in building upon the language of transnational solidarity already being deployed by Palestinian, Native American, and black activists. From the call for solidarity with Palestine and indigenous communities in the United States by the Movement for Black Lives to the sharing of anti-repression tactics by residents of Ferguson and Gaza, a settler colonial perspective encourages allies/accomplices to understand movement histories in its their own terms, determining the best ways to mobilize resources that build intersectional capacity (Allen 2018; Davis 2016; Ndugga-Kabuye and Gilmer 2016).

CONCLUSION

Using intersectionality alongside settler colonial and abolitionist frameworks and critiques of anti-blackness does not offer neat, finite solutions or formulas to the messy ethical and political puzzles of solidarity. Rather, these frameworks facilitate intersectional consciousness raising that can guide allies/accomplices in understanding our own multiple complicities, with the ultimate aim of mobilizing politically. Among allies/accomplices, intersectionality can also be a tool for self-reflexively determining when and how to "root" within particular aspects of our identity and when to "shift" so as to form broader coalitions. Alongside intersectionality, these frameworks can also help allies/accomplices build rhetorically upon the framing already being deployed by social movement actors. Finally, use of these multiple frameworks helps allies/accomplices voice how various "intersecting struggles" are gendered, even when movements may not overtly invoke the language of gender or feminism. In this way, intersectional analysis can facilitate not only a structural understanding of the status quo but also a prefigurative imagining of feminist, queer, and intersectional futurities.

Significantly, none of these frameworks alone are able to grasp or represent a social totality. Rather, in particular contexts they help illuminate the multiple workings of power and oppression across lines of gender, sexuality, race, nation, and class. In this way, intersectionality is a "nodal point" for studying social movements rather than a "closed system" of political analysis (Cho, Crenshaw, and McCall 2013, 788). As a point of departure, intersectionality can illuminate the power dynamics inhering within a given site of inquiry, whether this site be the systems of oppression leading to the formation of social movements, the hierarchies of leadership within movements themselves, or the differential processes of consciousness raising within and across organizations. Precisely because intersectionality is not a "closed system," but rather a starting point for mapping power relations, it multiplies, rather than delimits, the frameworks through which researchers can understand social movements. The complementarity of intersectionality with other frameworks for understanding oppression can widen the sites the researcher looks to study a given phenomenon and the cases the researcher may consider studying to understand gendered struggle and feminist resistance.

My analysis also suggests that researchers should attend to the ways social movements engage in finding voice—in deploying intersectional messaging, framing, and analysis, even when intersectionality may not explicitly be invoked. Though JVP does not frame Deadly Exchange as a campaign of feminist liberation, an intersectional lens reveals how police exchanges between Israel and the United States are inherently gendered, requiring disruptions of gendered violence by actors at the cross-section of multiple complicities. Finally, just as intersectionality can be a tool for critical self-reflexivity among allies/accomplices, so, too can it be used by the researcher to understand her own intersecting complicities with the academy. Producing social movement research that can be useful to movements themselves requires first locating ourselves as embodied subjects with personal and political stakes in the work that we do and historical relationships of power with the movements we study.

NOTES

1. I use both the terms "ally" and "accomplice" throughout this chapter. "Ally" has traditionally denoted actors who aspire to enact solidarity with oppressed individuals, collectivities, and communities, often because they benefit from particular privileges resulting from the very systems oppressing others. In recent years, activists and scholars have begun to use the term "accomplice" to move away from a "savior" model of purported solidarity based upon the presumed dependency of the oppressed. In contrast, an "accomplice" takes on the legal, political, and social risks necessary to achieve total liberation, thus becoming complicit in struggles of resistance (see Indigenous Action Media 2015).

2. See also Bilge (2013); Collins and Bilge (2016); Jibrin and Salem (2015).

3. Our direct action at the St. Louis ADL offices involved attempts to deliver the JVP national petition with over 20,000 signatures of Jewish Americans asking the organization to end its sponsorship of police exchanges, a demonstration, and the writing of an op-ed.

Chapter 9

Enacting Intersectional Solidarity in the Puerto Rican Student Movement[1]

Fernando Tormos-Aponte

On the morning of April 21, 2010, hundreds of college students woke up ready to execute their decision to strike and occupy the University of Puerto Rico (UPR). For the next sixty-two days, they were able to disrupt regular operation of the Río Piedras Campus until the demands of the student movement had been met. While not the first attempt to shut down the university as a pressure tactic, it was the most successful mobilization executed by the Puerto Rican student movement. Why? What was different? I argue that intersectional solidarity played a vital role. From 2005 to 2017, the Puerto Rican student movement shifted its agenda, leadership, and structure to include and prioritize the issues of intersectionally marginalized groups. Intersectional solidarity, which encapsulates both intersectional consciousness and praxis, enhances a movement's ability to broaden its base and exert political influence (Tormos 2017a). Adopting this organizing approach allowed the movement to sustain coalitions across different identity groups and increase their legitimacy in the public eye.

This chapter draws from my participant observation of the Puerto Rican student movement to examine the challenges and political consequences of enacting intersectional solidarities in social movements.[2] I trace the processes by which the movement in defense of public higher education in Puerto Rico deployed an intersectional organizing approach and analyze its impact on Puerto Rico higher education policy. The first section of this chapter provides a brief introduction to the use of intersectionality for the study of social movements. In the second section, I present the context and case of the Puerto Rican student movement, and, in the final section, I conclude by discussing the challenges that the colonial condition presents for the movement demanding education as a human right in Puerto Rico.

INTERSECTIONAL SOLIDARITY AND
SOCIAL MOVEMENTS

Social movements increasingly use intersectionality as a heuristic that informs their activist organizing approaches (Chun, Lipsitz, and Shin 2013; Collins and Bilge 2016; Greenwood 2008; Lapperière and Lépinard 2016; Roberts and Jesudason 2013). As discussed in the introduction to this volume, intersectionality can be a means of cultivating broad and inclusive representation of different groups; a means of understanding and framing problems and solutions; and a means of facilitating and advancing coalition building. All of these are a part of what I refer to as intersectional solidarity, "an ongoing process of creating ties and coalitions across social group differences by negotiating power asymmetries" (Tormos 2017a). Intersectional solidarity requires an intentional consciousness that is attentive to multiple and intersecting forms of oppression and the marginalities it creates but also a praxis that maintains and translates these concerns into action, both in the internal practices within the group and in its external political actions. Below I address the importance of both an "intersectional consciousness" and an "intersectional praxis" as part of an intersectional solidarity model of mobilization.

Intersectional Consciousness

Intersectionality is a way of understanding how the social world is constructed in ways that shape individuals' attitudes toward other groups and their propensity to engage in activism. Intersectional political consciousness stems from a person's recognition of the intersecting systems of oppression that contour their lived experience. While membership in and self-identification with intersectionally marginalized groups is not a prerequisite for developing an understanding of inequality through the lens of intersectionality (Curtin et al. 2015), an individual's location at the intersection of multiple disadvantaged social groups may lead them to think critically and develop ways of bridging divides within activist collectives (Barvosa 2008). The value of intersectional awareness, Curtin et al. (2015) argue, is that anyone can be aware of, and critique, intersecting forms of inequality.

Intersectional forms of solidarity and the durability of intersectional mobilization require the development of intersectional consciousness and awareness. These are based on individual and movement-wide sensibilities to differences that emerge among social groups due to their distinct lived experiences, which are conditioned by the interaction of multiple systems of oppression (Cole 2008; Greenwood 2008). Developing intersectional consciousness enhances movements as it attenuates the potentially negative effects of social movement diversity (Greenwood 2008). Movements driven by an intersectional consciousness and awareness recognize, represent, and provide spaces for the leadership and agency of intersectionally marginalized groups in collective action.

Intersectional consciousness can intensify activism and deepen engagement from multiple constituencies, particularly intersectionally marginalized activists (Greenwood 2008; Perry 2016). Despite the long-standing erasure of their work, intersectionally marginalized activists recurrently demonstrate the important role they play in movements, acting as political translators for their movements and communities (see the chapter by Nicole Doerr in this volume), doing the work of organizing movements at the frontline, and adopting leadership responsibilities in formal and informal social movement organizations (Cole 2008; Perry 2016). This political translation and interpretive work facilitate the development of intersectional consciousness and awareness and their enactment in practice.

Intersectional Praxis

An intersectional praxis refers to the actions that movements and individuals take to transform intersectional forms of oppression; it requires both recognizing *and* representing intersectionally marginalized social groups. Analyses of social movement organizations suggest that the adoption of an intersectional organizing approach enhances the likelihood of the longevity and political influence of mobilization (Tormos 2017b; Weldon 2006b). Previous scholarship on advocacy organizations has identified the pathways through which organizations may enact affirmative advocacy agendas that more adequately reflect the agentic proposal of intersectionality (Strolovitch 2007). This entails improving the status of intersectionally disadvantaged groups within the organization, diversifying and making organizational leadership more inclusive of intersectionally marginalized groups, prioritizing the issues affecting disadvantaged minorities, and actually allocating organizational resources to advocate on intersectional issues (Strolovitch 2007, 11). Studies on social movement organizations forward similar proposals for reassessing organizational structures and practices in light of the agentic implications of intersectionality. These proposals include organizing an inclusive decision-making structure and leadership, supporting the autonomous organization of distinct social groups within the movement, and advocating for social policies that address intersecting forms of oppression (Lapperière and Lépinard 2016; Roberts and Jesudason 2013; Weldon 2006b). Studies that examine the enactment of intersectional forms of praxis include movements for economic justice for low-income women of color (e.g., Carastathis 2013; Chun, Lipsitz, and Shin 2013) and anti-racial and gender discrimination advocacy (e.g., Carbado 2013; Verloo 2013).

Understandings of oppression and practices to upend it inform each other (Cho et al. 2013). Anti-oppressive movement groups have a priori understandings of oppression that evolve when they engage in collective action (Townsend-Bell 2011). A movement's openness to engaging in inclusive deliberations throughout the process of building and organizing social movements allows it to articulate agendas that address the issues of traditionally silenced subgroups within disadvantaged groups. While adopting inclusive deliberative norms may require significant investments of time and resources, enacting inclusive agendas secures the representation and continued engagement of intersectionally marginalized groups in social movements, thereby democratizing the movement, making it more legitimate in the eyes of the groups that they claim to represent, and increasing its likelihood of surviving over time (Doerr 2018a; Tormos 2017b).

Education as a Human Right in the Context of Puerto Rico

Since 1898, Puerto Rico has been a nonincorporated territory of the United States. It has been under uninterrupted colonial rule for over four centuries. In May of 1901, the US Supreme Court decided in *Downes v. Bidwell* that Puerto Rico, "inhabited by alien races," was a territory belonging to the United States but not a part of the United States.[3] This decision was among a series of Supreme Court decisions known as the Insular Cases. Together, the Insular Cases conferred Congress the power over the territory of Puerto Rico (Torruella 2013).[4]

Under this colonial regime, Puerto Ricans elected their own governor for the first time in 1944. In 1950, delegates elected to a constitutional assembly drafted the Constitution of Puerto Rico. The Constitution stipulates in its Bill of Rights that public education shall be a right of all peoples, and that it shall be offered for free at the primary and secondary level.[5] Since the 1960s, social struggles usually have been framed as human rights struggles, both in Puerto Rico and at the global level (Colón Morera y Alegría Ortega 2012, 13; Moyn 2010). In fact, the language of human rights is codified in the Constitution of Puerto Rico and in legislation that offer protections against discrimination.

Historically, social movements in Puerto Rico have also adopted this language, as is the case of the Puerto Rican student movement. The movement has called for a broad interpretation of the Constitution of Puerto Rico, including the right to higher education. Despite its limitations (see, e.g., Bilić 2014; Bilić and Krajinić 2016; Butterfield 2014; Stychin 2004), students found their voice in the discourse of human rights that reverberated in their marches and picket lines in the form of the chant "education is a right, not a privilege." This discourse resonated with movement participants and the general population, grounding the movement's demands in a language that lawmakers could understand and accept.

The constitutional convention that drafted the Constitution of Puerto Rico attempted to include a series of social justice provisions in Section 20 of the

Bill of Rights. On March 3 of 1952, 81 percent of votes approved of a version of the Constitution of Puerto Rico that included provisions on education as a right. As a result of the democratic deficit that characterizes the political status of Puerto Rico, the US Congress unilaterally amended the original draft of the Constitution of Puerto Rico to affirm that Section 20, which recognized certain social justice objectives, did not grant them judicially executable status (Ramos de Santiago 1970).[6] The Puerto Rican student movement has framed its struggle for education as a struggle for the right to education in spite of the US federal government's interpretation of the content of Section 20 as a social justice objective rather than a right granted to the Puerto Rican people by the Constitution of Puerto Rico.

Since its inception, the Puerto Rican government's enactment of social policies has been constrained by its colonial relation to the US federal government. The US government's unilateral elimination of Section 20 was one of the earliest examples of these obstacles. Yet, the Puerto Rican economy benefited from injections of US capital and, from the mid-1970s until the mid-2000s, also from federal government incentives. Namely, from 1976 until 2006, Section 936 of the US Internal Revenue Code gave corporations tax exemptions from revenue generated in US territories. When these incentives phased out in 2006, corporations fled, leaving Puerto Rico unable to sustain social policy expenditures. In response to this crisis, Puerto Rican ruling parties began enacting a series of neoliberal policies, including privatizing public services and corporations (e.g., communications, transportation, water, and, most recently, electricity generation) and reducing social policy-related expenditures in the areas of health care, labor, and education.

The detrimental social impacts of these policies and the economic crisis have been pervasive for the population of Puerto Rico as a whole but particularly for women, children, and nonwhite Puerto Ricans. Unemployment in Puerto Rico is consistently higher than in the United States and per capita income is half of the per capita income in the United States. In 2017, 43.5 percent of Puerto Ricans lived in poverty while 15 percent of people in the United States lived in poverty.[7] In 2018, women's labor participation rate in Puerto Rico was 17 percent lower than the male labor participation rate.[8] Also in 2018, unemployment for youth ages sixteen to nineteen was 43.8 percent and for those twenty to twenty-four years of age was 24.2 percent.[9] Fifty-six percent of children in Puerto Rico lived in poverty and 85 percent of children live in areas high in poverty in 2018.[10] Sixty-one percent of children in Puerto Rico lived in single-parent households, and 53 percent of children have parents who lack secure employment in 2018.[11] At the same time, 13 percent of children in Puerto Rico were neither in school nor working (highest in the United States).[12] Nonwhite Puerto Ricans live in poverty at higher levels than self-identifying white Puerto Ricans, who also perform better in terms of job opportunities, income, wealth, and educational attainment (Vargas-Ramos 2016).[13]

In the context of Puerto Rico, in which neoliberal austerity policies make access to education increasingly limited, the interplay between race, gender, and class dynamics has significant impacts on social mobility. Below, I detail how the student movement went from pushing an agenda centered on the question of class to adopting an intersectional approach to mobilization. Intersectionally disadvantaged groups took it upon themselves to engage in the political interpretive work that rendered visible the ways in which educational access, widely considered to be an issue of class, intersected with gender and racial hierarchies to further obstruct life chances for disadvantaged subgroups within the working class and for those living in poverty.

STUDENT MOVEMENT FOR THE RIGHT TO EDUCATION IN PUERTO RICO

During the period from 2005 to 2018, every Puerto Rican government administration has endeavored to address the fiscal crisis that has afflicted Puerto Rico by cutting the budget of higher education or raising the cost of tuition. These policies, in turn, ignited waves of student movement contention in 2005, 2010–2011, 2014, and 2017. The Popular Democratic Party (PDP) administration of Aníbal Acevedo Vilá (2005–2009) proposed tuition hikes shortly after its election to office, leading to the 2005 University of Peurto Rico (UPR) strike. The PNP Fortuño administration's Law 7 changed the funding formula for the UPR, thereby reducing its funding, implemented a tuition fee, and proposed to eliminate tuition waivers. The PDP García Padilla administration proposed a tax on private education and higher education budget cuts. In 2016, both the US-imposed Fiscal Oversight Board and the PNP Rosselló administration proposed substantial higher education budget cuts.

The 2005 Wave

In 2005, the UPR Board of Trustees under the Aníbal Acevedo Vilá administration announced that it would increase tuition costs for the UPR. The UPR Río Piedras Student Council called for a student assembly in which students approved motions to go on strike and to form a student negotiating committee with representatives from each college, the Comité Universitario Contra el Alza (CUCA) or "the university committee against the raise." Despite having representatives of students from each UPR Río Piedras College, the CUCA failed to adopt an intersectional organizing approach. CUCA leaders were criticized for having patriarchal, homophobic, and sexist approaches to mobilization (García

Oquendo 2010). Moreover, the CUCA articulated movement discourses that centered on the working class and did not address how other disadvantaged subgroups within the working class were barred from gaining access to higher education. This discourse did not resonate broadly, including among the LGBTQ community and feminist groups (García Oquendo 2010). The CUCA also could not sustain a democratic decision-making structure that allowed for inclusive internal deliberations. The CUCA steering committee's hasty approval of an agreement with UPR administrators without the consent of the plenary bodies that elected its delegates weakened engagement by multiple student movement groups. Ultimately, the CUCA's agreement with university administrators did not block the tuition hike but rather allowed students to defer the payment of tuition.

As indicated by table 9.1, the movement had a low level of influence on higher education policy in Puerto Rico. While it did not achieve the desired

Table 9.1. **Student Movement Demands and Policy Outcomes by Administration, 2005–2018**

	Government Policy Proposal	Movement Demand	Policy Outcomes	Movement Influence
Acevedo-PDP (2005–2008)	Tuition hike	Tuition freeze	Tuition hike payment deferral	Low
Fortuño-NPP (2009–2012)	Eliminate tuition waivers, tuition fee, budget cuts	Preserve tuition waivers, tuition fee repeal	Tuition waivers preserved, tuition fee, tuition fee scholarship, budget cuts	Moderate
García-PDP (2013–2016)	Tax on private education, budget cuts, phased-in tuition hike	Opposed tax on private education, UPR funding formula freeze, UPR governance reform	UPR governance reform, private education tax proposal dropped, UPR funding formula frozen momentarily, 2014 budget cut, phased-in tuition hike blocked	High
Rosselló-NPP under Fiscal Oversight Board (2016–Present)	Budget cuts, tuition hike	No budget cuts	Higher education budget cut, no tuition hike	Low

Source: Author's compilation

impact, the movement managed to push university administrators to allow students to defer the payment of tuition. Despite planting the seeds for future activist campaigns, the 2005 wave of contention was marked by a failure to sustain support across the diversity of groups that initially supported the movement. The failure to sustain solidarity across differences suggests that articulating a universalist, class-based discourse curtailed students' ability to mobilize and sustain activist engagement from disadvantaged subgroups within the working class.

The 2010–2011 Wave

Upon its inauguration in 2008, the center-right PNP Fortuño administration (2008–2012) launched a resolute attack on the Puerto Rico public sector, curtailing the power of unions and dismantling social policies. In the context of higher education, the Fortuño administration proposed a 25 percent higher education budget cut, tuition hikes, and the elimination of all tuition waivers, which were awarded to honor students, university band musicians, student athletes, and student workers. The conservative Fortuño administration was resolved to deal a blow to public education and altered the funding formula for the UPR, leading to a reduction in the UPR's budget. In order to make up for the UPR's funding shortfall, the Fortuño administration pushed UPR administrators to request financing from the Puerto Rico central bank. This loan was conditioned on an increase in the UPR's revenue, which UPR administrators sought to achieve through imposing a new tuition fee of $800 on UPR students and eliminating tuition waivers.

Most notably, the 2010–2011 campaign organizers learned from the strengths and failures of the 2005 wave. Student activist organizers at the UPR had worked on strengthening the movement's organizational infrastructure since 2008 and diversifying movement leadership (Laguarta Ramírez 2016; Garcia Oquendo 2010; Rosa 2015). In 2008, veteran student movement organizers, who had participated in the 2005 wave of contention, proposed a successful resolution at a student assembly in Río Piedras to begin forming direct action committees, known locally as "Comités de Acción." These action committees met multiple times per month, organized assemblies in each of the university's colleges, engaged in deliberations, and mobilized students to demonstrations. Comités de acción created the capacity to sustain mobilization in a highly repressive context and in a context that was marked by social group and ideological differences among movement participants.

Student leaders also strengthened and diversified movement organizations by recruiting newcomers from socialist groups (Unión de Juventudes Socialistas, J-23, and Organización Socialista Internacional), activist performance groups (Papel Machete and Sembrando Conciencia), pro-independence groups (Federación Universitaria Pro Independencia, Juventud Hostosiana, and the Juventud del Partido Independentista Puertorriqueño), a feminist group (Colectivo Masfaldas), and the anti-discrimination and LGBTQ rights Collective (Comité en contra de la Homofobia y el Discrimen). During a student assembly, students agreed to have feminist and LGBTQ representatives in the movement's negotiating committee.[14] This type of intersectional praxis allowed the movement to find voice. Movement leaders articulated a discourse that recognized how class intersected with race to mediate access to higher education. This discourse resonated with multiple sectors of the student movement and the general population, drawing widespread support. This support became visible when, in spite of the repression from riot police, people from multiple generations, political parties, and ideological perspectives came to the UPR boundary fences to toss food, water, and supplies over to students protesting inside.

In a moment that marked a shift in the discourse deployed by the student movement, a black working-class student movement leader, Giovanni Roberto, delivered a speech in the middle of a conflict that emerged between students and young black private security guards. A private security company had gone to the predominantly black and poor municipality of Loíza to hire guards to keep the gates to the Río Piedras UPR campus open. In his speech, Roberto identified himself as black and poor. Roberto criticized segregation in Puerto Rico as a manifestation of institutionalized racism. He told the security guards that they were not the enemies of the students. He described his personal history and said that this history of being brought up poor and black was the reason why the students were fighting for educational opportunities.[15] Students and guards embraced each other at the end of Roberto's speech.

During the 2010–2011 wave of contention, students deployed a diverse tactical repertoire that included lobbying, direct action, disruption, and artistic performances.[16] Most notably, the student movement launched strikes during the spring terms of 2010 and 2011 that spread across the vast majority of UPR campuses and succeeded in avoiding the elimination of tuition waivers. The 2010–2011 wave of contention marked a shift from the failure to adopt an intersectional approach evident during the 2005 wave of protest, as the movement articulated intersectionally conscious political discourse and translated this consciousness into practice by diversifying its leadership. Student movement participants overwhelmingly approved diversifying the movement's leadership at a student assembly that drew more than 3,000 attendees. Electing the movement's leadership was the first issue in the agenda for the assembly.[17]

The shift from the Fortuño to the García Padilla administration opened up new opportunities for the movement's political impact. While the Fortuño administration rejected negotiations with the student movement and repressed it heavily, the center-left opposition party, PDP, included in its platform a series of policies that mirrored student movement demands, such as the elimination of the tuition fees imposed by the Fortuño administration and freezing the funding formula for the UPR's budget (PPD Party Platform 2012, 154). The PDP exploited the Fortuño administration's questionable social and civil rights record on the campaign trail and included student demands in its platform in the 2012 election. Aiming to garner support from the left, the Popular Democratic Party (PDP) successfully challenged the Fortuño administration's bid for reelection by including a repeal of a $800 fee in its platform. Upon their election in 2012, the García Padilla administration eliminated the tuition fees imposed by the Fortuño administration and restored public funds to the UPR.

As stated in table 9.1, during the 2010–2011 wave of contention, the movement exerted moderate levels of policy influence, as it managed to block the university administration's proposal to eliminate tuition waivers but could not block the conservative Fortuño administration's $800 fee. Upon the election of the center-left PDP administration in 2012, the movement was able to exert high levels of policy influence. The movement seized the opportunity to exert influence over education policy during the 2012 electoral shift from the conservative PNP administration to the center-left PDP government. The movement's ability to seize this opportunity was possible because the movement had managed to sustain the support of PDP youth groups in spite of their ideological differences with more radical groups, including the socialist, pro-independence, and feminist groups. Student movement leaders from PDP youth groups, like Manuel Natal, used his good standing in the PDP party to push for the party's adoption of pro-movement proposals in its platform leading up to the 2012 election. Natal later became the first student movement leader to be elected to the Puerto Rico House of Representatives. Public higher education, however, was not safe from continued attacks.

The 2014 Wave

As the fiscal crisis became increasingly severe, barring the government from gaining access to foreign investment and lending, the center-left PDP's García Padilla administration (2012–2016) sought to impose austerity measures and a tax on education. Since 2010, public university student movement organizers recognized that their admission to public universities often stemmed from their privileges and that a hike in the cost of private higher education would also affect disadvantaged groups. Movement leaders of color and from working-class backgrounds had risen to prominence and garnered widespread support for building a movement that advocated to keep intersectionally disadvantaged people enrolled in the university and to open the university to those whose lived experiences barred them from gaining admission and attending. The groups involved in the opposition to the tax on education included a disability rights student group (Comité de Apoyo de Estudiantes con Diversidad Funcional) and the student movement group, Juventud Hostosiana, which had developed an intersectional solidarity organizing approach and included this approach as part of its mission statement.[18] At times, this form of intersectional solidarity met with the resistance of sectors of the movement that argued that the movement needed to focus on class issues and, specifically, the price of tuition in public universities.[19] Yet, since the 2010 wave of contention, intersectional consciousness and the commitment to intersectional praxis was more widespread among student activists, particularly within groups involved in the student movement (e.g., socialists, independence movement groups, and most prominently, within feminist groups).

Students in the 2014 protests built on the strengths developed in the 2010–2011 wave and organized coalitions with activist student groups in private educational institutions. In contrast to the US mainland, wealthy students in Puerto Rico attend public institutions of higher education while less wealthy students attend private universities. The majority of university students in Puerto Rico attend private universities and 20 percent of students in private universities are enrolled in institutions that only offer technical and associate degrees.[20] Educational inequality, however, is not only a class issue, as self-identified white Puerto Ricans are more likely to attain higher levels of education (Vargas-Ramos 2016).

Despite not being threatened by the IVA tax on private education, public university student organizers demonstrated what Yuval-Davis (1999) refers to as the practice of rooting and shifting. That is, "an exercise in empathy, in which participants bring with them a reflective knowledge of their own positioning and identity (rooting) but can also shift to put themselves in the situation of those with whom they are in dialogue and who are different from them" (introduction to this volume). The student movement managed to stop the private education tax after aiding in the organization of activist groups in private universities and assembling a heavily attended march that took their disapproval of the private education tax to the Puerto Rico Capitol. The García Padilla administration was more open to negotiating with students than the Fortuño administration and, after a series of protests and advocacy efforts, dropped the proposed tax on private education. The 2014 wave showed that the student movement had adopted a praxis that engaged in politically influential mobilization beyond the realm of public higher education. Student organizers, including those from privileged backgrounds, acted as bridge builders and political translators by articulating discourses that highlighted how the fiscal crisis would have pervasive effects on the lived experiences of young Puerto Ricans beyond the realm of public higher education.

The 2017 Wave

The political climate in which the student movement in Puerto Rico operated changed in June of 2016 when the US federal government passed the Puerto Rico Oversight, Management, and Economic Stability Act (PROMESA).[21] PROMESA gave a Fiscal Oversight Board, appointed by the US president, the authority over the territory's budget. Despite the less hospitable climate, the movement maintained its commitment to intersectional solidarity, largely due to the work of black and queer women organizers who, rather than organizing separately, continued to press the movement to develop an inter-sectional consciousness. The student movement was among many sectors of the Puerto Rican civil society decrying the imposition of a Fiscal Oversight Board that stripped Puerto Rico of its fiscal autonomy. Recognizing that PROMESA gave overarching fiscal powers to the Fiscal Oversight Board, the student movement targeted both the Puerto Rican government and the Fiscal Oversight Board itself.

In January of 2017, the board asked Governor Rosselló and the legislature to cut 300 million dollars from its annual higher education budget, which makes up 27 percent of the budget for higher education, in order to comply with their requirements for approving a balanced budget.[22] The Fiscal Over-sight Board proposed reducing higher education funding by raising tuition and cutting faculty and administrator jobs, among other measures. In March of 2017, the board raised the proposed amount of funds to be cut from the higher education budget and asked the governor to increase the cuts to higher education over the next five years by 450 million annually.[23] Students quickly organized assemblies in which they approved a proposal to go on strike on April 5, 2017. While the student movement succeeded in exerting some polit-ical influence, driving the Fiscal Oversight Board and the governor to reduce the amount of funds that they originally proposed to cut from the higher education budget, the movement failed to avoid all budget cuts. As indicated in table 9.1, the movement's level of policy influence in the 2017 wave of contention was low. In this highly repressive and anti-democratic policymak-ing context, the student movement did not achieve its desired outcome and, after a lengthy strike and a series of informal agreements with the UPR and Rosselló administration, students agreed to call an end to the strike in June of 2017. While intersectional praxis allowed for effective mobilization when political opportunities were open, it was (unsurprisingly) less effective when those opportunities closed.

INTERSECTIONAL SOLIDARITY

Over the past ten years, the student movement has been able to address internal differences and build capacity by developing an intersectional consciousness and adopting an intersectional solidarity approach. This entailed reforming its internal structure, adopting norms of inclusion for marginalized groups in the movement's leadership, and deepening its discourse for the right to education to emphasize the gendered, racial, and class dimensions of education. In the years leading up to the 2010 wave of contention, the movement developed an organizational infrastructure that relied on democratic decision-making norms. The movement's deliberative practices allowed it to (1) secure long-term commitment to their tactical decisions, including contentious direct action tactics; (2) decide on the terms of the negotiations with university administrators and government officials; and (3) ratify agreements made during negotiations with their targets (Tormos 2018). Inclusive and deliberative practices allowed the movement to *act politically*, which in this case entailed coping with divisive tactical choices and reaching agreements on movement proposals and demands.

Rather than continuing a tradition of elite, male-dominated, and pro-independence leadership, the movement learned from the experience of the 2005 Río Piedras strike and formed a negotiating committee that included a representative from the Committee Against Homophobia and Discrimination, a black working-class socialist student leader, and working-class women of color. The movement mirrored this inclusive and representative structure when it formed a national negotiating committee during the 2010 wave of contention. The development of a diverse and inclusive movement leadership was not the only demonstration of the movement's commitment to inclusion. The movement adopted norms of deliberation that democratized internal decision-making processes, thereby maintaining high attendance numbers at student assemblies and movement plenary sessions.

This diverse, inclusive, and democratic organizing approach allowed the movement to gain legitimacy in the public arena. Enactment of practices of democratic and inclusive internal deliberation in conjunction with work to develop a strong organizational structure allowed the movement to escalate its tactics and occupy the UPR's main campus for sixty-two days during the 2010 strike (Tormos 2018). Practices of democratic decision making, inclusion, and diversity gave the movement the ability to counter the government's discourse arguing that the movement did not represent the student body. By 2010, the movement had *created the capacity* to deploy tactics that required vast investments of time, resources, and coordination. Organizers from the

2004 protests had learned from the challenges of their organizational blight and had built movement organizations in each college of the UPR Río Piedras Campus and in most of the UPR campuses.

Government officials argued that a radical minority of the students led the movement, including leftist, "leaches" of the working class, and that a silent majority decried the movement's tactics and demands. This majority, government officials argued, kept silent and did not attend student assemblies due to the intimidation tactics of radicals in the student movement who resorted to violence to push their leftist political agenda. Yet, during a nationally televised student assembly in 2010, the stage was set for dispelling the notion that the movement was not representative of the student body. Government officials were so convinced of their perception of the lack of support for the movement that they actively pushed for an assembly in which students could vote to ratify or to end the 2010 student strike and provided the space for the assembly—the Puerto Rico Convention Center. Right-wing pundits and government officials argued that the movement always failed to achieve quorum in its meetings. On the day of the assembly, it was quickly evident that a large portion of the student body would attend. By the end of the assembly, movement members had successfully ratified the strike and seized the opportunity to march to the nearby Capitol building of Puerto Rico in San Juan.

Students in the 2014 protests built on the intersectional strengths developed in the 2010–2011 wave. Having found voice, they continued to engage in important cross-institution alliance formation that they could then translate into political action. They were well positioned to take advantage of the opportunities provided by the friendlier García Padilla administration. During the 2017 wave of contention, the movement became increasingly intentional about adopting an intersectional approach to solidarity and advocacy. During the student assemblies leading up to the 2017 strike, feminist groups within the student movement, including the Colectiva Feminista en Construcción and the Grupo de Trabajo de Género (working group on gender), successfully proposed discussing first the adoption of movement demands that addressed the gendered dimensions of austerity measures Ferrer-Núñez (2016). Specifically, feminist groups and gender studies collectives aimed to shed light on the feminization of the workforce, gender-based violence, and the ways in which austerity measures affected individuals at the intersection of gender, race, class, and sexuality Ferrer-Núñez (2016). These discussions and the movement's support for prioritizing the issues of intersectionally marginalized groups not only reflected the movement's development of an intersectional consciousness but also its willingness to translate this consciousness into action. These shifts toward intersectional mobilization were the results of years of political analyses, interpretive work, and organizing led by queer, black, and working-class student leaders.

The intersectional organizing approach adopted in the 2017 wave of contention entailed further diversifying the movement's leadership and reassessing its advocacy agenda so as to better include the claims of intersectionally marginalized groups. The inclusive, representative, and democratic character of movement assemblies and plenaries allowed it to embrace tactical diversity and cope with traditionally divisive tactical decisions, such as striking and occupying the university as a form of exerting pressure on university and government administrations. Beyond the student movement, veteran activists spilled over into other anti-oppressive organizing efforts. Outside of student movement organizing, student activists joined and formed new groups that were guided by an intersectional solidarity approach, such as the Colectiva Feminista en Construcción. Moreover, veteran student organizers pushed their political organizations outside of the movement to adopt intersectional feminist organizing commitments, as exemplified in the Juventud Hostosiana. Students also recognized the structural limitations to ensuring the recognition of their right to education and engaged in struggles to end Puerto Rico's colonial relation to the United States.

The student movement's adoption of an intersectional approach to organizing bore fruits by enhancing its ability to cope with internal differences, maintain the support of different social groups within the student community while also mobilizing external support, draw resources from multiple constituencies, and gain legitimacy with elected officials and the general population. Moreover, the diversity of civil society groups that supported the movement allowed it to thwart the continuous government efforts to repress it. The development of intersectional consciousness, awareness, and praxis within the student movement fostered the practice of rooting and shifting and led student organizers to spill over into feminist, labor, environmental justice, agroecology, and human rights activist groups and back into the student movement when it deployed new campaigns. While constrained by shifting political opportunity structure, adopting an intersectional solidarity organizing approach allowed the movement to sustain the support and engagement of marginalized groups while also allowing it to form alliances with powerful political actors without being subordinated to their strategies and goals, a risk that feminists have identified in the process of building alliances for intersectional activism (Friedman 2000; Seidman 1999).

CONCLUSION

The Puerto Rican student movement for the right of education faces a series of challenges due to the particular political and economic context in which it operates. Specifically, some of the major limitations to the political influence of the movement are the local governments' loss of fiscal autonomy and Puerto Rico's colonial condition as a nonincorporated territory of the United States. This particular political and economic context inhibits the Puerto Rican government from achieving the economic development that would enable it to fulfill the student movement's demand for education as a human right.

The Puerto Rican student movement has seized political opportunities to be politically impactful in a context characterized by electoral volatility. Piven and Cloward (1977) find that movements are likely to influence policy in times of electoral volatility. Yet, while the movement has been consistently influential, it has been constrained from achieving some desired policy outcomes due to the repressive character of the Puerto Rican political context, the fiscal crisis, and the local government's recent loss of fiscal autonomy under PROMESA. Ultimately, the colonial relationship of Puerto Rico to the United States and its political economy in times of fiscal crisis have thwarted student efforts to move beyond resisting austerity policies to pushing for the enactment of policies that address intersectional inequality. The case of the Puerto Rican student movement confirms previous studies arguing that developing an intersectional consciousness and awareness at individual and movement levels is a project that may take years to achieve (Curtin and Stewart 2011). Further, the benefits of enacting intersectional forms of mobilization can enhance a movement's political influence, internal cohesiveness in contexts of social difference, and commitments to intersectionally marginalized groups, but they may also be undermined by political and economic circumstances that exacerbate the inequality that anti-oppressive movements seek to contest. Beyond the limited opportunities in which the student movement operates, student activists have worked to strengthen movement capacity by enacting internally the just, societal relationships that they seek to bring about nationally and by adopting an intersectional solidarity organizing approach.

NOTES

1. I presented an earlier version of this chapter written in Spanish at the 2015 annual conference of the Latin American Studies Association in San Juan, Puerto Rico. I have since translated the text to English. I thank my fellow panelists and discussants at LASA for their feedback, including José Javier Colón, Carmen Concepción, Héctor Martínez, and Luis Rivera-Pagán.

2. I was actively involved in the Puerto Rican student movement from 2008 to 2010. I participated in routine organizing committee meetings, work stoppages, the 2010 student strike, demonstrations, and media work (radio and social media).

3. https://cdn.loc.gov/service/ll/usrep/usrep182/usrep182244/usrep182244.pdf.

4. Balzac v. Porto Rico, 258 U.S. 298, 309 (1922). "It is locality that is determinative of the application of the Constitution . . . not the [citizenship] status of the people who live in it" (cited in Torruella 2013, 73).

5. Note that this provision of the Puerto Rican Bill of Rights does not use the language of citizens in its allocation of these rights, but rather, it grants these rights to education to all people. In doing so, it avoids regulating the borders of political membership within the issue of education.

6. The Puerto Rican electorate's approval of this unilaterally imposed amendment was lumped together with the 1952 elections in Puerto Rico as a referendum. Puerto Rican civil society leaders questioned the fairness of such an act and the appropriateness of repeatedly consulting a Puerto Rican electorate that had overwhelmingly approved of the original draft of the Constitution.

7. https://www.census.gov/quickfacts/fact/table/pr/PST045217.

8. http://www.mercadolaboral.pr.gov/lmi/pdf/Grupo%20Trabajador/EMPLEO%20Y%20DESEMPLEO%20EN%20PUERTO%20RICO%20PROMEDIO%20A%C3%91O%20FISCAL%202016.pdf.

9. http://www.mercadolaboral.pr.gov/lmi/pdf/Grupo%20Trabajador/EMPLEO%20Y%20DESEMPLEO%20EN%20PUERTO%20RICO%20PROMEDIO%20A%C3%91O%20FISCAL%202016.pdf.

10. http://www.aecf.org/m/resourcedoc/aecf-2018kidscountdatabook-2018.pdf.

11. http://www.aecf.org/m/resourcedoc/aecf-2018kidscountdatabook-2018.pdf.

12. http://www.aecf.org/m/resourcedoc/aecf-2018kidscountdatabook-2018.pdf.

13. https://centropr.hunter.cuny.edu/sites/default/files/data_briefs/RB2016-10_RACE.pdf.

14. The Primera Hora newspaper chronicled the UPR strike day by day. It detailed the members of the student movement negotiating committee, which included members of the Committee Against Discrimination and Homophobia. See coverage at http://www.primerahora.com/noticias/gobierno-politica/nota/huelgaenlauprdia1minutoaminuto-382794/. Periódico Digital Puertorriqueño La Nación also chronicled the 2010–2011 UPR strikes. The following article provides the composition of the negotiating committee and the movement's demands: https://lanacionpr.wordpress.com/2010/04/24/exigencias-estudiantado/.

15. Roberto's speech is available at https://youtu.be/xXzpbYB7Ndo.

16. I observed each of these tactics deployed as part of my participant observation of the movement in 2010 and 2011. Moreover, I conducted interviews with students involved in lobbying efforts. These lobbying efforts are detailed further in the following article: http://pr.indymedia.org/news/2010/11/45614.php. Artistic performances are detailed with rich accounts and images in the following blog post: http://www.multitudenredada.com/2010/05/huelga-creativa-2010-en-la-upr-la.html. Direct action tactics are chronicled in the following article: https://occupyca.wordpress.com/2010/12/11/government-establishes-siege-following-successful-strike-at-upr/. Artistic performances during and after the strike are also elegantly exposed in the following text: https://static1.squarespace.com/static/580a34e6b8a79beb0e953352/t/58582a8ee6f2e1582c8722eb/1482173097332/smArtActionCatalog.pdf.

17. I attended and participated in this assembly. The following article documented occurrences at the assembly, including the election of the movement's leadership, setting movement demands, among other decisions: https://lanacionpr. wordpress.com/2010/04/24/exigencias-estudiantado/.

18. https://www.primerahora.com/noticias/gobierno-politica/nota/protestaran encontraderecortesaupr-1082352/.

19. Anonymous interview with student movement leader, June 24, 2018.

20. http://www.upr.edu/?mdocs-file=6079.

21. The text of PROMESA is available at https://www.congress.gov/bill/114th-congress/house-bill/5278/text.

22. The Fiscal Control Board's January 18, 2017, letter containing its proposed cuts to higher education is available at https://juntasupervision.pr.gov/wp-content/uploads/wpfd/50/ 587fea840f998.pdf.

23. The Fiscal Control Board's March 9, 2017, letter instructing Governor Rosselló to increase cuts to higher education is available at https://drive.google.com/file/d/1bQtefD1ovAsK69N4VYXt0WB9vsPqXkZl/view

Chapter 10

Activists as Political Translators?

Addressing Inequality and Positional Misunderstandings in Refugee Solidarity Coalitions

Nicole Doerr

In an external environment shaped increasingly by right-wing political backlash (Hark and Villa 2017; Sauer 2017), theories and practices of intersectional coalition work are key to the repertoire of progressive social movements. However, we know too little about the role of linguistic diversity overlapping with structural inequality, status hierarchies, and perceived "cultural misunderstandings" in coalition work involving citizens and refugees.[1] Nira Yuval-Davis has theorized the potential of self-reflective learning processes within transversal coalitions whose members connect their experiential knowledge and situated positioning (*rooting*) entering in dialogue with the positions of other groups—*shifting* (Yuval-Davis 2011, 199). Given the persistence of intersectional, linguistic, and structural boundaries for refugee solidarity coalitions, an open question for the praxis of dialogue within coalitions is how to address intersectional *positional misunderstandings* about inequalities and conflicts between coalition members and groups (Doerr 2018a). Unlike linguistic misunderstandings, *positional misunderstandings* are discursive processes through which dominant group members, including intercultural facilitators and leaders within coalitions, publicly deny disadvantaged groups the relevance of their political arguments for greater equality. Positional misunderstandings may be interpreted as "cultural" misunderstandings, yet the following empirical analysis reveals the structural inequalities that are often at their core.

I encountered the relevance of positional misunderstandings inductively during my eight-year ethnography of deliberative or discursive democracy in the European Social Forum (ESF), which formed part of the World Social Forum and the broader global justice movement (Della Porta 2005). Deliberation in the ESF enabled cooperation between global justice activists working together with migrants and disadvantaged groups in the multilingual, transnational arena of the ESF. ESF grassroots activists who were acting as volunteer linguistic interpreters/translators witnessed and sought to address inequality leading to what I term "positional misunderstandings" caused by subtle or more obvious power imbalances among the parties involved in the European assemblies. Building on their official role as the "Babels interpreters and translators" in these multilingual meetings, volunteer translators collectively and publicly resisted perceived unfair consensus decisions and temporarily interrupted their linguistic service to echo the voices of marginalized participants. This collective drew on volunteer translators' experiential knowledge of leaders and facilitators' continuing lack of taking seriously the arguments by less privileged participants in European meetings. A *political* translation practice emerged due to the translators' collective force as a heterogeneous multilingual and pluralist network, working to intervene as a disruptive *third* voice within the deliberation. I termed this practice *political translation*, distinct from linguistic translation, to describe a set of disruptive and communicative practices used collectively by volunteer translators in multilingual settings, in order to entreat powerful coalition members or institutional insiders to work together more inclusively with disempowered groups (Doerr 2018a).

An increasing number of professional linguistic translators and volunteer interpreters currently use their language skills to engage in social protest, engendering a need for research on how translators can influence political processes of discourse, deliberation, and democratic decision making in coalition work. This is a rich and generative field within which I have pursued one rather particular line of inquiry. Following translation theorist Moira Inghilleri, I use the notions of translating and interpreting interchangeably to emphasize the cultural component of the work of both interpreters and translators (Inghilleri 2012). Rather than focus on political ramifications of linguistic translation or interpreting per se, I look at political translation as a broad set of practices designed to address marginalization based on gender, class, race, and other differences—even within groups whose members speak the same language. For example, in a traditionally monolingual, national context, activists working on immigrants' rights, black feminism, and LGBTQ politics in the United States have used political translation to address positional misunderstandings related to issues of race/ethnicity and class (Doerr 2018b). Given that refugee solidarity coalitions struggle with linguistic difference and with ethnic and structural boundaries as well, I will explore in this chapter whether and under what conditions potential positional misunderstandings in solidarity coalitions encouraged activists to develop a practice of political translation.

My empirical analysis is based on a two-year ethnographic study of grassroots dialogue, democracy, and intercultural civic encounters between refugees and solidarity activists in Germany and Denmark. Following the long summer of migration in 2015 and the arrival of over 1 million refugees via the "Balkan route" (Della Porta 2018), thousands of citizens in Western Europe engaged in solidarity activism and participatory democratic processes organized for refugees (Della Porta 2018; Siim and Meret 2016). I focus on radical feminist and queer activist groups and "mainstream" civic organizations in Germany and Denmark, which invited refugee women and LGBTQ refugees to join them in creating solidarity encounters and dialogue on gender and sexuality and other themes.

In the years 2016–2018, I did research on eighteen civic associations and advocacy groups situated variously in large urban centers like Copenhagen or Berlin and rural areas in Western and Eastern Germany and Denmark. In all groups studied, paid staffers and civic volunteers interacted with refugees on a regular basis, supporting them in the asylum process, in the search for health care, housing, and labor and in organizing joint events for social interaction or political discussion. I interviewed a total of fifty staffers and volunteers who reflected about the challenges and the need to consider issues of race, ethnicity, class, national, linguistic, or gender-based marginalization—issues that also came up in my ten interviews with refugees.

The comparison of solidarity movements in two different host countries provides a broad impression of the challenges of intersectional coalition work on the issue of forced migration and asylum within the context of what is commonly referred to as European refugee crisis (Hamann and Karakayali 2016). Germany and Denmark are key destination countries for refugees and migrants (Siim and Meret 2016). While both German and Danish refugee solidarity activists have been inspired by dramatic media images, the local and national solidarity initiatives have also been shaped by variously hostile or welcoming political contexts and discursive and political opportunity structures (Daphi 2016; Della Porta 2018; Hamann and Karakayali 2016; Sauer 2017; Siim and Meret 2016).

To understand the challenges of intersectional coalition work and the issue of positional misunderstandings in a mass solidarity movement in two different national contexts, my analysis included groups whose agenda exhibited an explicit focus on intersectionality as well as groups that did *not* use conceptions or practices to consider intersectionality. Among the former groups were mostly radical feminist and queer organizations, and I aimed to understand how their members' potential awareness of interconnected forms of oppression and inequality related to citizenship status, gender, race, class, and sexuality would play out within their coalitions compared to other welcome and solidarity initiatives (Yuval-Davis 2011). Among the mass movement of religious and civic solidarity groups supporting refugees in Germany, feminist and queer organizations were a minority, and they involved fewer volunteers and staffers compared to the broader, institutionally funded mass movement of local solidarity initiatives emerging after 2015 (Lang 2015). In comparison, in Denmark, feminist and LGBTQ *themes* were "mainstream" and formed part of the moral codex of both institutional and grassroots refugee solidarity initiatives (Siim and Meret 2016). In Denmark, however, radical feminist and LGBTQ refugee solidarity organizations had difficulty getting funding if they did not fit the restrictive local government funding scheme based on "integration" measures by government and institutions operating in an increasingly conservative and right-wing populist political environment shaped by austerity politics (Ayoub 2019; Siim and Meret 2016).

To understand the challenges for intersectional coalition work in more open or hostile national and place-specific local political contexts, my case study included groups operating in liberal and cosmopolitan capital cities and urban centers like Berlin and Copenhagen as well as solidarity initiatives in rural, religious, or politically conservative regions or states like Bavaria, Brandenburg, and Sachsen in Germany and Jutland in Denmark in the years 2016–2018. For example, in conservative regions local groups, whose members experienced increasing pressure from local bureaucracies and institutions pushing deportation and decreased funding, sometimes internalized external stress. This led to intersectional oppression, marginalization, and conflict related to stereotypes of perceived gendered and cultural differences. Likewise, I consider conditions for local organizing in Copenhagen and Berlin as "best cases"; that is, these cities are known hubs of feminist and LGBTQ groups advocating for equality and inclusion of knowledge on gender and sexual diversity in mixed groups of citizens and refugees (Ayoub 2019).

My ethnography explores to what extent refugee women and LGBTQ refugees had an opportunity, depending on the solidarity group's local language, group culture, and social context, to express themselves and be included in the discussions and initiatives promoted by solidarity activists, including staffers and volunteers. Previous research on intersectionality, civil society, and social movements has shown that coalitions may fail to include grassroots members or target groups (such as socially disadvantaged women, minorities, refugees, resource-poor organizations, or poor people) if the format, location, or timing of meetings and events are chosen in inaccessible ways (Polletta 2002).

To address intersectional challenges of that kind, I first explored the basic question of whether and under what conditions refugee participants had opportunities to attend and participate in meetings by solidarity initiatives organized on their behalf. Second, I studied whether refugees could also effectively follow these public discussions in their own languages, and, third, could express their contributions in their own languages or an alternate, familiar language in order to participate in decision making. I analyze the outcome of such dialogue to determine to what extent decisions include positions by refugees and/or linguistic and sexual minority groups. That the latter groups have been included in intercultural civic dialogue and encounters can be assessed by exploring the outcome of decisions as well as by an analysis of shifts in the discourses that occur throughout the process of discussion (Wodak 1998; Young 1996). To get at the core of positional misunderstandings, including differences of material interest, I studied how such conflicts materialize during public debate when more powerful groups dismiss arguments made by the less powerful ones.

Most notably, I show how perceived cultural differences and intersectional boundaries within mixed groups of refugees and citizens came into tension within the context of increasingly restrictive asylum rules and decreasing funding. Refugees ceased attending joint encounters, and some volunteers externalized the stress they experienced by projecting it negatively onto the refugees, while others self-critically reflected on their own challenges of creating safe meeting spaces, activities, and egalitarian encounters in which refugees could feel comfortable and socialize with citizens.

FORGING ALLIANCES ON THE ISSUES OF GENDER AND SEXUALITY—FEMINIST AND QUEER COALITIONS

In each of the cities I studied, solidarity initiatives included organizations or informal networks working on gender and sexuality. In Germany, local LGBTQ rights and cultural associations as well as a certain number of institutional feminist NGOs and women's houses specialized in providing resources, knowledge, and facilities for hosting LGBTQ refugees or refugee women. While the women's movement was initially less broadly present within solidarity initiatives (Lang 2015), grassroots LGBTQ rights associations in smaller and medium-sized cities also became engaged early on. For example, a German LGBTQ rights organizer from a medium-sized town in southern Hesse said,

> We saw the TV images with all these people marching on the highways and heard that many young, single men were among the arrivers. We thought that naturally many of them must be gay. Because who can travel so easily? Who can leave behind their families and has nothing to lose if they leave? We met in our local association and we came up with a list of things we should do. We created flyers in Arabic, Farsi, English, Tigrinya and Kurdish so that queer refugees were aware that we are here to help. That was just in time. The day the flyer was ready we already went to help set up the gym for beds for refugees, they had arrived.[2]

As in this example, activists working on LGBTQ rights in numerous German cities took relative ad hoc actions to support the arrival of queer refugees. My interviews, however, also revealed that LGBTQ refugees who ended up in less progressive rural areas had almost no support. Thus, decentralized, newly emerging LGBTQ refugee solidarity initiatives worked across distances to connect queer refugees who had been placed in rural and often poorly accessible asylum housing. In Hesse, for example, Bavarian refugees traveled long distances to the more liberal towns near Frankfurt in order to connect to the local queer community there.

Large urban centers like Berlin experienced a rise of new activism among grassroots radical feminist and LGBTQ organizations. Existing groups created informal mentoring structures for refugees and so became aware of the multiple linguistic and institutional hurdles and racist practices refugees faced. A solidarity activist from an autonomous queer feminist housing project in Berlin said,

> I initially decided against mentoring as I thought I do not have the time to accompany someone to do all the bureaucratic stuff and get asylum, find housing, and a job. But now I take care of three young lesbians. It was like becoming pregnant unwillingly in old age. I am puzzled at the types of hurdles I encounter in intervening on behalf of them. I don't know how those who live in the asylum homes do it [who try to do things on their own], they can only become desperate. How do they succeed at this? You need to take humans by the hand and explain to them how it works.[3]

As this interviewee notes, grassroots feminist and LGBTQ activists in urban centers like Berlin, Frankfurt, Munich, Copenhagen, Roskilde, or Aarhus volunteered and hosted queer refugees and in the process became implicit mentors (Polletta 2002). More institutional feminist NGOs and grassroots organizations also engaged in solidarity actions with refugees (Lang 2015). As infrastructure and funding were available, feminist groups supported refugee women by providing shelters and housing opportunities specifically focusing on women who had experienced sexual violence or trauma either before or after arrival in the host country. Feminists engaged in civic education and training that enabled refugee women to feel at home in the host country. A feminist activist from Thuringia said, "For many of the [refugee] women learning to participate in our activities was completely new. They organized their own café and business, it is now running well but it was also something they had never done before back home.[4]

Cooperation within intersectional coalitions involving refugees and queer and feminist activists was itself a learning process. Moreover, volunteers as well as staffers reported how they learned through their intermediary positions as translators advocating on behalf of refugees dealing with officials and institutions. Rather than accepting their frustration with bureaucracies unwilling to listen to refugees, volunteers learned to "intervene" collectively by using their insider knowledge as citizens and activists to challenge the conditions for newcomers. Said a queer feminist activist from Berlin,

> I am incredibly angry at how job center employees, for example, in Eastern Berlin, treat refugees. I have written letters of complaint non-stop. It is an obstacle. They don't recognize refugees as humans, they don't react to the situation in front of their eyes, they all follow the rules by the book. "Our official language here is still German. We don't do that here." They don't want to be flexible. They don't want to welcome newcomers. . . . I also feel desperate often when I intervene. I already know the telephone numbers of the Treptow job center by heart. The way they treated refugees at the beginning is outrageous. In Kreuzberg, the job center is really cooperative; it is really often the culture within particular local institutions.[5]

The above volunteer describes her own process of learning to "intervene" as part of a broader collective of what I term "political translators," that is, groups who used their intermediary position and agency as a critical *third* toward local institutional insiders to open access to marginalized groups (Doerr 2018a). For example, this volunteer acted as part of an activist network whose members used their cultural capital and insider knowledge to support refugees to cooperate with officials on a more equal basis. What defines her intervention as an attempt of political translation is that the activist intervened *disruptively* toward officials unwilling to communicate with refugees who did not yet speak German and who wanted their cases to be processed. Activists also intervened virtually as a *critical third voice* on the phone when refugees experienced linguistic communication problems. For example, when a job center employee refuses to communicate with the German-speaking volunteer on the phone, the activist interviewed used her *disruptive* skills as an activist to "intervene," writing numerous letters of complaints to officials.

As political translators, activists challenge the ideals of neutrality and impartiality in situations where a dominant group or institution systematically ignores demands for equality and justice made by another, less privileged group, in short, during *positional misunderstandings* (Doerr 2018a). The positional misunderstanding between the refugee and the official at Treptow's local job center, beyond linguistic communication problems, was about power and civic status differences (Wodak 1998; Yuval-Davis 2011). Rather than being willing to cooperate with a German-speaking translator on the phone, the job center employee seemed unwilling—rather than unable—to communicate with refugees who were not fluent in German. As will be shown, positional misunderstandings also occur on a regular basis within refugee solidarity groups themselves. This anecdote also points to the limited influence of political translation given that its impact depends on the standing of the translator and the willingness of the official to accept working together with a critical third. Only a few of the groups and initiatives I studied had recognized this issue and the consequent need to build internal political translating capacities within their own coalitions in order to avoid situations in which dominant status groups or staffers marginalized disadvantaged community members.

GERMANY: WHY DON'T THEY COME TO OUR MEETINGS?

The present section discusses the challenge of intersectional inclusion focusing on positional misunderstandings about gender and sexuality and structural inequality in mainstream refugee solidarity organizations. In Germany, the experience of interaction with refugee women was new and unfamiliar for many volunteers who had joined solidarity initiatives in 2015–2016, and the majority of volunteers interviewed suggested that issues of gender may play a role in understanding why in particular refugee women did not attend meetings.

Outside the sector of feminist and queer groups, many organizers of refugee solidarity meetings for refugees whom I interviewed were middle class, majority German women, volunteers between thirty and sixty-five typical of the broader background of participants in the "welcome" movement (Hamann and Karakayali 2016). Interviewees stressed both their good intent and their difficulties in entering dialogue with refugee women not attending social encounters, meetings, and welcome gatherings that had been organized specifically on their behalf. Volunteers who were still engaged in local solidarity initiatives in 2017–2018 expressed their frustration at having repeatedly organized events for refugee women whose experiences were "very different" from their own culture. As an example, a volunteer who organized social encounters for several hundred refugees in a town in Bavaria said,

> Also all those enthusiast Germans who joined [volunteering] in 2015, many of them said goodbye in 2016, they are frustrated. . . . We have an open cafeteria for low level communication. I invite everyone who is coming to get vegetables for free at our kitchen table. Almost nobody comes [to our cafeteria meetings]. I have difficulties to understand that! Once they have arrived here they are no longer interested, we are just an instrument. In Afghanistan, the Middle East, and in many other African countries there is a "sitting culture." They sit at home a lot, also in the neighborhood, among each other, in the family, in the big clans, always like to visit each other, cook for each other; and our culture [in Germany] is very different. We have initially worked with intercultural translators, but this has also failed. . . . But I want to question whether we need any translators. Why should we Germans stretch ourselves? They have to adapt to our values, not the other way round.[6]

The above interviewee expresses frustration with and difficulty in "understanding" refugees' lack of interest in participating in social gatherings for "low-level communication" in German, which her group regularly organized. This highly engaged activist was critical of "racist" attitudes on the part of the Bavarian government, employers, and the general population. Yet despite her anti-racist ideology, the interviewee explained the failure of cooperation with refugees using stereotypical image of refugees and their families. The interviewee constructs a dichotomy between "our culture" in Germany and the alleged "sitting culture" of refugee "clans" "in Afghanistan, the Middle East, and . . . African countries." From an intersectional perspective, this statement is problematic. The speaker constructs culturalist notions of differences that essentialize negative and derogatory descriptions of refugees' behavior. The statement reflects cultural racism in its use of commonsensical and simplifying notions of "us" and "them" and blames refugees for not being interested in participating in social gatherings once they had been granted a permission of residency (Wodak 2015).

The above interview indicates the failure of intersectional coalition work in the absence of organizers' willingness to build political translation capacities. When I asked the interviewee whether her group had tried to work with linguistic or cultural translators, she argued that all attempts at multilingual or multicultural integration had failed or were counterproductive since refugees had to learn to assimilate.

Refugee women in Germany saw different reasons for the failure of joint encounters with German volunteers or staffers during solidarity meetings. For example, a member of the refugee network *Women in Exile* described the foundation of her network's interaction with German social workers and NGOs who [were perceived as] treating refugee women as less than equal partners: "We are often represented as vulnerable. So we decided we can do something [on our own]. If we have space and time, you can do something like learning German. I wanted to learn German and I was not allowed. They said no chance. No rights. Then we started a revolution."[7] As described by the *Women in Exile* activist, the sense of incomprehension—the intersectional *positional* misunderstanding—between German supporters and refugee women triggered the foundation of *Women in Exile*'s self-organized network—"a revolution" that challenged refugee women's experience of the patronizing, victimizing culture represented also in my interviews with some German volunteers. The self-organized form of resistance and protest by refugee women is a collective answer to the perceived ignorance of and racist representation of refugee women in German-led organizations?

Based on my interviews, in contrast to the perceived idea of a "sitting culture" in the countries of origin, the actual experiences of refugee women indicate other reasons that refugees had difficulty in maintaining a high level of social engagement with volunteers on a regular basis. Their financial situation and time availability decreased once they received asylum. This was true in both Germany and Denmark and applied to refugees from different countries of origin. A refugee from Iran said,

> When I got asylum it was the hardest time for me. They put pressure on me. They pushed me to work. I had such fear to be fired. Two months I worked every day, always under pressure. They pushed me away from my plan to finish my high school degree to make me work. They promised me that I'd have money to travel. Now I work for a Danish coffee chain but as I work part-time and get few hours every week, I have no money. I cannot travel. . . . When I got asylum I felt really bad. I cried when I woke up in the morning and when I went to bed. . . . I suddenly felt that it was my fault that my little brother cannot enjoy a childhood the way I did in Iran. He could not play. He had to interrupt his school because of me.[8]

Rather than "sitting" together and "cooking for each other" in "large clans," once they got asylum, refugees faced a lack of money, restrictive cultural integration programs, and high-pressure internships as well as mental health problems in the context of trauma. The interviewee, a refugee in her early twenties, mentions her serious health problems, trauma, and additional hurdles for participating in joint meetings with volunteers posed by a stressful integration and job activation programs that started after the actual asylum decision.

DENMARK: FROM WOMEN'S EMPOWERMENT TO DISCIPLINARY MEETINGS FOR JOB ACTIVATION

In comparison to Germany, most of the Danish solidarity organizers outside the sector of feminist and queer organizations showed comparatively more understanding for the difficulties of refugees, particularly women with small children, in attending meetings or participating in jointly organized events—at least in 2016. Danish activists' left-wing political ideas as well as their awareness of restrictive asylum policies made it clear to all engaged participants that refugees had a hard time attending any social gathering—in particular because the government had placed them in remote and inaccessible locations far from the capital, Copenhagen, and urban centers like Roskilde and Aarhus. However, in contrast to political and institutional support and relative availability of funding for emerging local German solidarity initiatives for women refugees in 2015/16 (Lang 2015), Danish refugee solidarity organizations supporting women suffered from restrictive working conditions in a hostile political environment as well as structural funding problems. Funding by the government was difficult to get and it was often connected to political mandates, leading organizations to apply instead for funding from private donors directed at "cultural integration" programs.

The hostile external environment fostered potential intersectional awareness among most of the Danish volunteers and staffers, who in interviews emphasized the difficulty for refugees in traveling from the remote locations where they had been placed in order to attend social gatherings. In the fall of 2017, the government decided to place all remaining asylum seekers in the countryside far from Copenhagen. They were to be transferred to remote, more politically conservative towns with more traditionally religious inhabitants in the Jutland region. This resulted in a perceived government crackdown on existing NGO structures and allied institutions supporting refugees in their daily lives. It also contributed to the sudden breakdown of long-existing and successful joint self-organized, cooperative solidarity activities, and meetings attended and organized by numerous refugees and volunteers.

Struggling with an increasingly hostile external policy environment, existing Danish solidarity organizations in 2017 transformed their initially egalitarian, dialogue-oriented grassroots democratic meetings for refugee women into semiofficial settings centered around "job activation." Where they had previously encouraged refugees and volunteers to exchange feminist stories of empowerment or to practice democracy in small group meetings, staffers now tried to teach and train refugee women to survive the pressure of the labor market in order to be able to leave the restrictive space of the camps. The effect, however, was that a part of the meeting spaces that had once provided refugees with what many initially perceived as an "open space" turned increasingly hierarchical and high-pressured, reflecting the very inequalities the organizations aimed to combat. The following example is from my observation of a "women's group" meeting at a grassroots democratic solidarity project in Copenhagen held in December 2017. The "women's group" organizers had just recruited a new staffer from the state-run unemployment center, whom staffers hoped would help "activate" women for the job market. The meeting opened as follows:

Women have filled their coffee cups and taken seats in the comfortable sofas.[9] Christian,[10] the new staffer recruited from a local public employment office, starts to introduce the changes that women will encounter in the next weeks if they want to continue to participate in activities at the self-organized house for refugees in Copenhagen, where many women did internships as cleaners.

Christian (new staffer): "You understand that the biggest challenge in Denmark is democracy. For that you have to learn to cooperate in teams. Our house needs to be clean. For that you have to meet at the beginning of the internship and discuss as a team."

Nobody reacts. Long silence (for about a minute).

Female staffer: "You have to independently decide how you're gonna clean it and how you do it."

Silence for about 30 seconds.

Male staffer: "Outside the self-organized house they expect you to work in a team. They will not instruct you how to do it."

Silence for about 30 seconds.

Female staffer: "The boss won't be there. She will expect you, the group, to do it on your own. By the way: how do you do it in Afghanistan?"

Afghan refugee translates for other Afghani women. Then she responds to the staffer's question: "In Afghanistan you are expected to follow instructions."

Refugee who translates for other women tries to voice dissent: "The problem [to understand why refugee women may not find the new rules for internships a good idea] is [cooperation between] people come from so many places. I propose [makes an alternative proposal against the toughening of rules for internships]."

Female staffer: "The style of internships will change in January. From then on we expect you to work as a team so they will take you more seriously."

Refugee who translates for other women: "I have a question. Maybe it's so hard to live in a camp. So hard that you don't find the energy for the internship. What do you say?"

Silence. No response by the staffers.

Refugee from African country (trying to voice critique): "There is an inside and an outside here, like in the camp."

Female staffer: "If you dream of working as secretary, for example, you need to learn the expectations of employers."

Male staffer: "So everything will change next year."

Silence.

A latecomer enters the meeting, Nawal.[11] Nawal is a refugee from North Africa who hugs the female staffer and apologizes in Danish for being late.

Female staffer (to all): "This is a very good example. Nawal came late and she apologized. Well done, Nawal, that you apologized yourself!" Nawal takes off her coat and takes a seat smilingly. Volunteers and most refugee women remain silent except that a refugee woman takes a furious look and crosses her arms in front of her breast.

To interpret these impressions from my field notes, I would argue that refugees expressed their critiques—verbally and nonverbally—without, however, being able to shape the outcome of the discussion in this meeting. In addition to the nonverbal signals of opposition by a refugee woman, the refugee who acted as translator questioned decision making by staffers on behalf of refugee women. However, the critical questions and the dissent expressed by the refugee translator were not noticed by the two staffers. With the activation policy for internships, the "free space" the NGO provided for women seemed to vanish. In fact, the policy also spilled over to the women's meeting itself where refugees had to prove their "punctuality" by showing up on time—even though the meeting was meant to give them a "free space".

Conflict escalated at the end of the women's meeting when the female staffer reimbursed refugees for their travel on public transportation that had enabled them to attend the meeting. Given refugees' lack of information about varying and fluctuating funding for reimbursement, this was a tense moment. Some refugees would find out only now that they may not get reimbursed to be able to attend future meetings—if there was insufficient funding. As a general rule, only refugees who engaged in "volunteer" internship activities like kitchen work or cleaning could be reimbursed. A refugee screamed at the staffer and expressed her frustration publicly. At the next meeting, the refugee who protested was indeed absent, and the female staffer commented on her absence as follows:

> In the last women's meeting there was some screaming going on and I still feel it in my bones. When the tickets are given out this can be very stressful but instead of yelling, talk calmly. (Silence). There are three rules . . . : First, no racism and sexism. Second, all are equal. Third, no violence. And no vodka. No hard alcohol. But also screaming can be violence. So let's practice not to scream but to talk about conflict like adults.[12]

While directed at de-escalating the conflict in the women's meeting, the staffer's self-reflective comments do not contain an apology; she instead projects the issue of "violence" toward the one refugee woman who yelled at her. The staffer's emphasis that "all are equal" omits the multiplicity of hierarchies of status, class, and language in the women's space.

My interviews with refugee women give further background to the failure of egalitarian dialogue in women's meetings for refugees in the high-pressure context of Denmark. I interviewed several who had participated in the meetings described and who experienced a sense of distance from the hierarchical group culture created by Danish staffers. For instance, a queer asylum seeker who had been placed in a remote town in Southern Denmark and who had refrained from attending the women's meetings said,

> In Denmark I don't experience a single place where human rights play a role. There is no place to complain. Every week we travel to the "women's group meetings" in Copenhagen. They organize the meetings, where they make plans, like, "yes, we want to make a revolution," but they do nothing. . . . I can tell about my problems but no one listens to me. The staffers are "official." We love that one day per week where we can travel to Copenhagen and meet people.[13]

Several participants interviewed experienced the "women's group meetings" as mixed at best—a venue that served to get them out of the camps and yet remained an ambivalent space with "official" elements and where their voices were not truly "listened" to.

Within the context of increasingly restrictive immigration rules, NGOs and grassroots democratic organizations in Copenhagen, like those sponsoring the mentioned "women's meetings," transformed their own meeting culture into a work-activation and job integration space. In the observation above, this is illustrated by the way that staffers justify their patronizing practices and disciplining of refugee women with a discourse on "democracy in Denmark" and "team work" as well as by imposing rules for punctuality on refugee women only but not on volunteers who attend meetings. The one-sided disciplinary discourse on work activation, "stricter" internships, and "punctuality" also potentially made solidarity between participating volunteers and refugee women harder as it created an additional invisible divide.

Attempts at individual, critical translation by refugee women themselves who intervened on behalf of others who did not speak English or Danish failed. Refugee translators were powerless where they also depended on the good will of staffers who acted as official facilitators of the women's group meetings and who ultimately had the discretion to decide whether they would reimburse refugees for their travel tickets or not.

FINDING VOICE: TRANSLATING BOUNDARIES TO MAKE MEETINGS MORE EGALITARIAN

In no meeting that I attended did refugees who translated on behalf of other refugees have the power to intervene critically and politically; but there was another group that succeeded in building critical political translation capacities within mainstream solidarity groups.

These were first- or second-generation migrants with stable incomes and residence status who intervened as critical, political translators while volunteering or working for different NGOs and organizations. Unlike refugees, these activist volunteer translators had more leverage in meetings and some of them could and did challenge positional misunderstandings favoring more powerful status groups like staffers or volunteers in meetings. For example, when I interviewed a resident migrant who volunteered as translator for a grassroots democratic NGO in Copenhagen, she described some of the critical interventions she was engaging in:

> Some of the staffers have this . . . it's almost like an arrogance. For example, in some of the NGOs they instruct refugees that democracy in Denmark is all about teamwork and about being punctual and about discussing everything with your boss before starting to work. They repeat it again and again. But honestly: It's not true! First, they aren't always punctual themselves and then it's also not always equal and democratic. It's like a show, a performance they put up, it's not the reality of life in Denmark. . . . But working with [staffer] Lasse[14] for me is like working in heaven. He helped all the people I know, he respects inside and outside, he respects all cultures. For example, we had a queer [refugee] from an African country who doesn't know whether [they] are woman or man. [They are identifying] not exactly [as] transgender but just [are] not sure. We want to make our [space] friendly as an environment for [them]. I saw that one of our most dominant [heterosexual refugee] couple wasn't friendly [to them] and went on marginalizing and humiliating that person here in our space! I told Lasse and Lasse intervened. He got so red in his face. He made sure that person is safe and that it will never happen again and that that person is not in the same camp as that couple.[15]

As quoted above, this volunteer translator, a resident migrant, criticized staffers' "arrogance" and their patronizing behavior toward refugees. However, without the critical intervention of the migrant-translator quoted, staffer "Lasse" would have been unable to notice that the "queer" or transgender refugee was being harassed. The leverage that volunteer translators like the interviewee quoted had was based on their close cooperation with Danish staffers like "Lasse" who were open to recognizing and putting an end to intersectional oppression. The agency of translators was fairly limited given that the sole power of decision making was with paid staffers, and again, volunteer translators to a certain degree depended on staffers who paid them a low salary for their linguistic services. Perhaps because of this status hierarchy, translators themselves almost exclusively expressed criticism of staffers behind the scene.

ACTING POLITICALLY: HOW BROADER, INTERSECTIONAL COALITIONS SURVIVED BACKLASH

I found that organizations and staffers who accepted that some of their members intervened as internal, critical, political translators for refugees and potentially disadvantaged groups developed a self-reflective group culture and were able to better address intersectional oppression within their own coalitions. While mainstream NGOs and volunteer organizations experienced decreasing participation by both refugee members and civic volunteers in the years 2017–2018, LGBTQ organizations in both Germany and Denmark survived or even grew, acquiring new members during that period. For example, a solidarity organizer who organized cooking encounters with LGBTQ refugees in Brandenburg said,

> Because of the increasingly restrictive asylum policy people now get only a year of residency—they are so worried and afraid of their future that they want to talk to us about residence status and work—and not sit around and have social encounters. . . . Some, however, come; they are interested to meet us rather than other asylum seekers.[16]

Where solidarity groups, like the LGBTQ initiative in Brandenburg, developed intersectional awareness of the multiple disadvantages and hurdles of participation for refugees, they succeeded in building regular encounters across intersections where different status groups could meet and socialize with each other.

One reason for the survival of these initiatives in both Germany and Denmark was that queer activists who had acquired the capacity to intervene as political translators on behalf of refugees changed their own working practices, having acquired more awareness of the challenges and intersectional oppressions that refugees experienced in their daily lives. For example, a Danish LGBTQ organizer from Copenhagen said,

> Forty percent of our asylum seekers are below middle class. They are particularly disadvantaged as they of course have difficulties translating their story into what a Western audience can understand, rational, ready for a court. We help them present their stories so that they have a chance in the asylum interview. We provide them with good lawyers. I am often among the first to hear their stories, and it is hard for [refugees] to believe that I, as a woman, am married with another woman and have children. Many are very young. When I hear people's stories I think that it could be me, in that place. It means questioning who we are.[17]

The practice of translating the stories of queer and women refugees for lawyers and court hearings was a new and transformative experience for volunteers who were often the first to hear refugees' traumatizing and painful life stories. The above interviewee's realization that "it could be me, in that place" suggests a moment of identification with queer asylum seekers who were not middle class and had often suffered trauma and oppression in their countries of origin because of their sexual identity. However, awareness of remaining differences and inequalities also increased. An LGBTQ activist from Roskilde described the challenges of equal cooperation in the multi-lingual, socially heterogeneous coalition of refugees and citizens that her organization had succeeded in building as follows:

> Even if we feel we are the same we are often very shocked about our differ-ences. For example, to be honest, we volunteers are rather liberal and radical leftists. The refugees are not left! They are neoliberal. They don't want to pay high taxes. We often grapple with realizing that. There are also other issues in our group. Of course we want it to be equal and democratic but that is of course not true. We have a big group of very young Afghan men who do not speak any English. In our meetings, we have many cultural misunderstandings because we are so diverse as a community. When we make joint workshops, for example about safe sex since some of our members use quite risky practices. But for some it is really important. Some people wanted to know how to use a condom so we used a banana to show. This is of course extremely boring for other people. Then there are also things we don't know. I realize this constantly. For example, I learned about a practice of [female sexuality] that some of our African members told us about. This is [empowering] knowledge about sex I had never heard about.[18]

Despite the sense of empathy and identification on the part of the Danish volunteers, the interviewee also reflects about her own ignorance and "cultural misunderstandings" that create lines of division and potential conflict between refugees and volunteers. However, rather than asking refugees to assimilate, LGBTQ activist groups experienced the arrival of refugees as a transformative moment that deeply challenged and renewed their activist communities, widening the class base and stretching the language repertoire of local queer communities to create broader, intersectional coalitions.

CONCLUSION

My analysis has shown that in a context of external political backlash and polemic public debates about gender and "cultural differences" in the years 2016–2018, mainstream refugee solidarity organizations in Denmark and Germany struggled with decreasing membership and internal positional mis-understandings between volunteers and refugees. During the same period, some grassroots feminist or LGBTQ solidarity groups succeeded in broaden-ing coalitions and enhancing their intersectional awareness and understand-ing of refugees beyond structural and perceived cultural lines of division. Regarding the challenge of positional misunderstandings in heterogeneous coalitions, my findings suggest a mixed picture of dialogue and informal

marginalization in solidarity organizations struggling with internal differences and multiple citizenship status hierarchies (Yuval-Davis 2011). While
less experienced volunteers and some members of mainstream solidarity
organizations blamed the failure of mutual dialogue and solidarity meetings
on refugees, others tried to organize funding for refugees to travel to meetings
and to provide mental health care services and other incentives that motivated
refugees to attend. As a result, the participation of refugees, in particular for
women and vulnerable populations such as LGBTQ refugees, increased.

Addressing a long-standing concern voiced by feminists, immigrants'
rights and people of color organizers, some refugee solidarity groups have
tried to work more inclusively within intersectional coalitions by developing
political translation capacities. Among all organizations analyzed, LGBTQ
organizers were the most successful in creating lasting encounters and relatively egalitarian meeting spaces involving both refugees and citizens. A first
systematic pattern to understand the key to these groups' development of
political translation capacities was potentially LGBTQ organizers' experiential knowledge of positional misunderstandings. In their role as critical, political translators, volunteers helped refugees to translate their sexual identities
into the dominant culture for Western asylum interviews and navigating local
institutions. Second, beyond structural and perceived cultural differences,
queer activists emphasized a feeling of connection to the traumatic experiences of discrimination and hurt that refugees had had. Their capacity to
imagine themselves in the place of a queer person born in another country
was a strength that facilitated mutual identification, trust, and understanding.
That capacity to imagine oneself as the other was missing in the experience
of activists who rejected to engage in building political translation capacities
in their groups. Rather than accepting marginalization of refugees in official
settings like job center encounters, queer activists acted as political translators who openly intervened as a *disruptive third* to challenge cultural and
linguistic power asymmetries between officials and refugees. Among queer
activist groups supporting refugees in Germany and Denmark, translation
became a model for political activism that also changed the way in which
organizers thought about their own intersectional coalition work. Where this
was the case, local organizations tried to change their own meeting cultures
and styles accordingly.

In mainstream solidarity organizations, migrant translators built collective
capacity and leverage using their accredited role as linguistic translators to
challenge intersectional status hierarchies and gendered and sexual marginalization where they cooperated in teams with staffers. However, attempted
critical interventions by individual refugees who spoke as political translators
on behalf of other vulnerable group members failed. This shows the continued relevance of intersectional oppression and marginalizing, exclusionary

dynamics caused by positional misunderstandings within mainstream solidarity organizations.

NOTES

1. I use the broad term "refugee" to refer to different categories of asylum seekers and refugees interchangeably.

2. Interview with a local LGBT rights educator and community organizer in Hesse, March 10, 2018.

3. Interview with a Berlin-based queer feminist activist, May 14, 2018.

4. Interview with a women's house staffer in Sachsen, March 6, 2018.

5. Interview with a Berlin-based queer feminist activist, May 14, 2018.

6. Interview with a refugee solidarity organizer in Bavaria, February 20, 2018.

7. Member of Women in Exile, public meeting on February 4, 2017, Humboldt Forum encounter between students of the course "The Right to Have Rights" and activist organizations.

8. Interview with a refugee, Copenhagen, November 2, 2017.

9. A women's meeting in Copenhagen, December 2, 2018.

10. Name changed.

11. Name changed.

12. Women's meeting, January 13, 2018.

13. Interview with a refugee, Southern Denmark, November 2016.

14. Name changed.

15. Interview with a voluntary translator, Copenhagen, November 10, 2017.

16. Interview with an LGBT rights organizer in the state of Brandenburg, March 16, 2018.

17. Interview with an LGBTQ refugee solidarity organizer, Copenhagen, October 30, 2017.

18. Interview with an LGBTQ refugee solidarity organizer, Copenhagen, October 30, 2017.

Chapter 11

Equality and Recognition or Transformation and Dissent?

Intersectionality and the Filipino Migrants' Movement in Canada

Ethel Tungohan

On October 23, 2009, during the "Spectres of Invisibility: Filipinos/as in Canada" conference in Toronto, I marveled at the numbers of Filipinos who filled the room. When Roland Coloma, who was an assistant professor at the Department of Social and Equity Studies at the University of Toronto, organized regular *Kritikal Kolektibo* (Critical Collective) meetings, I did not anticipate that our meetings would eventually lead us to organize a national symposium on Filipino studies in Canada. It was exciting for me, as a junior scholar and as a young community activist, to see Filipino academics and activists in the same room. Although academic spaces geared toward "Asian Studies" exist at the University of Toronto, I felt that those of us who are Filipino *and* who work on issues broadly related to the Philippines and the Philippine diaspora were unwelcome. That most of the people who attended these gatherings were not from the communities under study made these spaces uncomfortable for me, not because I think that only people of Asian descent should be part of "Asian Studies" but because of the scarcity of Asians present. I was excited by the "Spectres of Invisibility" conference, which promised to give a space for academics and activists who were interested in exploring the issues faced by Filipinos in Canada.

The excitement I felt, however, soon comingled with anxiety. It was energizing to be in a space where everyone present thought our project to explore forming a larger academic and social movement that centered Filipinos in Canada was necessary, but there was little consensus on what this should look like. In fact, there was much disagreement about how best to represent different groups of Filipinos with intersecting social locations. Audience members observed that Filipinos were fragmented by class, language, region, religion, and sexuality; that the project did not feature speakers from Filipino indigenous communities was also a gaping oversight. Yet it was the issues facing

Filipino migrant caregivers that elicited the sharpest divisions. I remember exchanging horrified glances with a friend when a heated debate emerged between prominent community leaders and academics on the issue of the Live-in Caregiver Program (LCP). The LCP has sharply divided the Filipino community. While it gives women from the Global South, most of whom come from the Philippines, the opportunity to apply for Canadian citizenship for themselves and their families, many members of the Filipino community saw this program as a form of indentured slavery. Why did this program exist when Filipino migrants in previous generations with similar skills and educational levels had the opportunity to immigrate permanently without having to experience the oftentimes demeaning process of live-in care work? Yet others contested this perspective, arguing that immigration programs have shifted and that the LCP—albeit not ideal—remains one of the few routes of entry for Filipina women hoping to obtain Canadian citizenship.

This was the debate that raged during the panel. As the people gathered rebuked each other, with some grabbing the mic to interrupt others to ensure that their positions were heard, audience members started whispering. I overheard the women behind me whisper furiously as a Filipina professor, who has long worked on migrant advocacy issues both as an academic and as a community leader, argued that rather than "scrapping the LCP"—a call that organizations such as the Philippine Women's Centre endorsed—perhaps the best route forward would be to reform parts of the program that were oppressive. The woman behind me rejected these comments out of hand, because the speaker was not a caregiver and was not working class. While they were whispering, another woman interjected. In a furious hiss, she chastised the women who were speaking, "Why would that matter? She's Filipino too, and she gets it."

The question of whose voices count and how to best deal with community members' intersecting social locations is at the heart of the debate that I address in this chapter. As someone who has been part of the Filipino migrants' movement in Canada for the past twelve years,[1] I have witnessed the tensions that exist when the movement has grappled with issues of allyship, social movement praxis, and intersectionality. In this chapter, I specifically consider the tensions and contradiction that arise within the Filipino migrants' movement in Canada when it strategically deploys different identities during specific campaigns, which at times necessitate forming coalitions with other social movements. Using an intersectional autoethnographic approach (Behl 2017) and participant observation (Gillespie and Michelson 2011), I ruminate on vital moments within the Filipino migrants' movement that illustrate the challenges of coalitionbuilding within the movement and with other movements. I consider whether and how actors within the Filipino migrants' movement embody "intersectional politics and practices" (see introduction). I specifically analyze the movement's attempts to grapple with the intersecting social locations of its members ("create intersectional capacity"), articulate its diverse needs ("find voice"), advocate for its members' needs ("act politically") *and* build coalitions with each other and with other social movements ("form alliances") (see introduction). Ultimately, I argue that the Filipino migrants' movement in Canada is divided between organizations that adopt a notion of intersectionality that adheres to Cohen's (1997) and Spade's (2013) vision of radical futurities, one that places a critique of interlocking powers at the center of their work and those organizations that prioritize legal equality.

METHODOLOGY AND POSITIONALITY

I base my arguments in this chapter on my individual experiences working within and studying social movements as a scholar-activist. Autoethnography remains marginal in political science. As a method, it is meant to add nuance to one's work by recognizing that researchers' *lived experiences* may strengthen theory building by "blending the personal and the scholarly" (Burnier 2006, 412). It responds to the following questions: "where is the flesh and blood scholar in the work? . . . where is context, place, situation? Where are the actual voices of the researcher and the researched? Where might narrative and biographical/autobiographical knowledge fit?" (Burnier 2006, 412). Patricia Hill Collins's (2015) trenchant observation that scholar-activists see intersectionality as being part of their "critical praxis" that "potentially constitute an important tool for political engagement" motivates my autoethnographic account, because appraising my complicated engagements with the Filipino migrants' movement from an intersectional lens may elicit insights about messy power dynamics. Neha Vora's autoethnographic account of being raised by a South Asian woman whom her parents had hired, which then became the basis of a discussion of her *own* complicity and entanglements in migrant domestic work, illustrates this well. In Vora's words, "Scholarship is about personal journeys and our own political investments, and feminist scholarship in particular has evolved from a refusal to adopt what Donna Haraway (1988) has called a 'view from nowhere" in favor of embedded, situated and reflexive knowledge production."

Similarly, intersectional autoethnography "challenges the subject—object separation by placing the researcher's experience at the center of the phenomenon under investigation," (Behl 2017, 584) but does so by focusing on the researcher's intersecting social locations. In this chapter, I use an *intersectional autoethnographic approach* where I foreground my intersecting social locations when analyzing the social movements with which I am active.

Through "critical reflexive attention to our own positionality" (Behl 2017, 592), I hope to draw closer attention to the workings of power within these social movements and reflect on the politics behind agendasetting, coalition-building, and allyship. Yet I also pair my autoethnographic insights as an activist within the Filipino migrants' movement with my observations of key public events such as International Women's Day marches and advocacy meetings, where I wrote field notes using participant observation. This, Gillespie and Micheson (2011) note, is a crucial method for helping illustrate political dynamics. By using both intersectional autoethnography and participant observation, I acknowledge my role as both a *part* of the movements that I am writing about and my role as a *scholar* of social movements, specifically of immigrant movements. In doing so, I try to foreground my self-identification as a scholar-activist, with my scholarly interest in understanding movement formation, activism, and strategizing and my political commitments in promoting greater social justice for migrant communities. Following the insight that intersectional analysis requires locating one's embodied social positions and experiences in relation to the production of knowledge, I take up this methodology to use my own personal experiences as jumping-off points for my theorizations.

I am a first-generation, middle-class immigrant to Canada from the Philippines whose family arrived in the country under Canada's "economic class" immigration program after living for four years in Hong Kong. I first became involved in Filipino community activism in Hong Kong, where I experienced daily forms of race- and gender-based discrimination. During my first year in Hong Kong, I came home in tears because my classmates in the international American school that I attended teased me mercilessly for my accent, my skin color, and for being "Filipino." I often spent time during the weekends at the *Bayanihan Centre*, a Filipino community center where my mother was the executive director. This made me aware that, despite the difficult experiences I faced as a Filipino teenager in Hong Kong, I was fortunate compared to the Filipina domestic workers in Hong Kong, who were vulnerable because of their intersecting race, gender, and class identities.

My awareness of Filipino migrants' experiences of vulnerability in Hong Kong led me, as a university student, to engage in community activism in Canada. I noticed that the Filipino migrants' movements in Hong Kong and in Canada were different in significant ways. The bigger and more active community of activists in Hong Kong focused primarily on *temporary* Filipino migrants' issues. In Canada, where there were more *permanent* immigrants, the Filipino migrants' movements grappled with issues of representation, employment and educational equity, and fair immigration policies. In my time as part of the Filipino migrants' movement in Canada, I have had to reflect on how being "Filipino," and thus a racial minority, makes me an "insider" in Filipino migrant community spaces. At the same time, my immigration history, which allowed me to come into Canada with my family, unlike many Filipino migrants who had to withstand prolonged periods of family separation, my acquisition of Canadian citizenship, my professional occupation as a graduate student and then as an assistant professor, and my relatively privileged economic situation gives me advantages that some advocates within the Filipino migrants' movement do not have. In addition, as a straight, married woman, I have been insulated from the homophobic and heterosexist attacks that have assailed many in the Filipino community (see, e.g., Diaz 2018).

Yet I have also observed that age can make participating in the Filipino migrants' movement difficult. Being a community member, first in my twenties and now in my thirties, I occasionally perceive that older community activists, many of whom are older men, are reluctant to give space to younger activists and in particular younger women. As I elaborate below, questions about who should speak for the Filipino migrants' community writ large are not easily resolved. Nor are questions about how to navigate internal tensions within the movement in light of the reality that being Filipino intersects with other social locations or how to work in coalition with other migrant and social justice movements in Canada.

INTERSECTIONALITY AND SOCIAL JUSTICE: "REFORMIST" V. CRITICAL APPROACHES?

When puzzling through the practice of intersectionality within the Filipino migrants' movement, I draw specifically from the works of Dean Spade, Cathy Cohen, and Erica Townsend-Bell. Spade's (2013) observations regarding social movements' engagement with reformist visions by seeking legal equality is a crucial component of my analysis. Spade argues that a focus on "legal equality" (Spade 2013, 1033) harms "intersectionally targeted" populations "by mobilizing narratives of deservingness and undeservingness, by participating in the logics and structures that undergird relations of domination, and by becoming sites for the expansion of harmful systems and institutions" (Spade 2012, 1032). Specifically, by citing examples of domestic violence, immigration, and anti-trafficking legal reforms that enforce "punishment-based solutions" to these specific problems, Spade shows how "reforms" actually perpetuate more harm on intersectionally targeted groups (Spade 2012, 1032). Legal reforms not only lead to limited and short-sighted solutions, they also rely on institutions, such as the police, that have a history of brutality toward oppressed people. Spade additionally argues that when campaigns are fought from a "single-axis" framework—as in the case of LGBT groups seeking "marriage equality" and disability rights groups arguing for greater access to "institutions and independent living"—social justice advocates end up prioritizing the needs of their more privileged members (Spade 2012, 1039–43).

Here, Cohen's (1997, 438) observations are salient. She notes that a "truly radical and transformative politics has not resulted from Queer activism" because of the tendency of the movement to "activate only one characteristic of their identity" and to "reject any recognition of the multiple and intersecting systems of power" (Cohen 1997, 440). For Cohen, using a "radical, intersectional, left analysis" allows social movements to push *beyond* the limitations of single-axis (or, as she calls it, "single-oppression") forms of organizing (Cohen 1997, 450). It does so by making unstable one's understanding of "identity" and of "community" such that one sees the "multiple social positions and relations to dominant power within any one category or identity" (Cohen 1997, 450) and, by placing at the center, *left* politics that "[emphasize] economic exploitation and class structure, culture, and the systemic nature of power" (Cohen 1997, 443). Cohen's vision of a radical, intersectional, left movement resonates closely with the Combahee River Collective's statement that "the liberation of all oppressed peoples necessitates the destruction of the political-economic systems of capitalism and imperialism as well as patriarchy" through a "socialist revolution" and a "feminist and anti-racist revolution" (1977).

It is not surprising that state-based institutions and nongovernmental organizations are generally resistant to such transformative visions of intersectionality and prefer instead the "narrower . . . goal of simply ameliorating social injustices to some degree" (Townsend-Bell 2014, 44). Townsend-Bell calls this tendency "ambivalent intersectionality" (2014), pointing specifically to how such organizations generally see the need for intersectionality, yet they are unsure or disagree about how to put intersectionality into effect. In addition, large bureaucracies face impediments when trying to enact social change because of their vast size. This is particularly true when facing restrictions from their funders on the types of activities they can legitimately support (INCITE! 2007). While it is tempting for grassroots organizations that are committed to the type of radical intersectional, leftist politics that Spade and Cohen endorse to disassociate themselves from funders, the realities of movement building frequently necessitate the formation of coalitions. Hence, for social movements that incorporate mainstream and grassroots organizations and that overlap with other movements, disagreements arise on normative goals and strategies and on understandings of intersectionality. When examining the Filipino migrants' movement, one wonders about the divisions that lead some participants and organizations to promote a radical and transformative agenda and others to promote a legal (reformist) approach.

THE FILIPINO MIGRANTS' MOVEMENT IN CANADA

At face value, it may appear hard to see what constitutes the Filipino migrants' movement in Canada and the common causes that can unite such a disparate group. In the introduction to "Filipinos in Canada: Disturbing Invisibility," the edited collection that emerged from the "Spectres of Invisibility" conference I discussed in the introduction, my coeditors and I highlighted how Filipinos are commonly associated with the "tropes of the victimized nanny, selfless nurse, and problematic gangster youth" (McElhinney et al. 2012, 5). Filipinos in Canada are "hyper-visible" in certain spaces based on these tropes. They also are automatically categorized as a "visible minority" according to Canada's census categories, which collapses "persons, other than Aboriginal persons, who are non-Caucasian in origin and non-white in colour" in one category, thereby "homogenizing" *all* "visible" (i.e., racialized minorities) as being "perpetual strangers to the nation" (McElhinney et al. 2012, 6). Yet Filipinos in Canada are simultaneously "invisible" because, beyond the aforementioned stereotypes, they inhabit a range of intersecting identities (McElhinney et al. 2012, 5).

In fact, scholars like Kelly (2006) emphasize diversity within the group because Filipinos in Canada occupy a range of educational, linguistic, class, and intersectional social locations. Filipinos have different immigration histories, having come to Canada in two main waves. The first wave occurred from the 1960s to the 1980s, during the heyday of the Points-System, when the Canadian state removed racial preferences in immigration selection. The new system admitted immigrants who scored the highest "points" when it came to language, income-earning potential, and other categories. As a result, the first wave was dominated by "skilled" professionals (Lacquian 1973). This group of Filipino immigrants was fragmented between those who supported Philippines' president Ferdinand Marcos's martial law regime and those who opposed him (McElhinney et al. 2012, 16). The second wave of immigrants came to Canada beginning in the 1980s. Although skilled professionals still entered the country, the entrenchment of the Philippines' labor export programs coupled with the establishment of programs such as the Foreign Domestics Movement (established in 1981) and the LCP (established in 1992) meant that more Filipino immigrants qualified for entry as "low-skilled" migrants (McElhinney et al. 2012, 10). This second wave of immigration included activists who sought refuge in Canada after being targeted by the Marcos regime.

Key differences exist between the two waves of immigrants. While Filipino immigrants in the first wave were settled in Canada with their families, later waves had to withstand extended periods of family separation (Lacquian and Lacquian 2008). Differences also exist in terms of professional standing. Although many immigrants in the second wave have university degrees and professional qualifications similar to the immigrants in the first wave, tightening immigration restrictions and higher standards of entry meant that their only chance to come into the country was to enter first as temporary migrants. Tension arises between these two waves of immigrants (Eric 2012), as I discuss below.

The substantive thrust of the Filipino migrants' movement's activities has concerned advocating on behalf of caregivers under the LCP and, to a lesser extent, the issues facing Filipino youth—many of whom are caregivers' children. The difficulties they face in Canada are in part connected to the tensions between "hyper-visibility" and "invisibility" and between different waves of immigrants. Because of these tensions, activists wished to address issues beyond those facing caregivers and youth since they feared that drawing attention to these issues would simply further entrench stereotypes that *all* Filipinos are "abject" nannies and their children. Nevertheless, these issues remain salient. In what follows, I consider the fraught and messy attempts by the Filipino migrants' movement to address Filipinos' concerns. I focus first on how organizations within the movement try to promote a radical, transformative vision of social justice that comes close to what Spade and Cohen discuss and then address how other organizations promote policy reforms.

Gabriela-Ontario and Radical, Intersectional Futurities

I felt inspired from the very first meeting that I attended at Gabriela-Ontario, which involved a health outreach session for caregivers at a community center in Toronto in 2008. Filipina community activists Petronila Cleto—or Tita (Auntie) Pet—and Cynthia Palmaria were involved, respectively, in anti-Marcos, feminist, and youth activism and were attempting to form a new organization, Gabriela-Ontario. In contrast to other Filipino activist spaces that I have entered, where there appeared to be an entrenched hierarchy and an ideology in place, Gabriela-Ontario was welcoming. Its organizing work involved directly advocating for its members, most of whom are caregivers, and creating spaces of support for them. These spaces became the starting point for developing a political consciousness about the interlocking nature of different struggles. Building the intersectional capacities of the organization was important, with much attention being paid to nurturing the lived realities of its diverse members.

But Gabriela-Ontario's advocacy was not dogmatic. I was drawn to the community it built among Filipinas in Toronto, which involved both marching in rallies, policy advocacy, and other "traditional" modes of movement organizing *and* frequent social outings such as apple picking and potlucks.

Through *kwentuhan* or storytelling, Gabriela-Ontario women, particularly caregivers, realize that their arduous employment and immigration situations are commonplace, thereby paving the way for the formation not only of bonds of friendship but also political education. During these gatherings, I, too, became politicized. Through multiple conversations, I finally understood the real-life implications of theories about the "feminization" of migration that I was reading about. The labor export regime in the Philippines, born out of global capitalist practices that placed countries in the Global South in a peripheral economic position, has led to the mass exodus of Filipina women. I saw that practices I believed were unique in my family—namely, frequently calling family members in the Philippines via Skype, listening to conversations between my mother and assorted female cousins who were thinking of opportunities to go abroad—were a routine part of other Gabriela-Ontario women's lives.

An important aspect of Gabriela-Ontario's work is to ensure that the migrants' movement includes diverse groups of migrant women. During a workshop on the history of the Filipino working-class women's movement, which I attended in 2009, I noticed the different ways Gabriela-Ontario members *strategically* deployed their social locations as racialized individuals, migrant "newcomers," marginalized youth, marginalized workers, Pinays, queers, linguistic minorities, and members of the working class, among many other social locations.

Gabriela-Ontario, like other Gabriela chapter organizations worldwide, uses an intersectional approach to its activism (Tungohan 2016). It began as a militant, anti-Marcos dictatorship organization in the Philippines, subsequently recognizing that the interlocking power structures of "imperialism, feudalism, and bureaucratic capitalism" interact with political, family, and religious institutions to oppress working-class Filipina women (Lee 1988, 218). This history means that a radical, left, socialist consciousness underpins its activities. For example, whenever migrant workers discussed their workplace and immigration experiences, those of us organizing with Gabriela-Ontario used these as an opportunity, first to stress that their experiences were commonplace and not their fault, and, second, that interlocking structural factors combined with individuals' intersecting social locations, made their situation more intractable. The Filipino migrants' movement is sometimes torn about how to advocate on behalf of Filipino nannies, nurses, and youth without resorting to stereotyping and reducing the issues faced by Filipinos in Canada to being only about the needs of these groups. Nevertheless, I have found that Gabriela-Ontario's intersectional approach links the situations of different types of migrants through its structural analysis, allowing for a productive way to ensure that different groups' *specific* needs are recognized alongside experiences of racism, sexism, and classism. Rather than only asserting that caregivers' abysmal situations result from bad employers or even from bad policies, Gabriela-Ontario links them back to institutions and structures that facilitate labor export, fragment migrant families, and entrench Global South countries into further poverty. These may not lead to easy conversations, because of the density of making these theoretical connections, but part of Gabriela-Ontario's work is to encourage deeper thinking.

Furthermore, through Gabriela-Ontario and its work with Migrante-Canada, which embodies an intersectional approach to activism (Tungohan 2016), its members' different social locations come to the fore depending on political context and activist strategy. Affirming Isoke's (2014, 354) observation that black women "organize from multiple and intersecting positions" and the volume editors' observation that some leaders of social movements invested in intersectionality pursue a "politicized identity strategy" (Introduction), Gabriela-Ontario and Migrante-Canada have been successful in framing key issues through specific lenses. When organizers with Gabriela-Ontario and Migrante-Canada speak at feminist events, such as during the International Women's Day march, they foreground how the issues facing Filipina migrant women have commonalities with the issues other women face, such as sexual violence, economic inequality, and political violence.

During the rally before the International Women's Day (IWD) march in March 2018, for instance, Gabriela-Ontario and Migrante-Canada shared their space with organizers from Kurdish women's organizations, with organizers from both groups addressing how political violence, as seen through land dispossession, is a women's issue. To bring further awareness of how women's issues globally are interlinked, organizers from Gabriela-Ontario, Migrante-Canada, and Anakbayan-Ontario ended their IWD 2018 presentation through a "one billion rising" (OBR) flash dance. During the dance, I distributed pamphlets to passersby and answered questions. I explained that OBR was a form of protest against gender violence, which in turn encouraged some to draw their own connections about how gender violence links different communities of women. After asking questions, they either kept watching or even participated in the dance themselves. By forming community through dance, OBR, which started in 2012, was a creative way to ensure that activism against gender violence becomes visible, and it was subsequently adopted by Gabriela chapter organizations to "link the struggle of women in the fight against global capitalist structures" (One Billion Rising 2018). When discussing Gabriela-Philippines's involvement with One Billion Rising, Gabriela-Philippines's Joms Salvador stressed that it is important to think about women's intersecting social locations. Salvador described "peasants, workers, indigenous people, migrants, youth, women human rights defenders" as working together to achieve their common goals of "ending the exploitation of women" (One Billion Rising 2018).

Gabriela-Ontario "acts politically" by engaging in multi-scalar forms of advocacy. The Gabriela-Ontario events I have attended and helped plan deliberately focus on both the situations of women in Canada (as seen through multiple events that are geared toward Filipina migrant domestic workers in Toronto) and in the Philippines (as seen through a picnic we organized in August 2017 with Gabriela-Philippines representatives to discuss the situations of how indigenous women—namely, the Lumad women—face violence under the present-day Duterte regime). They also organize transnationally (as seen through Gabriela-Ontario's participation in events such as the discussions on the creation of a Convention on Domestic Work in Geneva and in International League of People's Struggles events). In fact, its ongoing domestic and transnational work emphasizes the connections between the struggles facing women in the Global South and women in the more affluent Global North countries. Campaigns on behalf of Filipina migrant domestic workers, for instance, are tied to labor export programs in the Philippines, which in turn are described as having their roots in the structures of imperialism, feudalism, and bureaucratic capitalism. When Gabriela-Ontario organizes with grassroots migrants' networks such as the Migrant Workers Alliance for Change (MWAC), which shares its intersectional commitments, the focus is always on drawing these transnational connections and on the recognition that migrants themselves are settlers who need to work in solidarity with indigenous groups to ensure indigenous sovereignty. Building alliances with other social-justice organizations is thus crucial to its day-to-day work and to its normative goals. Their long-term vision rests on a belief in radical futurities that see the abolition of harmful structures, where alternatives to labor migration are established and where the harms caused by national borders are eliminated. Hence, Gabriela-Ontario and its allies embody the type of radical left intersectional revolution that Cohen (1997) discusses.

There were moments when I was organizing with Gabriela-Ontario that my intersecting social locations made me feel awkward. Being situated in academic spaces has allowed me to contribute to Gabriela-Ontario's work. For example, with a fellow academic, I co-taught research methods classes as part of a Gabriela-Ontario-led research project on the lives of migrant domestic workers after they transitioned out of the Live-in Caregiver Program (see GATES, 2014). There were moments when I was aware, however, that being an academic meant that I was insulated from some of the struggles other Gabriela-Ontario members faced. Unlike Gabriela-Ontario members who were domestic workers, I never had to experience onerous working conditions, nor did I have to live away from my children. In my organizing work with Gabriela-Ontario, I thus have tried to be self-reflexive to ensure that I did not attempt to take over the project with my own preferences.

I have become even more aware of my privileges relative to the group after Gabriela-Ontario members and I presented the results of our above-mentioned study to an audience of academics and government officials. Afterward, other academic members of Gabriela-Ontario and I were gently (and lovingly) called out by Tita Pet for uncritically presenting sensitive data that might have negative repercussions on the migrant domestic workers in our study. In this instance, I was reminded that "data" for me are "real-life" for migrant domestic workers. In this case, being an academic with Canadian citizenship led me to disregard the experiences of Filipina migrant domestic workers, some of whom were not Canadian citizens. While it was extremely difficult for me to hear what Gabriela-Ontario's founding member said—and thinking and writing about my actions right now makes me feel ashamed all over again—it was a crucial reminder of my privilege. Despite our common identities as Filipina women, working-class women with precarious migration status face experiences that I and my fellow academics are not able to relate to directly. Since then, I have been vigilant about ensuring that my organizing work remains rooted in the needs of the Filipina migrant women's community. Always making sure that the needs of the most "intersectionally disadvantaged" (Strolovitch 2007) members of our group are at the forefront of our advocacy work for me has become crucial.

Reformist Visions and Limited Intersectionality

My advocacy work with Gabriela-Ontario necessitates cooperating with other organizations within the Filipino migrants' movement. It is here that I have noticed the most tension. Because not all Filipinos share a commitment to intersectionality and consequently do not think about prioritizing the voices of the most "intersectionally-disadvantaged" within the community, questions emerge about who gets to speak for the Filipino community and whether and how advocates can give voice to the community's diverse needs. It is often difficult to overcome deeply entrenched divisions in terms of class, immigration status, gender, religion, region, and other intersecting social locations.

These tensions could best be observed when different organizations came together in 2014 to contest possible changes to Canadian immigration programs. During this time, members of the Filipino community across Canada were concerned about perceived targeting of Filipinos by the Conservative Party. Because of mainstream news reports that purportedly revealed how Canada's temporary foreign workers program led to Canadian workers being fired, there was a public backlash against all of Canada's temporary foreign worker programs, including the "low-skilled" Temporary Foreign Workers Program (TFWP) and in LCP. As a result, the Conservative government announced changes in both programs. The TFWP allowed workers from overseas to enter Canada on time-limited contracts, which many workers saw as an opportunity to later access Canadian citizenship by transferring to other immigration programs. It was also notorious for enabling debilitating working conditions because workers' immigration and employment status was tied to their employers (Polanco 2016). Similarly, the LCP also tied workers' immigration and employment status to their employers, thereby magnifying employers' power over their workers. It differed, however, from the TFWP in one important respect: after two years of live-in work, caregivers could then apply for Canadian citizenship for themselves and the families they left behind. In both cases, the carrot of potential citizenship—even though, as in the case of the TFWP, the odds of being able to transition to a permanent immigration program are slim—was enough to make the Filipino workers I met stay in abusive labor conditions. Because the majority of the workers in both the LCP and the TFWP were Filipino, there was the general feeling among the Filipino community in Canada that they were being scapegoated.

At the time that there was an outcry against temporary migrant labor in Canada, I was a postdoctoral fellow at the University of Alberta. I divided my time between Edmonton, Alberta, which had large numbers of Filipino temporary foreign workers because of the proximity of the city to the oil sands, and Toronto, Ontario, which had a large number of Filipina caregivers. Following news reports allegedly showing that Canadian workers were fired and replaced by temporary foreign workers, I noticed a visible rise in xenophobic attacks against temporary foreign workers generally and Filipino temporary foreign workers particularly. Many Filipinos felt under attack. Employment minister Jason Kenney's interview decrying Filipino families' alleged misuse of the LCP, which he claimed arose because Filipinos were hiring family members under the program, was, for many Filipinos, a form of racist dog-whistling that the Conservatives were using in order to garner electoral advantages. Even though hiring family members was allowed within the LCP, and was not as pervasive as Kenney claimed (GATES 2014), prevailing public sentiment was not receptive to nuance.

In response, Filipino migrants' movements in Edmonton and in Toronto strove to reverse negative stereotyping and to institute policy changes that would protect the interests of Filipino migrant workers. In Edmonton, Filipino migrants' organizations, led by Migrante-Alberta, attempted to form alliances with "progressive" groups such as labor unions, Filipino community organizations such as the University of the Philippines-Alberta alumni network, church groups, and even university-based organizations to push back against negative public sentiments toward the TFWP. I perceived that the older wave of Filipinos saw themselves as distinct from the later waves of Filipinos, since they had been in Edmonton for a longer time than the Filipino temporary foreign workers, who came primarily between the mid-2000s to the mid-2010s.

In their minds, they came to the country as *permanent* immigrants because of their "professional" qualifications. This sentiment persisted despite the fact that those entering the country under temporary labor migration programs did so with similar professional qualifications. It was the Canadian government that chose to prioritize temporary labor migration between the mid-2000s to the mid-2010s, leading to more temporary migrants entering than permanent immigrants. Eric's observations concerning the class gulf between different groups of Filipino immigrants in Hamilton, Ontario, resonates in this regard (2012). While some Filipino community organizations participated in disseminating a petition that called for the establishment of a Philippine consulate in Alberta, which would make it easier for Filipino temporary foreign workers to get consular assistance, they refused to participate in other more "radical" calls, such as discussions on the possible creation of sanctuary cities in Alberta.

This dynamic between those groups that embraced and those that opposed "respectability politics" was evident in Toronto from June to July 2014 during the Filipino migrants' movements' attempts to respond to the Conservative party's positions on caregivers. Convened by a Filipino "community leader" who was a pastor and the executive director of a settlement-services organization, meeting were held every week for a period of four weeks. Attending the meeting were different groups. At first glance, there was an attempt to build an intersectional coalition by involving various groups, each representing individuals from different socioeconomic demographics, religions, and immigration statuses. These more intersectionally oriented groups included members of Gabriela-Ontario (including myself) and other migrants' organizations that tried to apply intersectionality in their work. These more intersectionally oriented groups also shunned respectability politics or the belief that the only way for "marginalized classes [to] receive their share of political influence and social standing is . . . [if] they demonstrate their compatibility with the 'mainstream' or 'non-marginalized class' and shunned 'disruptive' actions, such as participating in protests" (Smith 2014). Other groups that attended included Filipino community leaders who, because of their professional accomplishments, were frequently asked to represent the community in political events. (Some of them had in fact run for public office.) Other attendees included members of church groups and other migrant domestic workers' organizations that adhered to a vision of respectability politics. Among the twenty individuals who gathered for these meetings, there were at most two women who were currently under the LCP. This was for me a stark contrast to Gabriela-Ontario meetings, where most of the members were current caregivers.

In these meetings, I was uneasy with the way men assumed positions of authority. In contrast to Gabriela-Ontario meetings and other social justice spaces that I had previously been part of, where women—and, in particular, migrant caregivers—took the lead, these meetings began with a prayer led by a male pastor. These prayers stressed gratitude to Canada for "opening its doors" to Filipino immigrants and praised the Filipino community for coming together. Rather than establishing common goals and agendas, those attending were asked to give comments on policy proposals on the caregiver program that were prewritten by three of the older community leaders, two of whom were lawyers and one of whom was a pastor. What struck me when reading these proposals was that they were used as starting points for the framework provided by the Conservative government, thereby echoing the discourses and policies being passed by populist far-right governments in countries such as Italy, the United Kingdom, and the United States, all of which decried the refugee "crisis." In these proposals, the importance of ensuring that migrant domestic workers are tied to specific employers was affirmed, an issue that Gabriela-Ontario and other migrant activist groups had fought against for years. Each of the proposals did advocate for shorter time periods of family separation for migrant caregivers and their families and endorsed the removal of the live-in requirement, which many migrant caregivers saw as trapping them into living *and* working for their employers. Nevertheless, the proposals fell short of what migrant caregiver groups sought, which is Canadian permanent residency on arrival.

More concerning for me was that they did not question Conservative government frameworks. I tried to diplomatically stress the importance of ensuring that migrant caregivers' perspectives were heeded since the policies in question, after all, affected them directly. I was silenced by others, however, who were upset that I might draw negative attention to the Filipino community by seeking policies that the Conservative government might deem unacceptable. In fact, in a heated email exchange, a group member stated that my proposals would "embarrass" the Filipino community because it would portray us as being "too demanding." Since the Conservative government sought to consult community members whom they identified as being allies on possible policy changes, it perhaps made sense, in retrospect, that some community members appeared to be reluctant to ask for "too much," lest their requests antagonize the Conservatives in power. The advocacy efforts by the Filipino migrants' movement in Toronto consisted of different groups of mostly Filipino community members with various intersecting social locations. Yet there was no recognition of the need to respond to the needs of the most intersectionally disadvantaged groups—in this case, the working-class Filipina women without Canadian citizenship—nor was there any desire or willingness to consider how to usher lasting social change. Rather, all of the substantive discussions concerned narrow policy changes.

To be clear, the Edmonton and Toronto coalitions led to short-term success. A Philippine consulate was established in the nearby city of Calgary.

In Toronto, the leaders of the group convening the meetings were invited to the Conservative government's consultations, with organizations that took a more critical stance, such as Gabriela-Ontario, and current caregivers left out. By being directly invited to provide feedback and suggest legal reforms, the Toronto migrant movement leaders ensured that their perspectives were dominant. While it is difficult to say whether their specific feedback was folded into the Caregiver Program, which replaced the Live-in Caregiver Program in 2014, that they were invited to the discussion meant the coalition succeeded in some measure.

After achieving these short-term gains, both coalitions fragmented.[2] There are drawbacks to prioritizing engagement within "state-regulated institutions and economic systems," which themselves foster "exploitation and violence" (Cohen 1997, 442). Without an underlying awareness of how institutions and structures themselves are flawed, the gains that were established primarily benefited those within the Filipino community with the most privilege. This is not to say that policy changes are unimportant but that an intersectional left analysis necessitates going *beyond* institutions and thinking about how to truly ensure social justice for all oppressed groups. As Cohen (1997, 443) argues, "Strategies built upon the possibility of incorporation and assimilation are exposed as simply expanding and making the status quo accessible for more privileged members of marginalized groups while the most vulnerable in our communities continue to be oppressed and stigmatized." For the Edmonton coalition, while the opening of a Philippine consulate in Alberta was undoubtedly helpful for temporary foreign workers who seek consular support, the fact that Filipino temporary foreign workers continue to face labor and immigration precariousness means that their everyday conditions have remained the same. In fact, the absence of any robust policies calling for sanctuaries for temporary foreign workers has meant that many have either become undocumented or have been deported (Lye 2015). For the Toronto coalition, although getting invited to decision-making meetings means that Filipino migrant communities are being consulted, the resulting Caregiver Program actually makes it harder for caregivers to acquire Canadian citizenship, in turn making the caregivers themselves more vulnerable.

CONCLUSION

Using Spade's, Cohen's, and Townsend-Bell's frameworks, it is clear that while the movement as a whole includes members with intersecting social locations, different organizations are divided on whether they subscribe to a more radical, left vision of intersectionality, as per Cohen's (1997) vision, or whether they adhere to more a reformist vision. In my engagements with the

Filipino migrants' movement, witnessing variations in advocacy strategies and normative inclinations was illuminating. It became clear that the question of who should speak for the group and whose voices should be the most dominant are contentious. Using an intersectional autoethnographic approach also highlights how there were instances when my positionality as a middle-class academic made me unaware of the precariousness facing Filipina caregivers and other instances when my positionality as a young, female community member made it hard to be heard.

There are other questions that emerge when assessing the Filipino migrants' movement's adherence to intersectionality. How can and how does the Filipino migrants' movement engage in the struggles of other social justice movements, such as the BlackLivesMatter (BLM) movement, the indigenous movement, and other migrants' movements? From my observations, it can be hard to organize Filipino community members who see their issues as needing more attention than issues facing other communities. Some key members of the Filipino migrants' movement have certainly worked in solidarity with other groups—with some Filipino activists supporting and promoting the work of BLM Toronto and marching in February 2017's "March Against Islamophobia," which was organized in Toronto after the mosque shootings in Quebec City and US President Donald Trump's "ban" against Muslim immigration.

Nevertheless, I cannot help but ask what a social movement consisting of robust and lasting alliances would look like. Cole (2008, 447) discusses how intersectionality can be a tool for the creation of alliances and includes a statement from an activist who argues that "the moment of intersection is really the moment of building a broader movement." Although it is true that the nature of social movement organizing is such that many alliances are temporary, is there a way for the Filipino migrants' movement to meet other movements and help build a broad, *long-term* alliance that links different social justice concerns together? Or is equating movement success with the ability of the Filipino migrants' movement to form broad, long-term alliances a limited perspective? Perhaps a more realistic approach is to see these short-term alliances as evidence that the Filipino migrants' movement can actually adapt to pressing political needs by mobilizing quickly in support of various concerns.

That said, while activists, including myself, have tried to think about how settler colonialism manifests itself transnationally—with my own advocacy taking pains to emphasize the transnational commonalities in how, for example, Canadian mining companies' ventures in indigenous land in the Philippines are push factors compelling Indigenous women to seek opportunities as migrant workers abroad, which in turn lead to further indigenous dispossession in places like Canada—it is a challenge to think more comprehensively about how settler colonialism interacts and reinforces anti-black racism and Islamophobia (to name just two examples of oppressions). Attempting to build a migrants' movement that works in solidarity with other oppressed groups and that sees the "interdependency among multiple systems of domination" (Cohen 1997, 442) remains an important goal.

NOTES

1. I deliberately use the term "Filipino" rather than "Filipinx," which many US-based activists have used to signal gender fluidity within the community and to disavow the purportedly masculinist implications of the term "Filipino." Because the mainstream Filipino migrants' movement in Canada has yet to truly engage with queerness in their activism—a critique that Diaz (2018) makes—using the term "Filipinx" to characterize the Filipino migrants' movement in Canada may mistakenly give the impression that homophobia, heterosexism, and transphobia do not exist within the movement.

2. The "progressive" groups that were part of the Toronto coalition convened their own meetings and organized a rally without inviting the Conservative groups. I, along with other activists, spoke during this rally.

Chapter 12

Sistas Doing It for Themselves

Black Women's Activism and #BlackLivesMatter in the United States and France

Jean Beaman and Nadia E. Brown

In *Their Eyes Were Watching God*, Zora Neale Hurston (1937) asserts that "black women are the mules of the world." This quote speaks to the significant challenges that women of African descent have faced because of racism, sexism, colonialism, and imperialism. Black women are strong, unprotected, and often used without regard to their own well-being. Michelle Wallace (1979) echoes the mule metaphor in her writing on the myth of the "superwoman" and marginalization of black women even within black social movements. Yet, black women's unique subject position at the intersection of multiple marginalities does not impede their political and social activism; rather, it enhances it. Wendy Smooth (2009) discusses the "participation paradox" in regard to black women's high electoral participation in the United States despite a societal positioning that predicts the opposite in traditional models of political behavior. In the context of social movements, black women's precarious social location has often led to their marginalization, but it has also contributed to them developing a particular intersectional consciousness that they exercise in their mobilization within and across social movements, as they passionately speak truth to power. In this chapter, we examine how black women across the globe are using this consciousness and voice to combat race-based, state-sponsored violence.

Since its inception, BlackLivesMatter, as well as its hashtag #BlackLivesMatter, has created a space for black communities to address state-sponsored violence.[1] While there is some disagreement as to the origins of the hashtag, many credit BlackLivesMatter as a social movement that was started by three black women,[2] two of whom are queer, following the acquittal of neighborhood watchman George Zimmerman for the murder in 2012 of Trayvon Martin, an unarmed seventeen-year-old African American. As the movement spread, black women have been on the forefront of leading BlackLivesMatter[3] as both an activist and organizing space and as an online community for dissemination of information. Intersectional inclusion has been a key component of this mobilization. We argue that this is consistent with the role that black women have played as "the mules of the earth," often doing the hard work that others (including black men and white women) seem less willing to do or may not even see as necessary. Black women as activists and politicians— often without thanks or acknowledgement—hold together and fight on behalf of communities that have been traumatized by state-sponsored violence.

In this chapter, we examine how black women have used their location at the intersection of multiple marginalities to mobilize against state-sponsored violence in the context of BlackLivesMatter, both within and outside of the United States. We argue that black women activists and candidates for public office draw on their race and gender identities as a primary means of connecting with their communities, advocating for social justice, and articulating why they are working to advance the movement for black lives. It is black women's identities and experiences that motivate their advocacy and activism against state-sponsored violence; it is central to how they enact intersectionality: finding voice, forming alliances, building capacity, and acting politically. The common connections of culture, history, and socialization serve to unite black women in a particular and unique way (Brown 2014). Strong perceptions of linked fate—the recognition that one's individual life chances are intimately connected to one's race as a whole (Dawson 1994)—and black feminist consciousness—the recognition that black women are marginalized because of their race and gender (Simien 2004)—contribute to black women understanding the world in unique ways (Collins 1990) and shape their political behavior. Conceptualizing women's statuses and actions within black communities calls for particular attention to the processes and conditions by which these aspects of their identities are primed (Brown 2014).

Viewing black women's politics and their responses to state-sponsored violence as either "gender politics" or "race politics" obscures the lived realities and material spaces that black women occupy. By examining black women as political actors and using their experiences as the key unit of analysis, we highlight the "messiness" and the "paradoxical" nature of black women's politics (Smooth 2006, 2009). We show how black women's intersectional identities are simultaneous sites of oppression and opportunity. These identities reflect social stratification that demonstrates how power relations operate among and within groups (Baca Zinn and Dill Thornton 1996). Taking black women's identities as the starting point for our analysis requires a sharp departure from traditional, hegemonic practices of social movement research that prioritize a monolithic identity or prioritize one salient identity over others (see Htun and Weldon 2018). Instead, we seek to elucidate how black women themselves, as agents of change and capable political actors, impact the systems and social structures that seek to oppress and marginalize them at every turn.

Using qualitative and comparative data, we take a transnational look at black women's activism asserting that the boundaries of black political and social activism are not nation-state based. Instead, because of the salience of race and anti-blackness, racism and colonialism are two sides of the same coin. We use the cases of black-identified women in Paris, France, and its *banlieue*s and in Ferguson, Missouri (USA), to demonstrate the unique role that black women play in advocating for black victims of state-sponsored violence. The women in our sample bring a powerful testimony to the role of social location—namely, gender, race, immigrant status, and socioeconomic status—to understanding how their identities are useful in advocating for their communities after experiences with state-sponsored violence. We draw connections between these two cases to show the interconnectedness of black women's identities as mothers, caregivers, and nurturers, which in turn shape their relationship to movement activism, community leadership, and politics.

In this chapter, we start with a brief discussion of black feminism, placing our contemporary analysis in historical context. We argue that it is necessary to foreground the historical experiences of black women in order to understand what motivates and shapes their intersectional politics and activism. Next, we provide illustrative examples of black women mobilizing against police violence against racial and ethnic minorities in both France and the United States, which we then use as a framework for understanding black women's positionality and activism in both contexts. We focused on the case of the death of Michael Brown (an unarmed eighteen-year-old African American fatally shot by a police officer) and the subsequent protests in Ferguson, Missouri, as a way to understand these dynamics and focused on its resonance in the greater St. Louis metropolitan area and in France. We selected these two sites for our study based on our individual research backgrounds (Brown had previously conducted research on race in the St. Louis area and Beaman had previously conducted research on race in France). Despite the very different political contexts, we see important commonalities as well as connections between these two cases.

The data presented in this chapter are drawn from a larger qualitative and comparative study, "BlackLivesMatter: Racial Tension and Police Violence in the Midwest and Beyond," which was funded by the Mellon Foundation's Humanities without Walls Global Midwest Initiative from 2016 to 2018. In this study, we conducted interviews with black women activists who are political elites, and the wider public to better understand the salience of blackness (and black feminist activism) in both the United States and France. We bring together our different disciplinary backgrounds—sociology, political science, and African American studies—to better understand the relationship between race, racism, state-sponsored violence, and race-gendered grassroots politics in the context of BlackLivesMatter. The larger study included traditional and social media content analysis, semi-structured interviews with black lawmakers in the St. Louis metropolitan area and with black activists in the Parisian metropolitan area, as well as participant observation in both sites. In this chapter, we draw primarily from interview data with black women lawmakers and activists. The intent is not to provide a thorough or systematic analysis of the movements but rather to explore the role that an intersectional black feminist identity has played in shaping the behavior of black women across time and space.

BLACKLIVESMATTER, BLACK FEMINISM, AND CENTERING BLACK WOMEN

Black feminist scholar and educator Anna Julia Cooper wrote in 1892 [in a *Voice from the South: By a Woman from the South*], "Only the Black woman can say 'when and where I enter, in the quiet undisputed dignity of my womanhood, without violence and without suing or special patronage, then and there the whole Negro race enters with me." This reference to women as the underpinning of black social activism and political life extends into the present moment, demonstrating the long and deep roots that inform black women's intersectional identity and activism. As both a social media hashtag and a broader social movement, BlackLivesMatter (BLM), in which black feminist leadership is central, is a critical and crucial intervention against state-sponsored violence toward black populations. It is a contemporary manifestation of what Cooper so eloquently articulated. BLM activist Alicia Garza, echoes this sentiment of creating entry points in her explanation of the movement, "We really felt like there needed to be a space that people could relate to that didn't blame Black people for conditions we didn't create."[4]

A key component to this activism, from the anti-lynching work of Ida B. Wells starting in the late 1800s to the present moment, has been the basic assertion of black humanity by black women. In August 2014, following eighteen-year-old Michael Brown's murder by white police officer Darren Wilson in Ferguson, Missouri, his mother Lesley McSpadden cried in front of television cameras. "You know how hard it was for me to get him to stay in school and graduate? You know how many Black men graduate? Not many." These words simultaneously draw attention to the value of black life as well as the challenges posed by state neglect and violence. Here, the role of mother, something that is race-gendered in this particular context, is particularly powerful. She is articulating the vital work of black women in trying to raise and protect their children in hostile environments and the grief experienced when they are unable to do so.

"When and where I enter" might also represent the challenge of locating black women's activism. Journalist and poet Alice Dunbar-Nelson, chronicling black women's contributions during World War I, wrote that "the problem of the woman of the Negro race is a peculiar one. Was she to do her work independently of the women of the other race, or was she to merge herself into their organizations?" (Rief 2004, 209). Black women's struggles with race- or gender-specific politics were evident as early as 1793 and 1809, when black women founded their own societies to provide care for each other and the community because white women's organizations excluded them or black organizations refused to let women vote or hold office (Scott 1990). It is necessary to disentangle homogenous analytical categories of race or gender to note that black women experience these categories in mutually constitutive parts. This recognition is paramount. Using a framework only through race or gender often renders black women invisible, which is why black women have often had to carve out their own spaces for resisting oppression. They have done this at the margins of or in the spaces between anti-racism and feminist movements.

Race-only and gender-only approaches are a particular form of violence that excludes black women's voices from the discussion of power and politics. Whether out of neglect or deliberate omission, it is a form of silencing when others do not pay attention to their specific cries for justice and equality. Just as in the epigraph of this chapter, Huston's protagonist, Janie, has a voice but her needs are seen as marginal to others. So too are the black women's struggles to be more than bearers of burdens. Centering black women's voices, moving from margin to the center (hooks 1984) requires and is part of a radical awareness that race- and gender- based experiences influence black women's understanding of the world. Furthermore, hooks argues that this positionality gives black women a particular perspective that enables them to criticize the "dominant racist, classist, sexist hegemony as well as to envision and create a counter-hegemony" (1984, 16). Therefore, black women's subject positions and vantage points allow them to speak truth to power by uniquely articulating the operation of power in a society. At its essence, BlackLivesMatter is a political project that uses the lens of location to challenge unjust and violent state institutions. It demonstrates that black women play a vital role as political agents, not as supporting actors behind the scenes or "the mules" of social movement but central and inimitable actors in efforts to disrupt systematic oppression.

In this project, we choose to center the voices and experiences of black women activists and those seeking elected office, as a deliberate means of calling attention to and resisting the disenfranchising of black women that has occurred within intersectionality studies (both as research subjects and scholars) (see also Mügge et al. 2018). As intersectionality has become more mainstream and theoretical, it has moved away from the black feminist standpoint tradition of highlighting experiences. Nikol Alexander-Floyd (2018) aptly demonstrates that relative inattention is given to black women within academic journals. She argues that in political science, black gender politics is nearly absent and calls for scholars to better incorporate a black feminist lens that resists the hegemonic gaze of viewing black women solely as a problem or the causes of their oppression. Julia Jordan-Zachary (2007, 257) argues for the use of narrative as a means of addressing the impact of intersectionality on the lives and work of black women not only in relation to the dominant society but also in relation to their own community. Women of color developed intersectionality as a concept to examine and document their own experiences with oppression, privilege, marginalization, and political agency, and it is imperative that scholars continue to center the voices of black women in our scholarly understandings of power.

We approach our study by centering black women as subjects and views politics from that vantage point. This black feminist perspective is similar to how canonical texts in black politics (Prestage 1991; Walters 2003) have centered social justice as a part and parcel of doing black political science and in which black women are centered as political actors. This type of research is concerned with black women's political strivings (Alexander-Floyd 2012). Making a place for black women as political actors within academic scholarship challenges the marginality of their experiences, voices, and ways of knowing the world. Drawing from sociologist Patricia Hill Collins, this type of framing highlights black women's struggles against domination and as central to understanding the operation of power and politics.

As political actors, black women challenge the structures that seek to erase them—both inside the academy and within the context of BlackLivesMatter. This is a decolonial project that addresses how we understand the production of knowledge and black women's political activism. Our goal is to make black women's voices in politics visible. Others have done this by challenging the prevailing paradigms—such as intersectionality approaches that often borrow from black women's experiences but do not always center their voices (Alexander-Floyd 2012)—to explore the liberatory nature of black feminist scholarship. In this chapter, we use post-positivist methods coupled with black feminist theoretical frameworks to demonstrate the value of examining black women's voices and actions to better understand how identity shapes their advocacy and activism against state-sponsored violence.

THE CASES: FERGUSON AND FRANCE

Located over 4,000 miles apart, Ferguson (a suburb of St. Louis, Missouri) and the arrondissements and *banlieues* of the Paris metropolitan region[5] covered in this chapter are in many ways distinct and different sociopolitical communities. Both, however, are characterized by segregated and stigmatized concentrations of racial and ethnic minorities who have been subjected to hyper-surveillance by the state. Furthermore, and of particular relevance to this study, both have had high-profile incidents of unrest after state-sponsored killings of black men. In this section, we first provide background information to orient the reader, identifying what makes Ferguson and France similar and different in order to contextualize our analysis of black women activism. Understanding the conditions in which the women were mobilized is the necessary first step in examining how their participation is transforming contemporary politics.

In terms of differences between the two contexts, Ferguson and the Parisian metropolitan region are characterized by different state-level ideologies regarding race and ethnicity. The United States operates under a multicultural model of identity politics and recognizes race and ethnicity as state-level categories. France does not. It applies an assimilationist model of identity politics in which everyone is seen as either French or not. French Republicanism dictates that individuals relate to the state as individuals and not members of identity-based groups or communities. As such, race and ethnicity are not acknowledged or measured as categories. This has different implications for, among other things, addressing racism and racial discrimination as well as mobilizing against race-related social problems such as police violence. In France, it is practically impossible to reference racism in any official capacity. The United States has a longer history of civil rights struggles and struggles for black liberation, more generally, than does France. Related, to this history, black political representation is stronger in the United States, where there are more black elected leaders than in France.

Ferguson is a majority black city in North St. Louis County, Missouri. White residents are 29 percent of the population. In contrast, the state of Missouri is 83 percent white and 11 percent black. According to the most recent census data,[6] the city is economically marginalized compared with other areas in Missouri. The median household income in 2016 was $42,571, which is nearly $10,000 below the rest of the state. The estimated house value in the city is $60,000 less than the median value of Missouri. Furthermore, 21 percent of the residents in this community live below the poverty line, which is more than 1.5 times the rate in the St. Louis metropolitan area. The average Ferguson resident earns two-thirds less than the average resident in the area at nearly $21,000 a year. However, the educational attainment rate for Ferguson residents is nearly identical to others in Missouri at a rate of 88 percent who have a high school degree or higher. At the time of Michael Brown's murder in August of 2014, the Ferguson police force employed fifty-three officers—fifty of whom were white. The police force for an overwhelmingly black community was 94 percent white and just 5.6 percent black. The lack of racial diversity among the police force is standard in U.S. The 2007 Department of Justice survey of local police departments identified the national average as 75 percent white.[7] At the time of Michael Brown's murder, the Ferguson city council was majority white, and today the council has a slight black majority.

Because France does not collect data on race and ethnicity, it is hard to make direct demographic and statistical comparisons across the two localities. Yet, the fact that the state does not officially recognize race as a relevant construct does not mean that its manifestations do not exist. "The outskirts of Paris are not-and perhaps have never been-neutral spaces" (Misra 2017). The term *banlieue*, although simply a French term for "suburb," has come to be understood in relation to the disenfranchised communities residing in particular areas of Paris. These residents are often working-class, immigrant-origin individuals of North African and sub-Saharan African descent. Ongoing and unaddressed racism contributes to disproportionately high levels of unemployment and poverty. Like Ferguson, many of these *banlieue* communities have been subject to hyper-surveillance. In contrast to the United States, however, police brutality and state-sponsored violence have not received as much attention in France as in the United States. Yet, it is a growing social problem. Disproportionate violence against populations racialized as black, whether they be North African or sub-Saharan African origin or Caribbean origin, is particularly challenging to confront in France due to the limitations of the Republican model (Beaman 2017). Scholars, including Didier Fassin (2013), have illustrated how the police acts as an agent of the state to maintain racial boundaries in a society where racial and ethnic categorization is not legitimated by the state. Because France does not collect ethnic and racial statistics, no official figures exist on the numbers of deaths of individuals at the hands of the police, but several estimates suggest about ten to fifteen deaths per year since the early 1980s.[8] While that number perhaps pales in comparison with US figures or estimates, activism in France regarding state-sponsored violence has increased in recent years, particularly in light of major incidents that have received increased media attention.

The different political contexts shape the political opportunity structures for the activism of black women. In Ferguson, Missouri, black women have been able to act both within and outside of the state. black women as elected officials or candidates for political office have mobilized as an important part and voice of the BlackLivesMatter movement. In France, this is less of an option for black women, who instead have had to mobilize outside of the French state. Our interviewees represent these differently positioned actors, one group as a part of the formal political leadership while the other as actors pushing from outside formal politics to enact political change. Despite these differences (along with the larger geopolitical ones), all the women with whom we spoke draw distinct connections to their race and gender to articulate how and why state-sponsored violence is detrimental to their communities. Although they use different tactics as well as vantage points and have different access to political power, they use their voices *as Black women* to challenge systems that oppress their families and communities after incidents of state-sponsored violence.

Black Women and BlackLivesMatter in Ferguson

On August 9, 2014, Michael Brown, Jr., an eighteen-year-old African American man, was fatally shot by a police officer in Ferguson, Missouri. The officer reported that the shooting was an act of self-defense that occurred when Brown stopped and charged him after a brief pursuit. Other witnesses argue that Brown had had his hands up in surrender, pleading to the officer, "Don't shoot." The event instigated protests (both peaceful and confrontational) in Ferguson. The police responded with riot squads, tear gas, rubber bullets, and curfews.

Black women mobilized in multiple ways in response to the shooting, choosing different sites to act politically. While some were a part of the street and online activism, others engaged more directly with the political system. Regardless of the location of their activism, their behavior was shaped by their identities as black women. In this section, we center the voices of women who chose elected office as a site for their activism.

Ferguson Councilwoman LaVerne Mitchum spoke of her experiences and efforts as a newly appointed representative. Councilwoman Mitchum shared that she saw how being a black woman aided her understanding of how to heal her community in the aftermath of #BlackLivesMatter activism surrounding Michael Brown's murder. She noted,

> So, we had citizens, and many of them were elderly, some of them were not, who were saying they didn't feel comfortable coming to their own council meeting. Now, as an African American—as a woman—the way that affected me and my thinking was Black people have gone through that for so long, you know, not being able to speak, being shut down. And see for me, Nadia, I don't want to see any human being mistreated, none. Now, I am very frank in terms of what Black people historically have gone through in this country and still go through. So I will let my White neighbors or my White friends, I will let them know.[9]

Because of the BlackLivesMatter protests at the Ferguson City Council meetings, many of the city's long-term residents felt uncomfortable attending meetings. Some of these residents were elderly, while other white residents voiced that they were unaware of racial biases in their community. As a resident of Ferguson for over twenty-five years, Councilwoman Mitchum understood the frustrations of her counterparts but fundamentally disagreed with their assertion that racism was not prevalent in their community. Instead, she used her influence to create a code of conduct for council meetings so that protestors and residents could respectfully engage with the council members and one another to voice their concerns. She credits this skill to her social positionality as a woman. Indeed, literature notes that women politicians are more adapt at listening, bringing more deliberations into legislative settings and building consensus (Kennedy 2003; Rosenthal 1998; Swers 2002).

> So, we had to come up with that [code of] conduct and, see, as a woman and as a city official—I think with women, with most of us, there's that sensitivity of anybody being mistreated. You know, it's something we have in us, that we're very sensitive, it may not be our child, or it may not be our friend, but if we see somebody being mistreated or done wrong, most women, I think it is something within us, we are highly sensitive to it. [That's] one of the reasons I was appointed.

Here Mitchem exercises the empathy that Yuval-Davis (2006) describes as a vital part of transversal politics. She simultaneously acknowledges aspects of her social location that set her apart from some of her neighbors while also still drawing on commonalities by recognizing them as a part of her community.

Cori Bush decided to run for office based on her experiences with the events of Ferguson. At the time of our 2017 interview, Bush was seeking election to the US House to represent the 1st Congressional District of Missouri.[10] Bush remembers personally witnessing the absence of black political leaders in Ferguson during the days immediately following Michael Brown's murder. She was appalled that Congressmen Lacy Clay did not meet with protestors in Ferguson until nearly a week into the civil unrest. Spending day after day on the frontlines on West Florissant Avenue, Bush noticed that not only were black political leaders missing from the protests but it was mostly black women who were activists in the movement for BlackLives. As a result, she decided to run for office noting that it is black women that are "already doing the work."

Then-candidate Bush was using her voice as a black woman to bring a sense of commonality, decency, and openness to public dialogue around BlackLivesMatter issues. She ran in a district that was overwhelmingly white; however, she took her comprehensive message for BlackLivesMatter with her as the focus of her proposed legislative agenda. Cori Bush framed her work as radical and seeking to normalize blackness. Furthermore, she wanted to help whites find political common ground. In this way, Bush appealed to the humanity in potential voters. At the heart of her plea is the call for recognition that BlackLivesMatter.

> We [she and her campaign volunteers] go into a rural town and, you know, we'll go into a room full of all White people. Rural, older, sometimes we are in Trump's America. But because I know my mission—and I'm very, very clear on my mission—it's okay with me going into those places. Because I gotta take—I gotta normalize Blackness, you know. I have to normalize Blackness in those places, so I go to those places because what they say to me doesn't really bother me, you know. Because I understand the place. I understand that somebody has to go in and speak that truth. And help them to understand that this is okay, you know, it's okay and it's okay that this is what it is. It's not white-washed, you know. I'm not trying to assimilate into any other group. I'm not trying to be anyone else, I'm being Cori that grew up in St. Louis and, you know, went to an all-black high school. And that's who I am and that should not scare you, you know. And then I go in and tell them about real issues that Black people face. And if they are able to see "Oh wait a minute, we face those issues so maybe were not so different," so yeah.

Bush's activism is informed by her positionality, a location she acknowledges and does not lose sight of, while at the same time, like Mitchem, she is trying to reach out and build broader understandings in other communities.

Ferguson councilwoman Ella Jones discussed the differences that black women elected officials bring to their communities in the wake of Black-LivesMatter activism, in a manner that seemed to reflect sentiments we heard from a majority of women in our larger sample. She spoke of how black female legislators turn their precarious social positioning into agency. For example, she lamented "being an African American woman, you have to do more than your counterpart. . . . When you are privileged, you feel like people are going to automatically follow you." For councilwoman Jones, this means that black women politicians "don't have a proven ground. Yeah, Black women have to prove everything." She noted that this stereotype never hurt her. Indeed, it has helped her advocate for people and to lead individuals. She said, "I've been called 'bossy' all my whole life, but it's okay." Similarly, literature on black women in politics demonstrates that voters appreciate this quality in black women as they are seen as strong and dynamic leaders (Hicks 2017; Livingston et al. 2003).

Directly speaking to her role as a Ferguson City councilwoman, Jones articulated the importance of having her particular skillset in the age of BlackLivesMatter. She urged residents and protestors to find a common ground, to keep pressure on elected officials, and to envision a community where justice and equity were foundational pillars.

> So, I had to go out there and still remind them that if we don't unite, the changes that you protest for will not come to the front because you can't just protest and go home. It is something you have to consistently do, you have to consistently bring it forward, you have to consistently bring it in front of the establishment and let them know that you're not going anywhere.[11]

These three women chose to advocate for their communities through political office. But even from this "inside" location, they engaged in activism that was shaped by their location as black women, doing the same type of work from a different vantage point. All three reference the responsibility they feel as black women to act on behalf of the racial communities to which they belong; yet, they do so by engaging transversally with the local white communities and community members. These women's voices demonstrate what other research has shown about how the race and gender of black women political elites change the nature of the political climate (Brown 2014). The difference that this group brings to political discourse is directly related to their own understanding of identity politics and social location. Furthermore, this desire to agitate is based on an articulation of inherently black feminist principles.

Black Women and BlackLivesMatter in France

On July 19, 2016, on his birthday, Adama Traoré, a twenty-four-year-old black construction worker, died under unusual circumstances after being arrested in the *banlieue* of Beaumont-sur-Oise, north of Paris. Adama was arrested for interfering in the arrest of his brother. The police first claimed that he had died of a heart attack and then later that he had a severe infection. His family asked for another autopsy asserting that Adama had no chronic health conditions prior to his death. Since his death, which one media account termed "France's Ferguson,"[12] there have been numerous demonstrations and uprisings demanding justice for Adama Traoré, including one demonstration outside of the local police station, which was met with tear gas from the police.[13] The week after Traoré's death, protesters gathered in the center of Paris and chanted "Black Lives Matter" in English and the hashtag #BLM-France went viral on Twitter.[14]

Leading the movement for justice for Adama is his older sister Assa Traoré, a thirty-two-year-old mother of three children and daughter of Malian immigrants. Assa and her family are alleging lack of assistance and willful neglect by the police as both contributing to his death and the failure to fully investigate his death. Assa grew up with her seventeen brothers and sisters in Beaumont-sur-Oise. Before Adama's death, she was working as a "educatrice" (or a teacher's assistant) in Sarcelles, a *banlieue* north of Paris. Assa co-wrote a book, *Lettre à Adama* [Letter to Adama], the funds of which she used to seek justice for her brother, including paying legal fees for four of her other brothers who have been in jail for various periods since Adama's death. Their incarceration has been interpreted by some as retaliation against this fight for justice for Adama's death; Assa has said publicly that she feels her family has been under attack ever since they contested the official explanation for Adama's death.

In less than two years, Assa has become an activist, one of the main people on the forefront of the movement against police violence and brutality in France. She has formed a collective, Justice pour Adama, which is also a hashtag. Assa regularly gives talks about police violence and her brother's death not just in France but also all over the world and has received support from various celebrities, including French rapper Mokobé, French feminist activist and political scientist Françoise Vergès, and activist Angela Davis. She sees her cause as not only about justice for her brother but for all marginalized populations in France, including other black and North African-origin individuals and residents of *quartiers populaires*, or working-class neighborhoods, who know the police only as an invading force. Assa supports other family members of victims of state-sponsored violence. She regularly leads demonstrations for justice for other victims of police violence throughout France, often under the banner "Sans justice, vous n'aurez jamais la paix" [No justice, no peace] and wearing a T-shirt stating "Justice pour Adama."

It is important to note, however, that this is not the first significant case of police brutality that has led to mobilization in France. In 2005, uprisings broke out in response to two teenagers of African descent who were electrocuted to death when fleeing police. The 2007 death of Lamine Dieng is also of important note, not only in regard to its occurrence but also the parallels in activism led by his older sister. Lamine Dieng, a twenty-five-year-old of Senegalese origin, died in the twentieth *arrondissement* on June 17, 2007. Following a struggle with multiple police officers, during which he was restrained face down on the street with his hands behind his back and his feet strapped together, Lamine was taken to a police van and transported to the police station. By the time he arrived, he was no longer breathing. The medical report stated that he died of asphyxiation, but Lamine's family and friends want a full investigation and punishment for the officers involved.[15]

Following her brother's death, Ramata Dieng, his older sister, started a collective, Vies Violées [or Stolen Lives], as a way to mobilize against state-sponsored violence and demand justice for its victims.[16] Through this collective, she and other activists align with friends and family members of other victims of police violence and also hold yearly demonstrations and commemorations each June on the anniversary of Lamine's death. During this commemorative march each June, Ramata recounts the events leading up to Lamine's death as well as allows family members and friends of other victims of police violence to recount those incidents.[17]

Ramata, who is forty-five years old, was not always an activist. But she has said that she felt compelled to act because Lamine was more than just her younger brother. She practically raised him as her parents worked multiple jobs as they grew up. In one media interview, she explained that being a woman in this struggle is an asset because women are not subjected as much to the daily, that is, patdowns and identity checks, by the police as are men. Rather, she understands the hyper-surveillance and police violence affecting her community more through the experiences of her brothers and the other men in her community. For her, Lamine could be anyone's brother, son, or cousin in her community.

Ramata explains that "police violence in France, really, is a racial question; it is racism of the state, because when you look at the list of victims, you see that essentially, more than 90 percent are blacks and Arabs. The remaining 10 percent are activists or militants, Roma, and what we say in quotation marks, as accidents. Whites [only die] by accident. Because they are not targeted, they are not the profile. There is a kind of profile for police violence, and the profile of victims is always the same profile: it's always young black men, between 20 and 40 years old, and . . . Maghrébins [North Africans] as well, between 20 and 40 years old."[18] This quote illustrates how state-sponsored violence is understood in relation to race and racism in France, even though the French Republican ideology disavows race and racism as salient factors in everyday life. Ramata is also inspired by activism against state-sponsored violence in the United States, namely as it relates to the BlackLivesMatter movement. In one conversation she explained to me, "Ferguson, Paris, it's the same thing."[19] While she is not always certain how to apply BLM to France because of the difference in identity politics between the two societies, she closely follows the high-profile incidents of police killings in the United States, including Tamir Rice and Michael Brown.

Both Ramata and Assa lead commemorative demonstrations each year on the anniversary of their brothers' deaths and they each attend and speak at each other's demonstrations. It is telling that despite the preponderance of men as victims of state-sponsored violence, it is women—as sisters, mothers, and so forth—who are doing much of the mobilization against this issue, rather than their brothers or uncles or fathers. As in Ferguson, black women activists navigate how to respond to police violence that disproportionately targets particular racial and ethnic minority populations in a context that does not acknowledge the relationship between state-sponsored violence and racism. They do so by locating the specificity of their identities as both black and women. Ramata feels that as a woman she is less likely to be the direct target of violence by police, yet this violence still impacts her because of her status as a racial and ethnic minority. Both Assa and Ramata are supported by men in their families and communities, but it is they who are on the forefront. This is a pattern that we see reflected not only in Ferguson but much more broadly. The activism of black women is not only motivated by their particular positionality, but it is also shaped by it. Gender is just as present as, and is inextricably intertwined with, racial identity, and both shape the possibilities and modes of mobilization.

CONCLUSION

We argue that we cannot understand BlackLivesMatter, and activism against state-sponsored violence more generally, outside of a black feminist and intersectional framework. We contend that black women's political behavior—in both formal and informal politics, in the United States and in France—is informed by connectedness to their identity as black women, which motivates them to represent the interests of black communities and shapes the way they do this. Theorizing from black women's experiences gives us the analytical tools to make connections between black women's identities and their roles in BlackLivesMatter advocacy and activism against state-sponsored violence. We have illustrated here how black women's social location is implicated across societal context. It matters that these are black women, not just for how they frame state-sponsored violence as a social problem but also for how they frame their roles in activism against it. Black women are experts and work from the expertise of their social locations to make this violence visible and to seek justice for its victims. Ignoring the activism of black women means misunderstanding their relationship to both formal and informal politics. Their activism "looks" different and comes from their unique social locations. The examples of women here draw upon their experience as black women to frame how activism and political priorities are intersectional.

These black women make a direct connection between their identity and achieving their goals of ending state-sponsored violence in black communities. Across cultures, nationalities and nation-state boundaries, these women demonstrate that drawing on black women's experiences and narrative are useful tools to address anti-black social and political agendas. The black women elected officials in Missouri, unlike the activist women in the France examples, may see running for office as a logical next step in their role as community organizers and politically active citizens. While the Ferguson women in our sample repeatedly noted that they are accountable to all city residents, they sought elected office out of their desires to help the community heal from state-sponsored violence. After the killing of Michael Brown, the subsequent uprisings, and the grand jury decision not to indict Officer Darren Wilson, the women placed a special emphasis on representing black constituents. For the Missourian women in this study, running for office was a particular strategy they pursued to change the pervasiveness of state-sponsored violence in their communities. Other black women, not included in this study, chose other means to engage with the social, political, and economic problems that Michael Brown's death made painfully apparent. In sum, the BlackLivesMatter movement has made room for black women in the United States to participate in formal and informal politics.

The women in France may never seek elected office. Their orientation toward politics is challenging the police and the state from outside the formal political arena—activism from the margins. This orientation is due, in part, to the different political structure in the United States and France. As we previously noted, American politics has relatively more descriptive representation of people of color who have been elected to government than in France. But like the women in Ferguson, their intersectional identity motivates their activism. Their narratives draw on similar themes that have echoed across generations of black women.

Black feminist scholars (along with other women of color feminists) have shown that women's organizing and activism is often indistinguishable from community, family, kinship networks, and their intersectional lived experiences (Flores-Gonzalez and Gomberg-Munoz 2013; Naples 1998; Pardo 1998). Women of color often take the community's problems and turn them into political goals with desired policy outcomes to improve the community (Pardo 1998). Thus, the congruency between community labor and seeking to better the community and running for political office are inseparable. Blurring the distinctions between community work and (elected) political work requires an intersectional lens to understand how black women see themselves in relationship to their communities and as goal-driven problem solvers.

More attention is needed to recognize the pivotal role they play with the community. More attention is also needed for the violence that they experience. The hashtag SayHerName was created to bring awareness to state-sponsored violence against black women and girls, which was popularly ignored in the larger #BlackLivesMatter conversations and activism (Threadcraft 2017). The invisibility of black women victims mirrors that of the black women activists and politicians in our study.

What we see in the examples of black women political elites in Missouri and black women activists in France is an articulation of intersectional political activism. These women are using their voices to draw attention to crimes largely seen as disproportionally affecting black boys and men. However, the violence done to these individuals has tremendous impact on the communities in which these boys and men belong to. These women are drawing from their social identities to assert a concern for the entire community, not just the individual victims of state-sponsored violence. They are making a connection to the larger systemic violence that is being done to black communities at the hands of the state. In the case of the political elites in Missouri, this is even more telling because they are agents of the state. Black women's subject positions enable them to uniquely see issues from a different vantage point that those with other and/or more privileged relationship to the state.

The ways that black women know the world—using a black feminist epistemology (Collins 1990)—empower black women to act as change agents within BlackLivesMatter movements because they bring a different perspective, one that is influenced by being on the margins of society. Sociologist Patricia Hill Collins's (1986) notion of the "outsider-within" in which individuals are simultaneously members of a society, yet kept on the margins of that society, is instructive here, as it also allows us to connect the positions of black women in different societies, with different histories and identity politics. How black women understand state-sponsored violence as a racism-related problem targeting black men is one manifestation of their standpoint or position as black women and the interlocking nature of oppression as both women and black. A focus on state-sponsored violence solely through the prisms of racism or sexism would be insufficient. What these black women are doing—in both the United States and in France—is using their positions as black women to mobilize for the betterment of their entire communities—both within and beyond constraints of the state. It is this work by black women that is crucial for the liberation of us all.

NOTES

1. By state-sponsored violence, we refer not only to killings of black individuals by the police but also to the systemic ways that black populations are devalued across various domains in society, including housing and public education, among others.

2. Alicia Garza, Patrisse Cullors, and Opal Tometti are often credited with starting the social movement BlackLivesMatter; however, the first use of the BlackLives-Matter hashtag was by sociologist Marcus Anthony Hunter (McKesson 2018).

3. To clarify, we use the term "BlackLivesMatter" to refer to the social movement affirming Black humanity primarily in the context of activism against police violence and the term "#BlackLivesMatter" to refer specifically to the social media hashtag related to this movement.

4. Blacklivesmatter.com.

5. To clarify, the Paris metropolitan region referenced in this chapter includes not only the banlieue or suburban outskirts of Paris but also the eighteenth, nineteenth, and twentieth *arrondissements* within Paris proper.

6. US Census Bureau. 2016. *American Community Survey 5-Year estimates*. Retrieved from *Census Reporter Profile page for Ferguson, MO* https://censusreporter.org/profiles/16000US2923986-ferguson-mo/.

7. https://www.bjs.gov/index.cfm?ty=pbdetail&iid=1750.

8. https://bastamag.net/webdocs/police/.

9. Brown conducted an interview with Councilwoman Mitchum in June 2017.

10. Brown conducted an interview with Candidate Bush in June 2017.

11. Brown conducted an interview with Councilwoman Jones in June 2017.

12. https://slate.com/cover-stories/2017/01/the-death-of-adama-traore-has-become-frances-ferguson.html.

13. https://www.bbc.com/news/world-europe-36854738; http://www.slate.fr/story/149028/mort-adama-traore

14. https://www.nytimes.com/2016/07/29/opinion/black-lives-matter-in-france-too.html.

15. http://www.leparisien.fr/paris-75020/mort-de-lamine-dieng-a-paris-la-justice-confirme-le-non-lieu-29–06–201v7–7098861.php; http://www.urgence-notre-police-assassine.fr/123663559.

16. www.viesvolees.org; https://www.facebook.com/collectif.viesvolees/.

17. Beaman did participant observation of this demonstration in both June 2017 and June 2018.

18. From July 2017, interview with Beaman in Paris.

19. From July 2017, interview with Beaman in Paris.

Chapter 13

A Mountain Skyline?

Gender Equality and Intersectionality in Supranational "Equality CSOs"

Petra Ahrens

Civil society organizations' (CSOs) participation is deemed crucial for democratic institution building in the social space between the European Union (EU) institutions and its citizens (Della Porta and Rucht 2013).[1] From the early 2000s on, the EU recognized CSOs as a tool to legitimize its activities, which resulted in partially legislating participatory democracy in the Lisbon Treaty (Sanchez Salgado 2014). The European Commission supported both the creation of supranational umbrella CSOs and their participation in EU policymaking (Johansson and Kalm 2015; Kröger 2013; Sanchez Salgado 2014), often as sources of expertise and information and as policy-implementation partners (Jacquot and Vitale 2014).

Yet, we know little about how CSOs mobilize intersectionally or about how they and EU institutions respond to the threat of "competition between inequalities" (Verloo 2006, 211). CSOs are not equal with regard to their resources, acceptance, access options, and alliances with other organizations. This chapter focuses on CSOs that—by definition—aim to improve citizenship rights and participation for groups that are often marginalized in the policymaking process. I call such CSOs "equality CSOs"[2] and purposefully limit this understanding to those that in their work explicitly refer to Article 19 of the Lisbon Treaty, forbidding discrimination on the grounds of sex, racial or ethnic origin, religion or belief, disability, age, or sexual orientation. Using Qualitative network analysis (QNA) embedded in expert interviews (Ahrens 2018b), I argue that institutional change affects networking among equality CSOs and that intersectionality in networks is co-constructed through top-down demands from EU institutions, on the one hand, and bottom-up mobilizations among equality CSOs, on the other. Like others, I argue that intersectionality may foster coalitionbuilding among activists to strategize for structural change by addressing several discrimination grounds at once (Cole

2008; Collins and Bilge 2016; Terriquez, Brenes, and Lopez 2018). Hence, networking may be understood as a basis for gendered and intersectional mobilization, shaping the dynamics between equality CSOs. My analysis shows which CSOs the EU is open to and to which it is not, where and what kinds of intersectional alliances exist, whether and why they are stable and what kind of meaning members give to them.

I start by introducing my methodological approach and how I conceptualize intersectionality in this context. Using the framework proposed by Irvine, Lang, and Montoya in the introduction of this volume, I then compare the literature on equality CSOs and the EU with the findings from my study, thereby drawing a comprehensive picture of networking among equality CSOs and of the roles gender equality and intersectionality play in their networks. I present the results on (1) acting politically in the EU's system of multilevel governance, with its changing political opportunity structures; (2) supranational funding structures and how they impact CSOs' capacity to act; (3) how specific movements found their voice; and (4) how collaborations and alliances are forged. The analysis shows that equality CSOs' access to EU institutions is hierarchically organized along class, then gender, then race, and that CSOs recognize and (unintentionally) replicate this order in their networks.

INVESTIGATING EQUALITY CSOS' NETWORKS USING QUALITATIVE NETWORK ANALYSIS

I use an inductive approach by asking equality CSOs how they engage with EU institutions and other CSOs and inquiring whether and how these engagements allow for gendered or intersectional mobilization. While formal EU-level procedures and the extent of CSO participation are covered well in the literature (Della Sala and Ruzza 2007; Friedrich 2011; Sanchez Salgado 2014), taking a micro-perspective on policy actors reveals which inequality grounds are considered important in CSOs' daily work. Taking the EU political opportunity structure into account, I ask how institutional changes shape CSO networks from the top down. To study gendered mobilizations, I ask how and why CSOs mention gender equality in their work. Regarding intersectionality, I investigate whether CSOs address intersecting inequalities in their activities and, if so, which categories. I am thus following what McCall (2005) called an intercategorical approach to studying the complexity of intersectionality. This approach allows for systematically comparing the relationships among the equality CSOs and examining coalition building as a form of "intersectional praxis" (Townsend-Bell 2011) or transversal politics (Yuval-Davis 2006, 2012).

For mapping the microcosm of equality CSO interactions, I use QNA, which builds on qualitative research methods such as interviewing and analyzing documents (Ahrens 2018b). QNA starts from the assumption that networks do not exist independently from individuals, that individuals are essential to any aspect of networks, and that networks enable as well as constrain individuals in their actions. QNA allows for examining what agency means in a given context, how policy processes and actors are connected, and which dynamics occur in (social) networks (Hollstein and Straus 2006). During the interviews I used the "method of concentric circles," initially labeled as "hierarchical mapping technique" (Hollstein and Pfeffer 2010; Kahn and Antonucci 1980), and asked my interviewees to draw a network map on a paper sheet about the CSO's contact frequency in three categories: stakeholders, European Commission, and other EU institutions (see figure 13.1).

I conducted semi-structured interviews from 2015 to 2018 with the following equality CSOs tackling one dimension of discrimination and organized around Article 19: the European Women's Lobby (EWL), the European Network Against Racism (ENAR), the AGE Platform, the European Disabilities Forum (EDF), the International Lesbian, Gay, Bisexual, Trans and Intersex Association (ILGA Europe), and the European Roma Grassroots Organisations Network (ERGO). Aside from these CSOs, organized around single dimensions, I also included the Social Platform and the European Trade Union Confederation (ETUC) as CSOs bridging several grounds of discrimination with the goal of transmitting the claims of identity-based CSOs into EU institutions.

The rich literature on (political) intersectionality sheds light on the complexity of how different forms of oppression, in this case defined by the different grounds of discrimination, interact (Collins and Bilge 2016; Crenshaw 1989; Hancock 2007). Recognizing intersectionality means recognizing that social structures create oppression, that different dimensions of oppression are constructed, and that identity groups are also internally diverse (Cole 2008). Exploring intersectionality and intersectional praxis thus is an empirical question that acknowledges specific contexts (Hancock 2007; Kantola and Nousiainen 2009). I started from the premise that there should be no hierarchy in the discrimination grounds, as these are mutually constitutive and do not simply add up (Hancock 2011; Yuval-Davis 2012), even though I also agree that discrimination categories do not operate on a structurally similar level (Verloo 2006). I assumed that equality CSOs' representatives would be able to reflect on the positionality and identity of their CSO (rooting), and that they would also recognize and accept the claims of the CSOs they collaborate with (shifting) (Yuval-Davis 2006, 2012).

Against this background, I analyzed the interviews in order to detect power relations and hierarchies among the CSOs, focusing in particular on resources and actions, access possibilities to EU institutions, and everyday

European Commission   Other EU institutions

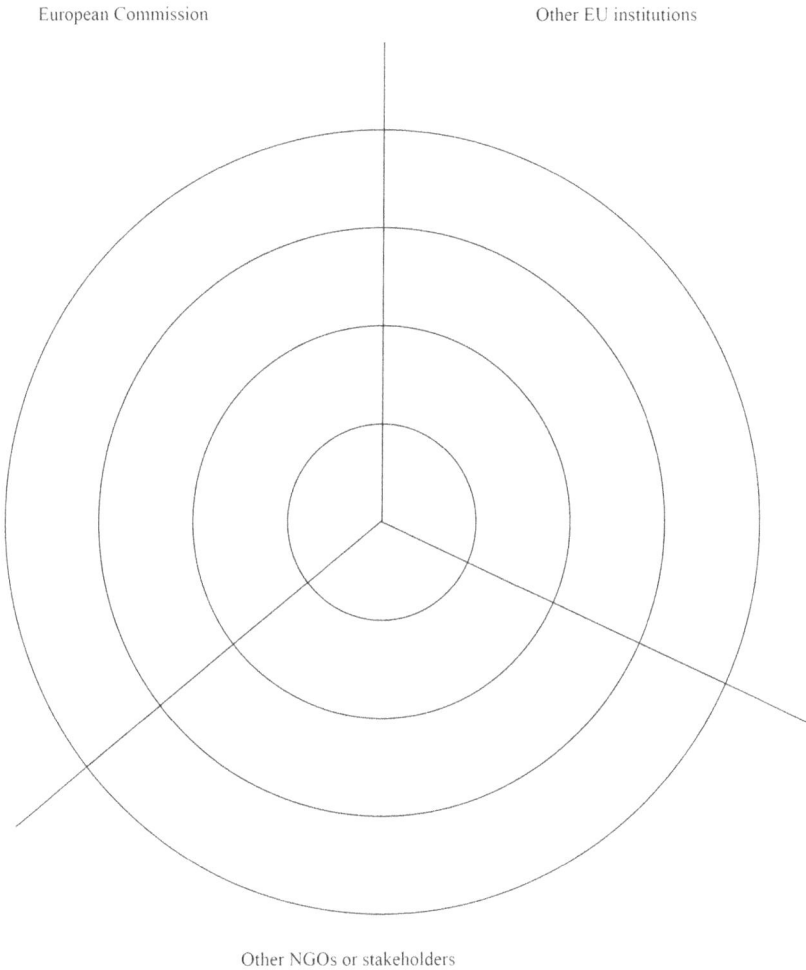

Other NGOs or stakeholders

Figure 13.1.   Network Map Example
Source: Author's design

communication and actions as a basis for mobilizing across networks and intersectionally. Moreover, I examined the roles gender equality and intersectionality play for each CSO. The network maps derived from the interviews reveal how equality CSOs organize, whether CSOs see differences in influence, and who is seen as the most influential. Della Porta and Parks (2013, 32) point out that leadership of CSO networks translates into visibility and into closer contacts to media and institutions, a precondition for strengthening one's network leadership (Diani and McAdam 2003). Thus, visibility increases influence among CSOs and toward EU institutions and determines which intersectional claims reach the political agenda. The network maps show us which equality CSOs are recognized, and lower contact frequency can be seen as an indicator of having less potential to make one's claims heard.

EU MULTILEVEL GOVERNANCE: SHAPING CSOS' ACCESS AND PERFORMANCE

Irvine, Lang, and Montoya (2019, this volume) highlight that acting politically depends on two sets of factors: on the way national and transnational institutions and structures allow for intersectional political action, on the one hand, and on the strategic choices and agency of movements, on the other. In this section, I focus on the former, as the latter will be covered in the section on alliances. The way supranational policymaking is organized influences CSOs' possibilities to act politically, regardless of their funding and often also their original intentions and strategies as political agents. EU policymaking is characterized by a large number of expert groups, committees, and semi-elected bodies designed by various institutions. Different policy fields also have different decision-making procedures, with some of them decided supranationally (e.g., agriculture), while others are regulated nationally (e.g., social security). The Commission, the European Parliament, and the Council decide who can participate at which point in time, for instance by inviting equality CSOs to expert groups, hearings, or consultations.

But what exactly are the EU structures that shape a CSO's access and how do they present challenges of (non)participation? Research is rich on how various interest groups access EU policymaking processes and how they are able to shape (EU) policies (Greenwood 2011; Sanchez Salgado 2014). An in-depth intersectional analysis, however, is still developing. Since the Treaty of Amsterdam, equality CSOs have had a legal basis for claiming rights vis-à-vis the European institutions (Verloo 2013). Yet the directives that were adopted in the treaty's aftermath created new hierarchies among discrimination grounds (Kantola and Nousiainen 2009). In the fields of gender equality and anti-discrimination, the Commission favored umbrella CSOs representing one ground of discrimination, which had problematic consequences for those not following this logic (Cullen 2010; Agustín 2013a). At first, this constraint was tolerated, if not welcomed, by the umbrella organizations (Agustín 2013b, 168). Verloo, however, pointed out that the EU formally treats all discrimination grounds the same way, "based upon an incorrect assumption of sameness or equivalence of social categories connected to inequalities and of mechanisms and processes that constitute them" (Verloo 2006, 223). Agustín and Siim (2014) further found that gendered citizenship as an important intersection of gender and ethnicity tended to be excluded from this economically oriented policy area. Consequently, only few women's or minority CSOs benefited from funding provided by the European Year, and none of these is intersectional in their outlook (Agustín and Siim 2014, 549). On another occasion, the Commission choose not to diversify funding to minority groups after it consulted CSOs; instead, it encouraged collaboration among CSOs regarding multiple discrimination grounds (Agustín 2013b, 168).

Acting politically—and thereby invoking the possibility to bring about political change—depends on the political opportunity structure shaping access to powerful EU institutions and on how willing these are to accepting new ideas (Mazey 2012). Equality CSOs started mobilizing supranationally quickly, as it was not until the early 2000s that the EU began to recognize CSOs as a tool to legitimize its activities, adopting participatory democracy elements in the Lisbon Treaty (Sanchez Salgado 2014). The literature on the opportunities and pitfalls of the EU's proposed ideal of participatory democracy and the role of CSOs therein is rich (Friedrich 2011; Kohler-Koch and Quittkat 2013), yet it lacks a focus on equality CSOs, with a few exceptions (i.e., Della Sala and Ruzza 2007). Overall, the relationship remains complicated: EU institutions exploit civil society for legitimation purposes and design the institutional structures and access points for CSOs to fit their interests. The Commission and the European Parliament (EP) are key in offering access to CSOs, whereas the Council, the political arena dominated by national governments, is often seen as closed to CSOs (Sanchez Salgado 2014). Equality CSOs have to take this into account when making choices about their political actions, leaving them not much room for maneuver.

As the main target and funder of equality policies until these were moved to the Directorate General (DG) Justice, DG Employment established close and exclusive relationships with umbrella organizations through their Social Dialogue with ETUC and their Civil Dialogue with the Social Platform, the European Platform against Poverty and Exclusion (meeting twice a year since 1995) (Sanchez Salgado 2014, 86), or the European Women's Lobby (which has advisory status in the Advisory Committee on Equal Opportunities). The EU, and particularly DG Employment, had long functioned as an ally for (gender) equality CSOs, and they collaborated in pressuring member states. During the past decade, EU (gender) equality policies started deteriorating and the close ties were cut (Ahrens 2018a; Jacquot 2015). As a consequence, the EU itself became a lobbying arena for equality CSOs (Ahrens 2018a). Hence, the changing scope of EU policies influences the channels for collaboration available between equality CSOs and EU institutions as well as those among CSOs.

The EU's legitimacy crisis of the early 2000s transformed not only the Commission's approach to CSOs but also those of the EP and the Council. Since 2000, the Social Platform has, for instance, been invited to attend meetings of the EU presidency trios[3] and since 2007 has also been invited to informal meetings of the Council of Ministers of Social Affairs (Sanchez Salgado 2014, 89). Committed femocrats in DG Employment accumulated expertise, established networks with feminist experts from member states, and developed close links with women's groups through the EWL (Jacquot 2015; Strid 2014). With the move to DG Justice, much of this expertise was lost, ties were cut, and the policy frame changed from economic and social affairs to anti-discrimination and human rights.

CSOs are affected to varying extents by institutional changes and the different strategies of DGs and EP committees. EU institutions seem to offer easier access for the Social Platform and ETUC than for those CSOs focusing on just one inequality ground. Social Platform and ETUC interviewees reported routinized meetings with the Commission, the EP, and to some degree with the Council or presidency, while the majority of other CSOs conveyed that they had to work hard to find the right contact, particularly after equality policies moved to DG Justice. The following quotes illustrate the difficulties they experienced due to the institutional change:

> So, that's what we are doing at the moment, we're kind of mapping our-selves. . . . There have been shifts and we have to see where exactly we should target our efforts. (Interview with EWL representative)
>
> I think [when we got to] Brussels, we were kind of: Ooh, thank you for letting us in and then sitting around the table with us. . . . And I think we're now slowly but surely trying to make small steps up for our members, for new staff. . . . We had a meeting with Jourovà, . . . that was the first meeting with the Commis-sioner and right when she took office, so she was completely new, completely open, and we were there discussing the whole strategy. (Interview with ERGO Network representative)
>
> We do not have a specific Unit in the Commission that works on our issue. So in DG Employment there was a Unit that had to do with aging, and this is not the case in DG Justice. (Interview with AGE Platform representative)

Its ability to act politically determines what kind of access a CSO has. Even though the EWL has observer status in the Advisory Committee, they found it difficult to select the correct institutional target to address their priorities, while AGE and ILGA lost their contacts and had to find new ones (Wood-ward 2007). CSOs new to the supranational level, like ERGO, had even bigger problems in figuring out where and how they could participate in policymaking. The next section illustrates how the diversified opportunities and challenges of EU multilevel governance actually shape equality CSOs' participation.

EU FUNDING, CSOS, AND THEIR CAPACITY TO ACT

CSOs can use different resources to extend their capacity to act, such as providing information to constituencies or expertise to policymakers, acquiring information on how other actors position themselves, and finding funding (Dür and De Bièvre 2007). Sanchez Salgado (2014) found that the funding of CSOs changed considerably over time and depended on their policy field and the Commission DGs in charge of it. Even though the number of expert groups and consultative committees involving interest groups keeps growing in the EU, they are not equally distributed among Commission DGs. Regarding the two most important DGs for equality issues, Employment and Justice, the former historically ran twice as many expert groups (Gornitzka and Sverdrup 2008, 735). In the early 2000s, DG Justice had not a single consultative committee, while DG Employment ran thirty—the second-highest number in the Commission (Mahoney 2004). EU funding also pushed CSOs to change their organization, for instance, by obliging them to use New Public Management tools, thereby adjusting the CSO's goals toward the political agenda regarding funding priorities and shifting them from using voluntary staff to hiring professionals (Mahoney 2004).

With regard to equality CSOs, the Commission has continuously contributed funding to setting up and maintaining the European Anti-Poverty Network (EAPN), the EWL, and the EDF starting in the early 1990s (Sanchez Salgado 2014), then in 1995 adding the Social Platform (Cram 2011), and in 1998 ENAR (Greenwood 2011). AGE, ERGO, and ILGA reported similar funding schemes in the interviews. The CSOs' self-reporting on their funding in the European Transparency Register[4] illustrates their strong dependency on the EU (see table 13.1). Given their restricted resources and their dependency on the Commission, equality CSOs must be characterized as weak groups in the broader context of EU interest groups and interest representation (Jacquot and Vitale 2014). Aside from the EU, the Open Society Foundations (OSFs) also fund equality CSOs, for instance, the European Roma and Traveller Forum (ERTF) (McGarry 2008), ENAR, and EWL—even though the OSF itself also lobbies in EU policymaking (Calligaro 2018).[5]

The move to DG Justice also changed funding responsibilities. This was not solely a technical detail, because aside from the changed policy frame, equality CSOs were also confronted with DG Justice's different funding traditions. Sanchez Salgado (2014, 84) found that CSO funding followed a specific life cycle: First, DGs pushed CSOs to apply for funding; second,

Table 13.1. Annual EU Funding of CSOs (Self-Reported)

	Total funding in €	EU funding in €	Share of EU funding (%)
AGE Platform	1,216,310	1,038,862	85,41
EDF	1,800,000	1,050,000	58,33
ENAR	1,124,423	899,523	79,99
ERGO	440,627	392,029	88,97
ETUC	No data	3,000,000	–
EWL	1,187,356	882,738	74,35
ILGA Europe	2,512,332	1,182,042	47,05
Social Platform	703,727	600,000	85,26

Source: European Transparency Register, 2018.

when more CSOs started applying, DGs introduced new funding management to control and regulate access; and third, DGs slowed down involving CSOs or even decreased funding and thereby the number of CSOs active on a supranational level. All this reduces CSOs' capacity to act in general but also intersectionally, because they constantly need to adjust to the changed institutional rules. While this process started at DG Employment early in the 1990s, DG Justice only commenced such processes at the end of the 1990s. With a view to equality CSOs, we can expect that those that received DG Employment funding early, such as ETUC and EWL, are better established in the EU system, and those that only started their activities after the Treaty of Amsterdam, such as ENAR, were faced with an already closed or at least complicated funding system. Moreover, most of the equality CSOs arrived at DG Justice at a time when new applicants to its budget were likely not appreciated. On the other hand, the Commission also faced problems when trying to withdraw funding once granted, as CSOs were good at mobilizing against such attempts (Sanchez Salgado 2014, 111), a likely advantage for longer-established equality CSOs. More recently established CSOs, by contrast, face more difficulties in trying to access EU funding, because they first need secure funding before being able to defend it. Aside from the changing funding cycle, the uneven coverage of different inequality grounds in the EU anti-discrimination directives (Givens and Evans Case 2014) and the move to DG Justice with its human-rights policy frame also added further complexity to possible intersectional mobilization. DG Employment had funded equality-CSO projects emphasizing multiple discriminations in employment situations, but DG Justice changed the funding landscape toward a policy focus on human rights, thereby providing a new setting for collaborations. Consequently, equality CSOs had to rethink their policy focus and the alliances they could set up to fit DG Justice's demands.

The current EU funding system for CSOs (see table 13.1) reveals a counterintuitive effect. Even though funding extends a CSOs' capacity to act in support of greater participation, it simultaneously implicitly limits their capacity to use contentious politics in the form of mass mobilizations or campaigns (Sanchez Salgado 2014, 175), as CSOs find that public strategies that are too contentious threaten their funding and also their credibility in the eyes of EU institutions. The only exception is the well-resourced ETUC, which still uses mass mobilization as a strategy (Sanchez Salgado 2014, 176). Furthermore, Lang (2013) found that current EU funding practices also tend to depoliticize movement discourses, practices, and goals.

EQUALITY CSOS FINDING THEIR VOICE IN SUPRANATIONAL POLITICS

Establishing supranational CSOs did not happen bottom up[6] but from the top down, with the Commission offering incentives through funding and access opportunities. Once established, equality CSOs still needed to find their voice in the European multilevel system, figuring out their answers to key questions such as the following: Who are they representing? Which international and member-state organizations should be included? What are their policy issues? Moreover, they do not only have to compete with each other over scarce resources, they also have to face the powerful business interest associations that dominate lobbying in the EU (Greenwood 2011). Kröger (2013, 592) characterizes those who represent "human constituencies such as the poor and socially excluded" as "weak interests," because they "generally do not enjoy the various sorts of capital necessary to organize themselves." This skewed starting point made it more difficult to find a voice on the supranational level, particularly as the main competencies for social issues are still located on the member-state level, resulting in different CSO interests depending on the state's welfare system (Kröger 2013, 596).

CSOs established their voice for different constituencies and policy issues. The ETUC and the Social Platform are well known for their social justice engagement (Cullen 2015a; Sanchez Salgado 2014), while little is known about their gendered or intersectional mobilization. The EWL successfully lobbied for the inclusion of gender mainstreaming in the Treaty of Amsterdam, but it has been less successful in applying it in its own work (Lang 2009, 2013) and the same applies to intersectional approaches (Pristed Nielsen 2013; Stubbergaard 2015). While the EWL is acknowledged as a creation of dedicated femocrats (Cullen 2015b), others raise concerns about its representation being largely limited to white, middle-aged, professional women, pointing to a lack of intersectionality (Jacquot and Vitale 2014) and about EWL's gatekeeper role in policymaking (Ahrens 2018a; Prudovska and Ferree 2004; Strid 2014). This gatekeeping role stands out compared to the more limited roles of the European Network of Migrant Women (ENoMW) and the European Forum of Muslim Women (EFoMW), both of which directly address gender and ethnicity-related intersectional issues. While the EWL actively contributed to setting up the ENoMW,[7] it remains dependent on the EWL, which functions as the main contact and also represents it in the Social Platform (Stubbergaard 2015). Whereas the ENoMW developed a strong and widely recognized identity based on multiple, migrant belongings, the EFoMW developed a strong, "Muslim women" identity and then faced disagreements with other women's organizations such as EWL and ENoMW about which identity to emphasize—women or ethnicity/religion; a disagreement that led EFoMW to forge stronger ties with ENAR instead (Stubbergaard 2015). LGBT movements in different European regions deliberately used the notion of "Europe" to forge a unified voice on LGBT rights with a specific understanding of EU rights (Ayoub and Paternotte 2014b). ILGA played a crucial role and made the LGBT movement voice heard by setting up close networks with the EP and the Commission (Ayoub 2016).[8]

While equality CSOs generally consider the intersectional aspects of their issues to a greater extent than EU institutions (Lombardo and Agustín 2011), my interviews show that gender mainstreaming and diversity paradigms have influenced intersectional consciousness differently depending on how long the CSO has been active: "Younger" equality CSOs seek to include more inequality grounds and/or intersectional aspects where appropriate and make efforts to link up with other movements, while the "old" movements are lagging behind. For instance, the EWL still predominantly emphasizes women's interests and intersectional claims if primarily labeled as women's issues. Addressing intersectionality seemingly became a necessary issue for their future strategy and was considerably strengthened with their website redesign in 2010 (Pristed Nielsen 2013). ENAR does not mention women in their self-description but distributes EWL press releases, references gender equality, generally "holds the most wide-ranging notion of diversity," and advocates for the nonhierarchy of inequality grounds (Pristed Nielsen 2013, 188ff). Overall, considering intersectional aspects seems to have advanced in CSOs' practices over the years.

ALLIANCES, COLLABORATIONS, AND THE ROLE OF UMBRELLA ORGANIZATIONS

Della Porta and Caiani (2009) have shown that actors' networks provide crucial opportunities and resources for mobilizing across movements, especially for those who want to influence the EU level. Established alliances contribute to easier mobilization and greater access to resources and make it possible to determine shared policy goals and new collective identities (Della Porta and Caiani 2009). This may lead to recognizing other CSOs' experiences and positions while being willing to define joint goals, a possibility in intersectional politics that Yuval-Davis (2012) has called "shifting." All equality CSOs are firmly established on a supranational level, have developed their distinct CSO voice, and created capacity to act by choosing a preferred strategy to get involved with EU institutions.[9] They are, however, constrained by the procedures of EU institutions.

For its Civil Dialogue(s), the Commission predominantly granted access to a core group of umbrella equality CSOs, the downside of which was that organizations that could be more representative on certain grounds of discrimination than umbrella organizations were excluded (Cram 2011). Remaining the most powerful and visible, the Social Platform and ETUC do not explicitly focus on one ground of discrimination but more broadly aim to influence EU (social) policies and tackle inequalities from a social-politics perspective. They function as a hub and coordinate joint actions with "satellite" CSOs. The Social Platform, for instance, reported taking initiatives from other CSOs to the Council of Ministers of Social Affairs meeting, with the aim of promoting them in EU institutions. The Social Platform was also often mentioned first by other CSOs and reported as their first-choice contact:

"Then, here in the stakeholder section would first be the Social Platform."
  (Interview with ILGA Europe representative)

Likewise, the Social Platform and ETUC both described that other organizations contact them and that they take less initiative:

"I don't see the [CSOs] in general, but they approach us more than we them."
  (Interview with ETUC representative)

All CSOs also acknowledged that the EWL is an adequate interlocutor for promoting gender equality, though not the only one. This finding is not an effect of the EWL's networking activities alone—many other CSOs depict the EWL as being in charge of advocating and mobilizing on the EU level, and therefore they themselves feel less of a need to take gender aspects into account or contact EU institutions on their own (Ahrens 2018a). The other equality CSOs always included the EWL in their network map, pointing to the EWL's core role in collaborating on gender equality. This recognition, however, is not necessarily directly mirrored by the EWL. When asked to map their connections to other organizations, EWL interviewees immediately included ETUC, the Social Platform, and the ENoMW, while other equality

CSOs were added stepwise when asked to include CSOs focusing on other discrimination grounds.

Thus, "shifting" among EU-level CSOs occurs mainly through cross-issue alliances and joint projects. The interviews show that equality CSOs focusing on one ground of discrimination take notice of other CSOs tackling related key issues, even if these other actors address these issues from a different perspective or a different ground of discrimination. Each movement is rooted in "their ground of discrimination" as its starting point and collaborates with others on interlinked other ground(s) or intersectional aspects of an issue. Similar to the findings from Cole (2008), shifting and coalitionbuilding among CSOs is driven by a shared vision for change. Equality CSOs practice intersectionality when the discursive framing is similar and problem definitions overlap (Verloo 2013). According to one interviewee, the AGE platform wanted to address disability policies and quickly found itself joining forces with the European Disabilities Forum because of the obvious issue overlap. Often the Social Platform might coordinate this collaboration, and the results of the cooperation might provide the building blocks for a joint statement (Cullen 2015a; Woodward 2007). Sometimes intersectional collaborations are actively encouraged—not to say prescribed—by funders. The OSF, for instance, developed calls for projects against Islamophobia with ENAR and decided to actively seek a partnership with the EWL to combine gender and religion in a joint project (Calligaro 2018).

Despite the broad variety of alliances, there appears to be a clear hierarchy of social movements, one that is notably created by the EU opportunity structure, with class—gender—race as descending levels. A good metaphor to describe the alliances among equality CSOs is therefore a mountain skyline. The highest peaks represent organizations focusing on inequalities more generally like ETUC and the Social Platform, while the lower peaks are dedicated to more specific discrimination grounds, like sex, race/ethnicity, (dis) abilities, age, and so forth. The height of the peaks and the distance between them indicate differences in power and resources available to the different equality CSOs: the higher the peak, the more power and resources are available to the organization. Similarly, the metaphor illustrates how the higher peaks are also the most visible, be that to other CSOs or EU institutions. If the peaks can be said to represent the equality CSOs, their bases are made up of their national member organizations. The more numerous or stronger these national organizations are, the higher the chance the peak will exceed the height (read, power and visibility) of CSOs with fewer or weaker national member organizations. Moreover, just as any mountain skyline descends and meets another's in the dip of a valley, so do CSOs' intersectional aspects, as they overlap and can offer the possibility for national CSOs or CSOs representing intersectional aspects to collaborate with different supranational organizations. For instance, the International Roma Women's Network (IRWN) is a member of the peaks EWL and ENAR, using both venues to promote their intersectional policy goals for Roma women (D'Agostino 2018). When considering this image, however, we have to acknowledge that it is constructed. It has not developed naturally but is a result of the perspective and actions of EU institutions toward equality CSOs and their originally strong preference for single-issue organizations (Cullen 2010; Agustín 2013a).

In the interviews, the CSO representatives did not mention or explicitly reflect on this hierarchy; it became predominantly visible by analyzing each interview and then by comparing the narratives. Concomitantly, the narratives indicated entangled factors that shaped the mountain skyline: issue attention span, the fluctuating availability of resources for CSOs, institutional change, and the political climate. As Lombardo and Agustín (2016) illustrated regarding issue attention, after the adoption of the anti-discrimination directives the equality CSOs' access to EU institutions varied over time with the changing policy issues. In the beginning, issues like age and demographic change were emphasized, then the focus shifted increasingly toward ethnicity, and here particularly to discrimination against Sinti and Roma.

At the time of the interviews, many member states still struggled with the fallout of the economic crisis, which lifted class- and poverty-related claims to a core concern in EU policies and consequently impacted access and resources. The Social Platform and ETUC tackle EU policies from the angle of social inequalities, with class as the (implicit) underlying framing, a policy problem euphemized as "social exclusion" (Agustín and Siim 2014). This policy frame guarantees access to different Commission expert groups, the Civil Dialogue(s) and the Social Dialogue, the latter even allowing them to propose directives. Both are accepted as major CSO voices, a classic dominant and superior position that, Cole (2008) warned, could wash out intersectional claims and be misunderstood as representing the universal. The social inequalities frame also resonated well with the policy context originating from the financial and economic crisis. While before the crisis social justice, broader equality issues, and intersectional claims were all acceptable to the institutions, the crisis made it impossible to be heard by all major EU institutions if issues were not framed in terms of economics. Rather than being open to rethinking economics from a sustainable, justice-oriented perspective, the claims that did not fit into the neoliberal austerity paradigm were institutionally ignored. One reason for this might be the differing importance member states attach to social justice issues, not to mention the fact that governing parties sometimes even oppose certain EU-level social welfare policies.

Class is followed by gender—not least because of long-established ties between the EWL and EU institutions and the different treaty articles. Gender equality as a proclaimed founding value of the EU can also be framed as economic policy and might have therefore remained on the agenda. The EWL stated that gender-equality claims were labeled as a luxury unless they provided an argument that their request would improve economic development. Moreover, connecting gender equality and economic policies resonated well with women's movement goals in some member states.

Finally, race appeared as the third important level of the mountain skyline, even though the interviews (particularly the one with ENAR) showed that there is no consensus among member states on what should be covered under the term and how urgent the need to fight racism is. Often, race was used interchangeably with ethnicity, pointing to the different member states' histories in tackling racial discrimination (Givens and Evans Case 2014).

Overall, the economic crisis further decreased funding opportunities while simultaneously narrowing policy frames. According to the interviews, funding cutbacks from EU institutions particularly affected CSOs focusing on anti-racism and/or LGBT issues.[10] Likewise, it seemed easier for CSOs focusing on social justice (Social Platform, ETUC) or disabilities (EDF) to keep their resources and funding stable. As a result, smaller and more critical voices have to constantly reorganize and refocus their main issues in order to push their interests forward. In addition, they need to rely more on the umbrella CSOs to promote their claims within the umbrella CSOs' general policies. In effect, those with longer-established ties such as the EWL are more often included in the lobbying attempts of umbrella CSOs.

Finally, the institutional change that took place in the European Commission with regard to (gender) equality in 2010, right after the crisis hit the EU, impacted CSOs' funding and alliances. DG Justice shapes the form and content of intersectional alliances by defining which issues are acceptable and providing resources along these lines. In particular, social justice claims face problems due to the new institutional context, because DG Justice is not responsible for employment and social policies. After 2010, lobbying often happened at the wrong DG. CSOs not focusing on employment, such as EDF and partly ILGA and ENAR, may find contact points at DG Justice, but if the main focus of a CSO is employment, DG Employment is the better contact— a fact that ETUC, the Social Platform, and also to a growing extent the EWL acknowledged. The EWL translated this challenge into splitting its actions by focusing on both DGs, which consumes a lot of their resources.

In addition to reduced funding opportunities, the "openness" of institutions also was impacted by changes in the overall political climate. According to interviewees, the rise of authoritarian and populist parties and governments across Europe reduced the receptiveness to race/ethnicity/migration issues in the typically consensus-oriented EU institutions. All equality CSOs faced constant threats, both nationally and supranationally, as a result of the growing anti-equality mobilization in member states and in the EP (Kemper 2014).

There is one important feature that the mountain-skyline metaphor does not render visible: It does not visualize the connections *between* the peaks, in other words how equality CSOs react to changes in the environment by forming flexible and needs-oriented alliances. Despite their different levels of power, CSOs claimed they did not fight over resources (see also Ayoub in this volume). While CSOs necessarily have to formally compete over the scarce resources available through EU funding, my interviews point to a uniting effect of limited funding. Instead of conflict, the CSOs turn to collaboration. They ally against racism, sexism, and homophobia alike and support each other as best they can, allowing for collaboration where possible. Interviewees stated, for instance,

> I mean, I do get a lot of support from my civil society colleagues. I think they're important for me, they're important as well for this, you know, kind of strategizing as well. (Interview with EWL representative)
>
> So we meet with, for example, the other non-discrimination networks like ILGA and ENAR and the EWL, so monthly to six-monthly. (Interview with EDF representative)
>
> And now for the other CSOs, we have very good contact—and again it depends on the topic—so for equality in particular we work with ENAR, ILGA, EDF, ERIO. (Interview with AGE Platform representative)
>
> I mean global synergies, diversified contributions, I mean contact between all types of movement, trade union, feminist movement, racial-equity movement, LGTBQI: everyone. (Interview with ENAR representative)

Notwithstanding the individual differences in policy-making power, as illustrated with the mountain-skyline metaphor, the collaborations between CSOs can be characterized as the kind of transversal politics that Yuval-Davis (2006, 2012) labeled intersectional praxis (Townsend-Bell 2011). The interviews furthermore speak to Yuval-Davis's (2012) concepts of rooting and shifting: equality CSOs are "rooted,"; that is, they are aware of their own positioning, and they allow for "shifting,"; that is, they recognize the positions of their allies and are willing to find a common ground to move issues forward on the supranational level. This also becomes visible on the network maps: equality CSOs tended to put all other equality CSOs on one level in their concentric circles. By putting them all on an equal level, each equality CSO determines the nonhierarchy of inequality grounds and acknowledges that possible allies arrive from different angles but with a similar interest in collaboration.

Summarizing intersectionality and gendered mobilization in equality CSOs in the EU, the findings are mixed. Intersectional alliances are common, in particular for joint EU-funded projects. The capacity to form such alliances, however, is highly dependent on institutional dynamics such as engaging with the same DG or receiving funds that ask for intersectional aspects in project execution. This, however, does not necessarily mean that gender equality plays a role in these alliances. The interviews highlight that gender equality is always an axis of concern when the EWL is involved, though in other cases it depends on the project's focus and also on the funding conditions that may or may not require a gender perspective to be included.

CONCLUSION

Intersectional mobilization as a basis for supranational policymaking between equality CSOs and EU institutions resembles a mountain skyline with a clear hierarchy of class—gender—race as descending levels. Even though the peaks are separate from each other, they are connected at the base to varying extents; this represents their overlapping policy issues that are addressed simultaneously by different equality CSOs. The interview analysis and secondary literature suggest that it is not a single factor but the simultaneous appearance of several factors that shape the mountain skyline.

Whether intersectional mobilization happens depends, first, on EU institutions or other funders inviting or positively sanctioning it. The changing nature and scope of EU policies influences the channels of collaboration available between equality CSOs and EU institutions. While the EU arena is open to social justice and gender equality claims, other inequality grounds have to frame their positions in a way that not only fits the EU policy context but also the objectives of broader and "bigger" CSOs such as the Social Platform. All equality CSOs originally started as identity-based CSOs and then slowly incorporated gender equality and/or intersectional aspects in their day-to-day business, although to varying degrees.

Second, the broader political context as well as available resources influences the acceptance and prioritization of one discrimination ground over another and hence shape intersectional mobilization and power structures. This means that some grounds of discrimination are more accepted on the EU level, such as disabilities and sex (women), while others, such as anti-racism or LGBT, meet more obstacles. Also, if and when CSOs act intersectionally depends on the time that movements have spent on the national and supranational levels, thus specifically the opportunity structure to build alliances over time. For instance, women's rights movements and organizations for persons with disabilities have a longer "official" history in many European countries compared to LGBTI organizations. Racism, on the other hand, is linked to ethnicity and religion and faces challenges because CSOs working for the interests of migrants, refugees, or ethnic minorities often only agree with a limited group of political parties. Authoritarian and populist parties who are on the rise across Europe are not among them.

Third, the effects of intersectional mobilization on institutional access are mixed: CSOs such as the Social Platform have taken up intersectionality and are also well integrated into the EU institutional system, while other, race-based CSOs, in particular, have to mobilize as outsiders. When resources are limited and movements need to decide which connections to promote and sustain, it may matter where their topics overlap and where they can join forces to lobby for the same issue from different perspectives. Here, national CSOs that mobilize intersectionally and are members of different supranational equality CSOs may point to future sources of deeper intersectional mobilization.

NOTES

1. This work received funding from the European Union's Horizon 2020 research and innovation program under the Marie Sklodowska-Curie grant agreement No. 702134. The author thanks Jill Irvine, Sabine Lang, and Celeste Montoya for their valuable comments and feedback.

2. CSO intersections may exist between (national and regional) equality CSOs and (different) supranational "equality CSOs."

3. Since the Lisbon Treaty (2009), the Council presidency rotates every six months among member states that work together in groups of three, called "trios."

4. The transparency register is a public database with information about lobbying actors. Accessed May 8, 2018, http://ec.europa.eu/transparencyregister/public/homePage.do?locale=en#en.

5. According to Calligaro (2018), aside from providing funding, the OSF also paid a professional consultancy to improve CSOs' management.

6. Except for ETUC: established in 1973 and crucial for the Social Dialogue, which allows for suggesting EU legislation in employment policies. ETUC is also the only CSO with sufficient resources for mass mobilization; other equality CSOs partner up but are not using mass mobilization as a strategy (Sanchez Salgado 2014, 176).

7. In the beginning, EWL hosted the ENoMW office and helped establish links with EU institutions and other movements.

8. For a detailed analysis of intersectional and transnational alliances of the European LGBT Movement, please refer to Ayoub in this volume.

9. CSOs did not mention how they resolve differences in alliances.

10. Cullen (2015b) provides a detailed account of how the economic crisis affected the EWL.

References

Abbasian, Saeid, and Carina Bildt. 2007. *Arbetsvillkor och Anställningsförhållanden inom Städbranschen i Stockholms Län*. Stockholm: Arbetslivsinstitutet.

Abortion Rights Campaign (ARC). 2015. *Annual Report*. Dublin. Accessed April 24, 2016. https://www.abortionrightscampaign.ie/2017/12/06/our-annual-report-2015/.

Abortion Rights Campaign (ARC). 2016. "Values and Inclusivity Statement." Accessed May 1, 2018. https://www.abortionrightscampaign.ie/2016/11/21/abortion-rights-campaign-values-and-inclusivity-statement/.

Abortion Rights Campaign (ARC). 2018. "Who We Are." https://www.abortionrightscampaign.ie/.

Aftonbladet. 2013. "Fick Största Applåder—för Feminismen." Aftonbladet. Accessed November 21, 2017, from http://www.aftonbladet.se/nyheter/article16702224.ab.

Agustín, Lise Rolandsen. 2013. "Transnational Collective Mobilization: Challenges for Women's Movements in Europe." In *Negotiating Gender and Diversity in an Emergent European Public Sphere*, edited by Birte Siim and Monika Mokre, 161–78. Basingstoke: Palgrave Macmillan.

Agustín, Lise Rolandsen. 2013a. *Gender Equality, Intersectionality and Diversity in Europe*. New York: Palgrave Macmillan.

Agustín, Lise Rolandsen. 2013b. "Transnational Collective Mobilisation: Challenges for Women's Movements in Europe." In *Negotiating Gender and Diversity in an Emergent European Public Sphere*, edited by Birte Siim and Monika Mokre, 161–78. Basingstoke: Palgrave Macmillan.

Agustín, Lise Rolandsen, and Birte Siim. 2014. "Gender Diversities—Practising Intersectionality in the European Union." *Ethnicities* 14 (4): 539–55.

Ahrens, Petra. 2018a. *Actors, Institutions and the Making of EU Gender Equality Programs*. Basingstoke: Palgrave Macmillan.

Ahrens, Petra. 2018b. "Qualitative Network Analysis: A Useful Tool for Investigating Policy Networks in Transnational Settings?" *Methodological Innovations* 11 (1). https://doi.org/10.1177/2059799118769816.

AkiDwA. 2018. "Repeal the Eighth without Further Delay." Accessed May 18, 2018. https://twitter.com/AkiDwA/status/995961582663487488.

Aksoy, Hürcan Aslı. 2015. "Invigorating Democracy in Turkey: The Agency of Organized Islamist Women." *Politics & Gender* 11 (1): 146–70.

Alcoff, Linda, and Elizabeth Potter. 1993. "When Feminisms Intersect Epistemologies." In *Feminist Epistemologies*, edited by Linda Alcoff and Elizabeth Potter, 1–14. New York: Routledge.

Alexander-Floyd, Nikol G. 2012. "Disappearing Acts: Reclaiming Intersectionality in the Social Sciences in a Post-Black Feminist Era." *Feminist Formations* 24 (1): 1–25.

Alexander-Floyd, Nikol G. 2018. "Why Political Scientists Don't Study Black Women, but Historians and Sociologists Do." In *Black Women in Politics: Demanding Citizenship, Challenging Power, and Seeking Justice*, edited by Julia S. Jordan-Zachery and Nikol G. Alexander-Floyd, 5–26. Albany: State University of New York Press.

Allen, Lori. 2018. "What's In a Link? Transnational Solidarities Across Palestine and their Intersectional Possibilities." *The South Atlantic Quarterly* 117, no. 1: 111–133.

Allians för Sverige. 2006. *En Politik för Arbete och Trygghet*. Stockholm: Allians för Sverige.

Altıok, Özlem, and Bihter Somersan. 2015. "Building 'A New Turkey': Gender Politics and the Future of Democracy." *Open Democracy*, March 23, 2015. https://www.opendemocracy.net/5050/%C3%B6zlem-alt%C4%B1ok-bihter-somersan/building-new-turkey-gender-politics-and-future-of-democracy.

Alvarez, Sonia. E. 1990. *Engendering Democracy in Brazil: Women's Movements in Transition Politics*. Princeton, NJ: Princeton University Press.

Alvarez, Sonia. 1999. Advocating Feminism: The Latin American Feminist NGO Boom. International Feminist Journal of Politics. Volume 1 (2): 181–209.

Alvarez, Sonia. E. 2009. "Beyond NGO-ization: Reflections from Latin America." *Development* 52 (2): 175–84.

Amos, Valerie, and Pratibha Parmar. 1984. "Challenging Imperial Feminism." *Feminist Review* 17: 3–19.

Anderson, Bridget. 2000. *Doing the Dirty Work? The Global Politics of Domestic Labour*. London and New York: Zed.

Anderson, Bridget. 2010. "Migration, Immigration Controls and the Fashioning of Precarious Workers." *Work, Employment and Society* 24 (2): 285–304.

Andrews, Kenneth T. 2001. "Social Movements and Policy Implementation: The Mississippi Civil Rights Movement and the War on Poverty, 1965 to 1971." *American Sociological Review* 66 (1): 71–95.

Anner, John. 1996. *Beyond Identity Politics: Emerging Social Justice Movement in Communities of Color*. Cambridge, MA: South End Press.

Anthias, Floya, and Nira Yuval-Davis. 1983. "Contextualizing Feminism: Gender, Ethnic and Class Divisions." *Feminist Review* 15: 62–75.

Anti-Defamation League. 2017. "Who We Are." https://www.adl.org/who-we-are.

Anzaldúa. Gloria. 1987. *Borderlands/La Frontera: The New Mestiza*. San Francisco, CA: Aunt Lute.

Anzaldúa, Gloria. 2015. *Light in the Dar/Luz en el Oscuro: Rewriting Identity, Spirituality, Reality*. Durham, NC: Duke University Press.

Arat, Yeşim. 1998. "Feminists, Islamists, and Political Change in Turkey." *Political Psychology* 19 (1): 117–31.

Arvin, Maile, Eve Tuck, and Angie Morrill. 2013. "Decolonizing Feminism: Challenging Connections between Settler Colonialism and Heteropatriarchy." *Feminist Formations* 25 (1): 8–34.

Atalay, Zeynep. 2013. "Civil Society as Soft Power: Islamic NGOs and Turkish Foreign Policy." In *Turkey between Nationalism and Globalization*, edited by R. Kastoryano, 165–86. New York: Columbia University Press.

Atalay, Zeynep. 2017. "Partners in Patriarchy: Faith-Based Organizations and Neoliberalism in Turkey." *Critical Sociology*. DOI: 10.1177/0896920517711488.

Axiarlis, Evangelia. 2014. *Political Islam and the Secular State in Turkey: Democracy, Reform and the Justice and Development Party*. London: I. B. Tauris.

Aydın-Yılmaz, E. Sare 2015. "A New Momentum: Gender Justice in the Women's Movement." *Turkish Policy Quarterly* 13 (4): 108–15.

Ayoub, Phillip M. 2015. "Contested Norms in New-Adopter States: International Determinants of LGBT Rights Legislation." *European Journal of International Relations* 21 (2): 293–322.

Ayoub, Phillip M. 2016. *When States Come Out: Europe's Sexual Minorities and the Politics of Visibility*. New York: Cambridge University Press.

Ayoub, Phillip M. 2019. "Intersectional and Transnational Coalitions during Times of Crisis: The European LGBTI Movement." *Social Politics: International Studies in Gender, State and Society* 26 (1): 1–29. https://doi.org/10.1093/sp/jxy007.

Ayoub, Phillip M., and David Paternotte. 2014a. "Challenging Borders, Imagining Europe: Transnational LGBT Activism in a New Europe." In *Border Politics, Social Movements and Globalization*, edited by Jennifer Bickham-Mendez and Nancy Naples, 230–60. New York: NYU Press.

Ayoub, Phillip M., and David Paternotte, eds. 2014b. *LGBT Activism and the Making of Europe: A Rainbow Europe?* Basingstoke: Palgrave Macmillan.

Bacchi, Carol. 1999. *Women, Policy and Politics: The Construction of Policy Problems*. London: Sage.

Bacchi, Carol. 2012. "Why Study Problematizations? Making Politics Visible." *Open Journal of Political Science* 2 (1): 1–8.

Bagić, Aida. 2006. "Women's Organizing in Post-Yugoslav Countries: Talking about 'Donors.'" In *Global Feminism: Transnational Women's Activism, Organizing and Human Rights*, edited by Myra Marx Ferree and Aili Mari Tripp, 141–65. New York: New York University Press.

Baltzer, Anna. 2017. "World without Walls Delegation Is On the Ground in Palestine!" October 9, 2017. US Campaign for Palestinian Rights. https://uscpr.org/worldwithoutwalls-delegation-in-palestine/.

Băluţă, Oana, Andreea Bragă, and Alice Iancu. 2011. *Impactul Crizei Economice Asupra Femeilor [The Impact of the Economic Crisis on Women]*. Bucureşti: Maiko.

Balzer, Carsten, and Jan Simon Hutta. 2014. "Trans Networking in the European Vortex: Between Advocacy and Grassroots Politics." In *LGBT Activism and the*

Making of Europe: A Rainbow Europe?, edited by Phillip M. Ayoub and David Paternotte, 171–92. Basingstoke: Palgrave Macmillan.

Banaszak, Lee Ann, Karen Beckwith, and Dieter Rucht, eds. 2003. *Women's Movements Facing the Reconfigured State*. Cambridge: Cambridge University Press.

Bandy, Joe, and Jackie Smith, eds. 2005. *Coalitions across Borders: Transnational Protest and the Neoliberal Order*. Lanham, MD: Rowman & Littlefield.

Bardon, Sarah. 2018. "Abortion: Taoiseach Defends 12-Week Plan Amid Cabinet Split." *Irish Times*, February 6, 2018.

Barvosa, Edwina. 2008. *Wealth of Selves: Multiple Identities, Mestiza Consciousness, and the Subject of Politics*. Texas: Texas A&M University Press.

Bassel, Leah, and Akwugo Emejulu. 2010. "Struggles for Institutional Space in France and the UK: Intersectionality and the Politics of Policy." *Politics & Gender* 6 (4): 517–44.

Bassel, Leah, and Akwugo Emejulu. 2014. "Solidarity under Austerity: Intersectionality in France and the United Kingdom." *Politics & Gender* 10 (1): 130–36.

Bassel, Leah, and Akwugo Emejulu. 2017. *The Politics of Survival: Minority Women, Activism and Austerity in France and Britain*. Bristol: Policy Press.

Bassichis, Morgan, and Dean Spade. 2014. "Queer Politics and Anti-Blackness." In *Queer Necropolitics*, edited by Jin Haritaworn, Adi Kuntsman, and Silivia Posocco, 191–210. New York: Routledge.

Beaman, Jean. 2017. *Citizen Outsider: Children of North African Immigrants in France*. Oakland: University of California Press.

Beamish, Thomas D., and Amy J. Luebbers. 2009. "Alliance Building across Social Movements: Bridging Difference in a Peace and Justice Coalition." *Social Problems* 56: 647–76.

Beckwith, Karen. 2000. "Beyond Compare? Women's Movements in Comparative Perspective." *European Journal of Political Research* 37 (4): 431–68.

Beckwith, Karen. 2007. "Mapping Strategic Engagements: Women's Movements and the State." *International Feminist Journal of Politics* 9 (3): 312–38.

Bedolla, Lisa García. 2007. "Intersections of Inequality: Understanding Marginalization and Privilege in the Post-Civil Rights Era." *Politics & Gender* 3 (2): 232–48.

Behl, Natasha. 2017. "Diasporic Researcher: An Autoethnographic Analysis of Gender and Race in Political Science." *Politics, Groups, and Identities* 5 (4): 580–98.

Beissinger, Mark R., and Gwendolyn Sasse. 2014. "An End of Patience? The Great Recession and Economic Protest in Eastern Europe." In *Mass Politics in Tough Times: Opinions, Votes and Protest in the Great Recession*, edited by Larry Bartels and Nancy Bermeo, 334–70. London: Oxford University Press.

Béland, Daniel. 2009. "Ideas, Institutions, and Policy Change." *Journal of European Public Policy* 16 (15): 701–18.

Benderly, Jill. 1997. "Feminist Movements in Yugoslavia 197–1992." In *State-Society Relations in Yugoslavia 1945–1992*, edited by Melissa Bokovoy, Jill Irvine, and Carol Lilly, 183–210. New York: St. Martin's.

Berg, Linda, and Andrea Spehar. 2013. "Swimming against the Tide: Why Sweden Supports Free Labour Mobility within and from Outside the EU?" *Policy Studies* 34 (2): 142–61.

Bernal, Victoria, and Inderpal Grewal, eds. 2014. *Theorizing NGOS: States, Feminism, and Neoliberalisms*. Durham, NC: Duke University Press.

Bickford, Susan. 1997. "Anti-Identity Politics: Feminist, Democracy, and the Complexities of Citizenship." *Hypatia* 12 (4): 111–31.

Bilge, Sirma. 2013. "Intersectionality Undone: Saving Intersectionality from Feminist Intersectionality Studies." *DuBois Review: Social Science Research on Race* 10 (2): 405–24.

Bilge, Sirma. 2014. "Whitening Intersectionality: Evanescence of Race in Intersectionality Scholarship." In *Racism and Sociology*, edited by Wulf D. Hund and Alana Lentin. Zurich, Switzerland: LIT.

Bilić, Bojan, ed. 2014. *LGBT Activism and Europeanization in the Post-Yugoslav Space*. London: Palgrave Macmillan.

Bilić, Bojan, and Sonja Krajinić, eds. 2016. *Intersectionality and LGBT Activist Politics: Multiple Others in Croatia and Serbia*. London: Palgrave Macmillan.

Bishwakarma, Ramu, Hunt Valerie, and Anna Zajicek. 2007. "Educating Dalit Women: Beyond a One-Dimensional Policy Formulation." *Himalaya*, 17 (2): 27–39.

Biţu, Nicoleta. 1999. *The situation of Roma/Gypsy women in Europe. Strasbourg: Council of Europe*. MG-S-ROM (99) 9e.

Blackwell, Maylei. 2011. *Chicana Power! Contested Histories of Feminism in the Chicano Movement*. Austin: University of Texas Press.

Blombäck, Sophie, and Jenny de Fine Licht. 2017. "Same Considerations, Different Decisions: Motivations for Split-Ticket Voting among Swedish Feminist Initiative Supporters." *Scandinavian Political Studies* 40 (1): 61–81.

Bohle, Dohrotee, and Béla Greskovitz. 2012. *Capitalist Diversity on Europe's Periphery*. New York: Cornell University Press.

Bohrer, Ashley J. 2018. "Intersectionality and Marxism: A Critical Historiography." *Historical Materialism* 26 (2): 46–74.

Borland, Elisabeth. 2010. "Crisis as a Catalyst for Cooperation? Women's Organizing in Buenos Aires." In *Strategic Alliances: Coalition Building and Social Movements*, edited by Nella Van Dyke and Holly McCammon, 241–65. Minneapolis: Minnesota University Press.

Broad-Wright, Kendal. 2017. "Social Movement Intersectionality and Re-Centring Intersectional Activism." *Atlantis*, 38 (1): 41–53.

Brown, Nadia. 2014. *Sisters in the Statehouse: Black Women and Legislative Decision Making*. New York: Oxford University Press.

Broz, Tajana. 2013. "(Pred)izborne kampanje ženskih i feminističkih organizacija." In *Širenje područja političkog: novi pogledi na političku participaciju žena*, edited by Zorica Siročić and Leda Sutlović, 143–93. Zagreb: Centar za ženske studije.

Buğra, Ayşe, and Ayşen Candaş. 2011. "Change and Continuity under an Eclectic Social Security Regime: The Case of Turkey." *Middle Eastern Studies* 47 (3): 515–28.

Bunce, Valarie J., and Sharon L. Wolchik. 2011. *Defeating Authoritarian Leaders in Post Communist Countries*. New York: Cambridge University Press.

Burnier, DeLysia. 2006. "Encounters with the Self in Social Science Research: A Political Scientist Looks at Autoethnography." *Journal of Contemporary Ethnography* 35 (4): 410–18.

Bustelo, Marıa. 2009. "Spain: Intersectionality Faces the Strong Gender Norm." *International Feminist Journal of Politics* 11 (4): 530–46.

Butterfield, Nicole. 2014. "Discontents of Professionalisation: Sexual Politics and Activism in Croatia in the Context of EU Accession." In *LGBT Activism and*

Europeanization in the Post-Yugoslav Space, edited by Bojan Bilic, 23–58. London: Palgrave Macmillan.

Çaha, Ömer. 2011. "The Kurdish Women's Movement: A Third-Wave Feminism within the Turkish Context." *Turkish Studies* 12 (3): 435–49.

Çaha, Ömer. 2016. *Women and Civil Society in Turkey: Women's Movements in a Muslim Society*. Abingdon: Routledge.

Čakardić, Ankica. 2015. "Women's Struggles and Political Economy: From Yugoslav Self-Management to Neoliberal Austerity." In *Welcome to the Desert of Post-Socialism: Radical Politics after Yugoslavia*, edited by Srećko Horvat and Igor Štiks, 417–46. London: Verso.

Çakır, Ruşen. 2000. *Direniş ve İtaat. İki İktidar Arasında İslamcı Kadın*. Istanbul: Metis.

Calleman, Catharina. 2011. "Domestic Services in a 'Land of Equality': The Case of Sweden." *Canadian Journal of Women and the Law* 23 (1): 121–39.

Calligaro, Oriane. 2018. "Une organisation hybride dans l'arène européenne: Open Society Foundations et la construction du champ de la lutte contre les discrimination." *Politix* 121 (1): 151–72.

Carastathis, Anna. 2008. "The Invisibility of Privilege: A Critique of Intersectional Models of Identity." *Les Ateliers de L'Éthique* 3 (2): 23–38.

Carastathis, Anna. 2013. "Identity Categories as Potential Coalitions." *Signs* 38 (4): 941–65.

Carbado, Devon W. 2013. "Colorblind Intersectionality." *Signs* 38 (4): 811–45.

Carby, Hazel. 1982. "White Woman Listen! Black Feminism and the Boundaries of Sisterhood." In *The Empire Strikes Back: Race and Racism in 70s Britain*, edited by The Centre for Contemporary Studies, 212–35. London: Hutchinson.

Çelik, Nihat, and Emre İşeri. 2016. "Islamically Oriented Humanitarian NGOs in Turkey: AKP Foreign Policy Parallelism." *Turkish Studies* 17 (3): 429–48.

Central Statistics Office (CSO). 2017. "The Proportion of Catholics in Ireland." http://www.cso.ie/en/releasesandpublications/ep/p-cp8iter/p8iter/p8rrc/.

Chenoweth, Erica, and Jeremy Pressman. 2017. "This Is What We Learned by Counting the Women's Marches." *Monkey Cage, The Washington Post*, February 7, 2017. https://www.washingtonpost.com/news/monkey-cage/wp/2017/02/07/this-is-what-we-learned-by-counting-the-womens-marches/?utm_term=.618df0520367.

Chetaille, Agnes. 2013. "L'Union Européenne, Le Nationalisme Polonais et La Sexualisation de La 'division Est/Ouest.'" *Raisons Politiques* 49 (1): 119–40.

Cho, Sumi, Kimberlé Crenshaw, and Leslie McCall. 2013. "Toward a Field of Intersectionality Studies: Theory, Application, and Praxis." *Signs: Journal of Women in Culture and Society* 38 (4): 785–810.

Chun, Jenifer Jihye, George Lipsitz, and Young Shin. 2013. "Intersectionality as a Social Movement Strategy: Asian Immigrant Women Advocates." *Signs* 38 (4): 917–40.

Cindoğlu, Dilek. 2011. *Headscarf Ban and Discrimination: Professional Headscarved Women in the Labor Market*. Istanbul: TESEV.

Clark, Ann Marie. 2001. *Diplomacy of Conscience: Amnesty International and Changing Human Rights Norms*. New Jersey: Princeton University Press.

Coalition to Repeal the Eight. 2017a. 'Campaign Launch Statement' Accessed September 18th 2017. https://repeal8.language.ie/citizens-assembly-urged-to-recommend-full-removal-of-eighth-amendment/

Coalition to Repeal the Eight. 2017b. Trapped in Time Round Table Discussion with '83 Anti Amendment Campaigners – 5th Oct. 2017 Dublin. Accessed November 12th 2017. https://repeal8.language.ie/1983-2017-trapped-in-time/..

Cohen, Cathy. 1997. "Punk, Bulldaggers, and Welfare Queens: The Radical Potential of Queer Politics?" *GLQ* 3: 437–65.

Cole, Elisabeth R. 2008. "Coalition as Model for Intersectionality: From Practice to Theory." *Sex Roles* 59 (5–6): 443–53.

Collins, Michael, and Mary Murphy. 2016. "Activation: Solving Unemployment or Supporting a Low-Pay Economy?" In *The Irish Welfare State in the 21st Century: Challenges and Changes*, edited by Mary P. Murphy and Fiona Dukelow, 67–92. Basingstoke: Palgrave Macmillan.

Collins, Patricia Hill. 1990. *Black Feminist Thought: Knowledge, Consciousness, and the Politics of Empowerment.* Boston, MA: Unwin Hyman.

Collins, Patricia Hill. 1993. "Towards a New Vision: Race, Class, and Gender as Categories of Analysis and Connection." *Race, Sex & Class* 1: 24–45.

Collins, Patricia Hill. 2008. *Black Feminist Thought: Knowledge, Consciousness, and the Politics of Empowerment.* New York: Routledge.

Collins, Patricia Hill. 2011. "Piecing Together a Genealogical Puzzle: Intersectionality and American Pragmatism." *European Journal of Pragmatism and American Philosophy* 3 (2): 88–112.

Collins, Patricia Hill. 2015. "Intersectionality's Definitional Dilemmas." *Annual Review of Sociology* 41: 1–20.

Collins, Patricia Hill, and Valerie Chepp. 2013. "Intersectionality." In *The Oxford Handbook of Gender and Politics*, edited by Karen Celis, Johanna Kantola, Georgina Waylen, and S. Laurel Weldon, 57–87. London and New York: Oxford University Press.

Collins, Patricia Hill, and Sirma Bilge. 2016. *Intersectionality.* Cambridge: Polity Press.

Colón Morera, José Javier, and Idsa Alegría Ortega. 2012. "Introducción." In *Puerto Rico y los Derechos Humanos: Una Intersección Plural*, edited by José Javier Colón Morera and Idsa Alegría Ortega. San Juan: Libros El Navegante.

Combahee River Collective. 1977. "Combahee River Collective: A Black Feminist Statement." In *Let Nobody Turn Us Around: Voices of Resistance, Reform, and Renewal*, edited by Manning Marable and Leith Mullings, 524–29. New York: Rowman & Littlefield.

Connolly, Linda. 2006. "The Consequences and Outcomes of Second Wave Feminism in Ireland." In *Social Movements and Ireland*, edited by Linda Connolly and Niamh Hourigan, 58–85. Manchester: Manchester University Press.

Conway, Janet M. 2012. "Transnational Feminisms Building Anti-Globalization Solidarities." *Globalizations* 9 (3): 379–93.

Coşar, Simten, and Aylin Özman. 2009. "Neoliberalismus, Nationalismus und Islam in der politischen Mitte der Türkei nach 1980." In *Debatten zur Globalisierten Türkei*. Wirtschaft, Politik, Gesellschaft, edited by F. E. Keyman and Nurhan Yentürk, 25–63. Berlin: Dağyeli.

Coşar, Simten, and İnci Özkan-Kerestecioğlu. 2017. "Feminist Politics in Contemporary Turkey: Neoliberal Attacks, Feminist Claims to the Public." *Journal of Women, Politics & Policy* 38 (2): 151–74.

Coşar, Simten, and Metin Yeğenoğlu. 2011. "New Grounds for Patriarchy in Turkey? Gender Policy in the Age of AKP." *South European Society and Politics* 16 (4): 555–73.

Cram, Laura. 2011. "The Importance of the Temporal Dimension: New Modes of Governance as a Tool of Government." *Journal of European Public Policy* 18 (5): 636–53.

Crenshaw, Kimberlé. 1989. "Demarginalizing the Intersection of Race and Sex: A Black Feminist Critique of Antidiscrimination Doctrine, Feminist Theory and Antiracist Politics." *University of Chicago Legal Forum* 1 (8): 139–67.

Crenshaw, Kimberlé. 1991. "Mapping the Margins: Intersectionality, Identity Politics, and Violence against Women of Color." *Stanford Law Review* 43 (6): 1241–99.

Crenshaw, Kimberlé. 2017. "Kimberlé Crenshaw on Intersectionality, More Than Two Decades Later." Columbia Law School, June 8. https://www.law.columbia.edu/pt-br/news/2017/06/kimberle-crenshaw-intersectionality. Accessed June 5, 2019.

Cullen, Pauline. 2005. "Conflict and Cooperation within the Platform of European Social NGOs." In *Coalitions across Borders: Transnational Protest and the Neoliberal Order*, edited by Joe Bandy and Jackie Smith, 71–94. Lanham, MD: Rowman & Littlefield.

Cullen, Pauline. 2008. "Irish Women's Organizations in an Enlarged Europe." In *Gender Issues and Women's Movements in the Expanding European Union*, edited by Silke Roth, 83–100. Oslo: Berghahn Press.

Cullen, Pauline. 2010. "The Platform of European Social NGOs: Ideology, Division and Coalition." *Journal of Political Ideologies* 15 (3): 317–31.

Cullen, Pauline. 2015a. "From Coalition to Community: Collective Identity Formation in the Social Platform." In *EU Civil Society. Patterns of Cooperation, Competition and Conflict*, edited by Hakan Johansson and Sara Kalm, 81–97. Basingstoke: Palgrave Macmillan.

Cullen, Pauline. 2015b. "Feminist NGOs and the European Union: Contracting Opportunities and Strategic Response." *Social Movement Studies* 14 (4): 410–26.

Cullen, Pauline. 2016. "The Irish Women's Movement." *Global Dialogue: Magazine of the International Sociological Association* 5 (2). http://globaldialogue.isa-sociology.org/category/volume-5/v5-i2/.

Cullen, Pauline, and Mary Murphy. 2016. "Gendered Mobilizations against Austerity in Ireland." *Gender, Work and Organization* 24 (1): 83–97.

Curtin, Nicola, and Abigail J. Stewart. 2011. "Linking Personal and Social Histories with Collective Identity Narratives." In *Social Categories in Everyday Experience*, edited by Shaun Wiley, Gina Philogène, and Tracey A. Revenson, 83–101. Washington, DC: American Psychological Association.

Curtin, Nicola, Abigail J. Stewart, and Elizabeth R. Cole. 2015. "Challenging the Status Quo: The Role of Intersectional Awareness in Activism for Social Change and Pro-Social Intergroup Attitudes." *Psychology of Women Quarterly* 39 (4): 512–29.

D'Agostino, Serena. 2018. Making, Unmaking and Remaking Spaces. Romani Women's Intersectional Activism in European Transnational Politics, paper presented at the 25th International Conference of Europeanists "Europe and the World: Mobilities, Values and Citizenship", organized by the Council for European Studies (CES), Chicago – Illinois (U.S.A.), 28–30 March 2018.

Dagens Arena. 2011. "Tid att avliva myter." March 28, 2011. Accessed January 25, 2017. http://www.dagensarena.se/opinion/tid-att-avliva-myter/.

Dagens Nyheter. 2004a "Lyckat Finskt Försök Trappar upp Pigdebatten Inför Nästa Val." October 26, 2004.

Dagens Nyheter. 2004b. "Ministerdebutant i Blåsväder." October 31, 2004. Accessed January 25, 2017. https://www.dn.se/nyheter/politik/ministerdebutant-i-blasvader/.

Daphi, Priska. 2016. "Zivilgesellschaftliches Engagement für Flüchtlinge und locale 'Willkommenskultur.'" *Aus Politik und Zeitgeschichte* 66 (14–15): 35–39.

Davidson-Schmich, Louise K. 2017. *Gender, Intersections, and Institutions: Intersectional Groups Building Alliances and Gaining Voice in Germany.* Ann Arbor: University of Michigan Press.

Davis, Angela Y. 1972. "Reflections on the Black Woman's Role in the Community of Slaves." *The Massachusetts Review* 13 (1/2): 81–100.

Davis, Angela Y. 1981. *Women, Race, and Class.* London: Women's Press.

Davis, Angela Y. 2003. *Are Prisons Obsolete?* New York: Seven Stories Press.

Davis, Angela Y. 2016. *Freedom Is a Constant Struggle.* Chicago, IL: Haymarket.

Davis, Kathy. 2008. "Intersectionality as Buzzword: A Sociology of Science Perspective on What Makes a Feminist Theory Successful." *Feminist Theory* 9 (1): 67–85.

Dawson, Michael. 1994. *Behind the Mule: Race and Class in African-American Politics.* Princeton: Princeton University Press.

De Jong, Sara, and Susanne Kimm. 2017. "The Co-Optation of Feminisms: A Research Agenda." *International Feminist Journal of Politics* 19 (2): 185–200. DOI: 10.1080/14616742.2017.1299582.

De Tona, Carla, and Ronit Lentin. 2011. "Networking Sisterhood, from the Informal to the Global: AkiDwA, the African and Migrant Women's Network, Ireland." *Global Networks* 11: 242–261.

Dean, Jodi. 2015. "After Post-Politics: Occupation and the Return to Communism." In *The Post-Political and Its Discontents*, edited by Japhy Wilson and Erik Swyngedow, 261–78. Edinburgh: Edinburgh University Press.

Della Porta, Donatella. 2005. "Making the Polis: Social Forums and Democracy in the Global Justice Movement." *Mobilization* 10 (1): 73–94.

Della Porta, Donatella. 2018. "Contentious Moves: Mobilising for Refugees' Rights." In *Contentious Moves: Solidarity Mobilizations in the "Refugee Crisis,"* edited by Donatella della Porta, 1–39. London: Palgrave Macmillan.

Della Porta, Donatella, and Dieter Rucht, eds. 2013. *Meeting Democracy: Power and Deliberation in Global Justice Movements.* Cambridge: Cambridge University Press.

Della Porta, Donatella, and Louisa Parks. 2013. "Contentious EU Politics: A Comparative Analysis of Protest Campaigns." In *A Political Sociology of Transnational Europe*, edited by Niilo Kauppi, 17–49. Colchester: ECPR Press.

Della Porta, Donatella, and Manuela Caiani. 2009. *Social Movements and Europeanization.* Oxford: Oxford University Press.

Della Sala, Vincent, and Carlo Ruzza. 2007. *Governance and Civil Society in the European Union, Volume 1&2.* Manchester: Manchester University Press.

DeWan, Jennifer K. 2010. "The Practice of Politics: Feminism, Activism and Social Change in Ireland." In *Irish Business and Society: Governing, Participating and Transforming in the 21st Century*, edited by John Hogan, Paul F. Donnelly, and Brendan O'Rourke, 520–36. Dublin: Gill & MacMillan.

Deželan, Tomaž, Jasminka Pešut, Zorica-Iva Siročić, Danica Fink Hafner, Leda Sutlović, Alenka Krašovec, Snježana Vasiljević, Slađana Krupljan, and Adis Velić. 2013. *Leveling the Playing Field: Monitoring Croatian Policies to Promote Gender Equality in Politics*. Ljubljana: Faculty of Social Sciences; Zagreb: Centre for Women's Studies.

Dhamoon, Rita Kaur. 2011. "Considerations on Mainstreaming Intersectionality." *Political Research Quarterly* 64 (1): 230–43.

Diani, Mario, and Doug McAdam, eds. 2003. *Social Movements and Networks. Relational Approaches to Collective Action*. Oxford: Oxford University Press.

Diaz, Robert. 2018. "Introduction: The 'Stuff' of Queer Horizons and Other Utopic Pursuits." In *Diasporic Intimacies: Queer Filipinos and Diasporic Imaginaries*, edited by Robert Diaz, Marissa Largo, and Fritz Pino, xv–xxxvi. Evanston: Northwestern University Press.

Diner, Çağla, and Şule Toktaş. 2010. "Waves of Feminism in Turkey: Kemalist, Islamist and Kurdish Women's Movements in an Era of Globalization." *Journal of Balkan and Near Eastern Studies* 12 (1): 41–57.

Dobrotić, Ivana, Teo Matković, and Sinisa Zrinščak. 2013. "Gender Equality Policies and Practices in Croatia—Interplay of Transition and Late Europeanization." *Social Policy and Administration* 47 (2): 218–40.

Doerr, Nicole. 2018a. Political Translation. *How Social Movement Democracies Survive*. New York: Cambridge University Press.

Doerr, Nicole. 2018b. "Translation and Democracy." *Routledge Handbook on Translation and Politics*, edited by Jonathan Evans and Fruela Fernandez, 64–78. London: Routledge.

Doolan, Karin. 2014. "Learning to be a Citizen through Policy Analysis and Protest: Citizenship in Southeast Europe." Accessed May 31, 2018, from http://www.citsee.eu/citsee-story/learning-be-citizen-through-policy-analysis-and-protest.

Dür, Andreas, and Dirk De Bièvre. 2007. "The Question of Interest Group Influence." *Journal of Public Policy* 27 (1): 1–12.

Dursun, Ayşe. 2018a. "Der Aufstieg von konservativen Frauen-NGOs in der 'neuen Türkei': Eine Analyse des Vereins für Frau und Demokratie." In *Patriarchat im Wandel: Frauen und Politik in der Türkei*, edited by Aslı Aksoy, 107–31. Frankfurt: Campus.

Dursun, Ayşe. 2018b. "Muslim Women's Movement in Turkey: An Intersectional Approach to Coalition Building." PhD diss., University of Vienna.

Dursun, Ayşe, and Nehir Kovar. 2018. "Trojanisches Pferd der Regierung: Konservative Frauen-NGOs in der Türkei." In *Nach dem Putsch. 16 Anmerkungen zur "neuen" Türkei*, edited by Ilker Ataç, Michael Fanizadeh, and Volkan Ağar, 204–14. Wien: Mandelbaum.

Duvander, Ann-Zofie, Tommy Ferrarini, and Sara Thalberg. 2006. "Swedish Parental Leave: Achievements and Reform Challenges" In *Reconciling Family and Work: New Challenges for Social Policies in Europe*, edited by Giovanna Rossi, 217–38. Milan: Franco Angelli.

Eder, Mine. 2010. "Retreating State? Political Economy of Welfare Regime Change in Turkey." *Middle East Law and Governance* 2 (2): 152–84.

Edwards, Robert, and John McCarthy. 2004. "Resources and Social Movement Mobilization." In *The Blackwell Companion to Social Movements*, edited by David A. Snow, Sarah A. Soule, and Hanspeter Kriesi, 116–52. London: Blackwell.

Ehrenreich, Barbara, and Arlie Russell Hochschild, eds. 2003. *Global Woman: Nannies, Maids, and Sex Workers in the New Economy*. New York: Metropolitan.

Ellison, Nick. 2000. "Proactive and Defensive Engagement: Social Citizenship in a Changing Public Sphere." *Sociological Research Online* 5 (3): 1–11.

Elomäki, Anna. 2012. *The Price of Austerity—The Impact on Women's Rights and Gender Equality in Europe*. Brussels: European Women's Lobby.

Emejulu, Akwugo. 2011. "Can 'the People' Be Feminists? Analysing the Fate of Feminist Justice Claims in Populist Grassroots Movements in the United States." *Interface: Special Issue on Feminism, Women's Movements and Women in Movements* 3 (2): 123–51.

Emejulu, Akwugo, and Leah Bassel. 2017. "Whose Crisis Counts? Minority Women, Austerity and Activism in France and Britain." In *Gender and Economic Crisis in Europe*, edited by Johanna Kantola and Emmanuela Lombardo, 185–208. New York: Palgrave.

Eric, Josephine. 2012. "The Rites of Passage of Filipinas in Canada: Two Migration Cohorts." In *Filipinos in Canada: Disturbing Invisibility*, edited by Roland Coloma, Bonnie McElhinney, Ethel Tungohan, John Paul Catungal, and Lisa Davison, 123–41. Toronto: UTP.

Ernst, Rose. 2010. *The Price of Progressive Politics: The Welfare Rights Movement in an Era of Colorblind Racism*. New York and London: NYU Press.

ERRC and Romani CRISS. 2006. "Shadow Report. United Nations Convention on the Elimination of All Forms of Discrimination against Women in Romania for Its Consideration at the 35th Session." May 15 to June 2, 2006. http://www.errc.org/uploads/upload_en/file/03/82/m00000382.pdf

Evans, Elisabeth. 2015. *The Politics of the Third Wave Feminisms: Neoliberalism, Intersectionality, and the State in Britain and the US*. New York: Palgrave MacMillan.

Expressen. 2010. "Invandrarna Behöver Städjobben." March 4, 2010. Accessed 25 January 2017. https://www.expressen.se/debatt/tobias-billstrom-invandrarna-behover-stadjobben/.

Fábian, Katalin. 2009. *Contemporary Women's Movements in Hungary: Globalization, Democracy, and Gender Equality*. Washington, DC: Woodrow Wilson Center Press.

Falcón, Sylvanna M. 2012. "Transnational Feminism and Contextualized Intersectionality at the 2001 World Conference against Racism." *Journal of Women's History* 24 (4): 99–120.

Falcón, Sylvanna M., and Jennifer C. Nash. 2015. "Shifting Analytics and Linking Theories: A Conversation about the 'Meaning-Making' of Intersectionality and Transnational Feminism." *Women's Studies International Forum* 50: 1–10.

Fassin, Didier. 2013. *Enforcing Order: An Ethnography of Urban Policing*. Malden, MA: Polity Press.

Feministiskt Initiativ. 2014. "Election Platform." Accessed November 21, 2017, from http://feministisktinitiativ.se/sprak/english/election-platform/.

Ferree, Myra Marx, and Silke Roth. 1998. "Gender, Class, and the Interaction between Social Movement." *Gender & Society* 12 (6): 626–48.

Ferrer-Núñez, Shariana. 2016. "Framing Intersectionality in Social Movements: The Puerto Rican Student Movement Case (2006–2016)." Presentation given at Purdue University on 7/27/16.

Filimonov, Kirill, and Jakob Svensson. 2016. "(Re)Articulating Feminism. A Discourse Analysis of Sweden's Feminist Initiative Election Campaign." *Nordicom Review* 37 (2): 1–16.

Fisher, Sharon, and Biljana Bijelić. 2007. "Glas '99: Civil Society Preparing the Ground for a Post-Tudjman Croatia." In *Reclaiming Democracy: Civil Society and Electoral Change in Central and Eastern Europe*, edited by Joerg Forbrig and Pavol Demes, 53–78. Washington, DC: German Marshall Fund.

Flores-Gonzalez, Nilda and Ruth Gomberg-Munoz. 2013. "FLOResiste: Transnational Labor, Motherhood, and Activism." In *Immigrant Women Workers in the Neoliberal Age*, edited by Nilda Flores-Gonzalez, Anna Romina Guevarra, Maura Toro-Morn, and Grace Chang, 262–276. Champaign-Urbana, IL: University of Illinois Press.

Fobear, Katherine. 2014. "Queer Settlers: Questioning Settler Colonialism in LGBT Asylum Processes in Canada." *Refuge* 30 (1): 47–56.

Frank, Ana. 2008. *Report Analysing Intersectionality in Gender Equality Policies for Croatia and the EU, QUING Project*. Vienna: Institute for Human Sciences (IWM).

Fraser, Nancy. 2009. "Feminism, Capitalism and the Cunning of History." *New Left Review* 6 (2): 97–118.

Fraser, Nancy. 2016. "Contradictions of Capitalism and Care." *New Left Review* 100: 99–117.

Friedman, Elisabeth J. 2000. *Unfinished Transitions: Women and the Gendered Development of Democracy in Venezuela 1936–1996*. University Park: Pennsylvania State University Press.

Friedrich, Dawid. 2011. *Democratic Participation and Civil Society in the European Union*. Manchester: Manchester University Press.

Gamson, William. 1961. "A Theory of Coalition Formation." *American Sociological Review* 26 (3): 373–82. https://doi.org/10.2307/2090664.

Gamson, William. 1988. "Political Discourse and Collective Action." *International Social Movement Research* 1: 219–44.

García Oquendo, José Enrique. 2010. "Huelga Estudiantil de Abril 2010: Una Huelga en Defensa de la Educación Pública Superior." https://www.facebook.com/notes/garc%C3%ADa-enrique-jos%C3%A9/huelga-estudiantil-de-abril-2010-una-huelga-en-defensa-de-la-educaci%C3%B3n-p%C3%BAblica-s/424789132025/.

Gay, Claudine. 2002. "Spirals of Trust? The Effect of Descriptive Representation on the Relationship between Citizens and Their Government." *American Journal of Political Science* 46 (4): 717–32.

Gill, Rosalind, and Christina Scharff. 2011. "Introduction." In *New Femininities. Postfeminism, Neoliberalism and Subjectivity*, edited by Rosalind Gill and Christina Scharff, 1–17. Basingstoke: Palgrave Macmillan.

Gillespie, Andra and Melissa R. Michelson. 2011. "Participant Observation and the Political Scientist: Possibilities, Priorities, and Practicalities." PS: Political Science and Politics 44(2): 261–265.

Gitlin, Todd. 1995. *The Twilight of Common Dreams: Why America Is Wracked by Culture Wars*. New York: Metropolitan.

Gitlin, Todd. 2012. *Occupy Nation: The Roots, the Spirit, and the Promise of Occupy Wall Street.* New York: It Books.

Givens, Terry E., and Rhonda Evans Case. 2014. *Legislating Equality: The Politics of Antidiscrimination Policy in Europe.* Oxford: Oxford University Press.

Goldstone, Jack A. 1980. "Theories of Revolution: The Third Generation." *World Politics* 32 (3): 425–53.

Göle, Nilüfer. 1998. "Islamism, Feminism and Post-Modernism: Women's Movements in Islamic Countries." *New Perspective on Turkey* 19: 53–70.

Göle, Nilüfer. 2000. "Snapshots of Islamic Modernities." *Daedalus* 129 (1): 91–117.

Gornitzka, Åse, and Ulf Sverdrup. 2008. "Who Consults? The Configuration of Expert Groups in the European Union." *West European Politics* 31 (4): 725–50.

Government Bill 2006/07:94 Sweden (SFS 2007:346). "Skattelättnader för hushållstjänster m.m.," Interpellation 2007/08:680 (2007) "Skattesubventioner för Hushållsnära Tjänster." Accessed October 11, 2013, from http://www.riksdagen.se/sv/Dokument-Lagar/Fragor-och-anmalningar/Interpellationer/Skattesubventioner-for-hushall_GV10680/.

Greenwood, Justin. 2011. *Interest Representation in the European Union.* New York: Macmillan.

Greenwood, Ronni Michelle. 2008. "Intersectional Political Consciousness: Appreciation for Intragroup Differences and Solidarity in Diverse Groups. *Psychology of Women Quarterly* 32 (1): 36–47.

Griffin, Penny. 2015. "Crisis, Austerity and Gendered Governance: A Feminist Perspective." *Feminist Review* 109: 49–72.

Grünberg, Laura. 2014. "Lived Feminism(s) in Postcommunist Romania." In *Theorizing NGOs: States, Feminisms, and Neoliberalism,* edited by Victoria Bernal and Inderpal Grewal, 248–65. Durham and London: Duke University Press.

Haaretz. 2018. "Durham, North Carolina Becomes First U.S. City to Bar Police from Training in Israel." *Haaretz,* April 19, 2018. https://www.haaretz.com/us-news/durham-becomes-first-u-s-city-to-bar-police-from-training-in-israel-1.6011720. Accessed June 5, 2019.

Hall, Lisa Kahaleole. 2009. "Navigating Our Own 'Sea of Islands': Remapping a Theoretical Space for Hawaiian Women and Indigenous Feminism." *Wicazo Sa Review* 24 (2): 15–38.

Hamann, Ulrike, and Serhat Karakayali. 2016. "Practicing Willkommenskultur: Migration and Solidarity in Germany." *Intersections East European Journal of Society and Politics* 2 (4): 69–86.

Hancock, Ange-Marie. 2007a. "Intersectionality as a Normative and Empirical Paradigm." *Politics & Gender* 3 (2): 248–54.

Hancock, Ange-Marie. 2007b. "When Multiplication Doesn't Equal Quick Addition: Examining Intersectionality as a Research Paradigm." *Perspectives on Politics* 5 (1): 63–79.

Hancock, Ange-Marie. 2011. *Solidarity Politics for Millennials: A Guide to Ending the Oppression Olympics.* New York: PalgraveMacmillan.

Hancock, Ange-Marie. 2017. *Intersectionality: An Intellectual History.* New York: Oxford University Press.

Haraway, Donna. 1988. "Situated Knowledges: The Science Question in Feminism and the Privilege of Partial Perspective." *Feminist Studies* 14 (3): 575–99.

Hark, Sabine, and Paula-Irene Villa. 2017. *Unterscheiden und herrschen. Ein Essay zu den ambivalenten Verflechtungen von Rassismus, Sexismus und Feminismus in der Gegenwart.* Bielefeld: Transcript.

Harris, Angela. 1990. "Race and Essentialism in Feminist Legal Theory." *Stanford Law Review* 42 (3): 581–616.

Harvey, Brian. 2014. *Are We Paying for That; Government Funding and Social Justice Advocacy.* Dublin: The Advocacy Initiative.

Harvey, David. 1996. *Justice, Nature and the Geography of Difference.* Oxford: Blackwell.

Hawkesworth, Mary. 2006. *Feminist Inquiry: From Political Conviction to Methodological Innovation.* New Brunswick, NJ: Rutgers University Press.

Healy, Grainne, Brian Sheehan, and Noel Whelan. 2016. *Ireland Says Yes: The Inside Story of How the Vote for Marriage Equality Was Won.* Dublin: Merrion Press.

Hemment, Julie. 2007. *Empowering Women in Russia: Activism, Aid, and NGOs.* Bloomington: Indiana University Press.

Hicks, Heather. 2017. "Intersectional Stereotyping and Support for Black Women Candidates." Presented at the American Political Science Association Annual Conference, San Francisco, CA.

Hobsbawm, Eric. 1996. "Identity Politics and the Left." *New Left Review* 217: 38–47.

Hollstein, Betina, and Florian Straus, eds. 2006. *Qualitative Netzwerkanalyse: Konzepte, Methoden, Anwendungen.* Wiesbaden: VS Verlag für Sozialwissenschaften.

Hollstein, Betina, and Jürgen Pfeffer. 2010. "Netzwerkkarten als Instrument zur Erhebung egozentrierter Netzwerke." In *Unsichere Zeiten. Verhandlungen des 34. Kongress der Deutschen Gesellschaft für Soziologie, 6.-10. Oktober, Jena.*, edited by Hans-Georg Soeffner. Wiesbaden: VS Verlag für Sozialwissenschaften. http://www.pfeffer.at/egonet/Hollstein%20Pfeffer.pdf.

hooks, bell. 1984. *Feminist Theory from Margin to Center.* Boston, MA: South End Press.

Horvat, Srećko, and Igor Štiks. 2010. *Pravo na pobunu: Uvod u anatomiju građanskog otpora.* Zagreb: Fraktura.

Hoskyns, Catherine. 1996. *Integrating Gender: Women, Law and Politics in the European Union.* London and New York: Verso.

Htun, Mala, and Laurel Weldon. 2012. "The Civic Origins of Progressive Policy Change: Combating Violence against Women in Global Perspective 1975–2005." *American Political Science Review* 106 (3): 548–69.

Htun, Mala, and S. Laurel Weldon. 2018. *The Logics of Gender Justice: State Action on Women's Rights around the World.* Cambridge: Cambridge University Press.

IHREC. 2017. *CEDAW Submission. Dublin IHREC.* https://www.ihrec.ie/documents/ireland-convention-elimination-forms-discrimination-women/.

INCITE! Women of Color Against Violence. 2007. *The Revolution Will Not Be Funded: Beyond the Non-Profit Industrial Complex.* Cambridge: South End Press.

Indigenous Action Media. 2015. "Accomplices Not Allies: Abolishing the Ally Industrial Complex." In *Taking Sides: Revolutionary Solidarity and the Poverty of Liberalism*, edited by Cindy Milstein, 85–96. Oakland, CA: AK Press.

Inghilleri, Moira. 2012. *Interpreting Justice: Ethics, Politics and Language*. London: Routledge.

International Parliamentary Union (IPU). 2018. *Women in National Parliaments*. Accessed April 1, 2018, from http://archive.ipu.org/wmn-e/classif.htm.

Irvine, Janice, and Jill A. Irvine 2017. "The Queer Work of Militarized Prides in the Balkans." *Contexts* 16 (4): 32–37.

Irvine, Jill A. 2007. "From Civil Society to Civil Servants: Women's Organizations and Critical Elections in Croatia." *Politics & Gender* 3 (1): 7–32.

Irvine, Jill A. 2013. "Electoral Breakthroughs in Croatia and Serbia: Women's Organizing and International Assistance." *Communist and Post-Communist Studies* 46 (2): 243–54.

Irvine, Jill A. 2018. "US Aid and Gender Equality: Social Movement vs. Civil Society Models of Funding." *Democratization* 25 (4): 728–46.

Irvine, Jill A., and Leda Sutlović. 2015. "Gender Equality in Croatia: Closing the Compliance Gap." In *Gender Equality and Gender Politics in Southeastern Europe, a Question of Justice*, edited by Sabrina P. Ramet and Christine M. Hassenstab, 62–86. London: Palgrave Macmillan.

Irvine, Jill A., and Nicholas Halterman. 2018. "Funding Empowerment: US Foundations and Global Gender Equality." *Politics & Gender*. https://doi.org/10.1017/S1743923X18000314.

Isoke, Zenzele. 2014. "Can't I Be Seen? Can't I Be Heard? Black Women Queering Politics in Newark." *Gender, Place and Culture* 21 (3): 353–69.

Jacquot, Sophie. 2015. *Transformations in EU Gender Equality: From Emergence to Dismantling*. Basingstoke: Palgrave Macmillan.

Jacquot, Sophie, and Tommaso Vitale. 2014. "Law as Weapon of the Weak? A Comparative Analysis of Legal Mobilization by Roma and Women's Groups at the European Level." *Journal of European Public Policy* 21 (4): 587–604.

Jewish Voice for Peace. 2015. *Jewish Voice for Peace on Boycott, Divestment and Sanctions*. Oakland, CA: JVP. https://jewishvoiceforpeace.org/jewish-voice-for-peace-on-boycott-divestment-and-sanctions/.

Jewish Voice for Peace (JVP). 2016a. *FAQ*. Oakland, CA: JVP. https://jewishvoiceforpeace.org/faq/.

Jewish Voice for Peace. 2016b. "Jewish Voice for Peace Responds to the Movement for Black Lives Policy Platform." Accessed August 4, 2016, from https://jewishvoiceforpeace.org/jvp4bl/.

Jewish Voice for Peace. 2016c. "Jewish Voice for Peace Supports the Standing Rock Sioux Tribe." Accessed August 29, 2016, from https://jewishvoiceforpeace.org/jewish-voice-for-peace-supports-the-standing-rock-sioux-tribe/.

Jewish Voice for Peace. 2016d. "Reflections on the School of the Americas Watch Convergence/Encuentro." Accessed October 21, 2016, from https://jewishvoiceforpeace.org/soaw/.

Jewish Voice for Peace. 2017a. "About Deadly Exchange." https://deadlyexchange.org/.

Jewish Voice for Peace. 2017b. "5777 Jewish Voice for Peace Annual Report." http://report.jewishvoiceforpeace.org/.

Jewish Voice for Peace. 2017c. "JVP: Mission." https://jewishvoiceforpeace.org/mission/.

Jewish Voice for Peace. 2017d. "The Road to Abolition." https://jvpchicago. org/calendar/2017/6/8/the-road-to-abolition-an-introduction-to-prison-industrial-complex-abolition.

Jewish Voice for Peace. 2018. "Imagining the World to Come." https://deadlyexchange. org/imagining-world-come-call-submissions/.

Jibrin, Reika, and Sara Salem. 2015. "Revisiting Intersectionality: Reflections on Theory and Practice." Trans-Scripts 5.

JOCSM. 2016. "Jews of Color Caucus Statement in Solidarity with the Movement for Black Lives." http://jocsm.org/jews-of-color-caucus-statement-in-solidarity-with-the-movement-for-black-lives-matter/.

JOCSM. 2017. "Stop Deportations and Grant Asylum to African Refugees in Israel." Accessed December 27, 2017, from http://jocsm.org/stopdeportingrefugees/.

JOCSM. 2018. "About This Blog." http://jocsm.org/about-us/.

Johansson, Hakan, and Sara Kalm. 2015. EU Civil Society. *Patterns of Cooperation, Competition and Conflict.* Basingstoke: Palgrave Macmillan.

Johnston, Hank, and Bert Klandermans. 1995. *Social Movements and Culture.* Minnesota: University of Minnesota Press.

Jordan-Zachery, Julia. 2007. "Am I a Black Woman or a Woman Who Is Black? A Few Thoughts on the Meaning of Intersectionality." *Politics & Gender* 3 (2): 254–63.

Jordan-Zachery, Julia. 2013. "Now You See Me, Now You Don't: My Political Fights against the Invisibility of Black Women in Intersectionality Research." *Politics, Gender, and Identities* 1 (1): 101–9.

Juris, Jeffrey S., Michelle Ronayne, Firuze Shokonooh-Valle, and Robert Wengronowitz. 2012. "Negotiating Power and Difference within the 99%." *Social Movement Studies: Journal of Social, Cultural and Political Protest* 11 (3–4): 434–40.

Kahn, Robert L., and Toni C. Antonucci. 1980. "Convoys over the Life Course: Attachment, Roles, and Social Support." In *Life-Span Development and Behaviour*, edited by Paul B. Baltes and Olim G. Brim, 383–405. New York: Academic Press.

Kajinić, Sanja. 2015. "Croatian Women's Movement and Domestic Violence Policy Change: Generational Approach." In *Mobilizing for Policy Change: Women's Movements in Central and Eastern European Domestic Violence Policy Struggles*, edited by Andrea Krizsán, 85–122. Budapest: Central European University, Centre for Policy Studies.

Kamenou, Nayia. 2018. "Social Movements and Europeanization: Resisting And Embracing Intersectionality in the Periphery." Presented at ECPR Joint Sessions, Nicosia, Cyprus.

Kantola, Johanna, and Emanuela Lombardo. 2017. "Gender and the Politics of the Economic Crisis in Europe." In *Gender and the Economic Crisis in Europe*, edited by Johanna Kantola and Emanuela Lombardo, 1–25. Basingstoke: Palgrave Macmillan. https://link.springer.com/chapter/10.1007/978-3-319-50778-1_1.

Kantola, Johanna, and Kevät Nousiainen. 2009. "Institutionalizing Intersectionality in Europe: Introducing the Theme." *International Feminist Journal of Politics* 11 (4): 459–78.

Kauffman, L. A. 1990. "The Anti-Politics of Identity." *Sociology Review* 90 (1): 67–80.

Kaya, Ayhan. 2014. "Islamisation of Turkey under the AKP Rule: Empowering Family, Faith and Charity." *South European Society and Politics*. DOI: 10.1080/13608746.2014.979031.

Keating, Ana Louise. 2009. "Recognizing Each Other: Towards a Politics of Interconnectedness." Paper presented at the National Women's Studies Association Conference, Atlanta, November 14.

Keck, Margaret E., and Kathryn Sikkink. 1998. *Activists beyond Borders: Advocacy Networks in International Politics*. Ithaca, NY: Cornell University Press.

Kelly, Liz. 2005. "Inside Outsiders: Mainstreaming Violence against Women into Human Rights Discourse and Practice." *International Feminist Journal of Politics* 7 (4): 471–95.

Kelly, Philip. 2006. *Filipinos in Canada: Economic Dimensions of Immigration and Settlement. Toronto: Joint Centre for Excellence for Research on Immigration and Settlement*. Toronto: CERIS.

Kemper, Andreas. 2014. *Keimzelle der Nation II. Wie sich in Europa Parteien und Bewegungen für konservative Familienwerte, gegen Toleranz und Vielfalt und gegen eine progressive Geschlechterpolitik radikalisieren*. Berlin: Friedrich-Ebert-Stiftung.

Kennedy, Carole. 2003. "Gender Differences in Committee Decision-Making." *Women & Politics* 25 (3): 27–45.

Kesić, Vesna. 2007. *Feminism and State*. Zagreb: CESI.

Kirby, Peadar, and Mary Murphy. 2011. *Towards A Second Republic: Irish Politics after the Celtic Tiger*. London: Pluto Press.

Kitschelt, Herbert P. 1986. "Political Opportunity Structures and Political Protest: Anti-Nuclear Movements in Four Democracies." *British Journal of Political Science* 16 (1): 57–85.

Knežević, Đurđa. 1994. "MI nasuprot JA." *Kruh i ruze* 1: 14–6.

Knežević, Đurđa, and Kristina Zaborski-čunović. 2000. *Izbori u Hrvatskoj 2000, 20% [ni]je dovoljno*. Zagreb: Ženska Infoteka.

Kohler-Koch, Beate, and Christine Quittkat. 2013. *De-Mystification of Participatory Democracy: EU-Governance and Civil Society*. Oxford: Oxford University Press.

Kontos, Maria. 2013. "Negotiating the Social Citizenship Rights of Migrant Domestic Workers: The Right to Family Reunification and a Family Life in Policies and Debates." *Journal of Ethnic and Migration Studies* 39 (3): 409–24.

Korac, Maja. 1998. "Linking Arms: Women and War in Post-Yugoslav States. Women and Nonviolence Series." *Uppsala Life and Peace Institute*, 6: 1–75.

Krizsán, Andrea. 2012. "Equality Architectures in Central and Eastern European Countries: A Framework for Analyzing Political Intersectionality in Europe." *Social Politics* 19 (4): 539–71.

Krizsán, Andrea, and Raluca Popa. 2014. "Frames in Contestation: Gendering Domestic Violence Policies in Five Central and Eastern European Countries." *Violence against Women* 20 (7): 758–82.

Krizsán, Andrea, and Conny Roggeband with contributions of Raluca Popa. 2018. *The Gender Politics of Domestic Violence: Feminists Engaging the State in Central and Eastern Europe*. New York: Routledge.

Kröger, Sandra. 2013. "Creating a European Demos? The Representativeness of European Umbrella Organizations." *Journal of European Integration* 35 (5): 583–600.

Kuhar, Roman. 2015. "Playing with Science: Sexual Citizenship and Roman Catholic Church Counter-Narratives in Slovenia and Croatia." *Women's Studies International Forum* 49: 84–92.

Kunac, Suzana. 2011. "Zagrebački prosvjedi—korak ka omasovljenju građanskih zahtjeva?" *Političke analize* 6 (2): 29–33.

Kurtz, Sharon. 2002. *Workplace Justice: Organizing Multi-Identity Movements*. Minneapolis: University of Minnesota Press.

Lacquian, Eleanor. 1973. *A Study of Filipino Immigration to Canada*. Ottawa: United Council of Filipino Associations in Canada.

Lag om Skattereduktion för Utgifter för Hushållsarbete SFS 2007:346. 2007. Swedish Code of Statutes.

Laguarta Ramírez, José A. 2016. "Struggling to Learn, Learning to Struggle: Strategy and Structure in the 2010–11 University of Puerto Rico Student Strike." PhD Diss., City University of New York. https://academicworks.cuny.edu/gc_etds/1359/.

Lalić, Drazen. 2011. "Politički Prosvjedi u Hrvatskoj. Klasične demonstracije, političko gibanje ili novi društveni pokret?" *Političke Analize* 2 (6): 23–8.

Lambda Legal. 2015. *Transgender Incarcerated People in Crisis*. New York: Lambda Legal. https://www.lambdalegal.org/sites/default/files/2015_transgender-incarcerated-people-in-crisis-fs-v5-singlepages.pdf.

Lang, Sabine. 1997. "The NGOization of Feminism." In *Transitions, Environments, Translations: Feminisms in International Politics*, edited by Cora Kaplan, Deborah Keates, and Joan W. Wallach, 101–21. London and New York: Routledge.

Lang, Sabine. 2009. "Assessing Advocacy: European Transnational Women's Networks and Gender Mainstreaming." *Social Politics* 16 (3): 327–57.

Lang, Sabine. 2013. *NGOs, Civil Society, and the Public Sphere*. New York: Cambridge University Press.

Lang, Sabine. 2015. "Testing Solidarities: German Women's and Migrant Activists in the Refugee Crisis." Paper presented at European Union Studies Association Meeting, Miami, Florida 2017.

Lang, Sabine, and Birgit Sauer. 2016. "European Integration and the Politics of Scale: A Gender Perspective." In *Gendering European Integration Theory*, edited by Gabriele Abels and Heather McRae, 217–36. Opladen/Berlin/Toronto: Budrich.

Lapperière, Marie, and Eléonore Lépinard. 2016. "Intersectionality as a Tool for Social Movements: Strategies of Inclusion and Representation in the Québécois Women's movement." *Politics* 36 (4): 374–82.

Laquian, Eleanor and Aprodicio Laquian. 2008. *Seeking a Better Life Abroad: A Study of Filipinos in Canada 1957-2008*. Manila, Philippines: Anvil.

Leahy, Pat. 2017a. "Eighth Amendment Referendum: Two Sides Now Marshal Forces." *Irish Times*, May 6, 2017.

Leahy, Pat. 2018a. "Anti-Abortion Campaigners Need Acceleration of Change to Secure Majority on May 25th." *Irish Times*, May 17, 2018.

Leahy, Pat. 2018b. "Yes Campaign's Outreach to Middle Ground Delivered the Land-slide." *Irish Times*, May 27, 2018.

Lee, Lynn. 1988. "The Contemporary Women's Movement in the Philippines." *Australian Feminist Studies* 3 (7–8): 217–23.

Lépinard, Eléonore. 2014. "Doing Intersectionality. Repertoires of Feminist Practices in France and Canada." *Gender and Society* 26 (3): 877–903.

Lewis, Gail. 2013. "Unsafe Travel: Experiencing Intersectionality and Feminist Displacements." *Signs* 38 (4): 869–92.

Livingston, Robert W., Ashleigh Shelby Rosette, and Ella F. Washington. 2012. "Can an Agentic Black Woman Get Ahead? The Impact of Race and Interpersonal Dominance on Perceptions of Female Leaders." *Psychological Science* 23(4): 354–58.

Lombardo, Emanuela, and Agustín. 2011. "Framing Gender Intersections in the European Union: What Implications for the Quality of Intersectionality in Policies?" *Social Politics* 19 (4): 482–512.

Lombardo, Emanuela, and Agustín. 2016. "Intersectionality in European Union Policymaking: The Case of Gender-Based Violence." *Politics* 36 (4): 364–73.

Lorde, Audre. 1982. *ZAMI: A New Spelling of My Name*. Freedom, CA: Crossing Press.

Luciak, I. A. 2001. *After the Revolution: Gender and Democracy in El Salvador, Nicaragua, and Guatemala*. Baltimore, MD: Johns Hopkins University Press.

Lugones, María. 2010. "Toward a Decolonial Feminism." *Hypatia* 25 (4): 742–59.

Lutz, Helma. 2011. *The New Maids: Transnational Women and the Care Economy*. London and New York: Zed.

Lye, Chandra. 2015. "Thousands of Temporary Foreign Workers Face Deportation Because of Program Changes." CTV News, March 21, 2015. Accessed April 10, 2018, from https://edmonton.ctvnews.ca/thousands-of-temporary-foreign-workers-face-deportation-due-to-program-changes-1.2291439.

Lynch, Kathleen, Sarah Cantillon, and Crean Magaret. 2016. "Inequality." In *Austerity in Recovery in Ireland. Europe's Poster Child in Recession*, edited by William K. Roche, Philip J. Connell, and Andrea Prohtero, 252–71. Oxford: Oxford University Press.

Lyshaug, Brenda. 2006. "Solidarity Without 'Sisterhood'? Feminism and the Ethics of Coalition Building." *Politics & Gender* 2 (1): 77–100.

McKay, Susan. 2018. "Ireland's Feminists Lost the Abortion Argument in '83. This Time We Can Win." *New York Times*, May 5, 2018. https://www.nytimes.com/2018/05/05/opinion/sunday/ireland-abortion-referendum.html, accessed May 19th 2018.

Maharawal, Manissa McCleave. 2012. "So Real It Hurts." In *Dreaming in Public: Building the Occupy Movement*, edited by Amy Shrager Lang and Daniel Lang/Levitsky, 154–60. Oxford: New Internationalist.

Mahoney, Christine. 2004. "The Power of Institutions. State and Interest Group Activity in the European Union." *European Union Politics* 5 (4): 441–66.

Mansbridge, Jane. 1999. "Should Black Represent Black and Women Represent Women? A Contingent 'Yes.'" *Journal of Politics* 61 (3): 628–57.

Martin F. Manalansan IV, Chantal Nadeau, Richard T. Rodríguez, and Siobhan B. Somerville. 2014. "Queering the Middle: Race, Region, and a Queer Midwest." *GLQ: A Journal of Lesbian and Gay Studies* 20 (1–2): 1–12.

Martinez, Elizabeth. 1993. "Beyond Black/White: The Racisms of Our Times." *Social Justice* 20 (1/2): 22–34.

May, Vivian. 2015. *Pursuing Intersectionality, Unsettling Dominant Imaginaries*. New York and London: Routledge.

Mazey, Sonia. 2012. "Policy Entrepreneurship, Group Mobilisation and the Creation of a New Policy Domain: Women's Rights and the European Union." In *Constructing a Policy-Making State? Policy Dynamics in the EU*, edited by Jeremy Richardson, 125–44. Oxford: Oxford University Press.

Mazur, Amy G. 2002. *Theorizing Feminist Policy*. New York: Oxford University Press.

McAdam, Doug. 1982. *Political Process and the Development of Black Insurgency, 1930–1970*. Chicago: University of Chicago Press.

McAdam, Doug. 1996. "Conceptual Origins, Current Problems, Future Decisions." In *Comparative Perspectives on Social Movements: Political Opportunities, Mobilizing Structures, and Cultural Framings*, edited by Doug McAdam, John D McCarthy, and Mayer N. Zald, 23–41. Cambridge: Cambridge University Press.

McAdam, Doug, Sidney Tarrow, and Charles Tilly. 2001. *Dynamics of Contention*. New York: Cambridge University Press.

McCall, Leslie. 2005. "The Complexity of Intersectionality." *Signs* 30 (3): 1771–1800.

McCammon, Holly, and Karen Campbell. 2002. "Allies on the Road to Victory: Coalition Formation between the Suffragists and the Woman's Christian Temperance Union." *Mobilization: An International Quarterly* 7 (3): 231–51.

McCarthy, John D., and Mayer N. Zald. 1977a. *The Dynamics of Social Movements*. Cambridge, MA: Winthrop.

McCarthy, John D., and Mayer N. Zald. 1977b. "Resource Mobilization and Social Movements: A Partial Theory." *American Journal of Sociology* 82: 1212–41.

McCarthy, John D., and Mayer N. Zald, eds. 1987. *Social Movements in an Organizational Society: Collected Essays*. New Jersey: Transaction.

McCarthy, John D., and Mayer N. Zald. 2001. *The Enduring Vitality of the Resource Mobilization Theory of Social Movements*. New York: Springer.

McElhinney, Bonnie, Lisa Davidson, John Paul Catungal, Ethel Tungohan, and Roland Coloma. 2012. "Spectres of (In)Visibility: Filipina/o Labour, Culture, and Youth in Canada." In *Filipinos in Canada: Disturbing Invisibility*, edited by Roland Coloma, Bonnie McElhinney, Ethel Tungohan, John Paul Catungal, and Lisa Davidson, 5–45. Toronto: UTP.

Mcgarry, Aidan. 2008. "Ethnic Group Identity and the Roma Social Movement." *Nationalities Papers* 36 (3): 449–70.

Mckesson, DeRay. 2018. *On the Other Side of Freedom: The Case for Hope*. New York: Viking.

Mendelson, Sarah E., and John K. Glenn, eds. 2002. *The Power and Limits of NGOs: A Critical Look at Building Democracy in Eastern Europe and Eurasia*. New York: Columbia University Press.

MERJ Migrants and Ethnic-Minorities for Reproductive Justice. 2018. "Together for Yes Supports Migrant Rights Groups Calling for the Removal of the 8th Amendment." https://www.togetherforyes.ie/together-for-yes-supports-migrants-rights-groups-calling-for-the-removal-of-the-8th-amendment/.

Meyer, David. 2004. "Protest and Political Opportunities." *Annual Review of Sociology* 30 (1): 125–45.

Mihálovics, Éva. 2013. "30 Minutes of Silence. Potential Intersections of Shame, Insecurities, and Fear on the NANE Helpline." MA Thesis, Central European University, Budapest.

Min-Ha, Trin T. 1989. *Women, Native, Other: Writing Post-Coloniality and Feminist.* Bloomington: Indiana University Press.

Mirza, Heidi Safia. 1997. *Black British Feminism: A Reader.* London and New York: Routledge.

Miškovska Kajevska, Ana. 2014. "Taking a Stand in Times of Violent Social Changes: Belgrade and Zagreb Feminists' Positionings on the (Post-)Yugoslav Wars and Each Other (1991–2000)." PhD Diss., University of Amsterdam.

Misra, Tanvi. 2017. "The Othered Paris." *CityLab*, November 16, 2017. Accessed June 6, 2019. https://www.citylab.com/equity/2017/11/the-othered-paris/543597/

Mitchell, Eve. 2013. "I Am a Woman and a Human: A Marxist Feminist Critique of Intersectional Theory." Accessed May 31, 2018, from https://libcom.org/library/i-am-woman-human-marxist-feminist-critique-intersectionality-theory-eve-mitchell.

Mohanty, Chandra. 2013. "Transnational Feminist Crossings: On Neoliberalism and Radical Critique." *Signs* 38 (4): 967–91.

Montoya, Celeste. 2013. *From Global to Grassroots: The European Union, Transnational Advocacy, and Combating Violence against Women.* New York: Oxford University Press.

Moon, Dreama, and Lisa A. Flores. 2000. "Antiracism and the Abolition of Whiteness: Rhetorical Strategies of Domination among 'Race Traitors.'" *Communication Studies* 51 (2): 97–115.

Moraga, Cherríe, and Gloria Anzaldúa, eds. 1981. *This Bridge Called My Back: Writings by Radical Women of Color.* Watertown, MA: Persephone Press.

Morgan, Jennifer L. 2004. *Laboring Women: Reproduction and Gender in New World Slavery.* Philadelphia: University of Pennsylvania Press.

Morgan, Kimberly. 2008. "The Political Path to a Dual Earner/Dual Career Society: Pitfalls and Possibilities." *Politics & Society* 36 (3): 403–20.

Morgensen, Scott Lauria. 2011. *Queer Settler Colonialism and Indigenous Decolonization.* Minneapolis: University of Minnesota Press.

Morgensen, Scott Lauria. 2012. "Queer Settler Colonialism in Canada and Israel: Articulating Two-Spirit and Palestinian Queer Critique." *Settler Colonial Studies* 2 (2): 167–90.

Motion 2003/04:Sk426. "Avdrag för Hushållsnäratjänster samt för Reparation, Om- och Tillbyggnad." Accessed January 31, 2015, from www.riksdagen.se/sv/Dokument-Lagar/Forslag/Motioner/Avdrag-for-hushallsnara-tjanst_GR02Sk426/?text=true.

Motta, Sara, Catherine Eschle, Cristina Flescher Fominaya, and Laurence Cox. 2011. "Introduction: Special Issue on Feminism." *Women's Movements and Women in Movements* 3 (2): 123–51.

Moyn, Samuel. 2010. *The Last Utopia: Human Rights in History.* Cambridge: Harvard University Press.

Mügge, Liza, Celeste Montoya, Akwugo Emejulu, and S. Laurel Weldon. 2018. "Intersectionality and the Politics of Knowledge Production." *European Journal of Politics and Gender* 1 (1–2): 17–36.

Murhem, Sofia, and Andreas Dahlkvist. 2011. "Arbetskraftsinvandring och Egenintresse—Arbetsmarknadens Parter och Liberaliseringen av det Svenska Regelverket för Arbetskraftsinvandring." *Arbetsmarknad & Arbetsliv* 17 (3): 37–51.

Murib, Zein, and Joe Soss. 2015. "Intersectionality as an Assembly of Analytic Practices: Subjects, Relations, and Situated Comparisons." *New Political Science* 37 (4): 649–56.

Murphy, Mary. 2017. "Irish Flex-Insecurity: The Reality for Low Paid Workers in Ireland Women, Migrants and Young People." *Social Policy & Administration* 52 (2): 308–27.

Murphy, Mary, and Pauline Cullen. 2018. *Feminist Response to Austerity in Ireland: Country Case Study Report for Rosa Luxembourg Foundation.* Brussels: Rosa-Luxembourg Institute.

Naples, Nancy. 1998. *Grassroots Warriors: Activist Mothering, Community Work, and the War on Poverty.* New York: Routledge.

Naples, Nancy. 2003. *Feminism and Method: Ethnography, Discourse Analysis, and Activist Research.* New York: Routledge.

Naples, Nancy A., and Manisha Desai, eds. 2002. *Women's Activism and Globalization. Linking Local Struggles and Transnational Politics.* New York: Routledge.

Naranđa, Ela. 2015. *Presjek ženskog aktivizma u Hrvatskoj danas. Libela—portal o rodu, spolu i Demokraciji.* Accessed May 22, 2018, from https://www.libela.org/vijesti/6335-presjek-zenskog-aktivizma-u-hrvatskoj-danas/.

National Women's Council of Ireland (NWCI). 2018. *Every Woman Affordable, Accessible Healthcare Options for Women and Girls in Ireland.* November 2017. Dublin: NWCI.

Ndugga-Kabuye, Ben, and Rachel Gilmer. 2016. "Invest-Divest—The Movement for Black Lives Policy Platform." Accessed June 10, 2018, from https://policy.m4bl.org/invest-divest/.

Negrón-Gonzales, Melinda. 2016. "The Feminist Movement during the AKP Era in Turkey: Challenges and Opportunities." *Middle Eastern Studies* 52 (2): 198–214.

Nesher, Talila. 2013. "Israel Admits Ethiopian Women Were Given Birth Control Shots." *Haaretz*, January 27, 2013. https://www.haaretz.com/israel-news/.premium-ethiopians-fooled-into-birth-control-1.5226424.

Newman, Janet. 2013. "Spaces of Power: Feminism, Neoliberalism and Gendered Labor." *Social Politics: International Studies in Gender, State & Society* 20 (2): 200–21.

Nyberg, Anita. 2012 "Gender Equality Policy in Sweden: 1970s–2010s." *Nordic Journal of Working Life Studies* 2 (4): 67–84.

Öberg, Lisa. 1999. "Ett Socialdemokratiskt Dilemma: Från Hembiträdesfråga till Pigdebatt." In *Kvinnor mot Kvinnor: Om Systerskapets Svårigheter*, edited by Christina Florin, 159–99. Stockholm: Norstedts.

Oirechtas. 2017. "Bill to Establish the Referendum on the Eight Amendment." https://www.oireachtas.ie/en/debates/debate/dail/2018-03-20/10/.

Okeke-Ihejirika, Philomina E., and Susan Franceschet. 2002. "Democratization and State Feminism: Gender Politics in Africa and Latin America." *Development and Change* 33 (3): 439–66.

One Billion Rising. 2018. "About One Billion Rising." Accessed August 4, 2018, from https://www.onebillionrising.org/about/campaign/one-billion-rising/

Öniş, Ziya. 2006. "Globalization and Party Transformation: Turkey's Justice and Development Party in Perspective." In *Globalizing Democracy: Party Politics in Emerging Democracies*, edited by Peter Burnell, 122–40. London: Routledge.

Özkan-Kerestecioğlu, İnci. 2004. "Women's Social Positions in Turkey: Achievements and Problems." In *The Position of Women in Turkey and in the European Union: Achievements, Problems, Prospects*, edited by Fatmagül Berktay, 35–53. Istanbul: KA-DER Press.

Pålsson, Anne-Marie, and Erik Norrman, eds. 1994. *Finns det en Marknad för Hemarbete?* Stockholm: SNS Förlag.

Pappé, Ilan. 2012. "Shtetl Colonialism: First and Last Impressions of Indigeneity by Colonised Colonisers." *Settler Colonial Studies* 2 (1): 39–58.

Pardo, Mary. 1998. *Mexican American Women Activists: Identity and Resistance in Two Los Angeles Communities*. Philadelphia, PA: Temple University Press.

Perry, Keisha-Khan Y. 2016. "Geographies of Power: Black Women Mobilizing Intersectionality in Brazil." Meridians: Feminism, Race, Transnationalism 14 (1): 94–120.

Piterberg, Gabriel. 2008. *The Returns of Zionism Myth, Politics and Scholarship in Israel*. New York: Verso.

Piven, Frances Fox, and Richard A. Cloward. 1977. Poor People's Movements: Why they Succeed, How They Fail. New York: Pantheon Books.

Platzer, Ellinor. 2006. "From Public Responsibility and Back Again: The New Domestic Services in Sweden." *Gender and History* 18 (2): 211–21.

Polanco, Geraldina. 2016. "Consent Behind the Counter: Aspiring Citizens and Labour Control under Precarious (Im)migration Schemes." *Third World Quarterly* 37 (8): 1332–50.

Polletta, Francesca. 2002. *Freedom Is an Endless Meeting—Democracy in American Social Movements*. Chicago/London: Chicago University Press.

Polletta, Franceca, and James M. Jasper. 2001. "Collective Identity and Social Movements." *Annual Review of Sociology* 27: 283–305.

Prestage, Jewel L. 1991. "In Quest of African American Political Woman." *Annals of the American Academy of the Political and Social Sciences* 515: 88–103.

Pristed Nielsen, Helene. 2013. "Collaborating on Combating Anti-Discrimination? Anti-Racist and Gender Equality Organisations in Europe." In *Negotiating Gender and Diversity in an Emergent European Public Sphere*, edited by Birte Siim and Monika Mokre, 179–200. Basingstoke: Palgrave Macmillan.

Promemorian. 2007. Remissammanställning på Promemorian Skattelättnader för hushållstjänster Fi 2006/7311 (2006).

Prudovska, Tetyana, and Myra Max Ferree. 2004. "Global Activism in 'Virtual Space': The European Women's Lobby in the Network of Transnational Women's NGOs on the Web." *Social Politics* 11 (1): 117–43.

Puar, Jasbir K. 2007. *Terrorist Assemblages: Homonationalism in Queer Times*. Durham, NC: Duke University Press.

Quilty, Aideen, Sinead Kennedy, and Catherine Conlon, eds. 2015. *The Abortion Papers Ireland: Volume II*. Cork: Cork University Press.

Ramos de Santiago, Carmen. 1970. *El Gobierno de Puerto Rico*. San Juan: Editorial de la Universidad de Puerto Rico.

Razavi, Shahra. 2001. "Women in Contemporary Democratization." *International Journal of Politics, Culture, and Society* 15 (1): 201–24.

Reagon, Bernice Johnson. 1983. "Coalition Politic: Turning the Century." In *Home Girls: A Black Feminist Anthology*, edited by Barbara Smith, 343–56. New York: Kitchen Table Press.

Reese, Ellen, Christine Petit, and David S. Meyer. 2010. "Sudden Mobilization: Movement Crossovers, Threats, and the Surprising Rise of the U.S. Antiwar Movement." In *Strategic Alliances: Coalition Building and Social Movements*, edited by Nella Van Dyke and Holly McCammon, 266–91. Minneapolis: Minnesota University Press.

Repeal the Eight October. 2017. https://www.repealeight.ie/1983-2017-trapped-in-time/.

Report of the Joint Committee on the Eight Amendment of the Constitution. December 20, 2017. https://data.oireachtas.ie/ie/oireachtas/committee/dail/32/joint_committee_on_the_eighth_amendment_of_the_constitution/reports/2017/2017-12-20_report-of-the-joint-committee-on-the-eighth-amendment-of-the-constitution_en.pdf.

Researching the American-Israeli Alliance and Jewish Voice for Peace. 2018. *Deadly Exchange: The Dangerous Consequences of American Law Enforcement Trainings in Israel*. Jewish Voice for Peace.

Rief, Michelle. 2004. "Thinking Locally, Acting Globally: The International Agenda of African American Clubwomen, 1880-1940." *The Journal of African American History* 89(3): 203–22

Riksdag Records of Proceedings in the Chamber 2006/07:116 (2007). Stockholm: Riksdag of Sweden. Accessed January 31, 2015, from www.riksdagen.se/sv/Dokument-Lagar/Kammaren/Protokoll/Riksdagens-protokoll-2006071_GU09116/].

Ritchie, Andrea J. 2017. *Invisible No More: Police Violence Against Black Women and Women of Color*. Boston: Beacon Press.

Ritchie, Jason. 2014. "Black Skin Splits: The Birth (and Death) of the Queer Palestinian." In *Queer Necropolitics*, edited by Jin Haritaworn, Adi Kuntsman, and Silivia Posocco, 111–28. New York: Routledge.

Roberts, Adrienne. 2013. "Financing Social Reproduction: The Gendered Relations of Debt and Mortgage Finance in Twenty-First-Century America." *New Political Economy* 18 (1): 21–42.

Roberts, Dorothy E. 2008. "Constructing a Criminal Justice System Free of Racial Bias: An Abolitionist Framework." *Columbia Human Rights Law Review* 39: 261–85.

Roberts, Dorothy, and Sujatha Jesudason. 2013. "Movement Intersectionality: The Case of Race, Gender, Disability, and Genetic Technologies." *Du Bois Review* 10 (2): 313–28.

Roggeband, Conny, and Bert Klandermans. 2017. *Handbook of Social Movements across Disciplines*. Cham: Springer.

Rohrer, Judy. 2016. *Staking Claim: Settler Colonialism and Racialization in Hawai'i*. Tucson: University of Arizona Press.

Rosa, Alessandra. 2015. "Resistance Performances: (Re)constructing Spaces of Resistance and Contention in the 2010–2011 University of Puerto Rico Student Movement." PhD Diss., Florida International University. http://digitalcommons.fiu.edu/cgi/viewcontent.cgi?article=2956&context=etd.

Rose, Fred. 1997. "Toward a Class-Cultural Theory of Social Movements: Reinterpreting New Social Movements." *Sociological Forum* 12 (3): 461–94.

Rosenthal, Cindy Simon. 1998. *When Women Lead*. New York: Oxford University Press.

Ross, Janell, and Trymaine Lee. 2011. "Occupy the Hood Aims to Draw People of Color to Occupy Wall Street." *Huffington Post*, October 14, 2011.

Roth, Benita. 2017. "Intersectionality: Origins, Travels, Questions, and Contributions." In *The Oxford Handbook of U.S. Women's Social Movement Activism*, edited by Holly J. McCammon, Verta Taylor, Jo Reger, and Rachel L. Einwohner, 129–149. New York: Oxford University Press.

Rottenberg, Catherine. 2014. "The Rise of Neoliberal Feminism." *Cultural Studies* 28 (3): 418–37.

Russell, Emma, and Bree Carlton. 2013. "Pathways, Race and Gender Responsive Reform: Through an Abolitionist Lens." *Theoretical Criminology* 17 (4): 474–92.

Ruyan, Ann Sisson, and V. Spike Peterson. 2018. *Global Gender Issues in the New Millennium*. New York: Routledge.

Ryan, Charlotte, and William A. Gamson. 2006. "The Art of Reframing Political Debates." *Contexts* 5 (1): 13–8.

Sáfrány, Réka. 2003. "Public and Political Discourse on Domestic Violence in Hungary: The Prospects and Limits of Feminist Strategies." MA Thesis. Budapest: Central European University.

Sahlin, Mona. 1996. Med mina ord. Stockholm: Rabén Prisma.

Salem, Sara. 2016. "Intersectionality and Its Discontents: Intersectionality as Traveling Theory." *European Journal of Women's Studies* 25 (4): 403–18.

Sanchez Salgado, Rosa. 2014. *Europeanizing Civil Society. How the EU Shapes Civil Society Organizations*. Basingstoke: Palgrave Macmillan.

Sandberg, Linn. 2013. "Backward, Dumb and Violent Hillbillies? Rural Geographies and Intersectional Studies on Intimate Partner Violence." *Affilia* 28 (4): 350–65.

Sandoval, Chela. 1991. *U.S. Third World Feminisms: The Theory and Method of Oppositional Consciousness in the Postmodern World*. Minneapolis: University of Minnesota Press.

Sauer, Birgit. 2012. "Intersektionalität und Staat. Ein staats- und hegemonietheoretischer Zugang zu Intersektionalität." *Portal Intersektionalität*. http://portal-intersektionalitaet.de/uploads/media/Sauer.pdf.

Sauer, Birgit. 2017. "Gesellschaftstheoretische Überlegungen zum europäischen Rechtspopulismus. Zum Erklärungspotenzial der Kategorie Geschlecht." *Gastbeitrag Politische Vierteljahresschrift* 58 (1): 1–19.

Scott, Anne Firor. 1990. "Most Invisible of All: Black Women's Voluntary Associations." *The Journal of Southern History* 56(1): 3–22.

Seidman, Gary. 1999. "Gendered Citizenship: South Africa's Democratic Transition and the Construction of a Gendered State." *Gender and Society* 13 (3): 287–307.

Sexton, Jared. 2010. "People-of-Color-Blindness: Notes on the Afterlife of Slavery." *Social Text* 28: 31–56.

Shalhoub-Kevorkian, Nadera. 2009. *Militarization and Violence Against Women in Conflict Zones in the Middle East: A Palestinian Case Study*. Cambridge, UK: Cambridge University Press.

Shmulyar Gréen, Oksana, and Andrea Spehar. 2014. "Caught in Vulnerability Trap: Female Migrant Domestic Workers in the Enlarged EU." *Baltic Worlds* 7 (4): 27–37.

Siim, Birte, and Monika Mogre, eds. 2013. *Negotiating Gender and Diversity in an Emergent European Public Sphere*. Basingstoke: Palgrave Macmillan.

Siim, Birte, and Susi Meret. 2016. "Right Wing Populism in Denmark—People, Nation and Welfare in the Construction of the 'Other.'" In *The Rise of the Far Right in Europe: Populist Shifts and "Othering,"* edited by Gabriella Lazaridis, Giovanna Campani, and Annie Benveniste, 106–36. Basingstoke: Palgrave Macmillan.

Simien, Evelyn M. 2004. "Gender Differences in Attitudes toward Black Feminism among African Americans." *Political Science Quarterly* 119 (2): 315–38.

Sirman, Nükhet. 1989. "Feminism in Turkey: A Short History." *New Perspective on Turkey* 3 (1): 1–34.

Smith, Barbara, ed. 1983. *Home Girls: A Black Feminist Anthology*. New York: Kitchen Table Press.

Smith, Jackie. 2014. "Transnational Network for Democratic Globalization." In *The Social Movements Reader: Cases and Concepts*, edited by Jeff Goodwin and James M. Jasper, 184–96. Hoboken, New Jersey: Wiley.

Smooth, Wendy. 2006. "Intersectionality in Electoral Politics: A Mess Worth Making." *Politics & Gender* 2 (3): 400–14.

Smooth, Wendy. 2009. "African American Women and Electoral Politics: Translating Voting Power into Officeholding." In *Gender and Elections: Shaping the Future of American Politics,* edited by Susan J. Carroll and Richard L. Fox, 167–89. New York: Cambridge University Press.

Snow, David A., E. Burke Rochford, Jr., Steven K. Wordern, and Robert D. Benford. 1986. "Frame Alignment Processes, Micromobilization, and Movement Participation." *American Sociological Review* 51: 464–81.

Snow, David A., and Robert Benford. 1988. "Ideology, Frame Resonance, and Participant Mobilization." *International Social Movement Research* 1: 197–217.

Snow, David A., and Sarah A. Soule. 2009. *A Primer on Social Movements*. New York: W. W. Norton.

Spade, Dean. 2013. "Intersectional Resistance and Law Reform." *Signs* 38 (4): 1031–55.

Špehar, Andrea. 2012. "This Far, but No Further? Benefits and Limitations of EU Gender Equality Policy Making in the Western Balkans." *East European Politics and Societies* 26 (2): 326–79.

Spillane, Alison. 2015. "The Impact of the Crisis on Irish Women." In *Ireland under Austerity, Neoliberal Crisis, Neoliberal Solutions*, edited by Coulter Colin and Angela Nagle, 151–70. Manchester: Manchester University Press.

Staggenborg, Suzanne. 1986. "Coalition Work in the Pro-Choice Movement: Organizational and Environmental Opportunities and Obstacles." *Social Problems* 33 (5): 374–90.

Staggenborg, Suzanne. 2010. "Research on Social Movement Coalitions." In *Strategic Alliances: Coalition Building and Social Movements*, edited by Nella Van Dyke and Holly McCammon, 316–30. Minneapolis: Minnesota University Press.

Staggenborg, Suzanne. 2015. "Building Coalitions and Movements." *Mobilizing Ideas*. Accessed November 3, 2015, from https://mobilizingideas.wordpress.com/2015/11/03/building-coalitions-and-movements/.

Stasiulis, Davia, and Nira Yuval-Davis. 1995. "Beyond Dichotomies: Gender, Race, Ethnicity and Class in Settler Societies." In *Unsettling Settler Societies: Articulations of Gender, Race, Ethnicity, and Class*, edited by Daiva Stasiulis and Nira Yuval-Davis, 1–38. London: SAGE.

Statistics Sweden. 2017. *Välfärd nr 1*. Stockholm: Statistics Sweden.

Stetson, Dorothy McBride, and Amy Mazur, eds. 1995. *Comparative State Feminism*. London: Sage.

Strid, Sofia. 2014. *Gendered Interests in the EU: The European Women's Lobby and the Organization and Representation of Women's Interests*. Saarbrücken: GlobeEdit.

Strolovitch, Dara Z. 2006. "Do Interest Groups Represent the Disadvantaged? Advocacy at the Intersections of Race, Class, and Gender." *Journal of Politics* 68 (4): 894–910.

Strolovitch, Dara Z. 2007. *Affirmative Advocacy: Race, Class, and Gender in Interest Group Politics*. Chicago: University of Chicago Press.

Strolovitch, Dara Z. 2012. "Intersectionality in Time: Sexuality and the Shifting Boundaries of Intersectional Marginalization." *Politics & Gender* 8 (3): 386–96.

Strolovitch, Dara Z. 2013. "Of Mancessions and Hecoveries: Race, Gender, and the Political Construction of Economic Crises and Recoveries." *Perspectives on Politics* 11 (1): 167–76.

Stubbergaard, Ylva. 2015. "Conflict and Cooperation: Interactions among EU-Level Civil Society Organisations in the Field of Gender Equality." In *EU Civil Society. Patterns of Cooperation, Competition and Conflict*, edited by Hakan Johansson and Sara Kalm, 119–36. Basingstoke: Palgrave Macmillan.

Stubbs, Paul. 2012. "Networks, Organizations, Movements: Narratives and Shapes of Three Waves of Activism in Croatia." *Polemos* 15 (2): 11–32.

Stubbs, Paul. 2017. "Review. Patrice C. McMahon. The NGO Game, Post Conflict Peacebuilding in the Balkans and Beyond." *H-Net Reviews in the Humanities and Social Sciences*. https://www.h-net.org/reviews/showpdf.php?id=50472.

Stychin, Carl F. 2004. "Same-Sex Sexualities and the Globalization of Human Rights Discourse." *McGill Law Journal* 49: 952–68.

Svenska Dagbladet. 2009. "De Flesta Stödjer Hemservice-avdrag." Accessed October 13, 2017. https://www.gp.se/de-flesta-st%C3%B6djer-hemservice-avdrag-1.1083053.

Svenskt Näringsliv. 2010. "RUT-avdraget Undanröjer Hinder för Jämställdhet." *Svenskt Näringsliv*, 18 March. Accessed October 11, 2017, from www.svensktnaring sliv.se/material/debattartikel/rut-avdraget-undanrojer-hinder-for-jamstalldhet_105226.html.

SVT Nyheter. 2010. "Rut-avdrag Splittar Feminister." *SVT Nyheter*, 3 March, 1905 hrs. Accessed January 31, 2015, from www.svt.se/nyheter/sverige/rut-avdrag-splittar-feminister.

Swedish Government Official Reports. 1975. Målet är jämställdhet. En svensk rapport med anledning av FN:s kvinnoår, SOU 1975: 58. Stockholm: Fritzes.

Swedish Government. 2018. "A Feminist Government." Accessed June 15, 2018, from https://www.government.se/government-policy/a-feminist-government/.

Swers, Michele L. 2002. *The Difference Women Make: The Policy Impact of Women in Congress*. Chicago: University of Chicago Press.

Tarrow, Sidney. 1998. *Power in Movement: Social Movements and Contentious Politics*. Cambridge: Cambridge University Press.

Tarrow, Sidney. 2005. *The New Transnational Activism*. Cambridge: Cambridge University Press.

Tarrow, Sidney. 2011. *Power in Movement: Social Movements, Collective Action and Politics*. New York: Cambridge University Press.

Taylor, Verta, and Nancy E. Whittier. 1999. "Collective Identity in Social Movement Communities: Lesbian Feminist Mobilization." In *Waves of Protest: Social Movements Since the Sixties*, edited by Taylor and Whittier, 169–94. New York: Rowman & Littlefield.

Terriquez, Veronica, Tizoc Brenes, and Abdiel Lopez. 2018. "Intersectionality as a Multipurpose Collective Action Frame: The Case of the Undocumented Youth Movement." *Ethnicities* 18 (2): 260–76.

Threadcraft, Shatema. 2017. "North American Necropolitics and Gender: On #Black-LivesMatter and Black Femicide." *South Atlantic Quarterly*, 116 (3): 553–79.

Together for Yes. 2018. "The National Campaign to Remove the Eight Amendment." https://www.togetherforyes.ie/about-us/who-we-are/.

Tormos-Aponte, Fernando. 2013. "Solidarity and Inclusion in the Global Movement against Sweatshops." Paper presented at the Annual Conference of the Midwestern Political Science Association, Chicago, Illinois.

Tormos, Fernando. 2017a. "Intersectional Solidarity." *Politics, Groups, and Identities* 5 (4): 707–20. https://doi.org/10.1080/21565503.2017.1385494.

Tormos, Fernando. 2017b. "Mobilizing Difference: The Power of Inclusion in Transnational Social Movements." PhD Diss., Purdue University, Indiana.

Tormos, Fernando. 2018. "The Politics of Survival in Puerto Rico: The Balance of Forces in the Wake of Hurricane María." Alternautas 5 (1): 79–94..

Tormos-Aponte, Fernando, and José Ciro Martínez. 2017. "Puerto Rico at the Precipice." *Jacobin*. https://www.jacobinmag.com/2017/10/ puerto-rico-hurricane-maria-trump-jones-act-colonialism.

Torpy, Sally J. 2000. "Native American Women and Coerced Sterilization: On the Trail of Tears in the 1970s." *American Indian Culture and Research Journal* 24 (2): 1–22.

Torruella, Juan R. 2013. "Ruling America's Colonies: The Insular Cases." *Yale Law & Policy Review* 32 (3): 57–95.

Townsend-Bell, Erica. 2011. "What Is Relevance? Defining Intersectional Praxis in Uruguay." *Political Research Quarterly* 64 (1): 187–99.

Townsend-Bell, Erica. 2014. "Ambivalent Intersectionality." *Politics & Gender* 10 (1): 137–42.

Tronto, C. Joan. 2002. "The Nanny Question in Feminism." *Hypatia* 17 (2): 34–61.

Tronto, C. Joan. 2011. "A Feminist Democratic Ethics of Care and Global Care Workers: Citizenship and Responsibility." In *Feminist Ethics and Social Policy: Towards a New Global Political Economy of Care*, edited by R. Mahon and F. Robinson, 162–77. Vancouver: University of British Columbia Press.

Tungohan, Ethel. 2016. "Intersectionality and Social Justice." *Politics, Groups, and Identities* 4 (3): 347–62.

Van Dyke, Nella. 2003. "Crossing Movement Boundaries: Factors That Facilitate Coalition Protest by American College Students, 1930–1990." *Social Problems* 50 (2): 226–50.

Ványa, Magdalena. 2006. *Making Domestic Violence: Gender, Collective Action, and Emerging Civil Society in Postcommunist Hungary and Slovakia*. Davis, CA: University of California, Davis.

Vargas-Ramos, Carlos. 2016. "Some Social Differences on the Basis of Race among Puerto Ricans." CUNY Center for Puerto Rican Studies Research Brief. https:// centropr.hunter.cuny.edu/sites/default/files/data_briefs/RB2016-10_RACE.pdf.

Vaughan, Dawn Baumgartner. 2018. "Israeli-Palestinian Conflict, Durham Policing to Come to a Head at City Council Meeting." *Herald Sun*, April 16, 2018.

Verloo, Mieke. 2006. "Multiple Inequalities, Intersectionality and the European Union." *European Journal of Women's Studies* 13 (3): 211–28.

Verloo, Mieke. 2013. "Intersectional and Cross-Movement Politics and Policies: Reflections on Current Practices and Debates." *Signs* 38 (4): 893–915.

Vlad, Ioana. 2013. "Coalition Building Inside and Outside the Romanian Women's Rights Scene." *European Public Policies Instruments, Models and Behaviour in the Public Space* 5: 259–76.

Wade, Peter. 2001. "Racial Identity and Nationalism: A Theoretical View from Latin America." *Ethnic and Racial Studies* 24 (5): 845–65.

Walby, Sylvia. 2011. *The Future of Feminism*. Cambridge: Polity Press.

Walby, Sylvia, Jo Armstrong, and Sofia Strid. 2012. "Intersectionality: Multiple Inequalities in Social Theory." *Sociology* 46 (2): 224–40.

Walsh, Shannon Drysdale, and Christina Xydias. 2014. "Women's Organizing and Intersectional Policy-Making in Comparative Perspective: Evidence from Guatemala and Germany." *Politics, Groups, and Identities* 2 (4): 549–72.

Walters, Ronald W. 2003. *White Nationalism, Black Interests: Conservative Public Opinion and the Black Community*. Detroit, MI: Wayne State University Press.

Waterman, Peter. 2005. "Talking across Difference in an Interconnected World of Labor." In *Coalitions across Borders: Transnational Protest and the Neoliberal Order*, edited by Joe Bandy and Jackie Smith, 141–62. Oxford: Rowman & Littlefield.

Weldon, Laurel. 2004. "The Dimensions of Policy Impact of Feminist Civil Society: Democratic Policy Making on Violence against Women in the Fifty U.S. States." *International Feminist Journal of Politics* 6 (1): 1–28.

Weldon, S. Laurel. 2006a. "The Structure of Intersectionality: A Comparative Politics of Gender." *Politics & Gender* 2 (2): 235–48.

Weldon, S. Laurel. 2006b. "Inclusion, Solidarity and Social Movements: The Global Movement on Gender Violence." *Perspectives on Politics* 4 (1): 55–74.

Weldon, S. Laurel. 2008. "The Concept of Intersectionality." In *Gender and Concepts*, edited by Amy G. Mazur and Gary Goertz, 193–218. Cambridge: Cambridge University Press.

Weldon, S. Laurel. 2011. *When Protest Makes Policy: How Social Movements Represent Disadvantage Groups*. Ann Arbor: University of Michigan Press.

Williams, Melissa S. 1998. *Voice, Trust, and Memory*. Princeton, NJ: Princeton University Press.

Wilson, Amrit. 1978. *Finding a Voice: Asian Women in Britain*. London: Virago Press.

Wodak, Ruth. 1998. *Disorders of Discourse*. London: Longman.

Wodak, Ruth. 2015. *The Politics of Fear: What Right-Wing Populist Discourses Mean*. London: Sage.

Wolfe, Patrick. 2006. "Settler Colonialism and the Elimination of the Native." *Journal of Genocide Research* 8 (4): 387–409.

Woodward, Alison. 2007. "Challenges for Intersectionality in the Transnational Organization of European Equality Movements: Forming Platforms and Maintaining Turf in Today's European Union." In *Gender Borders Unbound? Globalisation, Restructuring and Reciprocity*, edited by Ilse Lenz, Charlotte Ullrich, and Barbara Fersch, 167–85. Opladen: Barbara Budrich.

Young, Iris Marion. 1990. *Justice and the Politics of Difference*. Princeton, NJ: Princeton University Press.

Young, Iris Marion. 1996. "Communication and the Other—Beyond Deliberative Democracy." In *Democracy and Difference: Contesting the Boundaries of the Political*, edited by Sheyla Benhabib, 120–36. Princeton, NJ: Princeton University Press.

Young, Iris Marion. 2000. *Inclusion and Democracy*. New York: Oxford University Press.

Yuval-Davis, Nira. 1997. *Gender and Nation*. London: Sage.

Yuval-Davis, Nira. 1999. "What is 'transversal politics'?" Soundings (12): 94–98.

Yuval-Davis, Nira. 2006a. "Human/Women's Rights and Feminist Transversal Politics." In *Transnational Feminisms: Women s Global Activism and Human Rights*, edited by Myra Marx Ferree and Aili Mari Tripp, 275–94. New York: New York University Press.

Yuval-Davis, Nira. 2006b. "Intersectionality and Feminist Politics." *European Journal of Women's Studies* 13 (3): 193–209.

Yuval-Davis, Nira. 2007. "Intersectionality, Citizenship and Contemporary Politics of Belonging." *Critical Review of International Social and Political Philosophy* 10 (4): 561–74.

Yuval-Davis, Nira. 2012. "Dialogical Epistemology—An Intersectional Resistance to the 'Oppression Olympics.'" *Gender and Society* 26 (1): 46–54.

Ženska mreža Hrvatske. Politička platforma Ženske mreže. Accessed May 22, 2018, from http://www.zenska-mreza.hr/platforma.htm.

Zore, Paula. 2013. "rodno osviještena politika—utjecaj na feminističku teoriju i praksu." In *širenje područja političkog: novi pogledi na političku participaciju žena*, edited by Zorica Siročić and Leda Sutlović, 77–103. Zagreb: Centar za ženske studije.

Index

Note: Page references for figures are italicized

abortion rights, 10, 18, 26, 80; ECJ rulings on, 30; MERJ (Migrants and Ethnic-Minorities for Reproductive Justice), campaign, 38. *See also* Abortion Rights Campaign (ARC) Ireland; Ireland, reproductive rights activism in

Abortion Rights Campaign (ARC) Ireland, 10, 18, 26, 30–31, 33, 35, 36–37, 40; and Action for Choice (Ireland), 26, 31; intersectional dialogue in, 30, 31; and "March of Choice" protests, 30

AGE Platform (EU), *121*, 246, 250, *252*, 256, 259

Agustín, Lise Rolandsen, 46, 248–49, 257

AKDER (Women's Rights Association against Discrimination), 78, 82, 84, 85, 86–87; gender ideology in, 84, 85; headscarf issue in, 82, 85, 86; and Violence against Women Convention, 85–86

Alexander-Floyd, Nikol G., 4, 231

alliance formation, 13–15, 18, 27, 42–43, 57, 58, 74, 94, 112, 113, 159–60, 168–70, 210, 211, 224; and campaign reframing, 155, 159; financial crises, effect on, 111, 112; and intersecting struggles frame in, 159, 161, 169; and multiple identities, 95, 159–60, 169; rooting and shifting in, 15, 17, 27, 160, 161, 163, 169, 181, 255; threat and opportunity in, 111, 113–14; and transnational organizations, 14, 17, 112, 124. *See also* coalition building; JVC, Deadly Exchange campaign; LGBTQ, European movement inclusiveness study

Alvarez, Sonia, 45, 56, 96, 102

Amnesty International, 63, 69; and *Cries Unheard* 2007 report, 69

Amsterdam Treaty (EU), 248, 252, 253

anti-black violence, 155, 160, 162–63, 164, 240–42; and critiques of anti-blackness, 162–63, 164, 165, 167, 169; and Ferguson USA riots, 160, 228, 229, 231–37, 240–41; and JVC alliance campaigning, 155, 162–63, 160; and police repression, 160, 162, 167; women's invisibility in, 241–42. *See also* black feminism; Black-LivesMatter (BLM) movement; black women and activism

anti-Semitism, 158
Anzaldúa, Gloria, 2, 154, 156
autoethnographic approach, 21, 156, 209, 210–11; and intersectionality, 210–11, 224

Bassel, Leah, 2, 13, 14, 27, 27, 74, 111
Beckwith, Karen, 4–5, 96
Bilge, Sirma, 4, 172, 245, 246
black feminism, 7, 17, 22, 113, 154, 164, 165, 217, 226–42; academic attention to, 230; in Ferguson USA, 228, 229, 231–37; historical context of, 228, 229–30; intersectional identity/consciousness in, 226, 227, 229, 241; intersectional methodologies in, 154, 217, 231; LGBTQ connection with, 166; personal narratives, role in, 231, 240, 241; political translation, use of in, 190; role framing in, 240; and role of social location, 226, 228, 235, 237, 240; and "whiteness" self-reflection, 160–61, 165–66; women as "outsiders-within," 242. *See also* BlackLives Matter (BLM) movement; black women and activism; Chicana feminisms
BlackLivesMatter (BLM) movement, 14, 22, 148, 164, 165, 224, 226, 228, 229, 234, 235–36, 237, 239, 240–42; black feminist leadership in, 229, 230; intersectional consciousness in, 22; race/gender identity in, 22, 230, 240; origins of (US), 226–27; and transnational solidarity, 168. *See also* anti-black violence, and Ferguson USA riots; black women and activism
black women and activism: and assimilationist model, 232; BlackLivesMatter movement in, 22, 234, 235–37, 239; black women's leadership in, 239–40, 241; and Combahee River Collective, 2, 213; Ferguson in, 228, 229, 231–37, 240–41; and finding voice, 227, 230–31, 237; French *banlieues* in, 228, 232, 233, 234, 237–42; and interconnected identities,

228, 229; at intersection of multiple marginalities, 226, 227; Justice pour Adama collective in, 238; and multicultural model, 232, 241; personal narratives in, 234–40; and police violence, 233, 238, 239; political context of, 233; and political participation paradox, 226; socio-economic context in, 232–33; and Vies Violées collective, 238–39; women politician's leadership in, 235–37, 239, 240
Brown, Michael, 228, 229, 233, 234, 235, 239, 240–41

Canada: Filipino migrants' movement in, 13, 16, 17, 208–25; intersectionality/alliances in, 209–10, 212, 214, 215, 216–17, 219–21, 223–25; legal reformist approach use in, 13, 16, 21, 213, 219–24; Live-in-Caregiver Program (LCP), 209, 214, 215, 218, 219, 220, 221, 223; migrant opposition in, 219, 220, 222; radical futurities vision in, 13, 21, 210, 218; Temporary Foreign Workers Program, 219–20, 221; waves of immigration in, 214–15, 220–21. *See also* Gabriela-Ontario organization; Philippines, The; refugee solidarity movements
CEDAW, 58, 63, 66, 68, 70
Chicana feminisms, 7, 154; and repressive practices, 168
children's rights, 56, 62, 66, 68; and domestic violence activism alliance, 68–69, 71–72
Cho, Sumi, 4, 58, 154, 156, 169
Chun, Jenifer Jihye, 2, 3, 7, 14, 15, 74, 75, 138, 139, 172, 173
civil society mobilization: alliances and collaboration in, 245, 252, 254–55, 256, 259–60; and coalition building, 244–45, 256; economic crisis, effect on, 257–59, 260; equality CSOs in, 244, 245, 246, 249–61; EU access process in, 245, 248, 249, 250; finding voice in, 245, 253, 257,

258; and funding, 251–53, 258, 259, 260; gender equality in, 245, 247, 248–49, 254, 255, 258, 260; hierarchy of social movements in, 256–57, 259, 260; intersectional capacity and mobilization in, 252, 258, 259–61; network intersectionality in, 244, 245, 254, 256–57; network maps, use in, 246, *247*, 248, 259; shifting and rooting practices in, 255, 256, 259; social inequalities frame use in, 257–58; and supranational level, 245, 249, 253, 255, 261; visibility of, 247–48. *See also* European Social Platform; European Women's Lobby (EWL)

civil society organizations (CSOs), 244; and European Transparency Register, 251; role in EU, 244, 245–61

class inequality, 137–38, 258; and identity formation, 137, 138; and other dimensions of oppression, 137–38

coalition building, 14, 15, 32, 57, 58, 114, 189; definition of common interests in, 58; intersectionality in, 58, 137, 151, 171, 174, 192, 213; political opportunity structures in, 58; positional misunderstandings in, 189. *See also* alliance formation; intersectional solidarity

Cohen, Cathy, 210, 212, 213, 215, 218, 223, 225

Cole, Elisabeth R., 99, 136, 172, 173, 224, 246, 256, 257

collective action, 1, 2, 4, 26, 27, 39, 173; concept of voice in, 27; and intersectional consciousness, 173

collective identity, 74, 137, 139, 141. *See also* identity-based groups

Collins, Patricia Hill, 2–3, 8, 75, 113, 136, 137, 138, 139, 156, 172, 210, 227, 231, 242, 245, 246

colonialism, 13, 17, 20, 166–69, 226, 228; and decolonial liberation movements, 166; and settler-colonial framework, 20–21, 166–68, 224; and shared ideologies, 161. *See also* JVP,

Deadly Exchange campaign; Puerto Rico; settler societies

counter-intersectionality, 19, 74, 76–77, 89–90; discursive practices/strategies in, 76–77, 78, 89–90; and globalization, 89–90. *See also* intersectionality; Turkey, women's activism study

Crenshaw, Kimberlé, 2, 4, 8, 10, 58, 75, 78, 113, 138, 154, 156, 157, 159, 161, 165, 169, 246

crisis, notion of, 114; and alliance formation, 114–15, 130. *See also* financial crises

Croatia: Ad Hoc Coalition in, 97, 98, 99, 100; EU accession process in, 19–20, 93, 94; and Facebook Protests, 105–6; Fem Front (Feministički Front) in, 106; feminist social movements study, 16, 19–20, 92–109; gender equality law in, 101–2, 104; intersectionality in, 93, 98, 100, 101, 103–4, 108–9; legalistic approach in, 16, 19, 20, 93, 94, 96, 101, 102, 103, 104, 106, 108–9; liberal feminist critique in, 106–8; pro-democracy movements in, 19, 20, 96, 97, 99; professionalization effect on, 96, 102–3, 104, 109; rural inclusion in, 97–98, 100–101, 102; social reproduction concept reinstatement in, 106–7; 2008 economic crisis and protests in, 93, 104, 105–6; urban-rural divide in, 95–96, 97, 98, 102; Women's Front for Labor and Social Rights in, 107–8; Women's Network in, 97, 98, 100

Della Porta, Donatella, 189, 191, 244, 247, 254–55

Denmark, refugee solidarity activism in, 10, 21, 191–92, 198–203, 205, 206; feminist/LGBTQ groups in, 191–92, 198, 204; and funding issues, 192, 198–99, 201; hostile political and structural environment in, 198, 199; "job activation" focus in, 199, 202; political translation in, 202–3,

204; refugee women's meetings in, 199–202. *See also* refugee solidarity movements

disability activism/movements, 19, 29, 30, 31, 56, 59, 61, 124, 126, 181, 213; 256, 260; intersectional sensitivity in, 31, 35, 40, 61

domestic violence activism, 19, 56–60, 65, 71–72; and children's rights, 68–69; and disadvantaged groups, 59–60; gender equality approaches to, 59, 60, 65–66, 71–72; intersectional capacity in, 60, 64, 66, 72; and Law on Protection from Domestic Violence (Croatia), 101, 102; political intersectionality framework in, 57–58, 59, 70–71, 72; rights groups alliances in, 65–66, 67, 71–72; transnational networks in, 59, 60–61, 69, 72; universality claim in, 56. *See also* Hungary, domestic violence study; Romania, domestic violence study

domestic workers, 18, 42, 43, 44; and global care chain, 44; in Sweden, 44, 46, 51. *See also* Canada, Filipino migrants' movement in; Sweden, Domestic Service Tax Reform (RUT) in

Emejulu, Akwugo, 2, 13, 14, 27, 29, 74, 111

empathy, 8, 15, 181, 205, 235

European Anti-Poverty Network (EAPN), *121*, 251

European Disability Forum, (EDF), *121*, 246, 251, *252*, 256, 258, 259

European Network against Racism (ENAR), 116, *121*, 124, 246, 251, 254, 256, 257, 258, 259; and ILGA-Europe collaboration, 124; intersectionality in, 254, 257

European Social Forum (ESF), 189–90; positional misunderstandings, addressing of in, 190

European Social Platform, 114, 246, 249, 250, 251, *252*, 253, 254, 255, 256, 257, 258; inclusivity in, 261; social

exclusion policy frame in, 257; social policy influence strategy in, 255

European Trade Union Confederation (ETUC), 246, 250, *252*, 253, 255, 256, 258; inequality activism in, 255, 257; mass mobilization strategy in, 252

European Union: and accession process, 20, 58; CSOs role in, 244, 249–50; discrimination policy in, 248–49, 250, 252, 255, 257; economic crisis, effect on, 257; equality CSOs in, 244, 245, 246, 249–61; free movement of labor in, 44; funding practices, effects of, 11, 17, 251–53; legitimacy crisis in, 250; multilevel governance in, 245, 251; policymaking process in, 248. *See also* civil society mobilization, EU access process in; Croatia, feminist social movements study

European Union institutions: Council of Europe, 61, 120, 248, 250; economic crisis, policy effect on, 258, 260; European Commission, 61, 120, 244, 248, 249, 255, 257; European Court of Justice (ECJ), 30; European Parliament, 248, 249, 250

European Women's Lobby (EWL), 19, 60, 61, 70, 71, 116, *121*; and CSO equality study, 246, 249, 250, 251, 252, 253–60; gatekeeping role of, 254; gender equality promotion in, 255–56; gender mainstreaming lobbying in, 253; intersectionality in, 253–54

Evans, Elisabeth, 2, 11

feminist activism: alliance formation in, 27, 185; and feminist movements, 1, 3, 4, 5, 19–20, 22, 28–29; 44–45, 165; and Occupy groups, 143, 144, 148, 149, 150; and refugee solidarity, 191–92, 193–96, 199, 205, 206; and "whiteness" self-reflection, 160–61, 165. *See also* black feminism; black women and activism; Chicana feminism; Croatia, feminist social movements study in; gendered mobilization; Ireland, reproductive rights activism in; Roma women's activism; women's movements

financial crises, 6, 11, 15–16, 18, 111, 112, 115; EU CSOs effect on, 257–59; and intersectional consciousness, 111, 112; and resource scarcity, 114, 115; student movement protests (Croatia), 93, 104, 105–6; threat and opportunity in, 114–15, 130. *See also* LGBTQ, European movement inclusiveness study; resource mobilization theory

finding voice strategies, 11–13, 18, 94, 95–96, 108, 137, 154, 169, 210; campaign reframing, use in, 159; progressive stack method in, 147; and urban-rural identities, 95–96, 108; and voice diversification, 147

France: Republicanism in, 232, 233, 239. *See also* black women and activism, French *banlieues* in

Fraser, Nancy, 27, 42, 107

Gabriela-Ontario organization, 215–19, 221–22, 223; advocacy work in, 218, 219; intersectional approach in, 216–17; One Billion Rising activism in, 217; use of storytelling in, 216; transnational work of, 218. *See also* Canada, Filipino migrants' movement in

Gamson, William, 9, 112, 137

gendered mobilization, 5–6, 10, 16–17, 18, 25, 26, 77; and finding voice, 11–13, 27, 58, 77; intersectional solidarity difficulties in, 40, 43, 77. *See also* feminist activism, and feminist movements; women's movements

gender equality, 45, 46, 56, 78, 82–85; and "gender justice" notion, 83; and hierarchical leadership structures, 102–3, 106–7; and intersectional turn, 78; political approaches to, 93; and relationship to class, 109. *See also* civil society mobilization

gender violence. *See* domestic violence activism; violence against women

Germany, refugee solidarity activism in, 10, 21, 191, 193–98, 204, 205, 206; cultural tension in, 196–97, 205; feminist/LGBTQ organizational support in, 192, 193, 194–95, 204; political translators, role and capacity in, 195, 197, 204; and refugee asylum pressures/difficulties, 198, 204; and refugee self-organization, 197; and rural isolation, 194; and women refugee participation, 193, 196–98. *See also* refugee solidarity movements

globalization, 19, 89; effect on intersectionality, 89–90

global justice movements, 189–90

Hancock, Ange-Marie, 2, 3, 14, 15, 246

Haraway, Donna, 156, 210

human rights activism, 56–57, 58, 59, 66, 99, 100, 107, 124, 158, 185, 217; and EU LGBTI groups, 116–17; Human Rights Watch, 69; and transnational groups, 69. *See also* Jewish Voice for Peace (JVP); LGBTQ rights

Hungarian Women's Lobby, 60, 61, 63, 66; and Equal Treatment Bill, 61

Hungary, domestic violence study, 19, 57, 59, 60–61, 62, 63, 66–72; and children's rights groups, 68–69, 71–72; disability advocacy in, 61, 67; and ERRC/Women's Lobby report, 66, 68; intersectionality in, 19, 57, 59, 60, 61, 62, 63, 66, 67–72; Keret Coalition in, 63; organizational dynamics in, 70–71, 72; Roma/lesbian women's organizations in, 60, 61, 62, 63, 66, 68, 70; and transnational support, 60–61, 69; and UNUPR civil society participation, 67. *See also* Roma rights; Roma women's activism

identity-based groups, 7, 10, 13, 14, 15–16, 20, 135–39, 151–52; and intersectional consciousness, 136, 151; marginalization in, 135, 138–39, 151, 152; and movement failure, 136, 138; organizational limitations in, 138–39, 151; and single-axis movement disruption, 136–37; universal frames in, 138, 141; and visibility issues, 142. *See also* Occupy movement US study

identity formation, 9, 12, 137, 138, 157; and finding voice strategies, 11–13, 95–96, 137; multi-dimensionality in, 138; and solidarity/commitment, 137

identity politics, 2, 20, 135–38; axes of difference, use in, 137; and class considerations, 137; and constructionism, 159; critique of, 135–36, 137, 138, 139; fragmentation in, 136; rooting and shifting in, 138; and urban-rural division, 95–96

IGLYO (International Lesbian, Gay, Bisexual, Transgender, Queer and Intersex Youth and Student Organisation), 120, 122; and intersectionality "toolkit," 123

ILGA-Europe (International Lesbian and Gay Alliance), 14, 61, 116, 117, 122–25, 127, 128, 129, 246, 250, *252*, 254, 258, 259; capacity creation in, 125; finding voice networks in, 254; and INGO collaboration, 124; *Poverty and discrimination* report (2014), 119; 2005–2016 meetings, key terms, *123*; and 2016 intersectionality conference theme, 122–23; 2017 European Lesbian Conference, 127

immigrant rights, 1, 18, 190; political translation, use of in, 190. *See also* Canada, Filipino migrants' movement in; labor migration; migrant activism

indigenous activism: and Gabriela-Philippines movement, 217, 218; and Native Americans, 166, 167, 168. *See also* disability activism/movements; Palestinian rights and solidarity

indigenous people, 21, 155, 166–67; language frameworks used for, 155, 166; oppression/violence against, 21, 168; and transnational solidarity, 168, 218, 224. *See also* colonialism; land colonization

intersectional capacity, creation of, 10–11, 18, 21, 26, 27, 37, 60, 64, 94, 95, 124–25, 210; and multiple identities, 94–95; professionalization, effect of, 95, 109. *See also* political translation

intersectional consciousness, 7, 8–9, 10, 12, 15–16, 18, 22, 31, 47, 112, 130, 136, 139, 154, 162, 167, 169, 172–73; financial crisis, effect on, 112, 115, 130; multiple marginality recognition in, 139, 162, 172, 173–74; and political alliances, 16, 115, 122, 169; role of threat in, 114–15, 122; rooting and shifting in, 8–9, 17, 18, 162, 163, 169, 181; at transnational level, 112, 130. *See also* LGBTQ, European movements inclusiveness study

intersectionality: abolitionist lens in, 162–63, 168; academic research in, 2–4, 5, 6, 95, 154–55, 162, 210; campaign reframing in, 154–55, 159; and class inequality, 137; contextualization in, 161–62; definition/concept of, 2–3, 5, 75, 113; intercategorical approach to, 245; as intersecting struggles, 159, 161, 169; Marxist-feminist critique of, 107–8; as mode of mobilization, 2, 159; in multiple systems of oppression, 159–61, 246; origin of term, 2; and racial justice, 155, 159; scholar-activist approach to, 210–11, 218–19, 224; as tool of critical self-reflection, 160–61, 189, 163, 169, 211, 218; and universalizing claims, 168. *See also* counter-intersectionality; identity-based groups

intersectional political action, 15–17, 18, 57, 248; and institutional logics, 16–17; left critique of, 108; transnational emergence of, 17, 20. *See also* political intersectionality

intersectional praxis, 7, 8, 18, 56, 57, 93, 171, 172, 173–74, 181, 182, 246, 259; affirmative advocacy agendas in, 173; in coalitional politics, 8, 58, 245; inclusive deliberation in, 174; and political translation, 8; as transversal politics, 259

intersectional solidarity, 7–8, 21, 27, 40, 171, 172–74; intersectional consciousness in, 172; and praxis, 172. *See also* Puerto Rico, student movement study

Ireland: alliance formation in, 18, 31–32, 33–34; Coalition to Repeal the Eighth, 31–32, 34, 35, 36, 38–39; economic characteristics of, 27–28, 29; intersectionality in, 26, 27, 39–40; LGBTQ involvement in, 31; marriage equality campaign, 29, 32–33; migrant/ethnic women involvement in, 37–38, 39; and "Never Again" protests, 30; political culture in, 28, 30, 33, 39; reproductive rights activism in, 10, 25–26, 29–40; "Together for Yes" strategy in, 36–37, 38, 39, 40; universalizing messages use in, 32, 34, 35–37, 39, 40; women's representation in, 28; "Yes Equality" tactics in, 33. *See also* Abortion Rights Campaign (ARC) Ireland; National Women's Council of Ireland (NWCI)

Islamophobia, 122, 158, 256; and EU CSO collaboration, 256; Network Against, 158; OSF projects against, 256; and settler colonialism, 225

Israel, 155, 158, 166; African refugee oppression in, 158, 166, 167, 168; and Anti-Defamation League (ADL), 158, 160; land colonization in, 167, 168; Law of Return in, 156, 166; US security training in, 155, 158, 160, 163, 165, 167, 169; white settler perspectives in, 166, 167. *See also*

Jewish Voice for Peace (JVP); JVP, Deadly Exchange campaign; Palestinian rights and solidarity

issue framing, 9, 11, 13

Jewish Voice for Peace (JVP), 155–69; and ADL position, 158, 160; allyship/accompliceship in, 158–60, 167, 169; intersectionality formulations in, 158–59, 160–63; justice for Palestine campaign, 157, 158; and *Mizrahi* marginalization, 157, 158; organizational reframing in, 157, 158, 159–60; partnership groups in, 157, 158; racism/police brutality issues in, 157, 158, 160, 162–63, 167; self-reflective capacity in, 160–61, 163, 169; and US/Israeli collusion, 157, 163, 167, 169. *See also* JVP, Deadly Exchange campaign; Palestinian rights and solidarity

Jews of Color and Sephardi/Mizrahi (JOCSM) Caucus, 157, 158, 165, 166

JVP, Deadly Exchange campaign, 12–13, 20–21, 155, 163–70; abolition frame in, 155, 163, 164, 165, 168; and anti-blackness critiques, 155, 162–63, 164, 165, 168–69; intersecting struggles frame in, 159, 161, 169; intersectionality in, 155–56, 157–70; settler colonialism frame in, 155, 166–69; and US military/ ICE training, 155, 158, 160, 165. *See also* colonialism; disability activism/ movements; Jewish Voice for Peace (JVP); Palestinian rights; Palestinian rights and solidarity

KADEM (Women and Democracy Association), 78, 81–84, 85, 86, 87, 88; anti-violence discourse in, 86, 88; "gender justice," notion of in, 83

Kantola, Johanna, 43, 111, 246, 248

Kurdish women's movement, 19, 79, 80; conservative attitudes towards, 82;

ethnic feminism of, 80; women and violence campaign, 86

labor migration, 214, 216, 217, 218. *See also* Canada, Filipino migrants' movement in
land colonization, 21, 155, 167; frameworks used in, 155; in Palestine, 155, 158, 167; in USA, 155. *See also* Palestinian rights and solidarity
Lapperière, Marie, 2, 8, 12, 172, 173
Lépinard, Eléonore, 2, 7–8, 12, 172, 173
LGBT, use of acronym/terminology, 113
LGBTQ, European movement inclusiveness study, 20, 111–30; and alliance formation, 114, 115, 118, 119, 130; capacity creation in, 122, 124–25; domestic/transnational variation in, 125–26; financial crisis (2008), effect of on, 111, 114, 115, 118, 119, 121, 129–30; and INGO collaboration table, *121*; intersectional consciousness in, 20, 111, 112, 115, 117, *118*, 120–22, 126, 127–29; NGO focus in, 115–16, 117; resource cooperation in, 118, 120; transnational context in, 116, 118, 122, 124, 125–26, 128, 129. *See also* alliance formation; LGBTQ organizations; LGBTQ rights; IGLYO; ILGA-Europe; intersectional consciousness
LGBTQ organizations, 1, 3, 5, 11, 16, 17, 19, 56, 68, 71, 120–25, 127–30, 162–63, 213, 260; and black oppression politics, 162–63, 165; growth of, 119; impact of funding on, 11, 119, 120, 128, 129; inclusion of marginalized groups in, 120, 125, 127, 129; and Pride Parades, 16; and refugee solidarity activism, 191–92, 204, 205, 206; and single-axis organizing, 213; social movement visibility of, 142; and trans advocacy provision, 127
LGBTQ rights, 1, 19, 75, 124, 127, 254; and counter-intersectional politics, 19; European unified voice in, 254;

Irish "Yes Equality" campaign 2015, 32–33; The Netherlands, LGBTI HIV awareness campaign, 125; and Poland, Campaign against Homophobia (KPH), 126; political translation, use of in, 190. *See also* Turkey, women's activism study
Lipsitz, George, 2, 3, 7, 14, 15, 74, 75, 138, 139, 172, 173
Lisbon Treaty (EU), 244, 249
Lombardo, Emanuela, 46, 111, 254, 257

marginalization, 2, 10, 11, 13; in identity-based groups, 135, 138–39
McAdam, Doug, 9, 14, 92, 247
McCall, Leslie, 4, 14, 58–59, 89, 154, 156, 162, 169, 245
McCarthy, John D., 9, 114
Meyer, David S., 9, 58, 94
migrant activism, 13, 14, 21, 167; counter-intersectionality in, 84–85; and European Network of Migrant Women (ENoMW), 38, 254, 255; and feminization theories, 216; and gender ideology, 84; Hazar Association of Education, Culture and Solidarity, 78, 82, 84–85; and homosexuality, 84; in Hong Kong, 211; intersectionality in, 217; MERJ (Migrants and Ethnic-Minorities for Reproductive Justice) anti-abortion campaign, 38; Migrante-Canada, 217; Migrant Workers Alliance for Change (MWAC), 218; and Wo/men for women project, 87–88. *See also* Canada, Filipino migrants' movement in; refugee solidarity movements
Muslim women: and anti-violence discourse, 78, 85–89; and conservative gender ideology, 82–86; European Forum of Muslim Women (EFoMW), 254. *See also* AKDER; KADEM; Turkey, women's activism study in

Naples, Nancy, 96, 156, 241
National Women's Council of Ireland (NWCI), 25, 26, 28, 30, 31, 32,

34–35; "Every Woman" campaign, 34–36; reproductive rights activism in, 30, 32, 34–35

neoliberalism, 6, 27, 40, 75, 105, 109; austerity paradigm in, 257; concept of, 75; co-option of feminist projects by, 27; in Croatia, 105, 106, 107, 109; intersectionality, use of concept by, 162; in Puerto Rico, 175, 176; in Turkey, 75, 76, 79, 80, 89

Occupy movement US study, 14, 96, 135–37, 139–53; basic mobilization premise in, 135; and class inequality, 136–37, 147, 152; formation and purpose of, 141; framing and voice diversification in, 146–47; gender-based groups in, 144–47; identity-based organization in, 7, 10, 14, 15, 20, 96, 135–37, 139–43, 146; inequality issue focus in, 147–48; and intersectionality, 7, 10, 14, 136–37, 140, 149–52; leadership teams in, 142; LGBTQ visibility in, 142, 145, 149; male domination in, 142–43, 145, 150; multiple marginalities in, 140, 148, 149–50, 152; oppressive behaviour in, 145, 146, 149; racial representation in, 142, 143, 147, 148; "safe space" creation in, 143–46, 147, 149, 151, 152; single-axis organizing in, 149, 150–51; universal call and rally cry in, 135, 136, 140–41

Open Society Foundations (OSFs), 65, 251

Open Society Institute (OSI), 61

Organisation Intersex International (OII), *121*, 122, 127

Palestinian rights and solidarity, 20–21, 155, 158, 161, 163, 166, 167, 168; abolitionist framework, use in, 164; and BDS Movement, 158, 165; Black Youth Project 100 in, 160; and Demilitarize! Durham2Palestine Coalition, 160; Duke Students for

Justice in Palestine in, 160; Jewish American positions on, 164, 166; Jews of Color and Sephardi/Mizrahi (JOCSM) Caucus, 157, 158, 159; JVP campaign against US/Israel security collusion, 155, 157, 158, 160, 163, 165, 167; JVP Mexican anti-wall delegation, 167; and Movement for Black Lives, 168; Muslims for Social Justice in, 160; and School of the Americas Watch (SOAW), 167. *See also* colonialism; Israel; Jewish Voice for Peace; JVP, Deadly Exchange campaign; land colonization

participant observation approach, 21, 26, 93, 117, 171, 209, 211, 229. *See also* Canada, Filipino migrants' movement in; Ireland, reproductive rights activism in; Puerto Rico, student movement study

Philippines, The, 208, 209, 211; Canadian mining in, 224; indigenous communities in, 218, 224–25; and labor export, 214, 216; Marcos regime in, 214, 216. *See also* Canada, Filipino migrants' movement in

police oppression and brutality, 155, 157, 158, 162, 163, 164, 165, 167. *See also* BlackLivesMatter (BLM) movement; black women and activism, Ferguson in; black women and activism, French *banlieues* in

policymaking and intersectionality, 18, 42–43, 46; as finding voice process, 46. *See also* Sweden, Domestic Service Tax Reform (RUT) in

political intersectionality, 19, 26, 27, 39, 57–58, 59, 62, 69, 70, 71, 72, 113, 116, 119, 129; dimensions of, 119, 129; inter- and intra-categorical arenas in, 63, 72. *See also* alliance formation; intersectional consciousness; intersectionality

political translation, 8, 14, 21, 173, 190, 195–96; and intersectional capacity, 21; intervention techniques in,

195; and marginalization, 190, 196; and positional misunderstandings, 190, 195. *See also* refugee solidarity movements

Polletta, Francesca, 137, 138, 192, 194

prison reform: abolitionist intersectional approach to, 162; and BlackLivesMatter, 164, 165; and Critical Resistance, 164, 165; JVP involvement with, 165–66; and Occupy Baltimore, 148

protest, 1, 16, 17, 20; Arab Spring protests, 135; and collective identity, 141; and *los Indignados* (Spain), 135; and Trump's election, 152; and 2008 economic crisis (Croatia), 93, 104, 105–6. *See also* black feminism; black women and activism; JVP, Deadly Exchange campaign; Occupy movement US study; Puerto Rico, student movement study

Puerto Rico: class/race intersection in, 179, 180–81, 183, 185; coalition/alliances in, 181, 184; Colectiva Feminista en Construccion, 184, 185; Comité Universitario Contra el Alza (CUCA), 176–77; Constitution of, 174–75; higher education cuts in, 175, 178, 180, 181, 182; intersectionality in, 21, 171, 178, 179–80, 181, 182, 183–85, 186; Juventud Hostosiana in, 179, 181, 185; LGBTQ/feminist inclusion in, 177, 179, 182, 183, 184, 185; neoliberal austerity policies in, 175–76, 180, 182, 185, 186; and PROMESA Act (2016), 182, 186; protest waves and effectiveness of, 171, 176–78, 180–86; student movement study, 16, 21, 171, 174–86; unemployment/poverty in, 175–76; US colonial rule and expenditure in, 174, 175, 186. *See also* intersectional solidarity

racial discrimination and violence, 2, 17, 155–56, 161, 162, 164, 166, 226, 228, 241–42, 258; and black women's invisibility, 241–42; and JVP activism,

158; movements against, 56, 260–61; and 'whiteness' self-reflection, 160–61, 165. *See also* anti-black violence; black feminism; BlackLivesMatter (BLM) movement; black women activism; European Network against Racism (ENAR)

racial justice, 1, 6, 155, 158, 162; and abolitionist intersectional approach, 162; movement language used in, 155. *See also* black feminism; BlackLivesMatter (BLM) movement; black women and activism

racial liberation, 155, 232; and decolonial movements, 166. *See also* BlackLivesMatter (BLM) movement; Palestinian rights and solidarity

refugees, 6, 166, 22; and 'crisis' discourse, 222; 2015 European migration of, 191; and indigenous constructions, 166. *See also* refugee solidarity movements

refugee solidarity movements, 10, 16, 21, 189, 191; critical self-reflection in, 193, 204–5; and cultural tension, 193, 197, 205; discourse shifting in, 193; intersectional coalition work in, 191, 192, 194; political translation capacity in, 21, 190, 195–96, 197, 202–4, 206; positional misunderstandings in, 189–90, 191, 193, 195, 196, 197, 203, 205–6, 207; refugee participation in, 192–93, 206; refugee women/LGBTQ involvement in, 191, 193, 204, 205, 206; and safe space creation, 193; self-reflective group culture in, 204–5; *Women in Exile* network, 197. *See also* Canada, Filipino migrants' movement in; Denmark, refugee solidarity activism in; Germany, refugee solidarity activism in; political translation

representation: descriptive forms of, 139, 141–43; and intersectionality, 7–8, 10, 18, 58, 185, 221; of LGBTI, 113, 116, 127, 128, 129; of minority groups, 7–8, 10, 98, 197, 208, 211; substantive forms of, 139, 141; and supranational CSOs, 253–54, 255, 256–57; women's parliamentary, 28, 45, 100, 232. *See also* alliance formation; black feminism; black women and activism; finding voice strategies

reproductive rights, ECJ rulings on, 30; MERJ (Migrants and Ethnic-Minorities for Reproductive Justice) campaign, 38; New York Centre for Reproductive Rights, 34; reproductive justice, 38; and "Together for Yes" strategy, 36–37, 38, 39, 40. *See also* Abortion Rights Campaign (ARC) Ireland; Ireland, reproductive rights activism in

resistance movements, 1, 9, 28, 29, 108, 155, 161, 165, 166, 197, 189; reframing/finding voice in, 155. *See also* JVP, Deadly Exchange campaign; prison reform, and Critical Resistance

resource mobilization theory, 9, 10, 114; and collaborative alliances, 114

right-wing movements, rise of, 19, 89, 121; financial crisis, effect on, 121

Roggeband, Conny, 3, 57, 62

Romania, domestic violence study, 19, 57, 59, 60, 62, 63, 64–72; alliance formation in, 67, 68, 70, 71; and children's rights groups, 68–69, 71–72; ERRC/CRISS report, 66; and FILIA economic crisis report, 63, 64; human rights involvement in, 69; intersectionality in, 19, 57, 59, 60, 62, 63, 64–65, 68–72; organizational dynamics in, 71–72; Roma women's organizations in, 60, 63–64, 65, 66, 70; and transnational support, 60–61, 65, 66, 69; and 2011 coalition protest and manifesto, 63–65, 67, 71; and UPR report, 67–68; Women's Lobby (RoWL) in, 61–62; women's movements in, 61–62, 70. *See also* Roma rights; Roma women's activism

Roma rights, 59, 62, 64, 66, 67, 68, 71–72; and European Roma and Traveller Forum (ERTF), 251; and European Roma Grassroots Organisations Network (ERGO), 246, 250, *252*; and European Roma Rights Centre (ERRC), 14, 62, 66–68, 70; and forced sterilization, 63, 68; and Romani CRISS NGO, 60, 64, 66. *See also* Hungary, domestic violence study; Romania, domestic violence study

Roma women's activism, 60, 61, 62, 63–65, 257; Association of Gypsy Women, 60; Association of Roma Women, 60; and E-Romnja, 64, 65; and Hungarian rights and movements, 60, 61, 62–63, 66, 67, 68, 70, 71; International Roma Women's Network (IRWN), 257. *See also* Hungary, domestic violence study; Romania, domestic violence study

Sanchez Salgado, Rosa, 244, 245, 248, 249, 250, 251–52, 253

Sauer, Birgit, 17, 75, 189, 191

settler societies, 166–67; exceptionalism/racist narratives in, 166–67; ideal settler sexual construction in, 167–68; logic of elimination in, 166

Shin, Young, 2, 3, 7, 14, 15, 74, 75, 138, 139, 172, 173

Siim, Birte, 191, 192, 245, 248–49, 257

slavery, 155, 163, 209

social justice movements/organizations, 160, 212, 213, 218, 221–22, 224; black women activists in, 227, 231; and EU equality CSOs, 253, 257, 258, 260. *See also* BlackLivesMatter (BLM) movement; Canada, Filipino migrants' movement in; Puerto Rico, student movement study

social movements: access-influence model in, 94, 96, 108; action-reaction model in, 94, 108; identity framing

in, 137, 155; and intersectionality, 3–4, 6–8, 92, 94, 95–96, 138–39, 163, 169, 171, 172–74; marginalization in, 137–39; political context in, 94; professionalization, effects of, 95, 96, 109; research areas in, 2–3, 9, 92, 93–96; and resource mobilization, 9; scholar-activist role in, 210–11; universalizing impulses in, 141. *See also* Croatia, feminist social movements study; identity-based groups
social reproduction, concept of, 106–7
Snow, David, 127, 137
Spade, Dean, 155, 162–63, 164, 210, 212–13, 215, 223
Staggenborg, Suzanne, 14–15, 58, 113, 114, 130
Strid, Sofia, 75, 250, 254
Strolovitch, Dara Z., 8, 12, 58, 69, 114, 130, 138, 173, 219
Sweden: Confederation of Swedish Enterprise, 50; Domestic Service Tax Reform (RUT) in, 12, 18, 42–55; domestic workers in, 44, 46, 51; Feminist Initiative (Fi) in, 45–46, 50, 52; gender equality in, 42, 43, 45, 47, 48–49, 50–53, 54; 48–49; immigrant law/integration in, 44, 49, 53; intersectional approach in, 42, 43, 45, 46–47; intersectional consciousness/blindness in, 47, 54; leftist feminist critique in, 50–52, 53, 54; LGBTQ engagement in, 46. *See also* domestic workers

Tarrow, Sidney, 3, 9, 14, 16, 17, 58, 92, 112, 123, 136, 137
Townsend-Bell, Erica, 7, 58, 174, 212, 213, 223, 245, 259
Transgender Europe (TGEU), 61, *121*, 122, 127
transgender rights, 165–66
transversal politics, 8, 9, 27, 99, 151, 189, 235, 245, 259; and recognition, 9; rooting and shifting notions in, 8, 27, 189. *See also* intersectional praxis

Trump, Donald, 1, 152, 158, 167, 224; and US/Mexico wall issue, 167
Tudman, Franjo, 94, 97, 98, 99
Turkey: AKP party, rise of, 79, 80; conservative women's NGOs in, 75, 76, 77–78, 80, 81–88, 89; counter-intersectionality in, 19, 74–77, 78, 81–90; discursive dismantling practices in, 76, 77, 78, 86, 88; EU accession process in, 79, 80; feminist countermovement in, 74–75, 76; gender justice frame in, 82–85, 89; and 'headscarf issue', 78, 80–81, 82, 85, 86; Islamic-conservative society in, 74, 76, 80, 89; LGBTQ movements in, 19, 74, 75, 79, 80, 82, 84, 85, 86, 87; neoliberal state in, 75–76, 79; 2001 economic crisis in, 79; 2016 failed coup in, 84; violence against women approaches in, 78, 86–89; women's activism study, 19, 74–90; women's rights reforms in, 80. *See also* AKDER; KADEM; Kurdish women's movement

United Kingdom, 2, 222; feminist movements in, 2
United Nations, 61; Convention on the Rights of Persons with Disability, 61; Universal Periodic Review (UNUPR), 58, 67
United States: black political representation in, 232; Israeli security collusion, 155, 158, 160, 163, 165, 169; land colonization in, 155; police oppression/brutality issues in, 155, 157, 158, 163, 165, 166, 167; poverty levels in, 175; refugee reaction in, 167, 222; Women's March, 1. *See also* black feminism, in Ferguson USA; BlackLivesMatter (BLM) movement; land colonization; Occupy movement US study; Puerto Rico

Verloo, Mieke, 2, 12, 14, 58, 116, 173, 244, 246, 248, 257

violence against women: and black women invisibility, 241; Council of Europe Convention, 86–87; and Croatian activism, 96, 98–99, 101, 102; and land dispossession, 217; OBR flash dance, use in, 217; Occupy movement discussion on, 145; and Turkish conservative discourse, 78, 85–89. *See also* domestic violence activism

Walby, Sylvia, 56, 75
WAVE, 59
Weldon, Laurel, 2, 5, 8, 15, 56, 58, 138, 139, 173, 227

women's movements, 1, 4–5, 16, 27, 44–45, 260; finding voice in, 96; ideological divide in, 45, 95–96; legalistic strategies in, 93, 96, 108; neoliberal/ market forces co-optation of, 27. *See also* feminist activism; Croatia, feminist social movements study; Ireland, women's representation in; Turkey, women's activism study
World Social Forum, 189

Young, Iris Marion, 138, 139, 193
Yuval-Davis, Nira, 2, 8, 12, 15, 75, 160, 168, 181, 189, 191, 195, 206, 235, 245, 246, 255, 259

Contributors

EDITORS

Jill Irvine is Presidential Professor of International and Area Studies at the University of Oklahoma. Her teaching and research interests include social movements, political mobilization, and transnational activism, with a focus on gender. She is the author of *The Croatian Question, Partisan Politics in the Formation of the Yugoslav Socialist State* (1995); coeditor with Carol Lilly of *Natalija: Life in the Balkan Powder Keg, 1880–1956* (2007); and coeditor with Melissa Bokovoy and Carol Lilly of *State-Society Relations in Yugoslavia 1945–1992* (1997).

Sabine Lang is Associate Professor of European Studies at the Henry. M. Jackson School of International Studies of the University of Washington, where she directs the Center for West European Studies and the European Studies Program. Her research focuses on gender equality policies, the nongovernmental sector, and social mobilization. She is the author of *NGOs, Civil Society, and the Public Sphere* (2013) and *Politische Öffenlichkeit im Modernen Staat* (2001).

Celeste Montoya is Associate Professor of Women and Gender Studies at the University of Colorado Boulder. She studies how women and racial minorities mobilize to enact change, within and outside of political institutions, domestically and transnationally, and intersectionally. Her regional areas of specialization are Europe and the United States. She is the author of *From Global to Grassroots: The European Union, Transnational Advocacy, and Combating Violence against Women* (2013).

AUTHORS

Petra Ahrens is Guest Professor in Comparative Politics and Gender & Diversity at the University of Antwerp and Senior Researcher in the ERC-funded research project EUGenDem at the University of Tampere. She works on gender equality policies and politics in the European Union and Germany. She is the author of *Actors, Institutions, and the Making of EU Gender Equality Programs* (2018) and coeditor, with Lise Rolandsen Agustín, of *Gendering the European Parliament* (2019).

Phillip M. Ayoub is Associate Professor of Diplomacy and World Affairs at Occidental College. His research bridges insights from international relations and comparative politics, engaging with literature on transnational politics, sexuality and politics, norm diffusion, and social movements. Alongside several articles, he is the author of *When States Come Out: Europe's Sexual Minorities and the Politics of Visibility* (2016) and co-editor, with David Paternotte, of *LGBT Activism and the Making of Europe* (2014).

Jean Beaman is Assistant Professor of Sociology and affiliate faculty of African-American Studies, Global Studies, and American Studies at Purdue University. Her research focuses on race/ethnicity, racism, immigration, and state-sponsored violence in both the United States and France. She is the author of *Citizen Outsider: Children of North African Immigrants in France* (2017).

Nadia E. Brown (PhD, Rutgers University) is University Scholar and Associate Professor of Political Science and African American Studies at Purdue University. Dr. Brown's research interests lie broadly in identity politics, legislative studies, and black women's studies. She is the author of the award-winning book *Sisters in the Statehouse: Black Women and Legislative Decision Making* (2014) and coeditor, with Sarah Allen Gershon, of *Distinct Identities: Minority Women in U.S. Politics* (2016).

Rachel H. Brown is Assistant Professor of Women, Gender, & Sexuality Studies at Washington University in St. Louis. Her areas of scholarship include feminist political theory, carework and reproductive labor, migration, and citizenship and settler colonial studies. Brown's current book project is entitled Four Years, Three Months: Migrant Caregivers in Palestine/Israel. Brown received her Ph.D. in political theory from The Graduate Center, City University of New York.

Pauline Cullen is Lecturer in Sociology and Politics in the Department of Sociology, Maynooth University, National University of Ireland. Her research examines civil society mobilization on social justice and gender equality at national and European Union level, women's movements, and gender and political representation. This work has been published in the *Journal of Civil Society*, *Social Movement Studies*, *Gender Work and Organization*, and *Politics & Gender*.

Nicole Doerr is Associate Professor of Sociology at the University of Copenhagen. Her research investigates how and under what conditions increased linguistic and cultural diversity fosters democratic innovation in social movements, local democracy, and participation by migrants, refugees, and minorities. She is the author of *Political Translation—How Social Movement Democracies Survive* (2018) and coeditor, with Alice Mattoni and Simon Teune, of *Advancing the Visual Analysis of Social Movements* (2013).

Ayşe Dursun (PhD, University of Vienna) is a postdoctoral researcher at the University of Vienna, Department of Political Science. Her research areas include gender, women's movements, intersectionality, gender equality policies, and migration. She is the author of "Muslim Groups in the Gezi Park Protests: Identity Politics and Contentious Politics under Authoritarian Neoliberalism" in *Contentious Politics in the Middle East*, edited by Fawaz Gerges (2015).

Andrea Krizsán is Research Fellow at the Center for Policy Studies, Central European University, Budapest. Her research focuses on understanding equality policy change in countries of Central and Eastern Europe. Her current research is on the politics of policy backsliding in times of crisis and forms of feminist resistance to such reversal. She is coauthor with Conny Roggeband of *The Gender Politics of Domestic Violence: Feminist Engaging the State in Central and Eastern Europe* (2018) and coeditor, with Judith Squires and Hege Skjeie, of *Instituting Intersectionality: The Changing Nature of European Equality Regimes* (2012).

Raluca Maria Popa is a PhD candidate in comparative gender studies at the Central European University. She is a gender specialist at the International Development Law Organization (IDLO). In addition to the work in her dissertation on "State Feminism within State Socialism: Rethinking Communist Women's Activism in Romania, 1944–1989," she has published several book chapters and articles on gender violence.

Andrea Spehar is Associate Professor in political science and director of the Centre on Global Migration (CGM) at the University of Gothenburg, Sweden. Her fields of interest comprise migration and gender policy development in Europe. Her work has appeared, among others, in the *Journal of European Public Policy*, *Comparative European Politics*, *Journal of Women, Politics & Policy*, *Eastern European Politics & Societies*, and the *International Feminist Journal of Politics*.

Leda Sutlović is a PhD candidate and an external lecturer at the Department of Political Science, University of Vienna. She holds an MA from the Central European University and a degree from University of Zagreb in Political Science. Her thesis project focuses on (post)socialist transformations of Croatian gender policies, bringing together the approach of discursive and historical institutionalism with the role of knowledge and ideas in politics.

Fernando Tormos-Aponte (PhD, Purdue University) is a postdoctoral fellow with the Scholars Strategy Network and a research fellow of the Southern Methodist University Latino Center for Leadership Development. Dr. Tormos-Aponte specializes in social movements, identity politics, social policy, and transnational politics. Tormos-Aponte's work has appeared in *Politics, Groups, and Identities*, *Environmental Policy and Governance*, and in the edited volume *The Legacy of Second-Wave Feminism in American Politics*.

Ethel Tungohan is Assistant Professor in the Department of Politics at York University and a Canada Research Chair (Tier 2) in Canadian Migration Policy, Impacts, and Activism. Her research uses socially engaged research methodologies to examine migrant social movements and immigration policy, focusing specifically on temporary labor migration. Her work has been published in various academic journals and edited books. She is also the coeditor of *Filipinos in Canada: Disturbing Invisibility* (2012).